More Praise for *Access for All*

This book is essential reading for anyone interested in shaping a more livable world, from entrepreneurs to investors, corporates, nonprofits, and governments. Dr. Helms brings together the latest economic research and her own insights from 30 years in the field to show how market-based solutions are critical to pulling people out of poverty in developing markets. *Access for All* lights the way to a future of economic inclusion and challenges us to collaborate across private and public sectors to create a more prosperous and sustainable world. If you want to make the world a better place, read this book!

— Elizabeth Nelson, Chair of the Board of Managers, DAI

This book comes at a unique moment in history. The world's attention is finally zeroing in on deep economic divides in countries across the globe. At the same time, technology, globalization, and new business models now offer exciting new opportunities to pull previously excluded people across that divide quickly. Packed with real life stories in technology, the gig economy, mobile health care, education, and new agriculture, Brigit Helms has written a crisp and quick-paced tour of economic inclusion, from its roots in microfinance through to impact and SDG investing. Following the model of her first book at CGAP, *Access for All* is a refreshing and informative romp for development veterans and millennial entrepreneurs alike.

— Elizabeth Littlefield, Senior Counselor at Albright Stonebridge Group and Former Chairman and CEO of OPIC

Access for All tells the story of the revolution in economic development of the last 15 years. New technologies, new approaches, a new generation of entrepreneurs and social entrepreneurs, and policies that support all this have begun to unleash the greatest untapped resource: the human talent of the world's poor. We have come a long way but we have further to go, and *Access for All* maps the way ahead over the next 15 years.

— Daniel Runde, Senior Vice President; William A. Schreyer Chair and Director, Project Prosperity and Development, Center for Strategic & Interna

If you're looking to enter the world of inclusive economic development or you want to refresh your knowledge of it, *Access for All* covers everything you'd want to know. But it's much more than a primer. Comprehensive in its understanding of developing economies and the emerging solutions to problems encountered there, *Access for All* is packed with tips and full of ideas to design a more inclusive world. And it distills these ideas with a clarity and brevity that helps us learn and then apply our own thinking to the field.

— Toshiyuki Yasui, Guest Professor, Graduate School of System Design and Management, Keio University, Japan

In *Access for All*, Brigit Helms lays out both a call to action and a playbook for building inclusive economies. She explores the why and the how in layperson's terms—offering a way forward to help millions build a pathway out of poverty. Here's hoping that policy makers, international development experts, and, frankly, anyone who cares about building a more equitable global economy, read this book.

— Randall Kemper, Executive Director, Aspen Network of Development Entrepreneurs (ANDE)

Brigit Helms has crafted an excellent overview of the profound ways in which economies and economic opportunities are changing in today's world and equally profound implications of this for development assistance. She maps out how every major area—be it health, food, energy, finance, etc.—is transforming due to new technology, population shifts, and climate change and provides examples of new approaches that respond far more effectively to these changes than old-style, centralized, government-led programs. While she notes the new risks in this brave new world, she focuses on the new hopes and possibilities that innovations raise for truly eliminating poverty and raising living standards worldwide. She sets out a new agenda that companies (particularly SMEs), critical infrastructure providers, and governments should follow so that those left out of recent growth might finally be included—an agenda with very different roles and balance than has governed international development work to date. A must-read for all those committed to eliminating poverty in our lifetime.

— Matt Gamser, CEO, SME Finance Forum, International Finance Corporation (IFC)

Access for All

Access for All

Building Inclusive Economic Systems

BRIGIT HELMS

IN COLLABORATION WITH **DAI**

Access for All

Copyright © 2018 by DAI Global, LLC

Published by

DAI

Bethesda, Maryland

ISBN: 978-1-7327040-0-8

eISBN: 978-1-7327040-1-5

To my family, Andrew, Hugo, Paloma, and Rosie.

And to my mom, who always reminded me that this life
is not a dress rehearsal.

Acknowledgments

When I embarked on the *Access for All* journey in September 2017, my vision was to crowdsource much of the content—case examples, data, graphics, and evidence. With DAI's generous sponsorship, that dream became a reality. I relied on more than 30 colleagues across the company for their contributions, which ranged from drafting chapters or sections to brainstorming case examples to reviewing content to designing graphics to editing.

I would like to start by thanking DAI's Global Executive Team, especially Jim Boomgard, Jean Gilson, and Zan Northrip, for believing in this project and making the resources available to make it happen. Andre Averbug, Alex Brillman, Celia Garay, Colleen Green, and Erin Wigginton were major contributors on many chapters, and the quality of their writing was superb. Additional contributors include Estera Barbarasa, John Jepsen, Galia Nurko, Mark Rostal, and Georgia Taylor.

Technical reviewers helped me with quality control. Many thanks for this to Marcello Averbug, Anne-Marie Chidzero, Gerhard Coetzee, Xavier Faz, Randall Kempner, Ben Powell, and Alix Zwane. Any errors or omissions have nothing to do with these reviewers, however—they are all mine.

Steven O'Connor copyedited the book. Steven is the best editor with whom I've ever worked, and he channels my voice even better than I do. Alex Brillman, Amanda Naar, and Guthrie Renwick—crack interns all—offered proofreading and fact checking, while Maeghan Carpenter, Lauren Hillman, Josh Linden and Kitty Stone squeezed the design or replication of 100+ graphics into their busy workdays. Meg Karchner and Brian O'Connor mined the data for the funding chapter.

Krista Baptista, Chuck Chopak, Chuck Coon, Liz Drachman, Mike Field, Amy Fisher, Lara Goldmark, Jamal Al Jabiri, John Lindsay, Brian McMahon, Zaki Raheem, Jim Winkler, and Robin Young helped brainstorm great ideas and offered moral support along the way.

On the publishing side, Bethany Brown and Michele Healy of The Cadence Group, Kim Bookless, and Gwyn Snider at GKS Creative helped us push the manuscript through to production.

Last but not least, many thanks to my personal posse of readers and supporters, especially Andrew Mainhart.

The purpose of this book is to curate and collate the latest thinking and practice related to building inclusive economic systems, not to create new content. I hope the book organizes this material into an accessible, readable story line relevant to the nonexpert. Any success on this front is due to the tribe of supporters acknowledged here; any deficiencies are mine alone.

Contents

Figures

Boxes

Acronyms

ADC –Alternative Delivery Channels

AI – Artificial Intelligence

AML – Anti-Money Laundering

CCT – Conditional Cash Transfer

CFT – Combating the Financing of Terrorism

CIV – Corporate Impact Venturing

CSR – Corporate Social Responsibility

CVC – Corporate Venture Capital

DFI – Development Finance Institutions

DFID – Department for International Development

DRM – Domestic Resource Mobilization

EAP – Eastern Asia and Pacific

ECA – Eastern Europe and Central Asia

ERR – Economic Rates of Return

ESG – Environmental, Social, and Governance

FDI – Foreign Direct Investments

FRR – Financial Rate of Return

FTZ – Free Trade Zones

GHG – Greenhouse Gases

GIIN – Global Impact Investing Network

ICT – Information and Communications Technology

ICT4Dev – Information and Communication Technology for Development

ID4D – Identification for Development

IDB – Inter-American Development Bank

IFC – International Finance Corporation

ILO – International Labor Organization

IoT – Internet of Things

IPO – Initial Public Offering

IRIS – Impact Reporting and Investment Standards

LAC – Latin America and Caribbean

MDB – Multilateral Development Bank

MENA – Middle East and North Africa

MFI – Microfinance Institution

MNC - Multinational Corporation

MNO – Mobile Network Operator

MOOC – Massive Open Online Courses

MSME – Micro, Small, and Medium-Sized Enterprises

NGO – Nongovernmental Organization

ODA – Overseas Development Assistance

OECD – Organisation for Economic Co-operation and Development

OPIC – Overseas Private Investment Corporation

OTC – Over The Counter

PAYGO – Pay As You Go

PE – Private Equity

POS – Point of Sale

PPP – Public-Private Partnerships

RCT – Randomized Control Trial

SDGs – Sustainable Development Goals

SEZ – Special Economic Zones

SGB – Small Growing Business

SME – Small and Medium Enterprise

SSA – Sub-Saharan Africa

STEM – Science, Technology, Engineering, and Math

TVET – Technical and Vocational Education and Training

UNHCR – United Nations High Commission for Refugees

UCT – Unconditional Cash Transfer

VC – Venture Capital

VPO – Variable Payment Option

WASH – Water, Sanitation, and Hygiene

WFP – World Food Program

Foreword

For the first time in my career as a development professional—a career that goes back to the early 1980s—informed observers are talking in credible terms about ending extreme poverty, not just within our lifetimes but within the foreseeable future. These aspirations are reflected, to take just one example, in the United Nations' Sustainable Development Goals (SDGs).

No one factor accounts for this growing sense of promise. Not the rise of China and India, nor the globalization of the economy, nor the leveling and leapfrogging effects of digital technologies. But if there is one element that underlies the tectonic shift in the perceived prospects for global development, it is the pivotal role of the private sector: our realization, acceptance, and embrace of the notion that ending poverty ultimately depends on channeling the massive force of commercial actors driven by commercial incentives to create viable businesses and productive jobs.

Governments increasingly (albeit reluctantly in some cases) accept that a vibrant and inclusive private sector is the key driver of development. Experience has taught us that public sector institutions simply do not have the incentives or capabilities to do more than facilitate the development aspirations and activities of others. Likewise, international donors are beginning to embrace their role as catalytic enablers rather than prime movers in the development story— if only because the funds at their disposal are so small in the grand scheme of international financial flows.

And the nice part of this story is that the private sector itself has a powerful incentive to play the very role that is expected of it. The SDGs alone represent a $12 trillion business opportunity, according to recent estimates.

But the beauty of this story may be beguiling. While the convergence of opportunity and incentive could yield the economic growth we all want, there is no guarantee it will be the *inclusive* growth we all hope for. To put it in the terms of this book, there is no guarantee that the roaring engines of change in developing markets come with "access for all."

Brigit Helms has made a career at the intersection of inclusiveness and economic growth. As a development thinker, as a field worker, as an impact investor and an entrepreneur in her own right, she has striven to understand how markets work in developing countries, how they can work better for all citizens, and how the dizzying and evolving array of market actors are coming together to shape opportunity in frontier economies.

That's why DAI sponsored this book. DAI's roots are deep in the loam of economic development, and it is clear to us that this soil has never been richer or more fertile, particularly when it comes to engaging the private sector. As I write, six of the world's 10 fastest growing countries are in Africa. In Africa and elsewhere, DAI finds itself working in exciting new ways: running innovation centers and entrepreneurship hubs, bringing down risk and encouraging private capital toward emerging markets through "blended finance," accelerating the adoption of transformational technology, facilitating regional and international trade, and working directly for multinational firms on assignments that support their investments, underpin their social license to operate, upgrade local suppliers, and generate local jobs.

At the same time, we are working with country governments on what is known as domestic resource mobilization—fairer and more efficient taxation and revenue generation—so they can finance their own development programs as economic growth takes flight.

Brigit's book asks the right questions for this propitious moment. In our quest to create more inclusive economic systems, what works and why, and how do we measure it? Who exactly are the poor and how do we open doors for them? At various levels of the economy, who are the major and emerging players, and how are they engaging? Full of examples, the book is both a snapshot of the current scene and an inventory of what we know about inclusive growth. Rather than grasping for an exhaustive summary of an inexhaustible subject, however, it curates the most telling trends, examples, and data, highlighting the most interesting and innovative developments in the field.

Most importantly, it does all this in the language not of the development economist but of the layperson. Because "access for all" applies not only to the people who must be included in the growth picture but also to the range of players who must play a part in making inclusive growth a reality—the people, we hope, who may be drawn to this book.

Whether you are a government official, a fund manager, or a corporate executive; an academic, an impact investor, or a civil society leader; a venture capitalist, a philanthropist, or an NGO officer; an entrepreneur, an everyday citizen, or even—yes—an old development professional, you are the subject and the audience of this book, and you deserve to read it in a language we can all understand.

I hope *Access for All* gives you a fresh look at the exciting world of inclusive economics. And I hope something in it inspires you to find your place in that world.

James J. (Jim) Boomgard
President and Chief Executive Officer, DAI Global

Chapter 1. Introduction

Zakia Bakari is a 23-year-old Kenyan woman born and raised in Mombasa, the country's second largest city. Her father sells produce at the Mariki Market in Old Town on Digo Road; her mother stays home and takes care of the family. Neither has any formal education. Zakia and her two younger brothers are the first generation in the family to finish school, having received primary and secondary education at the nearby government-funded schools. Zakia graduated from the Mtongwe Girls Secondary School at age 18 and never attended university. She had a different vision for her future.

When she was 16, Zakia began helping her father and other vendors in the market after school and on weekends. At her graduation celebration, her family and her Mariki Market friends held a *harambee* (fundraiser) and they collected enough money for her to buy a refurbished laptop. Armed with her new computer and a gateway to the wider world, she began accessing free internet services at Swahili Pot, a Kenyan government project that supports technical innovation and the arts, located on donated land near Fort Jesus in Old Town Mombasa.

Zakia had always been a talented visual artist and one day she followed Google links to an Indian-produced Massive Open Online Course (MOOC) on graphic design. She enjoyed it so much that in the following months she tore through every free online course she could find on graphic and web design. After finishing one of these courses, she was prompted to an ad about Fiverr, an online freelancer platform where people with abilities like hers could sell their services to clients all over the world. She began designing

1

logos and brochures for clients in the United States and Europe, charging between $5 and $30 per job and receiving payments directly into her new PayPal-linked Equity Bank account. After just a few weeks, she was earning more money than her father.

Zakia's reputation grew offline, too, and local businesses started contracting her design services. Demand grew so fast that she added two of her cousins, one who lives in Nairobi and the other in Kisumu, to the team. They cooperated online using Red Pen, an app that facilitates remote designer collaboration. Her cousins soon needed computers with greater processing speeds to manage the increasing complexity of the work and Zakia took a microloan from zidisha. org, a peer-to-peer lending platform, to finance the new equipment. Zakia pays her cousins using M-Pesa, a mobile money service that electronically transfers cash quickly and seamlessly without the need for bank accounts. Her growing business currently nets an average of $2,000 a month after paying her cousins and other expenses.

Zakia is a character composed of an amalgam of real-life stories. And although her story may not be the norm in developing and emerging economies, it serves as an inspirational example of what is possible to achieve with the resources available today. Over the past decade, we have witnessed a sea change in how we think about poverty in developing and emerging markets. We now understand the power of activating private businesses and markets to make real change happen. Access to services and job opportunities, powered by digital technologies and sound policies, can transform lives.

A New Agenda for International Economic Development

In 2006, C. K. Prahalad published *The Fortune at the Bottom of the Pyramid*, a book that changed the way we think about impoverished people. The book argues that companies must revolutionize how they do business in developing and emerging markets. Poor people could be viable customers of products and services they value rather than simply beneficiaries of charity. Businesses could consequently "do good and do well" by creating business models that serve the billions of people at the "bottom of the economic pyramid."

The past decade or so has seen several new milestones in the thinking and practice of inclusive economics (see the timeline in Figure 1.1). These new economics go beyond grandiose top-down policies and embrace the bottom-up creation of equal opportunity, with the aspiration that all members of society should participate in all aspects of economic life—as employees, entrepreneurs, consumers, and citizens.

Recent years have consolidated these new ideas into a mandate for the private sector. For instance, in 2015 the Finance for Development conference in Ethiopia proclaimed that if we are truly to address the intractable social and environmental problems facing the planet, we need to shift the mind-set from investing billions of dollars to *trillions* of dollars. Traditional funders such as governments and international development agencies simply cannot fill this gap. Corporate social responsibility is not enough either. Private capital and viable business models need to kick in and scale.

The main events around climate, such as the Conference of the Parties, similarly point to the need for the private sector to play an integral role in achieving global development goals—in this case, reducing the planet's vulnerability to huge climate shifts. Companies of all sizes need to find new business models that put them and the planet on a new, more sustainable trajectory. Policy makers need to create the incentives to nudge private sector actors in the right direction. The urgency to create a green economy is particularly acute in cities—as the world becomes increasingly urban, how can we ensure that our cities become more livable, resilient, and sustainable?

Technology, especially digital, is upending the landscape everywhere. But nowhere is this transformation more dramatic than in low-income countries where digital technology enables them to leapfrog costly infrastructure investments and offer essential services for the first time. In 2016, the World Economic Forum proclaimed the advent of a Fourth Industrial Revolution based on this flourishing technology (the first industrial revolution liberated humans from animal power, the second leveraged electricity to create mass production, and the third harnessed electronics and information technology to automate production).[1] Yet the extent to which this revolution will include poor and vulnerable populations in the economy remains an open question.

---

1 Klaus Schwab, January 14, 2016, "The Fourth Industrial Revolution: what it means, how to respond," World Economic Forum, https://www.weforum.org/agenda/2016/01/the-fourth-industrial-revolution-what-it-means-and-how-to-respond/.

Figure 1.1: Milestones in Inclusive Economics

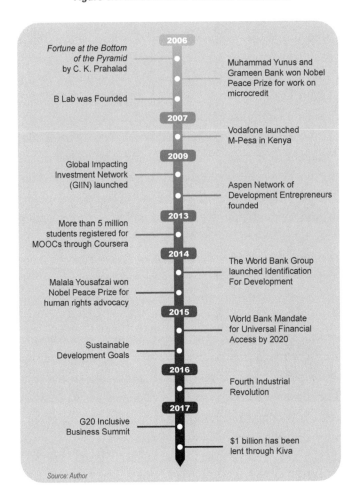

Source: Author

Finally, the Sustainable Development Goals, known as the SDGs or Global Goals, have captured the hearts and minds of people and organizations across the world (see Figure 1.2).[2] They are the new, universal set of goals, indicators, and targets that UN member states have committed to achieve by 2030 through their policies and agendas.

2   United Nations, "Sustainable Development Goals," United Nations, https://www.un.org/ sustainabledevelopment/sustainable-development-goals/.

4

The United Nations, large corporations, and national governments, both Global North and South, are scrambling to ensure that the 17 Global Goals are met by 2030. Tapping the ingenuity, initiative, and capital of the private sector will be crucial to achieving that objective, whether we are talking about poverty, health, education, climate, or any of the other Goals. Indeed, the UN estimates that we face a $2.5 trillion shortfall in the annual funding required to meet the Goals, a figure that dwarfs tax revenues and aid.[3] Recent estimates suggest that realizing the Goals will open up business opportunities worth a conservative total of $12 trillion by 2030.[4] However, to seize this opportunity in the future, businesses must invest today.

Figure 1.2: The Sustainable Development Goals

Source: United Nations Sustainable Development Goals

One thing is certain: for companies and organizations to fulfill their promise, we cannot rely on business as usual. Not for the private sector and not for the traditional development community. Indeed, we need innovation and disruption to address the social and environmental challenges we face. What's more,

---

3   Global Reporting Initiative, August 9, 2017, "Growing role for the private sector in the 2030 agenda," Global Reporting Initiative, https://www.globalreporting.org/information/news-and-press-center/Pages/Growing-role-for-the-private-sector-in-the-2030-Agenda.aspx.

4   Business & Sustainable Development Commission, January, 2017, "Better Business, Better World Executive Summary," Business & Sustainable Development Commission, http://report.businesscommission.org/uploads/Executive-Summary.pdf.

no one actor or type of actor can do it alone. Partnerships, often among un-easy bedfellows, hold out the only hope to execute on innovative solutions that promote inclusion. This need for partnerships further complicates an already complex set of problems and solutions.

Why do we care about inclusiveness? Because an inclusive economy means that the economic system incorporates everyone, so all can live productive lives, and because when large swaths of our societies are left out of the economy, everybody suffers. This is true both when we think about excluded people as consumers of the vital goods and services they need to reach their potential and as workers contributing to vibrant, growing industries. Inclusive economic systems are essential to bringing people out of poverty and creating a more prosperous and sustainable world.

The bad news is that we still have a long way to go to establish inclusive economies across the globe. The good news is that innovation and disruption are happening everywhere. We will explore many of these "new generation" collaborative solutions in this book.

Pathways Out of Poverty: Access to Services and Jobs

In this book, when we talk about economic inclusion, we refer to two main pathways that offer the poor and vulnerable a route out of poverty: access to services and jobs.

The first pathway entails access to goods and services that improve productivity and quality of life. A prominent example is access to financial services. Many of the most exciting innovations have occurred in this space—for instance, using mobile phones to make payments conveniently and cheaply. Significant innovations have also occurred in areas such as energy (cookstoves and solar panels), education (teaching girls to code), and sanitation (last-mile water connections). However, too many poor and vulnerable people still lack necessary products and services because they are not physically or culturally available, not good enough to deliver the desired outcomes, and/or too expensive.

When it comes to the second pathway—jobs—the reality is that many people in developing and emerging markets make their livelihoods through low-paying, insecure, and often dangerous occupations in the informal sector. These jobs are barely sufficient to eke out a subsistence living. Increasingly, though, new models are emerging for low-income people to integrate into national and international value chains.

The term value chain refers to all the activities that firms and workers undertake to bring a product or service from conception to end use. Value chains can be contained within a single firm or divided among a variety of firms and suppliers, both local and global. Agriculture remains critically important in the developing world, given the predominance of smallholder agriculture among poor and low-income people. Value chains in manufacturing, technology, and other services can offer powerful opportunities as well.

The way that the digital revolution evolves will drive the degree of economic inclusion, both for services and jobs. Increased access to mobile technology and the internet can promote the inclusion of previously unregistered and underserved populations (for example, via universal biometric identification), drive efficiency by lowering the cost to serve large numbers of customers (e-commerce, for example), and foster pro-poor innovation (such as peer-to-peer lending).[5] However, this growth in access has been slower than expected to deliver a digital dividend in terms of inclusive economic growth. In addition, frontier technologies such as robotics and artificial intelligence will almost certainly increase global productivity at exponential rates, but their impact on employment and overall inclusiveness may well be bleak.

Inclusive Economic Systems Framework

The framework employed in this book updates the one used in an earlier book, *Access for All: Building Inclusive Financial Systems*, while extending the analysis to incorporate topics beyond the financial system. The framework recognizes that excluded people will be empowered only if the pathways out of poverty—access to services and jobs—are incorporated into the three levels of the economic system: micro, meso, and macro (see Figure 1.3).

---

5   World Bank, 2016, "World Development Report 2016: Digital Dividends," World Bank, http://bit.ly/2IP3y2m.

Figure 1.3: Inclusive Economic Systems Framework

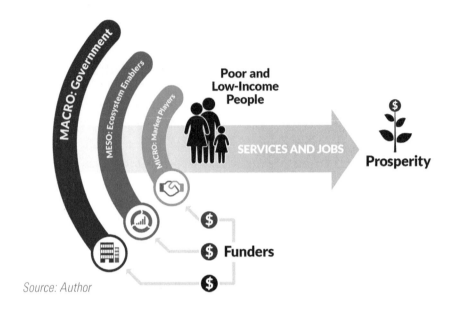

Source: Author

The components of this framework are as follows:

People. Poor and low-income people and households should be at the center of an inclusive economic system. Their demand for services and jobs should drive the actions of those at all the other levels.

Micro. Market players comprise the backbone of the economic system. They directly offer services and job opportunities to poor and low-income people. These micro-level market players run the gamut from microfinance institutions to commercial banks, small businesses, large multinational companies, civil society, and everything in between. Small and medium companies are particularly essential service providers and employers for poor and low-income people. The book addresses a range of different players, as discussed in Box 1.1.

Box 1.1: The Small and Medium-Sized Company Spectrum

Small and medium-sized companies can be grouped in different ways according to their stage of development, number of employees, purpose, and sales and/or assets. Four of the most common definitions—which often overlap—are small and medium-sized enterprises (SMEs), small growing businesses (SGBs), startups, and social enterprises.

SMEs are usually defined according to two main indicators: number of employees and level of revenue. Definitions vary by country and can range from as little as five employees and a few thousand dollars in revenues for "small" to up to 300 employees and $15 million in sales for "medium-sized" enterprises.[6] The SME definition is the broadest of the four categories and encompasses others such as SGBs and most social enterprises.

SGBs are defined as commercially viable businesses with five to 250 employees and significant growth potential and ambition.[7] An SGB actively searches for growth opportunities, while a typical SME remains small or medium-sized and is run as a subsistence or lifestyle business. SGBs often look for growth capital, typically in the range of $20,000 to $2 million.

Startups are new companies, as the name would imply. But for the purposes of this book, these are not just any early-stage companies; they work on innovative and/or high-growth-potential products or services. A startup searches for a replicable and scalable business model.[8] These are usually pre-revenue or low-revenue endeavors, often developing sophisticated and even groundbreaking concepts. They search for early-stage funding (usually equity) from angel investors and venture capital funds to prove concepts, pilot new ideas, and bring them to market. As a rule of thumb, a company is believed to have left "startup stage" after having achieved a cash flow break-even point and hired about 150 employees.

Social enterprises can be defined as organizations that develop market-based solutions to social, economic, or environmental problems. They can be for-profit or not-for-profit but must have a sustainable, revenue-generating business model. While size does not factor into their definition, most social enterprises are in fact SMEs.

---

6   Tom Gibson and H.J. van der Vaart, September, 2008, "Defining SMEs: A Less Imperfect Way of Defining Small and Medium Enterprises in Developing Countries," Brookings Global Economy and Development, http://seaf.com/wp-content/uploads/2014/10/Defining-SMEs-September-20081.pdf.

7   Aspen Network of Development Entrepreneurs, "What Is A Small And Growing Business (SGB)?," Aspen Network of Development Entrepreneurs, http://www.andeglobal.org/?page=aboutandesgbs.

8   Steve Blank, January 25, 2010, "What's A Startup? First Principles," *Steve Blank*, https://steveblank.com/2010/01/25/whats-a-startup-first-principles/.

Meso. Ecosystem enablers "grease the wheels" of an inclusive economic system. Examples include business incubators and accelerators, information brokers (such as credit bureaus and universal identification systems), workforce development providers, business associations, and knowledge providers. These enablers reduce transaction costs, increase outreach, build skills, and foster transparency across the entire economic system. Some of these entities can transcend national boundaries and include regional or global organizations.

Macro. Governments can play an important role in building—or thwarting—an inclusive economy. Appropriate legal and regulatory policies are necessary to allow innovation at the micro and meso levels, as well as attract the right kinds of finance to the system. Governments may also play a role in service delivery and influence markets via expenditure and through their procurement, licensing, and concession policies. Finally, public-private partnerships (PPPs) are becoming increasingly critical for improving services to underserved populations.

Funders. In addition to the three levels of the economic system, international and domestic funders play a key role. The funding landscape for inclusive economic systems is rapidly changing. To date, traditional donor funding and investments have played an important role in ensuring that capital reaches service providers and ecosystem players. Increasingly, however, nontraditional players such as venture capital funds, impact investors, corporates, and millennials are stepping up their support. Domestic capital markets are also being tapped to pay for services and opportunities.

This Book

The dizzying pace of change and multiple sources of information available online make it challenging to keep on top of the trends in inclusive economics. This book compiles the latest thinking and practice.

This is not a technical handbook, nor is it a chronicle of the history of development economics. Instead, it curates disparate sources of information to gather what we know today into a single place, relying on the "crowd"—a network of those working closely in the space at DAI and elsewhere—to provide compelling evidence, examples, and insights.

The principal audience is the general reader, the layperson who may be curious about inclusive economics. The book attempts to use plain language to explain the practical implications of a fairly murky concept—inclusive economic systems—by making a comprehensive argument about what we know now, what we need to find out, and where we need to go for further information.

This chapter presents key concepts that will be essential in understanding the remainder of the book, provides an overview of poverty and exclusion in frontier and emerging markets, and explores the current state of knowledge about the impact of inclusive economic initiatives.

Chapter 2 begins with a discussion of the poor and low-income people who are at the center of it all. Who are they? What are the services they currently use? What are their aspirations?

Chapters 3, 4, and 5 examine in turn the micro, meso, and macro level players in the economic system. Each chapter offers an overview of the diverse actors at each level, including information about what works to encourage inclusive economies, what does not work, and where more learning is needed. These chapters focus on innovative developments from the past decade or so to describe promising models and practices.

Chapter 6 analyzes the role of international funding sources, emphasizing the newer funders and investors who have entered the scene over the past few years. It highlights the characteristics and roles of concessional, impact-oriented, and commercial funders, and how they can complement each other to fuel economic inclusion.

Chapter 7 looks at cross cutting and frontier challenges that have an important impact on building inclusive economic systems. These deep dive topics include women's economic empowerment, the refugee crisis, consumer and worker protection, advanced technology, urbanization and climate change.

Finally, Chapter 8 sums up what we have learned and points to the challenges that await. Tackling the core challenges described throughout this book will ultimately result in inclusive economic systems that deliver on the promise of access for all.

Emerging and Developing Markets Today

Globally, poverty, particularly extreme poverty, has been on the decline. Extreme poverty dropped from 35 percent in 1990 to 11 percent in 2013—that accounts for around 1.1 billion people lifted out of dire conditions.[9] Figure 1.4 shows that most of this improvement has occurred in Asia, and that extreme poverty has actually increased in Sub-Saharan Africa.[10]

Figure 1.4: Global Poverty

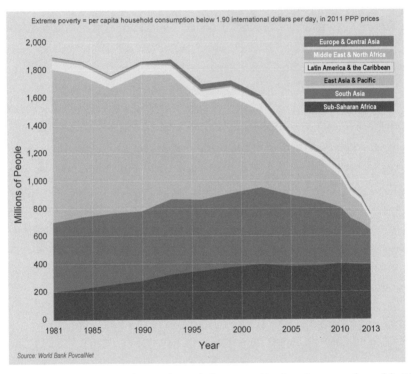

Additionally, Figure 1.5 shows that while inequality has improved worldwide, it has been growing in some places, especially in Africa, and may continue to deepen unless appropriate action is taken.[11] Populist movements, including the

---

9   World Bank, April 11, 2018, "Poverty Overview," World Bank, http://www.worldbank.org/en/topic/poverty/overview.

10   PovcalNet, "Research," World Bank, http://iresearch.worldbank.org/PovcalNet/povOnDemand.aspx.

11   Gapminder Data, "List of Indicators in Gapminder World," Gapminder, https://www.gapminder.org/data/.

Arab Spring and political shifts in the United States and United Kingdom, reflect an unsustainable sense of exclusion and disenfranchisement among significant constituencies in the global economy (see Box 1.2 for a discussion of poverty and inequality in the United States and Europe). Economic inclusion is an important factor in other issues plaguing the planet, too, from violence and conflict to the mass displacement of marginalized people.

Figure 1.5: Global Inequality

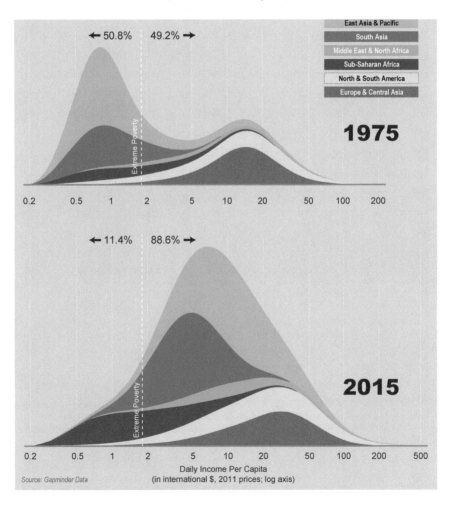

Box 1.2: Inequality in Rich Countries

While the focus of this book is on how to pave the pathways out of poverty in emerging and frontier markets, we can't forget that poverty and inequality are global phenomena. Among OECD countries, in 2015, total poverty rates were particularly high for the United States (16.7 percent), Spain (15.3), Canada (14.2), Italy (13.7), Portugal (12.6), and Poland (11.1).[12] The widening gap between the rich and the poor is also a widely contested issue in the United States and Europe. The median net worth of a high-income household in America is now 75 times that of a low-income household, up from 40 times in 2007 and 28 times in 1989.[13] There is also a geographic dimension to inequality—you will find more pockets of poverty in Appalachia than Silicon Valley in the United States, and the increasing cost of urban living is quickly pricing many people out of some cities. For instance, in San Francisco, a household earning $117,000 annually is now considered low income.[14]

Poverty also deepens racial divides in the global North. African Americans are far more likely to be poor than white Americans and they face structural barriers such as a lack of financial literacy. In the United States, 45.8 percent of black children live in poverty, compared to 14.5 percent of white children.[15] In Europe, inequality is less pronounced, but there is a growing tension between social groups based partly on racial and ethnic factors. Immigrants are more likely to be unemployed than natives, and even those who are employed are twice as likely to live in poverty.[16] Inequality depresses demand, lowers wages, and creates social problems. Also among the reasons for the alarming levels of poverty and inequality are the fast pace of globalization and high-skill-biased technological change. The global trend of rising income inequality will be another major challenge for governments in the coming decades.

---

12   Statista, "Poverty rates in OECD countries as of 2015," Statista, https://www.statista.com/statistics/233910/poverty-rates-in-oecd-countries/.

13   Lydia DePillis, November 3, 2017, "America's wealth gap is bigger than ever," CNN Money. http://money.cnn.com/2017/11/03/news/economy/wealth-gap-america/index.html.

14   Emmie Martin, June 28, 2018, "In San Francisco, households earning $117,000 qualify as 'low income'," CNBC, https://www.cnbc.com/2018/06/28/families-earning-117000-qualify-as-low-income-in-san-francisco.html.

15   State of Working America, "Poverty," State of Working America, http://www.stateofworkingamerica.org/fact-sheets/poverty/.

16   Michael Forster, Ana Llena Nozal, and Celine Thevenot, January 26, 2017, "Understanding the Socio-Economic Divide in Europe," OECD Centre for Opportunity and Equality, https://www.oecd.org/els/soc/cope-divide-europe-2017-background-report.pdf.

Figures 1.6a–f provide a snapshot of the world's developing regions, presenting a few key indicators that shed light on demographics, employment rates, entrepreneurial activity, and digital and financial inclusion.[17] Wide variations exist across and within regions.[18] Inclusive economics help close the gap not only between Boston and Mombasa but also within countries—between rural areas or slums, say, and the dynamic central districts. There are pockets of Silicon Valley around the world, but also pockets of depression or isolation. Notwithstanding these significant internal disparities, each global region possesses its own characteristics and challenges that determine the boundaries of what can be possible in terms of increasing access to services and jobs.

Eastern Europe and Central Asia (ECA) has enjoyed high levels of connectivity for some time. Back in 2006, the region already enjoyed mobile penetration of 82 percent; today, many people have more than one account and the figure stands at 130 percent. Internet penetration is the highest among emerging and developing regions, currently at 67 percent. Bank account ownership stands at a high 59 percent and ECA is the closest to gender equality in account ownership. ECA has an active ecosystem of micro, small, and medium-sized enterprises (MSMEs), with 18 such businesses for every thousand people. Conversely, unemployment has posed a major challenge over the past decade, stubbornly hovering around 8 to 9 percent, with youth taking the strongest hit at 19 percent. The region has the lowest share of youth in the population, with only about 44 percent of people younger than 29 years old. Given its strong levels of digital and financial inclusion, coupled with a well-educated population, ECA has favorable conditions for promoting inclusive growth.

---

17   World Bank, Development Indicators, World Bank, http://databank.worldbank.org/data/reports. aspx?source=world-development-indicators. Data for charts 1.6a–f and regional discussions come from World Bank Development Indicators.

18   For the complete list of countries per region, please see: World Bank Data, "World Bank Country and Lending Groups," World Bank, https://datahelpdesk.worldbank.org/knowledgebase/articles/906519-world-bank-country-and-lending-groups.

Figure 1.6a: Eastern Europe and Central Asia (ECA)

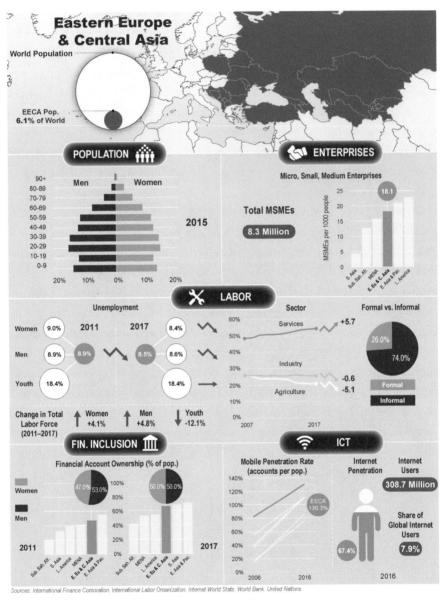

Sources: International Finance Corporation, International Labor Organization, Internet World Stats, World Bank, United Nations

Kazakhstan's market for freelance work is emblematic of the potential in the ECA region. Dissatisfied with the village life of their parents and grandparents, many young Kazakhs are joining the "digital nomad" style of work that has become commonplace in the West. Kazakhstan is nestled between Europe and Asia, and opportunities for freelance work abound in both regions.[19] Freelancer.com, a popular job-matching site, has more than 1,000 job categories, so freelancers can turn a wide array of skills into gigs.[20] At the same time, connectivity is growing in Kazakhstan. Accelerating technological modernization through programs such as "Digital Kazakhstan" is the first pillar of the government's ambition to become one of the top 30 most developed countries. Digital Kazakhstan includes the creation of new industries in areas such as 3D printing, robotics, and an international startup technological park.[21]

The Middle East and North Africa (MENA) is one of the youngest regions, with about 57 percent of the population under 29 years of age. Beset by war, conflict, decreasing oil prices, and consequent sluggish economic growth, the region suffers unemployment rates stagnating at close to 11 percent, with a staggering 30 percent of young people jobless in 2017. Informal employment dominates, accounting for 80 percent of the labor market. This situation, if not reversed, can be a recipe for continuing political and social instability. On the upside, women have acquired a stronger role in the economy. Their growth in labor force participation over the past six years is higher than that for men, and they have become more financially included, as shown by the rapid increase in the share of women with bank accounts in the past three years. Mobile and internet penetration have grown exponentially in the past decade, although MENA remains roughly average compared to the other regions on both dimensions. Digital technologies might be a key gateway to opportunities for unemployed youth to connect to global sources of knowledge (such as e-learning) and value chains (for example, through online outsourcing), to become more economically included.

In Morocco, women are beginning to increase their standing in the labor force in industries including tourism, one of the largest sectors of the economy.

19 Yerbolat Uatkhanov, February 10, 2017, "Freelancing in Kazakhstan: both stepping stone and ultimate prize," *The Astana Times*, https://astanatimes.com/2017/02/freelancing-in-kazakhstan-both-stepping-stone-and-ultimate-prize/.

20 Yerbolat Uatkhanov, March 17, 2017, "Kazakhstan is fascinating place for freelancers, experts believe," *The Astana Times*, https://astanatimes.com/2017/03/kazakhstan-is-fascinating-place-for-freelancers-experts-believe/.

21 Aigerim Seisembayeva, February 1, 2017, "Kazakh Leader Outlines Five Priorities of Kazakhstan's Third Stage of Modernisation," *The Astana Times*, https://astanatimes.com/2017/02/kazakh-leader-outlines-five-priorities-of-kazakhstans-third-stage-of-modernisation/.

Tourism accounted for 8.1 percent of Morocco's gross domestic product in 2016.[22] Tourism is projected to become an even larger sector of the economy as the country lowers visa requirements and the number of tourists who visit Morocco increases annually.[23] [24] The Moroccan government aims to double the number of tourism sector jobs by 2020 and will need qualified young Moroccans to fill these positions. Tourism offers a way for women to enter the formal economy; however, Moroccan tourism has historically benefited men more than women. To address this disparity, the National Confederation of Tourism Morocco has designed affirmative action policies to enhance female participation.[25] Challenges to gender parity still present enormous obstacles in Morocco; unemployment for everyone, not just women, is high across the MENA region.

22 Rochelle Turner and Evelyne Freirmuth, 2017, "Travel & Tourism Economic Impact 2017," World Travel & Tourism Council, https://www.wttc.org/-/media/files/reports/economic-impact-research/countries-2017/morocco2017.pdf.

23 Morocco World News, June 24, 2017, "Numbers of Tourists Visiting Morocco on the Rise," *Morocco World News,* https://www.moroccoworldnews.com/2017/06/221042/numbers-tourists-visiting-morocco-rise/.

24 Morocco World News, July 23, 017, "Moroccan Tourism Industry Resilient Despite Conjuncture: Oxford Business Group," *Morocco World News,* https://www.moroccoworldnews.com/2017/07/224074/moroccan-tourism-industry-resilient-despite-difficult-conjuncture-oxford-business-group/.

25 Yuko Morikawa, 2015, "The Opportunities and Challenges for Female Labor Force Participation in Morocco," Brookings Institute, https://www.brookings.edu/wp-content/uploads/2016/07/female-labor-force-participation.pdf.

Figure 1.6b: The Middle East and North Africa (MENA)

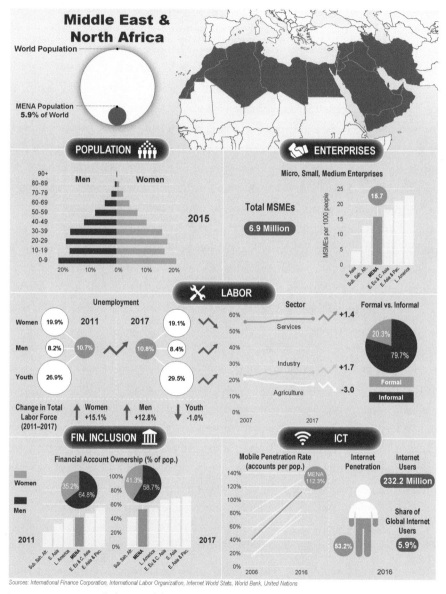

Sources: International Finance Corporation, International Labor Organization, Internet World Stats, World Bank, United Nations

Latin America and the Caribbean (LAC) is the most entrepreneurial region, with 23 MSMEs for every 1,000 people. In fact, businesses with fewer than 100 employees employ more than 50 percent of the workforce in the region, and MSMEs

19

remain an important driver of economic growth and inclusion.[26] The region is building an ecosystem of savvy entrepreneurs and creating a positive culture of risk-taking and innovation. Still, unemployment in the past decade has oscillated between 6.5 and 8.6 percent, with young people being the most affected (between 14.1 and 18.3 percent unemployed). LAC has the largest share of informal jobs at 87 percent. The great majority of the workforce labors in suboptimal conditions and without the benefits that accompany formality, such as labor rights, health insurance, retirement, and fringe benefits. People in LAC are well connected, with mobile penetration at 111 percent and internet at 61 percent. LAC is a region that can benefit greatly from business environment reforms that allow the private sector—and especially MSMEs—to take on a stronger role in driving the economy.

The financial sector in Brazil is likely to undergo enormous change as 200 financial technology companies (known as "fintech") compete with Brazil's large, traditional financial institutions. The top five banks in Brazil hold 84 percent of total loans, but this proportion will likely shrink, as these new fintech companies are estimated to generate $24 billion in revenue over the next decade.[27] Mobile banking is an increasingly popular option for Brazilian consumers, comprising 54 percent of the bank transactions made in Brazil in 2015.[28] Already, newcomers are changing the space by forcing established banks to adapt new technologies, reduce fees, and merge with or acquire startups. New types of institutions, such as the digital bank Conta Simples, which was founded by hackers and software engineers, are poised to gain market share despite the changes in traditional banks' business strategies.[29] Another pioneer in digital finance, Nubank, also has potential to gain standing in Brazil. Nubank's adept navigation of regulations and rejection of brick-and-mortar infrastructure have allowed it to pass savings on to its customers in the form of lower interest rates, resulting in 3 million card-carrying customers. Other fintech startups are disrupting the market across

26 Juan Carlos Thomas, June 14, 2016, "3 unorthodox lessons for Latin America's entrepreneurs," World Economic Forum, https://www.weforum.org/agenda/2016/06/3-unorthodox-lessons-for-latin-america-s-entrepreneurs/.

27 Vinod Sreeharsha, May 15, 2017, "Goldman Sachs Sees Big Potential for Fintech in Brazil," *The New York Times*, https://www.nytimes.com/2017/05/15/business/dealbook/goldman-sachs-sees-big-potential-for-fintech-in-brazil.html.

28 FintechLab, 2017, "Brazil FintechLab Report," Fintech Brazil, http://fintechlab.com.br/wp-content/uploads/2017/09/Report_Fintechlab_2017_ENG.pdf.

29 Team Fintech Brazil, September 15, 2017, "Brazilian digital banks: shortlist," Fintech Brazil, http://fintechbrazil.com/brazilian-digital-banks-shortlist/.

LAC countries: Mexico is home to more than 150 fintech startups, and Colombia is catching up with nearly 100.[30]

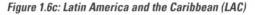

Figure 1.6c: Latin America and the Caribbean (LAC)

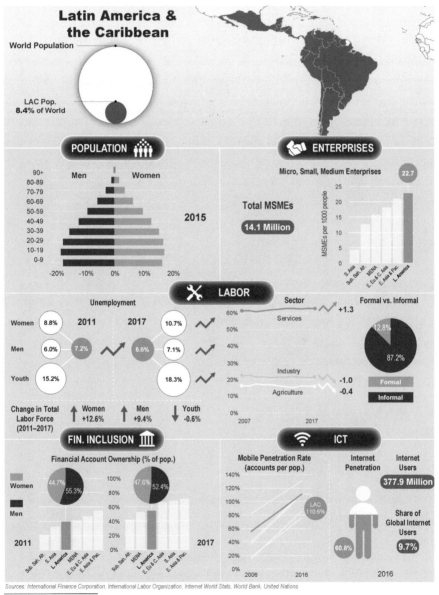

30   Chris Skinner, "The State of Fintech in Brasil," 2017, *The Finanser*, https://thefinanser.com/2017/09/state-fintech-brasil.html/.

East Asia and the Pacific (EAP) makes up nearly 30 percent of all global internet users—even though it represents just under 24 percent of the global population—with an internet penetration rate of 56 percent. Mobile penetration is also solid at 111 percent and EAP leads bank account ownership at 69 percent. The region has by far the most formal labor market, with only 24 percent of jobs in informal sectors. Unemployment is also low, normally around 4.5 percent, although among young people it reaches 12 percent. The region is generally seen as entrepreneurial, with 21 MSMEs per 1,000 people, and willing to implement reforms to improve its business climate. The World Bank recently referenced the region's progress in enabling entrepreneurship through reforms, with lagging countries offered the opportunity to learn from more developed neighbors.[31] With annual economic growth rates often exceeding 6 percent, EAP has the potential to continue to lift people out of poverty through access to services and jobs.

Trends in business climate reform in the region have stimulated economic growth. Indonesia implemented a series of reforms that caused it to rise from 114th to 72nd in the World Bank's *Doing Business* indicators rankings from 2014 to 2017. These reforms include a reduction in business startup fees and in the land transfer tax, as well as 14 stimulus packages, which eliminated red tape and fostered investment. Indonesia had one of the EAP region's highest foreign direct investment inflows in 2016, a trend that is likely to continue in the wake of increased deregulation.[32] [33]

31   World Bank, October 31, 2017, "East Asia and Pacific Economies Adopt 45 Reforms to improve business climate: Doing Business Report," World Bank, http://www.worldbank.org/en/news/press-release/2017/10/31/east-asia-and-pacific-economies-adopt-45-reforms-to-improve-business-climate-doing-business-report.

32   World Bank, June 20, 2016, "Reforms Strengthen Indonesia's Economic Resilience: World Bank Report," World Bank, http://www.worldbank.org/en/news/press-release/2016/06/17/reforms-strengthen-indonesias-economic-resilience-world-bank-report.

33   Aliyahdin Saugi, 2016, "Indonesia – further reforms in 2017 to promote economic growth," BNP Paribas, https://investors-corner.bnpparibas-am.com/investment-themes/indonesia-economic-recovery/.

Figure 1.6d: East Asia and Pacific (EAP)

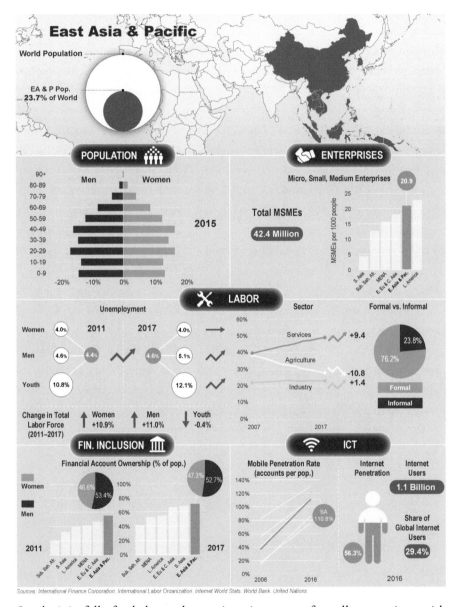

South Asia falls far below other regions in terms of small enterprises, with only 4.3 MSMEs per 1,000 habitants. On the other hand, unemployment is relatively low, hovering at only 4 percent over the past decade. Job informality, while still high, is not as acute as in other regions, and agriculture is the leading employment generator (44 percent) followed by services (33 percent). While South Asia is currently one of the least connected regions in the world in terms of mobile and internet penetration (86 and 34 percent, respectively), it is the fastest growing region in terms of mobile penetration growth (a stunning 576 percent in the past 10 years). In fact, South Asians love being online. They are among the most active online freelancers, performing online outsourcing work for clients across the globe. The region's low number of MSMEs suggests a strong potential for small enterprise-led growth, which could be unleashed by business-friendly reforms and improved access to finance.

Increased mobile penetration in Bangladesh is transforming the economy by increasing economic growth and connecting Bangladeshis with jobs and services in the mobile market. The mobile industry is projected to generate $17 billion in value by 2020, an increase of 30 percent compared to 2015. The industry contributed 10 percent of the government's revenue in 2015.[34] In addition to creating thousands of jobs, mobile access allows SMEs to obtain funding through an increasing number of financial service applications. This is vital for the continued expansion of Bangladesh's economy, as access to finance is a major barrier to entry for small and growing businesses in the country. Lack of financial inclusion harms female entrepreneurs disproportionately, so increased mobile access helps alleviate gender-based disparities.[35] [36] Finally, mobile penetration increases the productivity of workers, reduces the digital divide, and promotes social cohesion.[37]

---

34 GSMA Press Release, January 18, 2017, "GSMA Reveals Economic Impact of Mobile in Bangladesh," GSMA, https://www.gsma.com/newsroom/press-release/gsma-reveals-economic-impact-mobile-bangladesh/.

35 Ibid.

36 Mustafizur Rahman, March 19, 2017, "The SME sector has the highest opportunity to create employment in Bangladesh," Centre for Policy Dialogue, http://cpd.org.bd/sme-sector-highest-opportunity-create-employment-bangladesh-mustafizur-rahman/.

37 Barney Lane, April, 2006, "The Economic and Social Benefits of Mobile Services in Bangladesh," GSMA, http://www.dirsi.net/english/files/Ovum%20Bangladesh%20Main%20report1f.pdf.

Figure 1.6e: South Asia

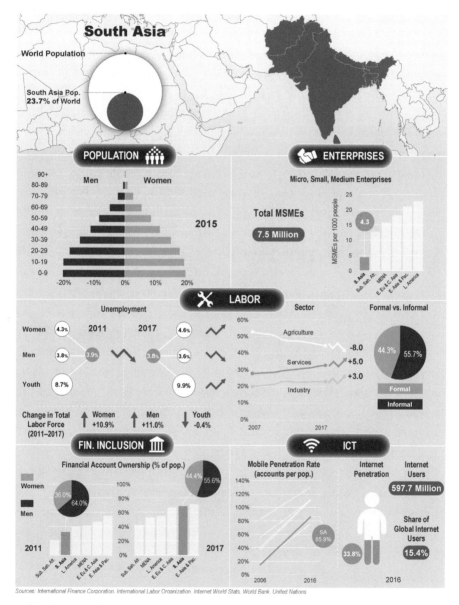

Sub-Saharan Africa (SSA) remains dependent on agriculture for formal employment, with 53 percent of workers in the sector. Unemployment has fluctuated at around 8 percent in the past decade, with 12 percent among the youth.

SSA is the youngest of all regions, with about 71 percent of the population younger than 29 years old. The region lags in connectivity. As of 2016, mobile penetration stood at only 76 percent and internet penetration at 29 percent. At the same time, SSA is growing quickly in terms of mobile penetration (430 percent growth between 2006 and 2016). The region ranks worst in formal financial inclusion, with only 34 percent of the population claiming a bank account. However, actual financial inclusion might be underrepresented by bank account ownership, since new technologies such as mobile payments and transfers, peer-to-peer (P2P) lending, and other nonconventional financial solutions have increased significantly in SSA. While still low in absolute terms, the number of entrepreneurs developing market-based solutions for Africa's problems has grown over the past decade, supported by an improving ecosystem that includes business incubators, technical assistance providers, and funders such as angel investors, international donors, and impact funds.

Although the region as a whole lags behind the rest of the world in terms of mobile connectivity and internet access, increasing access to these mobile services in Ghana has fostered the creation of business incubators and accelerators. For example, the Meltwater Entrepreneurial School of Technology (MEST) teaches skills to help enterprising young West Africans break into the software business. MEST has helped provide seed funding to 15 startups, and the incubator has seen several of its startups receive additional funding from elite Silicon Valley firms.[38] Other incubators, such as the Savannah Fund, work to reduce the skills and experience gap among local entrepreneurs to create long-term value.[39] Ghanaian startups cover a range of sectors and goals. Trotro Tractor connects farmers and tractor operators on a specialized platform; the company Developers in Vogue helps women in science, technology, engineering, and math (STEM) fields enhance their skills; and Soronko Solutions provides software development services for SMEs looking to grow their online presence.[40] These startups, and more than 200 others in Ghana, look to be the future of the region.

---

38 Martin Greenberg, September, 2014, "The Ghanaian Startup Ecosystem," Meltwater, http://meltwater. org/wp-content/uploads/2014/09/Ghanaian_Startup_Ecosystem_Report.pdf.

39 Ibid.

40 Michael Alimo, June 2, 2017, "13 Tech Startups from Ghana You Need to Know About in 2017," *Techflier*, https://www.techflier.com/2017/06/02/13-tech-startups-from-ghana-you-need-to-know-about-in-2017/.

Figure 1.6f: Sub-Saharan Africa (SSA)

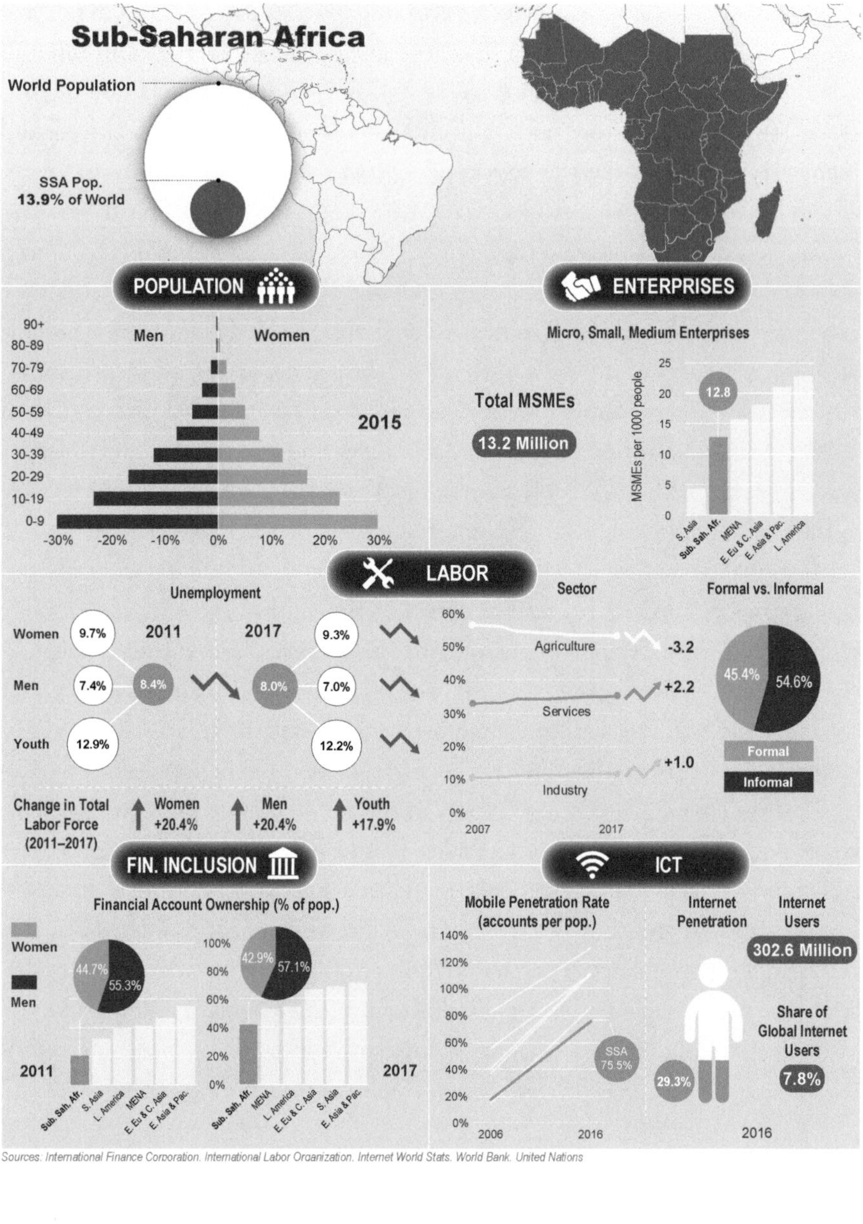

Sub-Saharan Africa

World Population

SSA Pop.
13.9% of World

POPULATION

Men / Women

2015

90+
80-89
70-79
60-69
50-59
40-49
30-39
20-29
10-19
0-9

-30% -20% -10% 0% 10% 20% 30%

ENTERPRISES

Micro, Small, Medium Enterprises

Total MSMEs

13.2 Million

MSMEs per 1000 people

25
20
15
10
5
0

12.8

S. Asia / Sub. Sah. Afr. / MENA / E. Eu & C. Asia / E. Asia & Pac. / L. America

LABOR

Unemployment

	2011	2017	
Women	9.7%		9.3%
Men	7.4%	8.4% 8.0%	7.0%
Youth	12.9%		12.2%

Change in Total Labor Force (2011–2017): Women +20.4% / Men +20.4% / Youth +17.9%

Sector

60%
50% Agriculture -3.2
40%
30% Services +2.2
20%
10% Industry +1.0
0%
2007 2017

Formal vs. Informal

45.4% 54.6%

Formal
Informal

FIN. INCLUSION

Financial Account Ownership (% of pop.)

Women
Men

2011: 44.7% / 55.3%
2017: 42.9% / 57.1%

100%
80%
60%
40%
20%
0%

Sub. Sah. Afr. / S. Asia / L. America / MENA / E. Eu & C. Asia / E. Asia & Pac.

ICT

Mobile Penetration Rate (accounts per pop.)

140%
120%
100%
80%
60%
40%
20%
0%

2006 2016

SSA 75.5%

Internet Penetration: 29.3%

Internet Users: **302.6 Million**

Share of Global Internet Users: **7.8%**

2016

Sources: International Finance Corporation. International Labor Organization. Internet World Stats. World Bank. United Nations

What Works and How to Measure It

What makes us believe that inclusive economies will pull people out of poverty and make them less vulnerable? Various stakeholders—ranging from international development agencies such as the World Bank and bilateral aid organizations to impact investors, corporations, and academics—have spent time and money trying to measure the impact of access to services and jobs.

The discussion on what works best, where, and how is a vibrant debate and the answers depend largely on the context. Nevertheless, a few insights have been drawn repeatedly, based on decades of evidence. In recent years, researchers have conducted a new generation of studies to better understand the impact of economic inclusion initiatives on the lives of the poor, their households, and their communities. Most of these studies have focused on two areas: financial inclusion, such as the provision of microcredit, savings, and other financial services; and pro-poor graduation and cash transfer programs, which seek to raise extremely poor people to the level that they can begin to connect to the market economy.

Microfinance was arguably the first major market-based solution explicitly targeting the poor and, for that reason, is the experiment that enjoys the largest body of evaluation work. Studies on microfinance have reached mixed conclusions. On the one hand, randomized control trial (RCT) studies on traditional microcredit programs did not find significant improvements in welfare, education, health, or women's empowerment (see Box 1.3 on measurement methodologies).[41] In addition, an evaluation of seven such programs did not find evidence of increased incomes or consumption among households. On the other hand, the latter and other RCTs conducted over the past decade found that microcredit borrowers tended to invest in and expand their businesses, and that expanded access to credit did, in fact, afford households more freedom in how they earn and spend money.[42]

Other studies suggest that small adjustments to financial products and services—expanding them to include savings, insurance, and money transfers—result in significant benefits for clients in terms of investments, resilience, and

---

41 Abhijit Banerjee, Esther Duflo, and Rachel Glennerster, 2010, "Evidence from a Randomized Evaluation: The Miracle of Microfinance?," Innovations for Poverty-Action, https://www.poverty-action.org/study/miracle-microfinance-evidence-randomized-evaluation.

42 Dean Karlan., October 5, 2016, "Making Microfinance More Effective," *Harvard Business Review*, https://hbr.org/2016/10/making-microfinance-more-effective.

income smoothing while also improving financial institutions' performance.[43] Evidence also shows that successes of microfinance and other financial inclusion schemes are at least partly due to the fact that clients are typically women, who tend to spend money more responsibly and for the benefit of their families.[44]

Box 1.3: Impact Measurement Tools

There are several ways to measure the development impact of projects, programs, and policies on the intended beneficiaries and the economy more broadly. Two of the most commonly used methodologies are randomized control trial (RCT) and economic rates of return (ERR).

An RCT is run like a scientific experiment, offering the targeted intervention to one group but not another similar (control) group. By comparing the outcomes of the two groups, RCT studies can reveal impacts perhaps not readily apparent and analyze an intervention from an unbiased perspective. However, it can be difficult in social experiments to control the characteristics of sample populations or the leakage between groups, so RCTs require careful sample selection and isolation techniques to be effective.

Other studies calculate the economic rates of return (ERR), which incorporate quantifiable social, economic, and environmental impacts into the traditional cash flow analysis that generates the financial rate of return (FRR) of a project. ERR is often used, for example, in project finance interventions in sectors such as energy and transportation. If a project's ERR is greater than its FRR, then the project has a positive impact on society, the environment, or the economy. Comparing the ERR to the FRR helps investors and entrepreneurs ensure that they undertake projects that contribute to the greater good rather than detract from it through pollution, unfair labor practices, or health violations (as examples).

Studies on savings and insurance show they provide poor people with benefits such as being able to more easily cope with health shocks and invest in children's education. Mobile money, in turn, is revealed not only to reduce transaction costs for households but also to improve people's ability to share risk, especially during hard times.[45] These financially enabled risk-mitigation and coping techniques are critical to preventing poor households from falling into

---

43 Ibid.

44 Katherine Esty, January 10, 2014, "5 Reasons Why Muhammad Yunus Focuses on Lending to Women," Bill & Melinda Gates Foundation, https://www.impatientoptimists.org/Posts/2014/01/5-Reasons-Why-Muhammad-Yunus-Focuses-on-Lending-to-Women.

45 Ibid.

extreme poverty due to shocks, such as natural disasters and illness, as well as building opportunities for children's futures.

The other poverty reduction approach that has been widely adopted with some success is the graduation approach, which has proven to complement microfinance services and to enable people to move out of extreme poverty. A graduation program entails a sequenced set of interventions including food to ensure basic consumption, skills training, capital and opportunities to start up a business or find a job, financial education and savings support, and mentoring to boost confidence.[46] Graduation programs—implemented in more than 30 countries—have been evaluated carefully and shown to be cost-effective while yielding long-lasting change.[47]

For instance, the BRAC Targeting the Ultra-Poor project, implemented in Bangladesh in the mid-2000s, had a positive effect on savings, financial behavior, and food security.[48] Another review of seven programs across South Asia, Africa, and Latin America suggests that graduation programs increase participants' assets by 12 percent and savings by 96 percent on average one year after they ended. These assessments also indicate that participants spent more time working, went hungry less, and were less stressed and healthier.[49] These types of programs play a key role in reducing dependency on social safety nets—where they exist—and in leading participants into a productive life with access to services and jobs.

Another popular poverty-reduction intervention in emerging and developing countries, especially in the past decade or so, has been the conditional and unconditional cash transfers (CCTs and UCTs) to support poor households. The main difference between the two is that the former requires participants to fulfill conditions such as keeping children in school or keeping up with prenatal health visits. In 2016, 130 countries implemented UCT programs and 63 countries

46 Syed M. Hashemi and Aude de Montesquiou, December 12, 2016, "Graduation Pathways," CGAP, http://www.cgap.org/publications/graduation-pathways.

47 Tony Sheldon, February 7, 2017, "Can the Graduation Approach Help to end Extreme Poverty?," Yale School of Management, http://insights.som.yale.edu/insights/can-the-graduation-approach-help-to-end-extreme-poverty.

48 BRAC, January 15, 2016, "Research," BRAC, http://www.brac.net/targeting-ultra-poor/item/753-research.

49 Munshi Sulaiman, December, 2016, "Eliminating Extreme Poverty: Comparing the Cost-Effectiveness of Livelihood, Cash Transfer, and Graduation Approaches," Access to Finance Forum, http://www.cgap.org/sites/default/files/Forum-Eliminating-Extreme-Poverty-Dec-2016.pdf.

CCT programs. These programs aim to help poor families access basic services such as education and health care and improve nutrition and economic well-being. A recent study found that cash transfers reduce income poverty, raise school attendance, encourage access to health services, diversify diets, improve economic autonomy, reduce child labor, and empower women in decision making.[50] Cash transfers can boost savings and productive investments suggesting that they can both reduce poverty and help poor people attain more autonomy and control their economic destinies.[51]

The spread of digital systems enables electronic transfer payments, translating into advantages in cost and convenience. Transfer programs are more efficiently operated using digital technologies and are more effective where access to high-quality services already exist. Yet while studies demonstrate that graduation and cash transfer programs can be effective at moving people out of poverty, they are not sustainable business models and require operational subsidies or major public expenditures. Therefore, these programs must be transitional and coupled with market-based interventions that create advancement opportunities through jobs and entrepreneurial activity.

Building on the lessons of microfinance—in terms of sustainability, outreach, and impact—diverse private sector solutions are emerging to deliver a range of essential services to the poor. These solutions vie for the attention and resources of funders who increasingly require data to demonstrate impact. They have often fallen within the ambit of impact investing, which refers to investments that seek to generate social and environmental impact and financial returns.[52] Several organizations connected to the impact investing community have developed indicators and tools to measure and report on impact. To date, the diverse range of sectors and impact investor priorities has resulted in a plethora of indicators from which to choose.

The Global Impact Investing Network (GIIN) manages the Impact Reporting and Investment Standards (IRIS), a catalog of generally acceptable metrics and key performance indicators for measuring development effectiveness.

---

50   Jessica Hagen-Zanker, July, 2016, "Understanding the impact of cash transfers: the evidence," Overseas Development Institute, https://www.odi.org/sites/odi.org.uk/files/resource-documents/11465.pdf.

51   Ibid.

52   Global Impact Investing Network, "About Impact Investing," Global Impact Investing Network, https://thegiin.org/impact-investing/.

Depending on the sector or purpose, IRIS offers a menu of options to investors and social entrepreneurs for their measurement needs.[53] The goal is to eventually provide the market with a standard set of indicators and monitoring and evaluation practices that can be compared across the board.

Another notable impact measurement tool is the B Impact Assessment tool, developed by B Lab. This tool targets companies that want to measure their impact and compare it to similar companies for benchmarking purposes. They use the tool to assess their social and environmental impact, as well as their governance practices, treatment of workers and customers, and interaction with the community. They can then compare their scores with other similar businesses and identify opportunities for improvement.[54]

In short, although the debate around what works is not fully resolved, the past decade or so has shown that market-based solutions can have a strong impact in poverty reduction and economic inclusion. We have also witnessed solid growth in measurement practices targeted at private sector initiatives. The use of these tools supports the trend toward inclusive business and the generation of market-based opportunities for the poor to access much-needed services and build productive careers.

---

53   The GIIN has been managing the development of IRIS since 2009. Prior to that, IRIS was jointly managed by the Rockefeller Foundation, Acumen Fund, and B Lab, which began the development of IRIS in early 2008 with support from Hitachi, Deloitte, and PricewaterhouseCoopers. See more at Global Impact Investing Network, "What is IRIS?," https://iris.thegiin.org/.

54   B Impact Assessment, "About," http://bimpactassessment.net/.

Chapter 2. Poor and Low-Income People

Poverty is multidimensional and complex. It affects men, women, girls, and boys in different ways at different times. It deprives people of the freedom to shape their own lives and decide their own paths. Traditionally, poverty has been defined narrowly—around income and assets—but poverty is in fact conditioned by a host of factors, including lack of access to education, health care, land, security, finance, power, voice, and freedom of choice. In some regions, poverty is directly tied to food security and compounded by worsening climate change and/or other global economic shocks.

Over the past decade, we have deepened our understanding of poverty. Research has confirmed that rather than being a homogeneous group, poor people exhibit a complex array of characteristics. If you are poor, you're more likely to be a woman or child living in a rural village in Sub-Saharan Africa or South Asia, with little to no education and working in the informal sector, especially in subsistence agriculture—and you are likely to have access to a mobile phone. (See Figure 2.1).[1]

Expanding the pathways out of poverty—access to services and jobs—starts with a comprehensive understanding about those who are poor. Those pathways will depend on the starting point for each major segment of poor people.

---

1 World Bank, "World Bank Development Indicators," World Bank, http://databank.worldbank.org/data/reports.aspx?source=world-development-indicators.

Figure 2.1: If the World's Poor Were 100 People

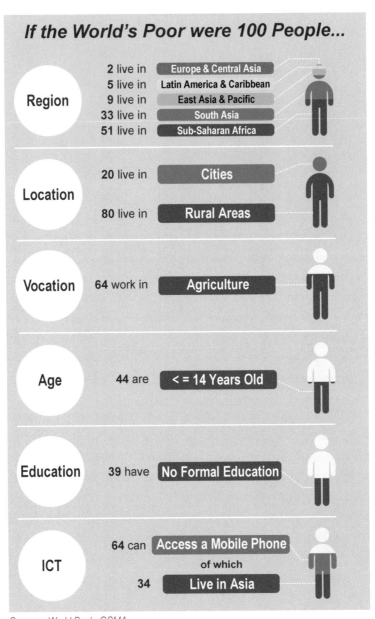

Sources: World Bank, GSMA

Characteristics and Segmentation

Income, Assets, and Food Security

Poor and low-income people share a defining characteristic: limited income, assets, and food security. The World Bank defines the extreme poor as those living on less than $1.90 per day in local purchasing power parity (dollars adjusted to the cost of living in each country—see Box 2.1). According to this definition, approximately 767 million people, or roughly 11 percent of the global population, lives in extreme poverty.[2] More than 2 billion people, or 28 percent of the world, falls below $3.20 per day, the threshold that defines moderate poverty.[3] Although this ratio is far lower than historical levels, it reflects the persistence of poverty and inequality over time.

Box 2.1: What Does the International Poverty Line Mean?

The international poverty line equals the equivalent of $1.90 adjusted for price-level differences across countries. To understand what this means in practice, think about what a person can buy for $1.90 a day. She can't afford proper nutrition, health insurance, or shelter. Entertainment and luxury goods are unattainable. Globally, over 900 million people live below this threshold.

While the poverty line categorizes people as "poor" or "not poor," poverty is not either/or. Someone who has $3.30 a day to spend likely faces similar challenges as someone with $3.20. Both individuals may not have enough income to buy medications, send children to school, or obtain a loan. Instead, poverty can be viewed as a spectrum, encompassing those who are chronically poor and struggling to purchase fundamentals, as well as those who have low incomes and are vulnerable but can envision pulling themselves and their families into a brighter future (see Figure 2.2).[4]

---

2   World Bank, "Poverty Overview," October 2, 2016, World Bank, http://www.worldbank.org/en/topic/poverty/overview.

3   Global Basic Income Foundation, "Facts," http://www.globalincome.org/English/Facts.html.

4   V. Kasturi Rangan, Michael Chu, and Djordjija Petkoski, June, 2011, "The Globe: Segmenting the Base of the Pyramid," *Harvard Business Review*, https://hbr.org/2011/06/the-globe-segmenting-the-base-of-the-pyramid.

Figure 2.2: The Spectrum of the Poor

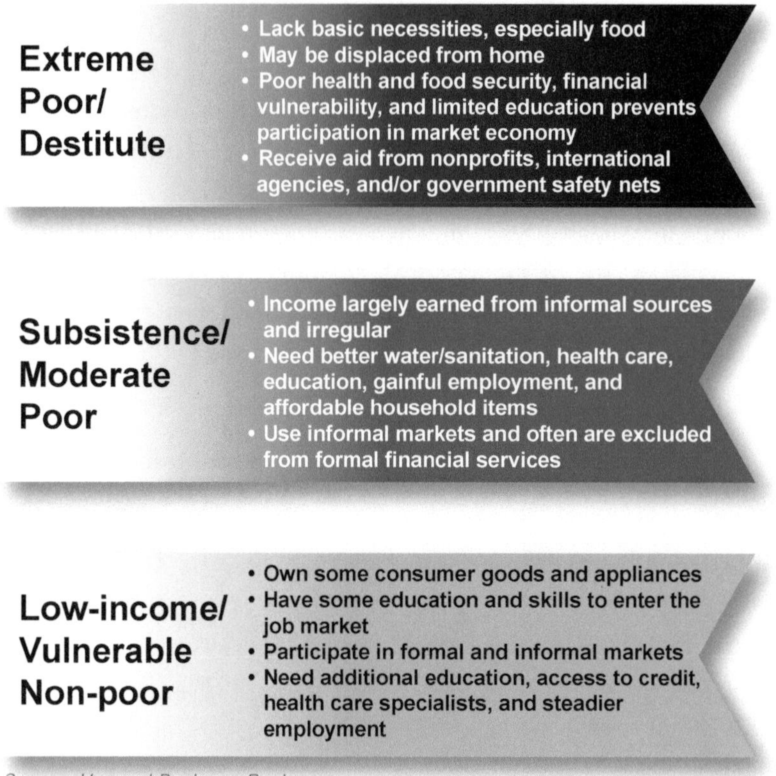

Extreme Poor/ Destitute
- Lack basic necessities, especially food
- May be displaced from home
- Poor health and food security, financial vulnerability, and limited education prevents participation in market economy
- Receive aid from nonprofits, international agencies, and/or government safety nets

Subsistence/ Moderate Poor
- Income largely earned from informal sources and irregular
- Need better water/sanitation, health care, education, gainful employment, and affordable household items
- Use informal markets and often are excluded from formal financial services

Low-income/ Vulnerable Non-poor
- Own some consumer goods and appliances
- Have some education and skills to enter the job market
- Participate in formal and informal markets
- Need additional education, access to credit, health care specialists, and steadier employment

Source: Harvard Business Review

People residing along this spectrum share a desire for better services and employment opportunities, yet their specific needs vary depending on their relative position. For example, while the difference between $2.00 and $2.50 a day may seem inconsequential to high-income observers from the developed economies, this 25 percent difference equates to $182.50 over a year. Having this much extra each year can make a significant difference in an individual's ability to purchase better food (proteins in addition to staples, for example), pay for household or productive assets (an improved roof, a cook stove, farming implements), invest in education, save money, or plan for catastrophes. Measuring poverty is indeed complex. Box 2.2 describes a tool that helps us understand who is poor, beyond the numbers.

Box 2.2: How Do We Know Who Is Poor? The Progress Out of Poverty Index

The collection and analysis of comparable data on poverty is critical to ending extreme poverty, and that entails using simple but robust data collection methods to yield context-specific information. Measurement tools such as the Progress Out of Poverty Index (PPI) aim to contextualize poverty for businesses and other organizations. The statistically sound tool uses 10 questions about a household's characteristics and asset ownership that are scored to compute the likelihood that the household is living below the poverty line—or above it by only a narrow margin. The survey should take no more than 5–10 minutes to complete. Sample questions include "What material is your roof made out of?" and "How many of your children are in school?" Possible responses are tailored to the country in question. For example, one country might include tin and thatched rooves as possible responses, where others might include more modern building materials.[5] PPI has developed 66 national tools that help contextualize poverty in those countries.

Irregular Income

Asserting that a poor person makes $2 per day does not mean that she makes $2 per day consistently every day. See Figure 2.3 for a typical household's uneven income and expenditure flow.[6] Many low-income people juggle the irregular incomes associated with seasonal labor, seasonal or rainfed agriculture, and forms of migrant labor. Often, irregular income means that households suffer from hungry periods where they must cope with less food and fewer resources. Globally, only 40 percent of adults have fixed employment for more than 30 hours per week. Fixed employment is usually held by individuals with greater education levels and skills.[7]

---

5   Piroska Bisits Bullen, "Measuring poverty using the Progress out of Poverty Index," tools4dev, http://www.tools4dev.org/resources/progress-out-of-poverty-index-tool-review/.

6   Jamie Anderson and Wajiha Ahmed, February, 2016, "Smallholder Diaries: Building the Evidence Base with Farming Families in Mozambique, Tanzania, and Pakistan," CGAP, https://bit.ly/1pl5QNA.

7   Jon Clifton and Ben Ryan, August 12, 2014, "Only 1.3 Billion Worldwide Employed Full Time for Employer," Gallup, http://news.gallup.com/poll/174791/billion-worldwide-employed-full-time-employer.aspx.

Figure 2.3: Tanzania Smallholder Net Income and Household Expenditures

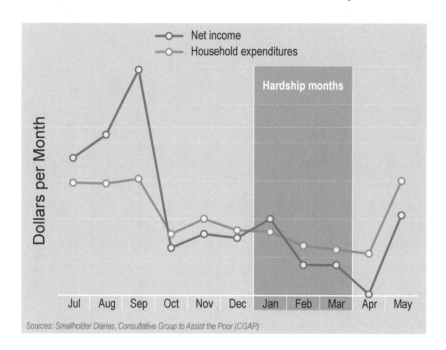

Without specialized knowledge, education, and capabilities, the poor must rely on multiple and diversified streams of income to survive. Low-income households in Kenya, for example, had an average of 10 sources of inflows, and these inflows fluctuated month to month by 55 percent.[8] Recent research found that farmers in Pakistan, Mozambique, and Tanzania relied on many nonagricultural endeavors for their net cash income. In Mozambique, 93 percent of the sampled households obtained net cash income from sources other than agricultural production, compared to 74 percent in Tanzania and 58 percent in Pakistan. Consuming what they grow is also vital for these families. Mozambican families, for example, consumed nearly all of what

---

8   Julie Zollman, 2014, "Kenya Financial Diaries – Shilingi kwa shilingi, the financial lives of the poor," FSD Kenya, http://fsdkenya.org/publication/kenya-financial-diaries-shilingi-kwa-shilingi-the-financial-lives-of-the-poor/.

they produced.[9] While maintaining multiple sources of income can offset some of the risk posed by dry spells in any one income stream, overall income remains unpredictable, which complicates the ability of individuals and households to manage finances and plan for the future (see Box 2.3).

Box 2.3: Diversifying Income Sources: An Important Coping Strategy for the Poor

In Guntar, a slum in Southern India, many women begin their mornings making dosa on griddles and selling them on the street. After breakfast, women turn to their next venture, whether it's collecting trash, selling saris, making other meals for purchase, or working as laborers. Similar patterns exist in rural areas. In Mozambique, for example, people work on and off farms as day laborers; run small, informal businesses; and/or depend on remittances from family members.[10] Each day is a balancing act of activities that, taken together, add up to what they hope is a livable wage.

Food Insecurity

When households lack sufficient resources to purchase or grow enough food for consumption, they are food insecure. Within market economies, there is no guarantee that enough income will be earned and distributed across the population to enable everyone to purchase food. Price volatility poses an enormous challenge for the poor, who may not be able to afford food when prices surge. Under turbulent market conditions, this food insecurity exacerbates poverty.[11] Currently, 815 million people suffer from undernourishment (up from 777 million in 2015); of this group, 155 million are children under the age of 5 who suffer from stunting (more than two standard deviations below ideal weight), which increases their risk of infection or death, impaired cognitive abilities, and poor school and work performance. While stunting rates are dropping globally, food insecurity is

---

9   Jamie Anderson and Wajiha Ahmed, February, 2016, "Smallholder Diaries: Building the Evidence Base with Farming Families in Mozambique, Tanzania, and Pakistan," CGAP, https://bit.ly/1pl5QNA.

10   Ibid.

11   Will Martin, November 5, 2010, "Food Security and Poverty – a precarious balance," World Bank, http://blogs.worldbank.org/developmenttalk/food-security-and-poverty-a-precarious-balance.

worsening in some areas of Sub-Saharan Africa, Southeast Asia, the Middle East, and Western Asia due to climate-related shocks.[12]

Other Dimensions of Poverty

In addition to income-related characteristics, other factors contribute to poverty. Examples relate to aspects such as geography, gender, and demographics.

Geography

While people living in extreme poverty can be found everywhere, they are concentrated in Sub-Saharan Africa and South Asia. Sub-Saharan Africa alone contains more than half of the world's poor.[13] Of the 10 countries with the greatest number of people living in poverty, six are in Sub-Saharan Africa, and of the 10 countries with the greatest population ratios of people living in poverty, all are in Sub-Saharan Africa.[14] In addition, those living in the region tend to fall further below the poverty line than individuals living elsewhere. In brief, poverty is more widespread and severe in Sub-Saharan Africa than in the rest of the world. Figure 2.4 illustrates the distribution of poverty by region and by country.[15]

Rural versus Urban

Low-income people also tend to be located in remote and rural areas, with estimates ranging from 80 to 85 percent of the world's poor living in rural areas.[16] Unsurprisingly, almost two-thirds of people living in poverty work in ag-

---

12   FAO, IFAD, UNICEF, WHO and WFP, 2017, "The State of Food Security and Nutrition in the World 2017, "Building resilience for peace and food security," http://www.fao.org/state-of-food-security-nutrition/en/.

13   World Bank, 2016, "Poverty and Shared Prosperity 2016: Taking on Inequality," World Bank, https://bit.ly/2cL20LI.

14   Ibid.

15   Max Roser and Esteban Ortiz-Ospina, March 27, 2017, "Global Extreme Poverty," Our World in Data, https://ourworldindata.org/extreme-poverty/#the-demographics-of-extreme-poverty.

16   Sabina Alkire, June 2014, "Poverty in Rural and Urban Areas: Direct comparisons using the global MPI 2014," Oxford Poverty & Human Development Initiative, https://bit.ly/2GtxkOa.

riculture, mainly on small- and medium-sized farms.[17] In fact, agricultural workers are over four times more likely to be poor than people working in other sectors.[18]

Figure 2.4: Distribution of Global Poverty in 2013

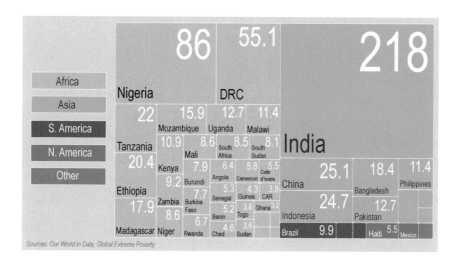

Sources: Our World in Data, Global Extreme Poverty

While poor people have traditionally resided in remote and rural areas, they increasingly migrate to cities and urban areas where they believe more job opportunities await them. After seeing their families struggling on farm incomes, young people are particularly drawn to the possibility of formal sector employment and higher salaries. Families may also encourage a move in the hope that migrants will send home a portion of their earnings, known as remittances, to support the family. Yet moving does not guarantee better livelihoods. Competition for higher-paying jobs is often fierce, and urban dwellers face their own challenges. Approximately 880 million people reside in urban slums with inadequate housing, com-

17   World Bank, 2016, "Poverty and Shared Prosperity 2016: Taking on Inequality," World Bank, https://bit.ly/2cL20LI.

18   Ibid.

fort, and sanitation.[19] Although many cities are working to upgrade infrastructure to accommodate this growth, an expected 40 percent of the world's future urban population will live in slums.[20] Currently, 54 percent of the world's population lives in urban areas, and this percentage is expected to rise to 66 percent by 2050.[21]

Women

As shown in Figure 2.5, women are disproportionately represented among the ranks of the extreme poor, especially single-mother heads of household and older women living alone.[22] Women are also more likely to work in low-pay, low-productivity, undervalued jobs in the informal sector and subsistence agriculture—jobs that are unprotected by labor laws.[23] In agriculture, women are less likely to control land and they have limited access to inputs, seeds, extension services, and finance. They also bear greater responsibility for unpaid work, including childcare occupying one to three hours more per day than men, and they are disproportionately responsible for household food preparation. Women spend a greater percentage of their incomes on expenditures that benefit children and the household.[24]

19   Selim Jahan, 2016, "Human Development Report 2016," United Nations Development Programme, http://hdr.undp.org/sites/default/files/2016_human_development_report.pdf.

20   Ibid.

21   United Nations Department of Economic and Social Affairs, 2014, "World Urbanization Prospects: The 2014 Revision, Highlights," United Nations, https://bit.ly/2gYlppO.

22   United Nations Stats, 2015, "The World's Women," United Nations, https://unstats.un.org/unsd/gender/chapter8/chapter8.html.

23   Rafael Diez de Medina, June 2012, "Statistical update on employment in the informal economy," ILO Department of Statistics, https://bit.ly/2q2pboJ.

24   World Bank, 2012, "World Bank Development Report 2012: Gender Equality and Development," World Bank, http://bit.ly/2NtmF4S.

Figure 2.5: Women Are More Likely to Fall Into Extreme Poverty Than Men

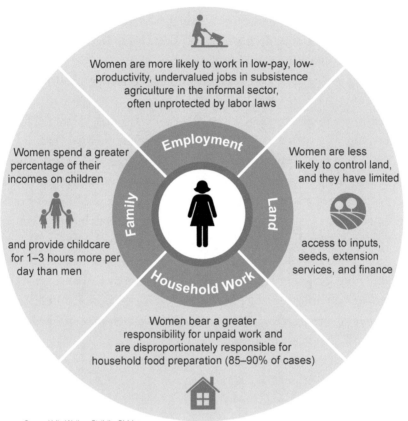

Source: United Nations Statistics Division

Closing the gender gap in workforce participation by 25 percent by 2025 could increase global GDP by US$5.3 trillion.[25] Across developed and developing countries, women are paid less than men, earning between 60 and 75 percent of a man's wages depending on the country. Contributing to this underpayment is the fact that women are more likely to be wage workers and unpaid family workers; they are more likely to work in the informal sector, with fewer options to transfer to formal employment than men.[26]

25   International Labor Organization, 2017, "ILO What Works Research Brief: Economic Impacts of Reducing the Gender Gap," International Labor Organization, https://bit.ly/2C2Ujsx.

26   World Bank, 2012, "World Bank Development Report 2012: Gender Equality and Development," World Bank, http://bit.ly/2NtmF4S.

Other benefits accrue from increased income equality for women. For example, increasing women's and girls' education contributes to higher economic growth.[27] One study presenting data from 175 countries found that childhood mortality decreased by 9.5 percent for each additional year of education for women of reproductive age.[28]

Becoming a wife does not protect a woman from poverty. In fact, early marriage of girls before their 18th birthday is correlated with multiple factors that contribute to generational poverty. For poor families, arranging for their daughters to be married early can relieve immediate financial pressures but has the longer-term result of keeping that girl locked in extreme poverty by limiting her education. Moreover, the cycle is more likely to continue because a mother who is under 18 has a 60 percent higher risk of her own child dying in its first year of life or suffering from a low birth weight, poor nutrition, and late physical and cognitive development.[29]

In addition to earning less than men, married women are frequently excluded from economic decision making in the home. About one in three married women from developing countries has no control over household spending on major purchases, and about one in ten is not consulted on how her own cash earnings are spent.[30]

Gender-based violence has affected or will affect one in three women in their lifetime and has personal, social, and economic outcomes for those women. While violence affects women of all socioeconomic backgrounds, research suggests that men who live in poverty are more at risk of perpetrating such violence. Countries that are war or conflict affected, fragile states that have experienced economic collapse, and places where large portions of the

---

27 Organisation for Economic Co-operation and Development, May, 2012, "Gender Equality in Education, Employment and Entrepreneurship; Final Report to the MCM 2012," Organisation for Economic Co-operation and Development, https://www.oecd.org/employment/50423364.pdf.

28 Emanuela Gakidou, 2010, "Increased Educational Attainment and its Effect on Child Mortality in 175 Countries between 1970 and 2009: A Systemic Analysis," *The Lancet*, http://bit.ly/2L9m0ce.

29 Lorriann Robinson, July 8, 2014, "Early marriage and poverty: Why we must break the cycle," ONE, https://www.one.org/us/2014/07/08/early-marriage-and-poverty-why-we-must-break-the-cycle/.

30 United Nations Department of Economic and Social Affairs, 2015, "The World's Women 2015: Trends and Statistics," United Nations, https://unstats.un.org/unsd/gender/downloads/WorldsWomen2015_report.pdf.

population have been displaced are all more prone to suffer from poverty, income insecurity, and gender-based violence.[31]

Most countries in the world have laws that restrict women's economic participation to some degree, such as laws excluding them from a particular type of employment, enshrining a husband's right to object to his spouse working, or preventing women from accepting a job.[32]

Youth

Young people make up the largest segment of global poverty. Approximately 44 percent of the extreme poor are 14 years old or younger, with the greatest concentration in Sub-Saharan Africa, which houses more than half of extremely poor children worldwide.[33] In general, much of the developing world has a median age under 30. This "youth bulge" has in many instances resulted from a reduction in infant mortality due to improved access to health services and pre- and postnatal care, accompanied by a consistently high fertility rate among women. Figure 2.6 shows the median age of people across the globe, highlighting the growing youth bulge.

---

31   World Health Organization, Media Centre, November, 2017 "Violence against women," World Health Organization, http://www.who.int/mediacentre/factsheets/fs239/en/.

32   World Bank, 2014, "Women, Business and the Law 2014, Removing Restrictions to Enhance Gender Equality," World Bank, https://bit.ly/2q29Fdp.

33   UNICEF and World Bank, October 3, 2016 "Nearly 385 million children living in extreme poverty, says joint World Bank Group – UNICEF study," UNICEF, https://www.unicef.org/media/media_92856.html.

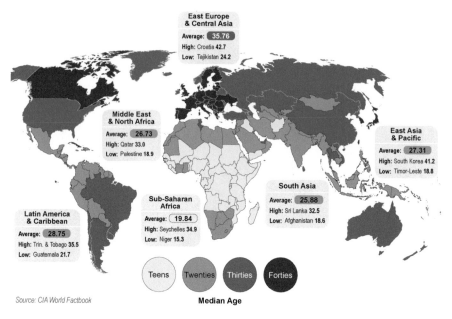

Figure 2.6: World Median Ages and the Growing Youth Bulge

Source: CIA World Factbook

Many children living in poverty suffer from malnutrition and undernutrition. Undernutrition contributes to nearly half of all deaths in children under five in Asia and Africa—a total of about 3 million lives lost every year.[34] For those who survive, undernutrition can also contribute to stunting, which diminishes cognitive performance and, over the long term, earning potential. It also leaves children more vulnerable to infections and disease.

In addition, many of these children and young people are out of school. In 2015, 264 million children and young people were not in school, with a disproportionate number located in low-income countries or countries with conflict. Sub-Saharan Africa has the highest out-of-school rates, as illustrated in Figure 2.7.[35] [36] Without a strong education, children risk entering an increasingly competitive global economy as illiterate and unskilled workers, further entrenching themselves in poverty.

---

34   UNICEF Data, "Nutrition," UNICEF, https://data.unicef.org/topic/nutrition/malnutrition/.

35   Global Partnership for Education, "Education Data," Global Partnership for Education http://www.globalpartnership.org/data-and-results/education-data

36   UNESCO, Institute for Statistics, June, 2017, "Reducing global poverty through universal primary and secondary education," UNESCO https://bit.ly/2gOP6zn.

Figure 2.7: Percentage of Children Not Enrolled in School in Sub-Saharan Africa

See Box 2.4 for a more detailed description about the effects of illiteracy and innumeracy. Today, 39 percent of the poor have no formal education.[37]

Box 2.4: Illiteracy and Innumeracy

Illiteracy and innumeracy carry an enormous economic cost in the developing world. Countries waste billions annually on education spending. Billions more in foregone economic benefit results from lower productivity of illiterate populaces. Policies and products are frequently designed without considering this segment of the population. For example, while bank accounts can be an excellent tool for providing bottom of the pyramid people with a pathway toward financial inclusion, merely having a bank account is not enough. To reap the benefits of inclusion, it is essential for people to be able to use and understand their accounts. The benefit of having cash available in a bank account is greatly diminished when one cannot use an ATM. Services can be provided to the illiterate if they are well designed with inclusion in mind. My Oral Village strives to create usable financial records for illiterate and innumerate adults through oral information management tools. These tools include cellular interfaces that use

---

37   World Bank, 2016, "Poverty and Shared Prosperity 2016: Taking on Inequality," World Bank, https://bit.ly/2cL20LI.

icons to indicate meaning, voice-assisted interfaces for mobile money payments, and contracts and documents for financial services providers that use simplified language and symbols.[38] [39]

At the same time, in some regions of the world the population is aging, causing the number of elderly affected by poverty to rise. Unlike other developing regions, Latin America and the Caribbean has seen higher growth rates among its elderly cohort than among its youth. By 2030, the 65-and-older population will reach at least 10 percent in most countries in the region.[40] If the elderly poor are unable to support themselves in the informal economies to which they typically have access, then the absence of adequate social programs means we could see a rising number remain in or slip into poverty.

Refugees and Displaced Persons

The numbers of refugees, asylum seekers, and internally displaced people have reached levels unseen since World War II. There are currently more than 71 million displaced people in the world—a population greater than that of the United Kingdom.[41] At the root of these movements of people are conflicts, violence, and natural disasters, which drive people from their homes and force them into an existence of uncertainty and vulnerability. Given the increasingly protracted nature of conflicts and frequency of natural disasters, people are living outside of their homes for longer periods of time too. Refugees in 2015 had spent an average of four years uprooted from their lives.[42]

---

38 Brett Matthews, July, 2017, "Design for Oral Financial Inclusion," Briefing Note #2, My Oral Village http://myoralvillage.org/research/publications/.

39 Brett Matthews, October 31, 2014, "Oral Information Management Tools: Lighting the Path to Financial Inclusion," My Oral Village, https://bit.ly/2uLpb20.

40 Paola Scommegna and Marlene Lee, April, 2014, "Aging in Latin America and the Caribbean," Population Reference Bureau.

41 Adrian Edwards, June 19, 2017, "Forced displacement worldwide at its highest in decades," UNHCR, https://bit.ly/2GxspHE.

42 Xavier Devictor, September 15, 2016, "How many years do refugees stay in exile?," World Bank, http://blogs.worldbank.org/dev4peace/how-many-years-do-refugees-stay-exile.

When people flee their homes, they typically leave behind almost all their assets. While some may have lived comfortable lives before the crisis that uprooted them, displacement often eliminates people's security and leads them into poverty. Away from their homes and possibly their native countries, it becomes even more difficult for the displaced to rebuild their lives. Whether living in a formal refugee camp or informally in an urban area, they often face significant barriers to employment and education that hinder people's ability to rebuild their lives. Among the Syrian refugees in Jordan and Lebanon, for example, the unemployment rate is 60 percent and 36 percent, respectively.[43]

Indigenous Populations

Indigenous people are defined as those people with specific rights derived from their historical ties to a specific territory and who are culturally distinct from other, often politically dominant, populations. About 370 million indigenous people live across the globe and they represent 15 percent of the extreme poor, and one-third of the rural poor. The poverty of indigenous populations is more severe than the poverty of nonindigenous populations because of geographic and political exclusion, historic oppression and discrimination by majority populations, insecure land tenure and lack of property rights, the effects of climate change, and exclusion from public services such as health care and education. As a result of this discrimination, the indigenous poor are also excluded from access to opportunities.[44] Figure 2.8 shows the percentage of indigenous populations in major regions and countries around the globe.[45]

43 Alex Dziadosz, November 21, 2016, "Syrian exiles in Lebanon seek a refuge in work," *The Financial Times*, https://on.ft.com/2q4kgnS.

44 Gillette Hall, August 9, 2016, "Poverty and exclusion among Indigenous Peoples: The global evidence," World Bank, https://blogs.worldbank.org/voices/poverty-and-exclusion-among-indigenous-peoples-global-evidence.

45 Gillette Hall, April, 2010, "Indigenous Peoples, Poverty, and Development," Cambridge University Press http://siteresources.worldbank.org/EXTINDPEOPLE/Resources/407801-1271860301656/full_report.pdf.

Figure 2.8: Indigenous Populations Around the World

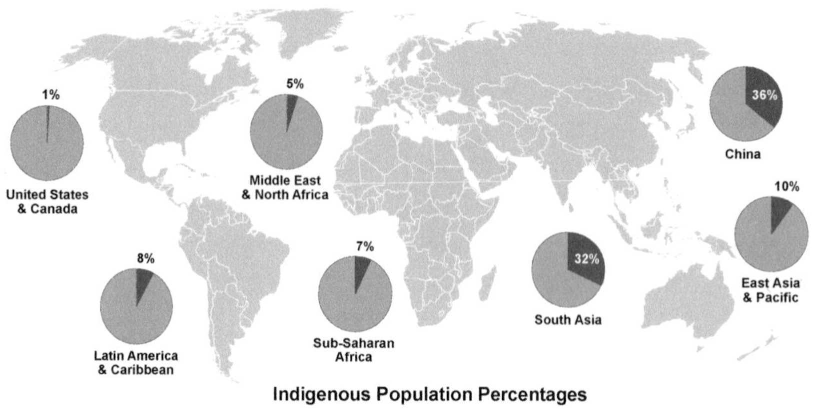

Indigenous Population Percentages

Source: Gillette Hall, Indigenous Peoples, Poverty and Development

Needs and Spending Patterns

One of the common struggles among poor people is the need to meet and balance daily and periodic spending demands. Given the scarcity of resources and the need to stretch their money, considerable time is spent on financial decision making. These decisions are stressful, which itself can contribute to less efficient financial decisions. Poor people weigh three courses of action when considering an expenditure:

• Go without, despite the risks this may pose to one's well-being,
• Raise money to complete the purchase by selling assets, or
• Use savings or credit to fund the expense.[46]

For people in extreme poverty, meeting basic needs becomes the sole focus. Food, in particular, represents a large proportion of low-income people's spending. In a study across 13 countries, households were found to spend 56 to

---

46   Daryl Collins, Jonathan Morduch, Stuart Rutherford and Orlanda Ruthven, December 19, 2010, "Portfolios of the Poor: How the World's Poor Live on $2 a Day," Princeton University Press.

78 percent of their income on food.[47] With rising incomes, the proportion of income spent on food drops and people direct cash toward other purchases including investment in their business. In fact, it is useful to think about the non-day-to-day expenditures of the poor in three buckets: life cycle events, emergencies, and opportunities (see Box 2.5 for an example).

Box 2.5: The Impact of Lifecycle Expenses

Bertha was a single mother in Tanzania raising five children. She provided for her family by selling potatoes, eggs, and maize; collecting and selling grasses and timber; working on other farms; and receiving money from family members living in the capital city. In 2014, her sister-in-law needed an operation during childbirth and her brother was forced to borrow $343 to pay for the operation. Bertha's brother soon fell ill and was unable to pay back the loan. Bertha took on the responsibility and started borrowing from four informal groups, two local shops, a group of four family members, and friends. She was also forced to take on additional work to cover her payments. By this point, her income barely covered her debts and expenses. Fortunately, Bertha could manage the loan payments and help her brother but, as her situation demonstrates, another unexpected event such as a failed harvest, natural disaster, or illness could have plunged her family into further debt. As she was already maximizing her ability to pay off the loans, this situation would have been disastrous for Bertha's financial stability.[48]

Life cycle events include those once-in-a-lifetime occurrences (birth, marriage, death) or recurrent incidents (school fees, religious holidays, harvest time) that every household faces. In Bangladesh and India, the dowry system makes daughters' marriages an expensive business. In parts of Africa, burying deceased parents can be quite costly. Other life cycle events include home building, widowhood, old age, and passing a lump sum inheritance to heirs. These needs can usually be anticipated, even if their exact date is not always known. The awareness that such outlays await is a source of great anxiety for many poor people.

---

47   Abhijit V. Banerjee and Esther Duflo, October, 2006, "The Economic Lives of the Poor," Massachusetts Institute of Technology, https://economics.mit.edu/files/530.

48   Jamie Anderson and Wajiha Ahmed, February, 2016, "Smallholder Diaries: Building the Evidence Base with Farming Families in Mozambique, Tanzania, and Pakistan," CGAP, https://bit.ly/1pl5QNA.

Emergencies include personal crises such as sickness or injury, the death of a breadwinner or the loss of employment, and/or theft. Many emergencies are completely outside the control of the household, such as war, floods, fires, cyclones, and (for slum dwellers) the bulldozing of their homes by the authorities. All these emergencies create a sudden need for cash.

Opportunities to invest in businesses, land, or household assets also occur from time to time. Business investments are only one of several kinds of investments that poor people make. They also want to invest in costly items that make life more comfortable—energy, better roofing, better furniture, a fan, a smartphone, a tablet.

The way that individual households and poor communities handle regular and intermittent expenditures is influenced by a myriad of factors, not all of which are purely economic or financial in nature. Box 2.6 discusses the importance of psychological and social factors as behavioral science has revealed them in recent years.

Box 2.6: Are the Poor Worse Spenders Than the Other People? Learning from Behavioral Science

Policy makers, development theorists, program managers, and other development actors have long argued about the capacity of the poor. Some more libertarian-minded advocates have argued that the poor are resilient, creative, and value-conscious entrepreneurs and actors whose capacity can be harnessed to build pro-poor businesses that can serve the poor and alleviate poverty. Others have highlighted the poor choices that the poor make, choosing to spend their limited earnings on, say, celebrations instead of improved nutrition. Increasingly, though, policy makers are turning to behavioral science for insights that will help them address intractable policy challenges, from increasing household savings rates to improving decision making around nutrition or sanitation practices. Behavioral science looks broadly at the social, cultural, psychological, economic, and even biological factors that influence how people think and act, without assigning moral judgement or bias. It also identifies the details in the systems, technologies, and services that often get overlooked but—when corrected—can enhance the design and implementation of programs in developing countries.

An example of how behavioral science has been applied to poverty programming is the World Bank's 2014 review of 19 studies that detail the impact of cash transfers on overall consumption (that is, considering consumption associated not just with the transfer but also from other income). The researchers focused on two items—alcohol and tobacco—because these items are frequently cited by critics of cash transfer programs as examples of expenditures that increase when cash is provided to the poor. The study found that in 82 percent of cases, there was no increase in alcohol and tobacco expenditures among recipients.[49] Part of the explanation lies in a substitution effect where participants increase spending in other areas to meet the requirements of the program. For example, parents may need to spend less money on alcohol to send their children to school and qualify for the transfers. In addition, many of these programs targeted women who have been shown to invest more money in children and productive expenditures.

A GiveDirectly randomized evaluation of an unconditional cash transfer program in Kenya found similar results. Poor households received one-off mobile payments ranging from $404 to $1,520. The study found that even 14 months after the payment was received, households were spending more on food, health, and education than those who did not receive payments. Spending on alcohol and tobacco did not increase, which may be due to productive spending that led to rising incomes and lower stress levels.[50]

Spending is also influenced by geography. Urban areas have greater markets for water, ICT, and housing, given the dense concentration of people and the more advanced digital infrastructure. Cities also enjoy larger markets for transportation and energy, except in most of Asia. Rural areas, on the other hand, have the most demand for food and health care markets.

Over the past 15 years, the private sector has increasingly looked at low-income and poor consumers' spending to identify business opportunities. Although the purchases of this segment of the population often have small monetary values, the "base of the pyramid" encompasses 4 billion people living on less than $3,000 a year in local purchasing power (see Figure 2.9).[51] Therefore,

---

49   David Evans, May 27, 2014, "Do the Poor Waste Transfers on Booze and Cigarettes? No," *Development Impacts*, https://blogs.worldbank.org/impactevaluations/do-poor-waste-transfers-booze-and-cigarettes-no.

50   Charles Kenny, September 25, 2015, "Give Poor People Cash," *The Atlantic*, https://www.theatlantic.com/international/archive/2015/09/welfare-reform-direct-cash-poor/407236/.

51   Allen L. Hammond and William J. Kramer, 2007, "The Next 4 Billion: Market Size and Business Strategy at the Base of the Pyramid," International Finance Corporation and World Resources Institute, https://bit.ly/2q1v9Hj.

the aggregate volume of their purchases is significant and translates into an impressive $5 trillion global consumer market.[52] As more businesses begin exploring how to tap into such markets, the products available to poor consumers are likely to grow in number and variety and may influence how the poor allocate their resources.

Figure 2.9: Estimated Base-of-the-Pyramid Market by Sector

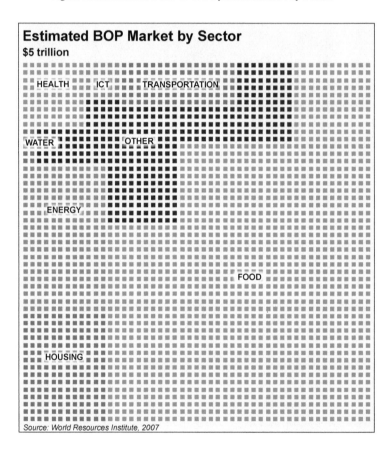

Estimated BOP Market by Sector
$5 trillion

HEALTH ICT TRANSPORTATION

WATER OTHER

ENERGY

FOOD

HOUSING

Source: World Resources Institute, 2007

Access to Services

Poor and vulnerable households need basic services such as education, health care, electricity, water and sanitation (WASH), finance, ICT, and transport to live full and healthy lives. Access to these basic services also enables people

---

52 Ibid.

to be active contributors to the economy, building opportunities for others and fueling economic growth. People need access to education to obtain good jobs, earn a decent income, and be productive for their employers. Basic health care helps to combat illness, heal injuries, and prevent sickness and disease, keeping workers and students healthy and on task. Power enables households, businesses, and communities to have light, heat, and air conditioning, fueling machines and enabling a range of useful services now taken for granted in the developed economies. Infrastructure and the internet facilitate the flow of goods, services, and information, providing people with tools to improve their lives. Financial services help poor people manage their financial flows and obligations, whether it is through completing purchases, setting aside savings, managing risks, or making investments. Public and private transport systems enable them to get to jobs and move goods to buyers and marketplaces. Unlike wealthier people in their communities, the poor often lack access to these services, as shown in Figure 2.10.[53]

Figure 2.10: Poor People Lack Access to Basic Services

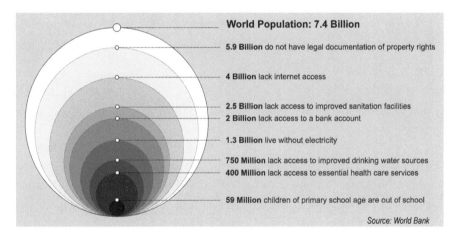

World Population: 7.4 Billion

5.9 Billion do not have legal documentation of property rights

4 Billion lack internet access

2.5 Billion lack access to improved sanitation facilities
2 Billion lack access to a bank account

1.3 Billion live without electricity

750 Million lack access to improved drinking water sources
400 Million lack access to essential health care services

59 Million children of primary school age are out of school

Source: World Bank

In the past, governments have been the main providers of many of these services, but this pattern is changing as public-private partnerships are being built across all sectors to improve the delivery of services to the poor and to the last mile. A recent study followed the experiences of 20 companies that

---

53   World Bank, "World Bank Development Indicators," World Bank, http://databank.worldbank.org/data/reports.aspx?source=world-development-indicators.

deliver energy, sanitation, health care, housing, and education to people living on less than $2.50 per day and found that many of the companies reach this market.[54]

Poor people often encounter three key barriers when they seek to access essential goods and services: availability, quality, and affordability (see Box 2.7). This section explores the state of access to—and critical gaps in—services to the poor.

Box 2.7: Availability, Quality, and Affordability: What Do We Mean?

Availability refers to access to the service at all times. Poor people often reside and work in remote, rural, or otherwise cutoff areas with substandard roads (if any), electricity grids, and water systems. This lack of infrastructure makes it difficult if not impossible to physically reach poor customers. In some instances, availability is also driven by politics, where majority groups use their power to limit access to minority groups.

Quality refers to the grade of excellence of the service being provided. Poor service might take the form of discriminatory pricing or the dumping of poor or expired product (especially in health care). Very often, one aspect of poor service is an underlying assumption that poor people do not have the right to expect better or to complain.

Affordability refers to the cost for the service. Given the low income and remote location of poor people, the cost of a service is often prohibitively high.

Energy

Some 1.3 billion poor people lack access to high-quality energy, making them "energy poor." Improving access to energy services can enable progress across a range of important dimensions related to the home, work, and community: agricultural productivity, education, gender, health, livelihoods, and quality of life and jobs.

Energy poverty forces people to manage the hours of electric power available, but this burdensome task is often compounded by unpredictability, which in turn wreaks havoc on their home lives and businesses, particularly in places with erratic weather. Poor customers must cope with a lack of control over the electrical power for the machines that heat, cool, cook, process,

54   Michelle Larivee, Kristen Dobson, and Allie O'Shea, June 2017, "Reaching Deep in Low-Income Markets," Deloitte, https://bit.ly/2GtiQxH.

and manufacture. Moreover, lack of power also impairs the quality of community services such as health care, education, policing, water, and local government services generally.[55]

Water and Sanitation

Poverty and access to safe water and sanitation are inextricably linked; access to water and sanitation is required to reduce poverty. Currently, 2.3 billion people live without adequate sanitation and 844 million without basic drinking water services, defined as water sources that can be accessed in a 30-minute round-trip or less.[56] Any further away and people spend excessive time or money to obtain them or to make them safer (through boiling untreated water, for instance). Globally, millions of women spend up to four hours gathering water *each day.*[57] Moreover, waterborne diseases are a constant threat to health, keeping people out of the workforce, out of school, and in poverty.

Water and sanitation are also crucial parts of a healthy economy and employment environment, essential to everyone from the subsistence farmer to a large company working in agriculture, services, or manufacturing. Water is critical to processing food, textiles, and other manufactured goods, from coffee to cotton to steel. It is also critical to employees, who otherwise must leave their place of employment to find water or a public toilet. The same applies to schools, hospitals, and other community service providers. An estimated half of all hospital beds in the developing world are occupied by people with waterborne diseases.[58] Access to these important services provides for a safer, healthier, and more productive work environment that retains its employees.

55   Aaron Leopold, Lucy Stevens, and Mary Gallagher, 2014, "Poor people's energy outlook 2014," Practical Action, https://bit.ly/2uLI6d7.

56   Anna Grojec, July 12, 2017, "Progress on Drinking Water, Sanitation, and Hygiene," World Health Organization and UNICEF, http://www.who.int/mediacentre/news/releases/2017/launch-version-report-jmp-water-sanitation-hygiene.pdf.

57   Kevin Watkins, 2006, "Human Development Report 2016," United Nations Development Programme, http://hdr.undp.org/sites/default/files/reports/267/hdr06-complete.pdf.

58   The Water Project, August 31,2016, "Facts About Water: Statistics of the Water Crisis," The Water Project https://thewaterproject.org/water-scarcity/water_stats.

Health Care

Poverty is also inextricably linked with health. Poverty is a cause of poor health and a constraint to accessing better health care. The biggest barrier to better health care is affordability; the poor simply cannot afford to purchase goods and services required to maintain good health, including access to water and sanitation, nutritious food, and health care services. They often cannot afford out-of-pocket expenses for consultations, tests, and medical treatments provided by health care providers, nor the transport to get to the clinic. According to the World Health Organization, 400 million people lack access to essential health services and 6 percent of people in low- and middle-income countries are pushed further into poverty because of out-of-pocket health spending.[59]

When poor people fall ill, they lack the social benefits that cover the income from lost wages. Those who miss work to care for the sick also lose wages. Finally, health care poverty is exacerbated by a lack of information about healthy behaviors, which leaves the poor prey to misinformation, "quick fix" schemes, or other poor-quality services provided by untrained or undertrained professionals whose services are less expensive than those provided by qualified medical professionals.

Education

Lack of access to high-quality education has prevented millions of people from escaping the cycle of extreme poverty. Approximately 59 million children of primary-school age remain out of school, more than half of them girls or children living in the most remote, conflict-affected, or hardest-to-reach areas. UNESCO estimates that in Sub-Saharan Africa alone, 17 million primary and secondary teachers will be needed to achieve universal primary and secondary education by 2030.[60]

Poor people often cannot afford the fees required to send children to school, let alone out-of-pocket expenses for uniforms, school materials, and

---

59 World Health Organization and World Bank, 2015, "Tracking Universal Health Coverage: First Global Monitoring Report," World Health Organization, http://www.who.int/mediacentre/news/releases/2015/uhc-report/en/.

60 Kate Hodal, October 5, 2016, "UN warns universal education goal will fail without 69 million new teachers," *The Guardian*, https://bit.ly/2dQYBqR.

exam fees. As a result, significant percentages of adolescent girls do not get access to primary school, and early marriage and adolescent pregnancy remain obstacles to moving on to secondary school.[61] Low government spending on education constrains the number of schools built (the fewer the schools, the greater the distance many students have to travel), the payment of teachers, the availability of school resources and learning materials, and the access to clean water, latrines, and new technology. In Malawi, for example, the teacher-to-student ratio is 1 to 130. Poor access to education is also compounded by other dimensions of poverty such as poor nutrition, which has resulted in 155 million stunted children under the age of five whose cognitive abilities are affected.[62]

Digital Connectivity and the Internet

Digital connectivity is widespread among poor populations as well as rich. Today, mobile phones are widespread, enabling people to better communicate, shop online, bank, and access news. Through these channels, digital technologies connect people, save time and energy, and increase productivity. Almost two-thirds of the global population—more than 5 billion people—are mobile subscribers. By 2020, 620 million more will be mobile subscribers; three-quarters of the global population will be connected.[63] Remarkably, that's more people than have access to electricity. Mobile phone access and usage is even higher, thanks to phone sharing. For example, while approximately 17 percent of people in Sub-Saharan Africa do not own a cellphone, one study suggested that more than half of them have periodic access to one.[64] Low-income people are driving the increase in mobile subscribers. China and India are projected to represent 47 percent of the increase in mobile subscribers from 2017 to 2020, but Sub-Saharan Africa and developing countries in Asia also make up

61 UNESCO, July 2016, "Leaving no one behind: How far on the way to universal primary and secondary education?," UNESCO, https://bit.ly/29IlbFG.

62 UNICEF, World Health Organization and World Bank, 2017, "Levels and Trends in Child Malnutrition," https://data.unicef.org/wp-content/uploads/2017/05/JME-2017-brochure-1.pdf.

63 GSMA Intelligence, September 2017, "Global Mobile Trends 2017," GSMA, https://bit.ly/2h72M58.

64 Grace Dubush, July 27, 2015, "How Mobile Phones Are Changing the Developing World," Consumer Technology Association, https://bit.ly/29NCbtZ.

significant portions with 16 and 12 percent, respectively.[65] The benefits of connectivity extend to social and leisure activities too. In fact, users in developing countries are more likely to use social media than users in developed countries (see Figure 2.11).[66]

Figure 2.11: Internet Users in Emerging Markets

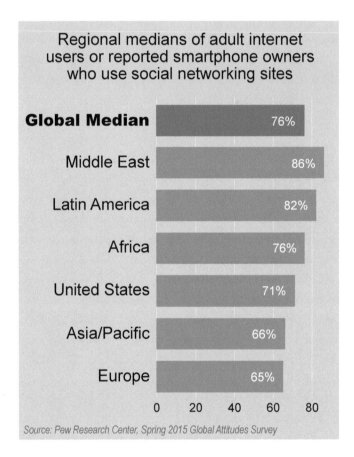

Regional medians of adult internet users or reported smartphone owners who use social networking sites

Global Median	76%
Middle East	86%
Latin America	82%
Africa	76%
United States	71%
Asia/Pacific	66%
Europe	65%

Source: Pew Research Center, Spring 2015 Global Attitudes Survey

65   GSMA Intelligence, September 2017, "Global Mobile Trends 2017," GSMA, https://bit.ly/2h72M58.

66   Jacob Poushter, February 22, 2016, "Smartphone Ownership and Internet Usage Continues to Climb in Emerging Economies," Pew Research Center, https://pewrsr.ch/1RX3Iqq.

Smartphone usage, while lagging behind feature phone usage, is also on the rise due in large part to decreases in smartphone costs. An estimated 2.4 billion people owned smartphones in 2017, an increase of almost 11 percent over 2016. Smartphone growth is expected to grow substantially by 2018, with more than 50 percent of mobile users expected to own smart phones.[67] Yet the spread of digital technologies has been uneven. In countries such as Ethiopia and Uganda, smartphone ownership rates are as low as 4 percent.[68] Within countries, people living in rural areas outside of 3G and 4G signals are underrepresented. In addition to physical infrastructure issues, obstacles to further cellular adoption include a lack of literacy, the cost of data, erratic electricity, language barriers, and lack of technical know-how.

Access to the internet either through the mobile phone or a computer has also increased substantially, with approximately 40 percent of the world's population able to access to the internet today. This access increased tenfold between 1999 and 2013, with the first billion reached in 2005, the second billion in 2010, and the third in 2014.[69] About half of the world's population, 3.7 billion people, are still not connected. Those that lack access are predominantly the poor and extreme poor. More than 60 percent of India's and Sub-Saharan Africa's populations are not yet on the internet, accounting for 42 percent of the world's unconnected; by comparison, 32 percent of Europeans remain unconnected.[70] The poor's lack of access is driven by limited infrastructure (telecom companies do not build the infrastructure in areas where they expect usage to be low), cost, and network quality, which tends to be better in urban areas and more developed countries.

---

67   David Murphy, February 4, 2017, "2.4BN Smartphone Users in 2017, Says Emarketer," *Mobile Marketing Magazine*, http://mobilemarketingmagazine.com/24bn-smartphone-users-in-2017-says-emarketer.

68   Drake Baer, February 22, 2016, "This map shows the percentage of people around the world who own smartphones," *Business Insider*, https://read.bi/1oDTDDp.

69   Internet Live Stats, "Internet Users," http://www.internetlivestats.com/internet-users/.

70   GSMA Intelligence, September 2017, "Global Mobile Trends 2017," GSMA, https://bit.ly/2h72M58.

Financial Services

Approximately 2 billion poor people worldwide still lack access to financial services. Credit, savings insurance, payment, and other services available to the better off are often lacking for the poor. Part of the issue is physical access: formal banks locate branches in urban areas, and given central bank regulations are not financially incentivized to build "brick and mortar" branches that serve few clients in rural areas. Other semiformal providers—microfinance institutions, credit unions, savings and credit cooperatives—operate in or closer to rural areas, but service quality varies, and products are often not tailored to the volatile income and cash flows of rural communities.

Meeting the requirements of financial institutions presents a problem for the poor. They often lack a birth certificate or national ID card required to conduct financial transactions with a financial institution that must meet know-your-customer requirements. They also are less likely to hold a title to their land or other formal collateral that is required as a pledge against loans. Finally, cost also drives the poor away from formal financial institutions that require a minimum amount for a deposit, account balances that do not go below a certain threshold amount, and monthly fees for account usage.

The issues around access, however, are changing with the growing use of mobile phones and mobile money to make payments, receive loans, and even collect deposits. As of 2016, there are 555 million registered mobile money accounts, and 92 countries now offer mobile money-related services, including mobile payment/money transfers, digital credit, and mobile-based insurance.[71] These new technologies have the potential to enable deeper penetration and therefore availability in more rural and remote areas and more affordable services because they require less investment in conventional branch infrastructure. New encryption technologies such as blockchain also offer the opportunity to provide the poor with access to a unique digital identity through which they can be identified and engage in financial transactions. While the potential of these technologies is great, challenges remain for the poor: agent networks that get built out to the "last mile"

---

71 Barbara Arese Lucini and Kalvin Bahia, September 22, 2017, "2017 Mobile Industry Impact Report: Sustainable Development Goals," GSMA, https://bit.ly/2JiIH9o.

must address the problems of limited liquidity in rural areas. They must also identify ways to engage poorer, less literate clients who may have fewer digital skills or lack access to or ownership of smart phones.

Access to Jobs

Typically, countries analyze their job markets by counting those people who have jobs, those who are unemployed, and those seeking jobs for the first time. A large segment of the poor, however, fall into uncounted categories—those who work but are unpaid (often family work) and those employed in the informal sector.

In emerging and developing countries, poverty and informality go hand in hand. Information and statistics on the informal sector—the part of the economy where businesses and jobs are not registered and where income is not measured, taxed, or captured in the gross domestic product of a country—is unreliable at best. When poor people work in the informal sector, they also do not benefit from new technologies, access to public services, or social protection. For example, as shown in Figure 2.12, informal employment makes up between 33 and 82 percent of nonagricultural employment in Sub-Saharan Africa, depending on the country, between 40 and 75 percent in Latin America and the Caribbean, between 42 and 84 percent in South and East Asia, and between 31 and 58 percent in North Africa.[72] If agricultural employment is included, the percentages rise, in countries such as India and many Sub-Saharan African countries, beyond 75 percent.

---

72 International Labor Office, 2013, "Women and Men in the Informal Economy: A Statistical Picture," International Labor Organization, https://bit.ly/1xDj9vG.

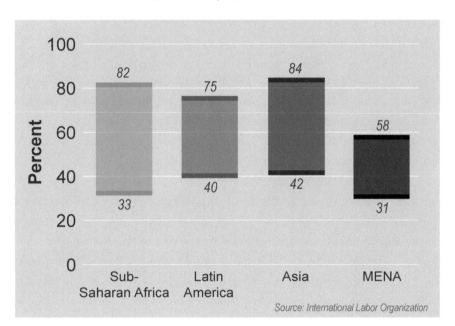

Figure 2.12: Informal Employment as a Percentage of Total Nonagricultural Employment (Estimated Ranges)

Source: International Labor Organization

Informal sector jobs are less attractive than formal sector employment for many reasons. First, the pay is usually lower and inconsistent. Second, workers lack legal protections that ensure a safe workplace, enforce contracts, and provide social security. Workers are limited in their ability to redress abuses and access benefits. Because employers face less government oversight, they may choose to exploit workers, placing them in dangerous working conditions that make health issues, hardship, and arrest more likely. Thus, while informal employees may earn wages, they still face significant instability.

In many developing countries, higher wages in the formal sector drive migration into cities, increasing the labor pool beyond the number of available positions and pushing new migrants into poorly paid informal jobs. There may also be barriers that limit local entrepreneurship, such as excessive regulation or high costs of business licensing and formalizations. These serve as disincentives to businesses to expand, further stifling job growth.

Even those who do obtain formal sector jobs continue to face insecurity. In fact, many low-income people piece together a mix of formal and informal jobs to support themselves. Formal sector jobs tend to have higher wages than informal sector positions, but these wages may still be insufficient to meet a worker's needs. Formal sector positions are also often short-term either by design (because the need is seasonal) or by necessity (because a business fails and must cut back). Furthermore, jobs, particularly those of unskilled workers, may even be eliminated by automation. Weak education and training institutions that do not prepare workers with 21st century skills in science, technology, engineering, and math (STEM) exacerbate this trend.

The global economy will struggle to create sufficient jobs. Between 2010 and 2030, the number of people between 15 and 64 years of age will rise by almost 1 billion in developing countries.[73] Most of these people will want to enter the workforce, and hundreds of millions of new jobs will need to be created to accommodate them. Based on current trends in population, education, and labor demand, it is estimated that by 2020 the global economy could face the hurdles outlined in Figure 2.13.[74]

Figure 2.13: Challenges in Matching Labor Supply with Demand

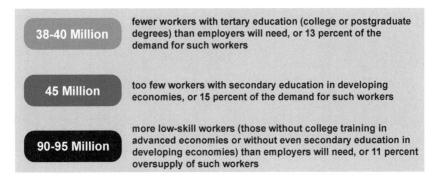

38-40 Million — fewer workers with tertiary education (college or postgraduate degrees) than employers will need, or 13 percent of the demand for such workers

45 Million — too few workers with secondary education in developing economies, or 15 percent of the demand for such workers

90-95 Million — more low-skill workers (those without college training in advanced economies or without even secondary education in developing economies) than employers will need, or 11 percent oversupply of such workers

Source: McKinsey Global Institute

---

73 The Economist Intelligence Unit, February 2015, "Global Trends Impacting the Future of HR Management: Engaging and Integrating a Global Workforce," SHRM Foundation, https://bit.ly/2uOlHeW.

74 Richard Dobbs, Anu Madgavkar, Dominic Barton, Eric Labaye, James Manyika, Charles Roxburgh, Susan Lund, and Siddarth Madhav, June 2012, "The world at work: Jobs, pay, and skills for 3.5 billion people," McKinsey Global Institute, https://www.mckinsey.com/global-themes/employment-and-growth/the-world-at-work.

Aspirations

Recent years have seen more attention paid to the aspirations of poor people, especially for good jobs, greater income, an improved future for their children, and an improved standard of living and social status. But the relationship between poverty and aspiration is complicated. On the one hand, those who aspire to a better life may find more strength to combat poverty. On the other hand, poverty itself can drain energy and crush dreams, leading to a vicious cycle. At the same time, aspirations can be influenced through exposure to success stories (see Box 2.8).

Box 2.8: Learning from Experiments that Aim to Foster Changes in Confidence and Behavior

A study conducted by the World Bank looked at how specially developed video content in Ethiopia could influence and shift the aspirations and behaviors of people by showing them what is possible. The video depicts four stories—featuring two men and two women—who despite their poverty improved their socioeconomic conditions. The videos capture their situation relative to others in the community but also chart the different path the portrayed individuals took to achieve success. The stories reflect some core characteristics of the successful protagonists—perseverance, determination, and reliability—and emphasize the feasibility of making these positive shifts.

The findings show that the videos have a great impact on people, especially in the six months following their viewing and especially on those viewers who went into the process with higher aspirations in the first place. They also found evidence of improved uptake of savings and credit behavior, better school enrollment, and more investments in children's schooling, suggesting that video messaging could change people's aspirations and translate those new aspirations into forward-looking behavior. Similar research is being conducted around the globe with the aim of tapping into new mechanisms that can help promote a growth mindset and agency (individual power to make things happen) among poor people.[75]

When it comes to jobs, the poor, especially younger poor people, aspire to much better opportunities. A recent survey of more than 7,000 young people found that:

---

75   Tanguy Bernard, April 21, 2014, "The Future in Mind: Aspirations and Forward-Looking Behaviour in Rural Ethiopia," World Bank, https://bit.ly/1lTkOp5.

- Despite uncertainty and change across the globe, 70 percent of young people are optimistic about their career prospects. Optimism is even higher in cities in developing markets.
- More often than not, there is a mismatch in the jobs youth have and what they want to do. Globally, 55 percent of employed young people are currently working in an industry in which they do not aspire to work. To find new opportunities, young people are craving on-the-job experience and professional and social connections.
- Seventy-eight percent of young people believe internships and apprenticeships are critical for success; however, 60 percent say there aren't enough of these opportunities.
- Young people have entrepreneurial hopes but are not starting businesses. Nearly 70 percent of young people surveyed aspire to be entrepreneurs, yet only 6 percent are actually entrepreneurs at present.
- Three out of four young people are willing to work long hours and take risks to achieve their career aspirations.[76]

As depicted in Figure 2.14, young people articulate the desire to shift from lower productivity work to higher value added, from low to high skill, informal to formal, and agricultural to office or urban-based jobs.

Figure 2.14: Young People's Work Aspirations

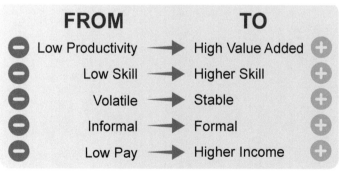

Source: Author

---

76 Brandee McHale, "Youth Optimism, Meet Opportunity: Bridging the Gap between Young People's Career Aspirations & Ability to Succeed," CECP, https://bit.ly/2JfOfkV.

Finding ways to tap into poor people's aspirations has been an ongoing endeavor. For example, global health programs have long used soap operas, serial dramas, and other mass media campaigns to model health seeking behaviors, conduct social marketing, and challenge social norms with the aim of promoting new ones. These tools are useful because they create an emotional connection to motivate people to seek new knowledge or change their viewpoint, attitude, or behavior. These same tactics are now applied to understanding the aspirations of the poor, seeking to identify those levers or nudges that enable people to remain optimistic, generate positive expectations for themselves and their families, and find the power and confidence to make things happen.

Chapter 3. Micro Level: Market Players

This chapter examines how the private sector directly supports economic inclusion by expanding access to services and better jobs—the two main pathways out of poverty. Innovative business models and market leaders with pro-poor value propositions are highlighted within the growing and diverse landscape of market players.

New business models promise to address the interconnected problems of availability, quality, and affordability, and thereby reach poor and low-income people with an expanded range of products and services (see Figure 3.1). From financial services to energy to sanitation and beyond, entrepreneurs are finding new ways to get closer to customers with more reliable, more relevant, and more affordable services. The private sector also offers formal-sector jobs, from low- to high-skilled, which lead not only to increased income but also in many cases to benefits such as health insurance, a retirement plan, and a step into the country's broader social safety net. Jobs elevate people's morale, sense of worth, and connectedness to the market and the wider world.

Figure 3.1: The Triple Challenge of Availability, Quality, and Affordability

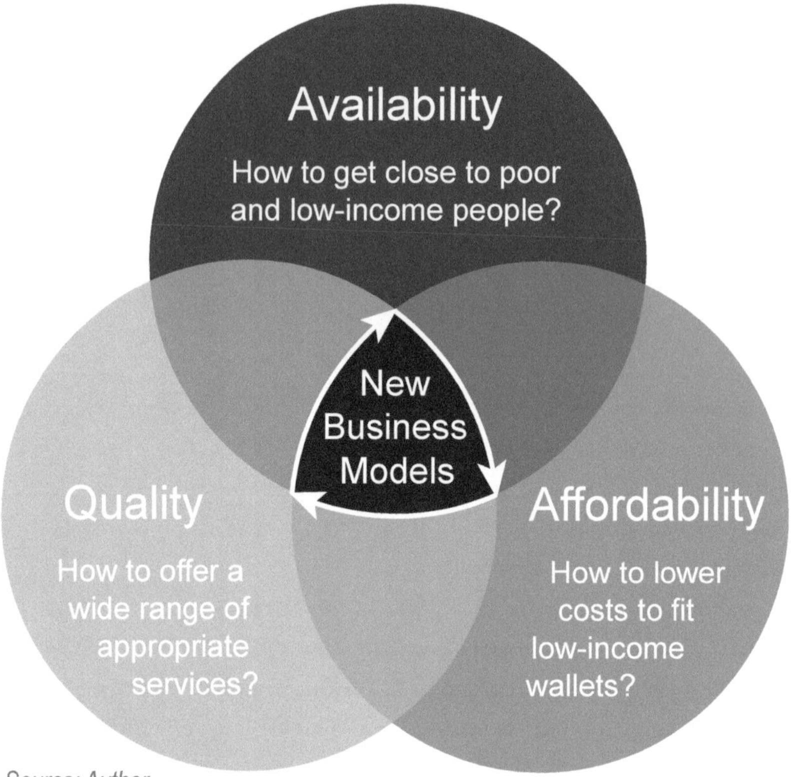

Availability
How to get close to poor and low-income people?

New Business Models

Quality
How to offer a wide range of appropriate services?

Affordability
How to lower costs to fit low-income wallets?

Source: Author

Service Providers

The financial services sector pioneered scalable and pro-poor business models, enabling poor and low-income people to manage their financial lives, save and invest in businesses, and pay for education, improved housing, and other expenses. Building on this success, a new generation of pro-poor business models has emerged, leveraging technology and taking advantage of mobile money and payments. These services help address cost, quality, and availability challenges, but their value goes even further: insights and information gained from these service providers have opened other essential services to poor and low-income people. At the same time, the spread of digital technology has enabled follow-on innovations that can be equally transformative.

Financial Services

Various service providers offer an increasingly diverse range of financial solutions, from informal savings groups in local neighborhoods, to enterprise loans from national and international banks, to mobile money offered by mobile network operators. Today, more than 3.7 billion people hold financial transaction accounts globally, with 1.2 billion new accounts opened between 2011 and 2017. Of these accounts, almost all are at banks, but some are from other formal financial institutions such as credit unions and microfinance institutions (see Figure 3.2, 3.3, and 3.4).[1][2][3]

Figure 3.2: Financial Account Penetration: Adults with an Account (%), 2017

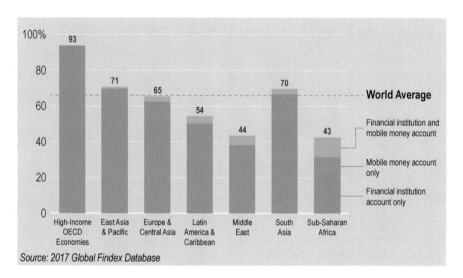

Source: 2017 Global Findex Database

---

1   Asli Demirguc-Kunt, Leora Klapper, Dorothe Singer, Saniya Ansar and Jake Hess, April, 2018, "The Global Findex Database 2017: Measuring Financial Inclusion around the World," World Bank http://bit.ly/2M6zHF9.

2   Susy Cheston, Tomás Conde, Arpitha Bykere and Elisabeth Rhyne, July, 2016, "The Business of Financial Inclusion: Insights from Banks in Emerging Markets," Institute of International Finance, https://bit.ly/29zWLM7.

3   Asli Demirguc-Kunt, Leora Klapper, Dorothe Singer, Saniya Ansar and Jake Hess, April, 2018, "The Global Findex Database 2017: Measuring Financial Inclusion around the World," World Bank http://bit.ly/2M6zHF9.

Figure 3.3: Account Penetration Around the World

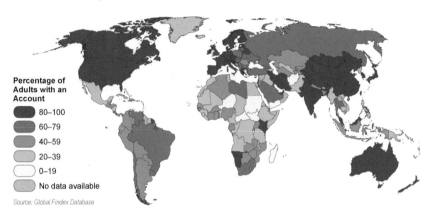

Percentage of
Adults with an
Account

80–100
60–79
40–59
20–39
0–19
No data available

Source: Global Findex Database

Figure 3.4: Mobile Money Account Penetration in Sub-Saharan Africa

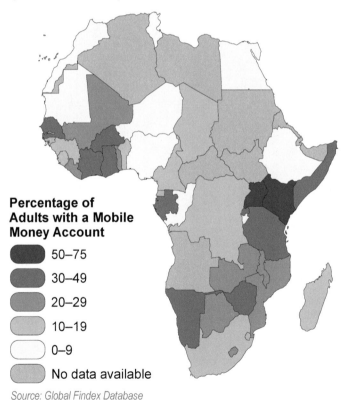

Percentage of
Adults with a Mobile
Money Account

50–75
30–49
20–29
10–19
0–9
No data available

Source: Global Findex Database

Despite dramatic increases in access to formal financial services, much of the world's low-income population continues to conduct financial transactions informally. Only 40 percent of adults in developing countries who saved money in 2014 report having saved formally at a commercial banking institution. This means that the majority relied on informal or semiformal service providers.[4] Poor and low-income people are most likely to be excluded financially: the highest-earning quintile of adults in developing countries is twice as likely to have a formal account as the lowest-earning quintile.[5] The challenges of availability, cost, and quality drive reliance on informal financial services, and new market players have begun to address these issues in innovative ways.

Landscape of Service Providers

From commercial banks and credit unions to savings groups and family members, financial service providers range from formal to informal, with players in each category sometimes collaborating with and reinforcing each other (see Figure 3.5). This section explores some of the most common types of service providers, as well as some key innovations and ideas that have underpinned success in this sector so far.

---

4   Ibid.

5   Asli Demirguc-Kunt and Leora Klapper, 2013, "Measuring Financial Inclusion: Explaining Variation in Use of Financial Services across and within Countries," Brookings Institute, https://brook.gs/2GPr83f.

Figure 3.5: The Spectrum of Financial Service Providers

	Informal	Membership-based	Formal
Who?	Moneylenders	Credit unions	Traditional banks
	Savings collectors	Savings groups	Microfinance institutions
	Pawnbrokers		
	Traders		
	Friends		
	Relatives		
Pros	Solves availability issues	Generally low risk	Subject to stringent laws
	Can be low interest	Transparency	Low risk of misappropriation
	Smaller, frequent payments	Low transaction costs	Financial inclusion awareness
	Low to no transaction costs	Can have charter	
	No credit history necessary	Can be subject to more laws	
Cons	Potential for loss/theft	Risk of member default	Not always accessible
	Borrowing limit	Irregular payouts	High transaction costs
			Can require credit history
			Lack information to BOP

Source: Author

Informal Financial Services

Individual informal providers include moneylenders, savings collectors, pawn-brokers, traders, processors, and input suppliers, but friends and relatives are the most commonly utilized individual informal providers. Informal providers solve problems of availability: they typically live or work close by and will offer services to people who may not be able to qualify for bank services. However, they can be very expensive, both financially and in terms of the social capital spent. Informally provided services also can be low quality due to relatively rigid repayment terms and the potential for lost or stolen money.

People in developing countries also often self-insure or try to save informally to hedge risk because premiums for insurance contracts from formal institutions tend to be high, particularly in areas or contexts with a higher perceived risk.[6] Additionally, current insurance processes tend not to match the needs of low-income people, as they don't allow for the smaller, more frequent payments typically desired by people with inconsistent income. Accepting these smaller but more frequent payments raises transaction costs for insurance companies, and thus the cost of services for their customers.[7]

---

6   Stefan Dercon, Tessa Bold and Cesar Calvo, 2008, "Insurance for the Poor?," UNICEF, https://www.unicef.org/socialpolicy/files/Insurance_for_the_Poor.pdf.

7   Ibid.

Membership-Based Financial Services

Membership-based financial services may be formal, such as credit unions, or largely informal, such as savings groups—a common saving or borrowing alternative in developing countries. In 2014, around 17 percent of savers in developing economies reported having saved through a semiformal or informal channel in the past 12 months.[8]

Informal savings groups enable people to borrow through a variety of community-based mechanisms instead of a formal financial institution. Participants make weekly contributions, and the funds collected are distributed to each member on a rotating basis. The funds are typically distributed to one contributor at a time each week.[9] Though they vary in structure and requirements, savings groups cost little to run, are transparent and easy to understand, and carry a low risk of misappropriation because they are often run for a short period to avoid bookkeeping issues and member disputes. As shown in Box 3.1, some savings groups are leveraging new technology to make their operations even more efficient and secure.

Box 3.1: Savings Group in Chad Gets a Mobile Upgrade

Cattle traders in Chad have gained a powerful tool for accessing financial services. Tigo Paare combines a mobile money platform (Tigo) with a popular savings group structure in Chad (Paare) to make it easier for members to make payments, receive funds, earn interest, and monitor group activity. Since the telecommunications company Millicom created it in 2015, Tigo Paare has expanded. It now aims to reach churches, women-led savings groups, and agricultural cooperatives. With 19,000 users two months after its launch and a waiting list of more than 27,000 groups, Tigo Paare is allowing members of informal savings groups to reap the benefits of formal savings services.[10] [11] [12]

---

8   Asli Demirguc-Kunt, Leora Klapper, Dorothe Singer, Saniya Ansar and Jake Hess, April, 2018, "The Global Findex Database 2017: Measuring Financial Inclusion around the World," World Bank http://bit.ly/2M6zHF9.

9   Francois I. Kabuya, August, 2015, "The Rotating Savings and Credit Associations (ROSCAs): Unregistered Sources of Credit in Local Communities," *IOSR Journal of Humanities and Social Science* 95, http://www.iosrjournals.org/iosr-jhss/papers/Vol20-issue8/Version-4/M020849598.pdf.

10   GSMA, "2015 Mobile Insurance, Savings & Credit Report," 2015, GSMA, https://bit.ly/2v3b8Fd.

11   Millicom, 2015, "How a mobile money solution is born," Millicom, http://www.millicom.com/mediaroom/blogs/blog-tigo-paare/.

12   Balancing Act Africa staff, November, 2015, "Group TigoPaare accounts in Chad may lead to Peoples' Banks for communities across Africa," Balancing Act Africa, https://bit.ly/2qoHiFp.

Credit unions represent a formalized option for membership-based financial services, usually with charters falling under cooperative or credit union laws.[13] In some countries, credit unions can be licensed and supervised by the banking authority and have developed sophisticated consumer and small business financial services. Credit unions are often more affordable than commercial banks and other consumer financing options.

Formal Financial Institutions

Several barriers limit access for poor and low-income people to banks, microfinance institutions, or other formal institutions. Some of the most common reasons people remain unbanked include distance from bank outlets, religious objections, lack of required identification, and an incomplete or nonexistent credit history.[14] Financial realities also can be limiting, as people without bank accounts often report not having enough money to make opening an account worth their while, or they may feel they are unable to afford the services.[15] The sheer cost of formal sector transactions like remittances, for example, keeps many potential customers in the informal sector (see Box 3.2).

Box 3.2: The High Cost of Remittances

Many low-income and poor people rely on money transfers and remittances from family members who migrated to find employment and other income-generating opportunities. However, a slow pace of innovation coupled with increased scrutiny of money transfers in many countries (due to anti–money laundering and anti-terrorist protections) have made these transactions prohibitively costly for many recipients. Among the three largest money transfer operators, the average cost of a single transaction equals $18—an expensive fee considering the typical migrant sends only $200 per transaction. Remittance fees provide just one example of why many poor people cannot afford to operate within the formal financial sector.[16]

---

13 Francois I. Kabuya, August, 2015, "The Rotating Savings and Credit Associations (ROSCAs): Unregistered Sources of Credit in Local Communities," *IOSR Journal of Humanities and Social Science 95*, http://www.iosrjournals.org/iosr-jhss/papers/Vol20-issue8/Version-4/M020849598.pdf.

14 World Bank, April 5, 2017, "Financial Inclusion Overview," World Bank, http://www.worldbank.org/en/topic/financialinclusion/overview.

15 Asli Demirguc-Kunt and Leora Klapper, 2013, "Measuring Financial Inclusion: Explaining Variation in Use of Financial Services across and within Countries," Brookings Institute, https://brook.gs/2GPr83f.

16 Olav Kjorven, September, 2011, "Remittances, Towards Human Resilience: Sustaining MDG Progress in an Age of Economic Uncertainty," United Nations Development Programme, https://bit.ly/2EAukK0.

Over the past decade, commercial microfinance has evolved into a broader concept known as financial inclusion. Commercially viable microfinance institutions, banks, and nonbank financial institutions, including insurance companies, have increasingly adapted their business models to offer services that are more relevant to previously excluded populations. From modernizing state-owned agricultural, developmental, and postal banks to offering mobile financial products, licensed and regulated finance companies have been able to offer a range of services to low-income and marginalized market segments. These microfinance initiatives and institutions also have been profitable, sustaining the sector. The initial public offering (IPO) of Compartamos in Mexico in 2007, for example, caught the attention of capital markets and bankers alike and drove more resources into the microfinance sector (see Box 3.3).

Box 3.3: IPOs Hit Microfinance

The IPO of Compartamos represented a tipping point in terms of proving the profitability of microcredit. Compartamos began as an NGO in 1990 and made collateral-free loans to a variety of small businesses, many of them women owned. The NGO became a for-profit company in 2000, and costs fell as efficiencies increased. High demand led to an extremely successful IPO in 2007. Share prices increased by 22 percent on the first day of the IPO, and perhaps more important than the actual metrics is the makeup of the investors who participated. Purely commercial investors (not only impact investors) bought most of the shares. The success was not short lived because its return on equity in 2008 was triple the average for commercial banks in Mexico, and investors were seeing upwards of 100 percent returns on their investment due to the high interest rates charged by Compartamos.[17]

On the one hand, Compartamos showed that socially conscious enterprises could compete with and even outperform traditional financial institutions. On the other, enormous rates of return and high interest rates have caused some to question whether these high rates are defensible and whether Compartamos is truly helping the poor. Compartamos charges borrowers interest rates that are far above what it needs to break even, and this is a cause for concern among some microfinance professionals. The precise amount of

---

17   Richard Rosenberg, June, 2007, "CGAP Reflections on the Compartamos Initial Public Offering," *CGAP*, https://bit.ly/2v1GxYt.

profit an institution like Compartamos can ethically make will remain contentious going forward, especially as other companies globally find similar success. But the fact remains that Compartamos has 840,000 customers, and its loans have provided a valuable service that has elevated the socioeconomic status of thousands of Mexican entrepreneurs.[18]

Traditional private banks have begun to view financial inclusion as a core function of their business and can offer developed infrastructure, fast transaction processing, and international linkages (see Figure 3.6 for an illustration of how banks are increasing their footprint in the financial inclusion space).[19] For some financial institutions with an eye toward social impact, inclusion fulfills corporate social responsibility (CSR) goals. But the fundamental lesson over the past decade or so is that financial inclusion transcends CSR and can be a profitable business line for banks and other financial service providers. Box 3.4 illustrates a few insurance examples.

Box 3.4: Insurance for All

The insurance market is changing as new technologies come online and more people have access to smartphones and, thus, financial services. Satellites and drones allow insurance companies to verify damages without causing customers to go through a claims process. Transaction costs are decreasing, and instant enrollment increases the insurance pool.[20] Banks are increasingly choosing to collaborate with insurance companies to offer insurance products to poor and low-income people. For example, in India, the State Bank of India (SBI) issues the RuPay debit card to low-income customers free of charge. The RuPay Card carries free accident insurance coverage to account holders with any sort of a bank account, and by early 2016, almost 15 million customers had enrolled in accident insurance coverage for less than a dollar a year. Around 4 million customers had enrolled in high-quality life insurance for only $5 per year.[21] Davivienda in Colombia

18   Ibid.

19   Susy Cheston, Tomás Conde, Arpitha Bykere and Elisabeth Rhyne, July, 2016, "The Business of Financial Inclusion: Insights from Banks in Emerging Markets," Institute of International Finance, https://bit.ly/29zWLM7.

20   CFI Staff, January 18, 2018, "How Technology Is Propelling Inclusive Insurance," Center for Financial Inclusion, https://cfi-blog.org/2018/01/18/how-technology-is-propelling-inclusive-insurance/.

21   Susy Cheston, Tomás Conde, Arpitha Bykere and Elisabeth Rhyne, July, 2016, "The Business of Financial Inclusion: Insights from Banks in Emerging Markets," Institute of International Finance, https://bit.ly/29zWLM7.

offers DaviPlata, a mobile-based platform for purchasing insurance. Customers pay an annual premium of $10 for a $1,000 life insurance product payable upon the death of the policyholder or relative.[22] These innovations and partnerships have led to explosive growth in the insurance market. Nigeria, to take another example, has seen an average annual growth of 106 percent over 10 years. Insurers should continue to take note; the untapped market for insurance amongst women in the developing world could be worth as much as $870 billion in premiums.[23]

Figure 3.6: Increasing Access to Accounts Globally

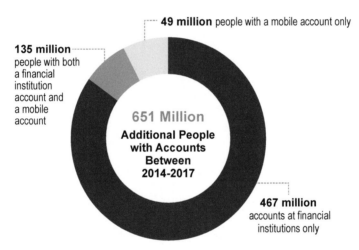

49 million people with a mobile account only

135 million people with both a financial institution account and a mobile account

651 Million Additional People with Accounts Between 2014-2017

467 million accounts at financial institutions only

Sources: Global Findex Database 2017, United Nations

Alternative Delivery Channels, Financial Technology, and Mobile Money

Many game-changing innovations have spurred dramatic increases in financial inclusion over the past decade or so. These innovations address all three of the customer challenges: availability, quality, and cost (although probably most relevant for availability and cost). Three of these innovations

---

22 Susy Cheston, January, 2018, "Inclusive Insurance: Closing the Protection Gap for Emerging Customers," Center for Financial Inclusion at Accion and Institute of International Finance, https://bit.ly/2GNVWRV.

23 Ibid.

are alternative delivery channels (ADCs), financial technology (fintech), and mobile money. These innovations are interrelated, as shown in Figure 3.7, but not interchangeable. Some ADCs are "low tech," leveraging retail-level shops across countries. In addition, some fintech solutions address issues outside of delivery, such as applications that leverage big data and data analytics to predict the creditworthiness of clients. Mobile money, on the other hand, straddles both ADCs and fintech—it is the ultimate technology solution that delivers financial services directly into the hands or pockets of consumers. This section addresses each of these innovations in turn.

Figure 3.7: The Relationship Between ADCs, Fintech, and Mobile Money

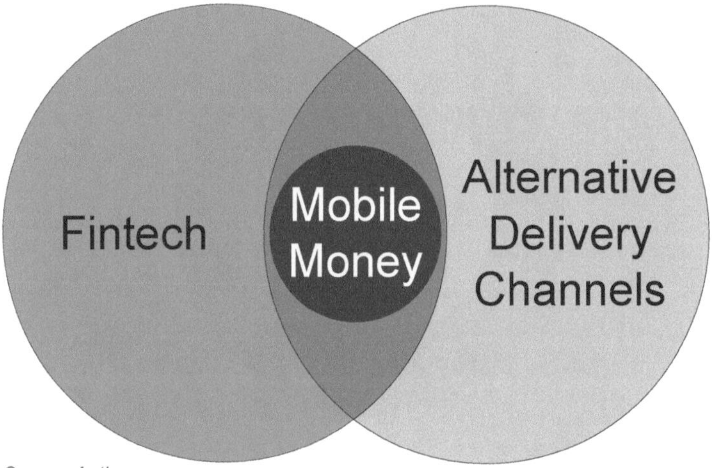

Source: Author

Alternative Delivery Channels

The high cost to serve is a key impediment for formal service providers to expand access, especially in more remote areas. ADCs have expanded availability, improved quality, and reduced the cost of service. An ADC is a financial channel that expands the reach of traditional brick-and-mortar banking outlets by using technology without compromising quality. Figure 3.8 delineates the services and functionalities of different types of ADCs.[24] Cost savings can be significant

---

24   Andrew Lake, 2014, "Alternative Delivery Channels and Technology Handbook," International Finance Corporation, https://bit.ly/2ILytNM.

for both financial institutions and customers, and new technologies in ADCs have reduced waiting times and improved quality of services available to customers.[25] The popular convenience store chain OXXO in Mexico, for example, collaborated with a large Mexican bank, Banamex, to issue alternative accounts with no minimum balance for which customers easily can apply at thousands of OXXO stores across the country. The system, called Saldazo, gives customers a bank-issued, card-based account that they can use at OXXO stores to transfer, deposit or withdraw money, and pair with mobile payments and purchases.[26]

Figure 3.8: Types of ADCs

	Type of Channel		Who/what customer interacts with to transact	Sample functionality of channel
ATM		Self-service	ATM	3rd party agent, merchant, phone, POS, mobile
Internet Banking		Self-service	Computer, phone, tablet, kiosk	Enquiries, transfers, payments
Agent Banking		OTC	3rd party agent, merchant, phone, POS, mobile	Cash in, cash out, payments
Extension Services (field staff, mini branch, etc.)		OTC	Bank staff, loan officer, susu collector, other FSP staff, POS, mobile	Account opening, cash in, cash out, loan applications inquiries
Mobile Banking		Self-service	Phone	Inquiries, transfers, payments
E-Wallet (m-wallets, prepaid cards)		Self-service + OTC	Phone, computer, merchant, kiosk, ATM agent, card	Cash in, cash out, payments, transfers
Call Center		OTC	Phone, customer service representative	Inquiries, transfers, payments

Sources: *International Finance Corporation, Alternate Delivery Channels and Technology Handbook* **Note:** *OTC = Over the Counter*

---

25   Ibid.

26   Gabriela Zapata Alvarez and Martha Casanova, November 30, 2016, "How a Retail Chain Became Mexico's No. 1 Bank Account Supplier," CGAP, https://bit.ly/2IFzxTi.

Branchless banking emerged in the mid-2000s, with several banks in Brazil leading the way. Since then, branchless or agency banking has grown across several geographies. This system enables people to conduct banking business in their hometowns or near their place of work, greatly increasing the convenience of the service. Introducing branchless banking into Autazes, Brazil, for example, transformed the small town, once largely unserved by formal banking structures, into a regional commercial and banking hub, leading to greater economic growth and a higher quality of life for the community.[27] Beyond expanding access, branchless banking services cost 19 percent less for customers than comparable services at a traditional bank and 38 percent less than banks for the transactions more typically used by lower-income people.[28] In addition, a number of new businesses have emerged to facilitate agency banking for existing bank clients as well as the unbanked. Box 3.5 provides the example of Zoona.

Box 3.5: Expanding Mobile Money Transfers in Africa with Zoona

In many developing economies, person-to-person money transfers are frequently costly, inefficient, or insecure. Zoona attempts to address this problem by managing a network of more than 1,500 money-transfer outlets that utilize mobile technology across Zambia, Malawi, and Mozambique. Each outlet staffs an agent, known as a Zoona entrepreneur, who will take the customer's money and transfer it electronically on the entrepreneur's mobile device through the Zoona platform. This means that customers do not need a financial account or even a mobile phone. The recipient then goes to another Zoona entrepreneur and collects his or her funds.[29] Zoona became profitable in 2014 and served 700,000 active users as of 2015; 2015; over 300,000 of these customers transact at least once a month.[30]

ADCs are effective in reaching clients at the base of the pyramid and the more general population, including retail clients and their customers. However, in

---

27   Claudia McKay, January 28, 2012, "Banking Services Transforming a Town in the Amazon," *CGAP*, http://www.cgap.org/blog/banking-services-transforming-town-amazon.

28   Claudia McKay, November 3, 2010, "Branchless Banking 2010: What Price?," *CGAP*, http://www.cgap.org/blog/branchless-banking-2010-what-price.

29   Kurt Dassel and John Cassidy, June, 2017, "Reaching deep in low-income markets," Deloitte, https://bit.ly/2qo6gVD.

30   Jungwon Byun, August, 2015, "Zoona: A Case Study on Third Party Innovation in Digital Finance," Financial Sector Deepening Zambia, https://bit.ly/2kBRhWS.

some markets, issues such as a lack of reliability or integrity among agents, undertrained agent staff, or a difficult regulatory environment can hinder ADCs. For example, FINCA DRC discovered and subsequently published six key risks for its ADCs, including strategic, political, technological, operational, fraud, and reputational concerns. Strategies to mitigate these risks include addressing connectivity issues, improving call center and automated processes, mitigating fraud, preempting regulatory changes, and formalizing risk management processes.[31]

Fintech: Bridging the Gap

The use of financial technology has exploded over the past several years, both in industrialized and developing countries. Rising mobile penetration rates and improved access to 3G and 4G service have accelerated this trend. As of February 2015, digital finance services were available through mobile phones in more than 80 countries.[32] Fintech has grown into a big business, with global investment in fintech ventures reaching $19 billion in 2016.[33]

Backed by venture capitalists and other investors, fintech has the potential to disrupt the financial industry in ways that can greatly improve access and reduce cost to the poor. In some cases, fintech companies compete directly with traditional banks and other financial service providers. However, fintech companies and mobile network operators (MNOs) are increasingly partnering with banks to find mutually beneficial solutions. By lowering underwriting costs for financial institutions, fintech companies have enabled banks to give smaller loans that previously would not have been very profitable.[34]

Designing innovative ways to assess creditworthiness, fintech can often reach rural or undeveloped locations, providing modern financial products and services to a range of previously unbanked people. Fintech innovations and ap-

---

31 Jeff Abrams, Maelis Carraro, Wajioha Ahmed, March, 2017, "Alternative Delivery Channels for Financial Inclusion," The Mastercard Foundation and Bankable Frontier Associates, https://mastercardfdn.org/wp-content/uploads/2018/06/BFA_ADC_FIpaper_April2017-Accessible.pdf.

32 Kate Lauer and Timothy Lyman, October, 2014, "Digital Financial Inclusion: Implications for Customers, Regulators, Supervisors, and Standard-Setting Bodies," CGAP, http://www.worldbank.org/en/news/press-release/2016/06/17/reforms-strengthen-indonesias-economic-resilience-world-bank-report.

33 Alex J. Alexander, Lin Shi, and Bensam Solomon, March, 2017, "How Fintech is Reaching the Poor in Africa and Asia," International Finance Corporation, https://bit.ly/2fus9xQ.

34 Allen Taylor, August 15, 2017, "The Growth of Lending-as-a-Service," Lending Times, https://lending-times.com/2017/08/15/the-growth-of-lending-as-a-service/.

proaches have improved the way consumers access financial services by offering tools for financial management, access to credit and lending, payment processing and remittances, cash management, trade analytics and finance, protective services such as blockchain, and anti–money laundering and machine learning (see Box 3.6 for an example in India).[35] These tools include virtual advisors, mobile banking, and pay-as-you-go systems.

Credit history assessments have evolved as fintech tools make it possible to use social media, data analytics, behavioral economics testing, and artificial intelligence to communicate with customers and analyze their behavior. The fintech app Tala has provided credit scores to people in Kenya and the Philippines based on nontraditional measures of creditworthiness via mobile phone data. Tala can identify qualified borrowers based on stable personal relationships, regular financial transactions, predictable movements within their community, and a diverse network of contacts. These mobile services also help customers qualify for formal financial services by helping to build their credit history, thereby giving people financial identities that can enable them to qualify for more services from traditional banks.[36]

Box 3.6: How Fintech Supports Payments to the Very Poor in India

Because their work is unregulated, informally employed domestic workers face significant risks—from financial risks to job insecurity and from long hours to safety concerns. One fintech startup in India, SERV'D, seeks to enhance protection for these workers through a mobile app that easily creates formal digital work contracts and allows users to make and receive payments electronically. Employees gain access to a documented record of their employment and income, which could help them qualify for loans or other services. SERV'D also can be used to vet potential employees, making the app beneficial for employers as well.[37]

---

35   James Manyika, Susan Lund, Marc Singer, Olivia White, and Chris Berry, September, 2016, "Digital Finance for All," McKinsey Global Institute, http://bit.ly/2xA0R37.

36   Shivani Siroya, February, 2016, "A smart loan for people with no credit history (yet)," TED, https://www.ted.com/talks/shivani_siroya_a_smart_loan_for_people_with_no_credit_history_yet#t-351517.

37   Casey Hynes, August 24, 2017, "India's Domestic Workers Have A New Ally In This Innovative FinTech Startup," Forbes, https://bit.ly/2EBnmEn.

Fintech also supports financial inclusion by offering more flexibility and security for people who migrate, experience natural disasters, or face other risks. Digital records follow people, even if they move or lose important personal documents. Fintech also provides a relatively easy way to go cashless, increasing the security and safety of users and making it easier to save, move money, and pay for goods and services in their daily lives. Digital finance often offers more flexible payment plans, such as pay-as-you-go installments for accessing critical goods and services, including solar panels or energy sources.[38] Figure 3.9 shows the array of fintech services available in the market.[39]

Figure 3.9: Beyond Banking Services

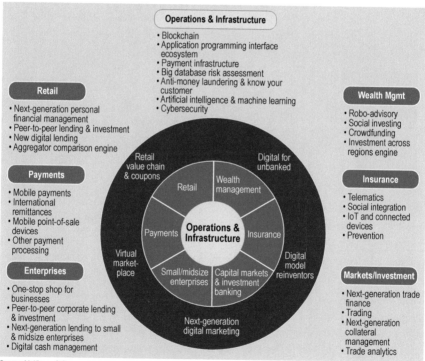

Source: McKinsey & Company

38   Y Media Labs, March 14, 2017, "Developing Nations Take Aim With Fintech: What Elite Economies Can Learn," Y Media Labs, https://ymedialabs.com/developing-nations-fintech/.

39   Miklos Dietz, Vivayak HV, and Gillian Lee, November, 2016, "Bracing for seven critical changes as fintech matures," McKinsey & Company, https://bit.ly/2qJTzFE.

Crowdfunding, a method of fundraising for a new business venture wherein the entrepreneur raises small investments from a large number of funders, is another important application of fintech with real implications for poor and low-income people. Box 3.7 offers a view on Kiva, one of the oldest and most established crowdfunding platforms for developing countries. A number of other crowdsourcing platforms have launched in lower-income countries as well. For instance, in Mexico, Torneo de Ideas provides graphic design solutions to small corporations in Mexico. Other countries are also seeing increased crowdfunding activity; for instance, Zoomaal and Aflamnah in the Middle East and North Africa, and Startup Africa and StartMe in Sub-Saharan Africa, are all making waves in the crowdfunding space.

Box 3.7: Crowdfunding Pioneer Kiva Surpasses $1 Billion Lent

Kiva is a nonprofit organization that provides microloans to low-income entrepreneurs in more than 80 countries. In July 2017, the peer-to-peer lending site achieved the milestone of lending US$1 billion to 2.5 million borrowers since its founding in 2005. Of Kiva platform users, roughly 80 percent are women, who borrowed nearly 73 percent of the total funds. While one arm of Kiva relies on a network of on-the-ground operators to distribute funds (including microfinance institutions, social businesses, and NGOs), Kiva Zip directly sends loans at zero percent interest to entrepreneurs through mobile payments platforms such as PayPal.[40]

Mobile Money

Mobile money, sometimes referred to as mobile wallets, enables transactions to occur electronically from one phone to another. M-Pesa, launched in 2007 in Kenya and Tanzania, is one of the most successful examples of mobile money. Developed after researchers noticed Kenyans transferred mobile airtime as a proxy for money, M-Pesa is a phone-based electronic money transfer service that allows users to deposit, withdraw, transfer funds, and pay for goods and services with their mobile device. A decade after its founding, M-Pesa has facilitated financial access for almost 20 million Kenyans, including for entrepreneurs who have created thousands of new small businesses.[41] [42] As shown in Box 3.8, mobile money also

40   Susan Price, July 6, 2017, "Lending Pioneer Kiva Hits the One Billion Mark And Launches A Fund For Refugees," *Forbes*, https://bit.ly/2HrMKzx.

41   Daniel Runde, August 12, 2015, "M-Pesa And The Rise Of The Global Mobile Money Market," *Forbes*, https://bit.ly/2HoFNPE.

42   Safaricom, 2014, "Safaricom Limited FY14 Presentation," Safaricom, https://www.safaricom.co.ke/images/Downloads/Resources_Downloads/FY_2014_Results_Presentation.pdf.

has spurred banks in Kenya to become more inclusive. While Kenya and Tanzania are trailblazers in the mobile money arena, being the first two countries to surpass 1 million active accounts, the rest of the world is quickly catching up.[43] [44]

Box 3.8: Bank Accounts Now Surpass Mobile Money in Kenya

By focusing on the development of services that can compete with mobile money, banks are mirroring essential services for the poor in their own way. PesaLink is a payments system that enables small transfers between its member institutions, more than 30 of whom are currently participating. Each transaction takes only 45 seconds.[45] A newly created bank-owned entity, Integrated Payment Systems Limited, now oversees the mechanism. The abundance of mobile money accounts through one of PesaLink's rivals, M-Pesa, has driven banks to coordinate more aggressively to compete in the marketplace. The result is a richer landscape of services available to poor people—not just through mobile money but also through banks that are incentivized and challenged to keep up.[46]

Sub-Saharan Africa still accounts for 100.1 million of 173.7 million active mobile money accounts, but the number of accounts in the South Asian and East Asia & Pacific regions is also growing, with nearly 50 million active accounts at the end of 2016.[47] The rest of the world, too, has shown consistent growth year over year, as shown in Figure 3.10.[48] Some 277 services now operate across 92 countries, and competition in some markets has helped to drive interoperability among mobile money operators, as well as other improvements and innovations for clients. Additionally, mobile money provides much more than person-to-person, or P2P, payment services. It allows for airtime top-ups, bill payments, sending money overseas, and commercial payments.[49] Mobile money allows low-income consumers to become more productive and elevate their socioeconomic status, becoming drivers of economic growth.

---

43   Ignacio Mas and Dan Radcliffe, 2011, "Mobile Payments go Viral: M-PESA in Kenya," *The Capco Institute Journal Of Financial Transformation*. https://siteresources.worldbank.org/AFRICAEXT/Resources/258643-1271798012256/M-PESA_Kenya.pdf

44   GSMA Staff, "State of the Industry Report on Mobile Money," 2016, GSMA, https://bit.ly/2DxsiPf.

45   PesaLink website, "What sets us apart?," https://ipsl.co.ke/pesalink/.

46   William Cook, October 3, 2017, "In Kenya, Bank Accounts Again More Popular Than M-Pesa," CGAP, http://www.cgap.org/blog/kenya-bank-accounts-again-more-popular-m-pesa---why.

47   GSMA Staff, "State of the Industry Report on Mobile Money," 2016, GSMA, https://bit.ly/2DxsiPf.

48   Ibid.

49   Ibid.

But these figures underestimate the true reach of mobile payments, as they count only mobile money accounts run by mobile network operators. Other fintech companies are entering into the game, and quickly. In China alone, 358 million citizens used their phones to make a purchase, through apps such as TenCent and AliBaba.[50]

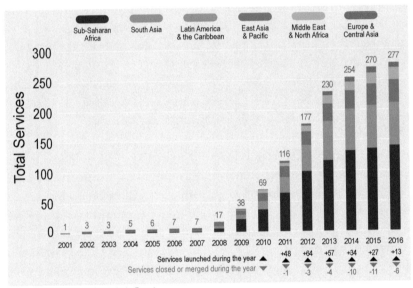

Figure 3.10: Mobile Money Services Growth

Source: 2016 GSMA State of the Industry Report

Pro-Poor Business Solutions

Advances in financial inclusion set the standard and demonstrated the potential of pro-poor business models. This section explores how a few of the more successful models resolve the challenges that poor and low-income people face—availability, quality, and affordability.

These market challenges, combined with rising private sector interest in base-of-the-pyramid business models, have highlighted a new opportunity in the quest for pro-poor business solutions. Pro-poor solutions are defined as products and services that enable poor and low-income people to enjoy safe,

---

50   Claire van den Heever, "China's Mobile Payment Revolution Is Going to Africa," *The Huffington Post*, https://www.huffingtonpost.com/claire-van-den-heever/china-mobile-payment-africa_b_9329126.html.

healthy living environments and benefit from broader economic inclusion. Pro-poor businesses target population segments such as women, youth, migrants, and displaced people; sectors such as agriculture or consumer goods; and needs such as energy and medical services. They are sometimes called "inclusive businesses," meaning that they profit from providing goods and services to people at the base of the pyramid. An inclusive business works with base-of-the-pyramid populations not only as customers but also as suppliers, distributors, and retailers. Essentially, an inclusive business is a revenue-generating enterprise that either sells goods to or sources products from those at the base of the pyramid in a way that helps to improve the standard of living of the poor.[51]

A recent study explored 20 pro-poor businesses, concluding that most of the enterprises reach base-of-the-pyramid populations successfully, and some reach surprisingly deep into the poverty spectrum to very poor customers. The study also found many of the enterprises are financially viable, with prospects for growth. However, many companies received some form of subsidy at an early stage, which helped mitigate startup risks and navigate challenging markets. Commercially priced, market-rate capital often replaced these subsidies in time, which means that the subsidy did not prevent businesses from becoming self-sufficient.[52]

This section looks more closely at private sector–provided pro-poor solutions and a small sample of the business models behind these opportunities. It looks at some of the most compelling cases in the rapidly changing areas of energy, water and sanitation, health, education, and agriculture. Figure 3.11 offers a summary of some of the most innovative businesses and indicates how they address the challenges of availability, quality, and affordability of services to the poor (note that many of these companies resolve more than one of the key challenges, but for simplicity they are categorized according to their strongest attribute). [53]

---

51   Guadalupe de la Mata, July 21, 2012, "What is inclusive business?: World Bank's definition and resources," Innovation for Social Change, https://innovationforsocialchange.org/what-is-inclusive-business-world-banks-definition-and-resources/.

52   Kurt Dassel and John Cassidy, June, 2017, "Reaching deep in low-income markets," Deloitte, https://bit.ly/2qo6gVD.

53   Icons made by Freepik from www.flaticon.com.

Figure 3.11: Innovative Pro-Poor Businesses

	Energy ⚡	WASH 🚰	Healthcare ➕	Education 🎓	Agriculture 🌱
Availability	**M-KOPA** Kenya, Uganda, Tanzania 600,000 homes illuminated through M-KOPA financing	**Sarvajal** India 4.3 million people served daily through water ATMS	**Living Goods** Kenya, Myanmar, Uganda 27% reduction in childhood mortality rates at villages	**FINALE** Mexico 2,000 students with degrees as a result of loan access	**Aldeia Nova** Angola 1.7 million customers receiving enough protein from Aldeia Nova eggs
Quality	**Ilumexico** Mexico 10,000 systems installed in rural areas	**SOIL** Haiti 84 metric tons of compost sold in 2016	**Livewell** Kenya 250,000 patients seen at Livewell clinics	**Bridge Intl. Academies** India, Kenya, Liberia, Nigeria, Uganda 10 million pupils by 2025	**Babban Gona** Nigeria 99.9% loan repayment rate of franchisees
Affordability	**d.light** 62 countries 12 million solar-powered products sold	**Aakar** India 300+ female entrepreneurs empowered through minifactories	**Life Saving Dot** India 16 cents for a woman's monthly dose of iodine	**UPM** 45 Countries 23 million lessons downloaded per month	**Mazzi** Sub-Saharan Africa 10% amount of bacteria growth compared to a traditional container

Source: Respective company websites

Energy

Unreliable energy provision forces consumers to use often expensive or even unsafe alternatives, such as kerosene or charcoal. In many developing countries, it falls to the private sector to provide reliable access to electricity and energy, especially last mile delivery. The private sector is beginning to provide energy solutions for the 1.2 billion people worldwide who live off the grid, such as financing for home solar systems and inexpensive tools for households to take advantage of innovations in solar power. The rise of clean energy alternatives for both homes and businesses has resulted in an estimated $50 billion spent annually worldwide on solar and other alternative energy sources. However, an additional investment of $45 billion each year is required to meet the goal of universal electrification.[54] The future is bright for this industry; the Global Off-Grid Lighting Association predicts that by 2020, the market for alternative energy projects will equal 100

---

54   Peyton Flemming, Fiona Messent, Christine Eibs Singer, and Stacy Swann, 2017, "Energizing Finance: Scaling and Refining Finance in Countries with Large Energy Access Gaps," Sustainable Energy for All, https://bit.ly/2HaB7PH.

million households (500 million people) worldwide, and continued interest and innovation will help firms meet this demand.[55]

One of the companies engaging in this market is M-KOPA, which manufactures and sells home solar systems that provide electricity to rural households in Kenya, Uganda, and Tanzania. M-KOPA's goal is to have solar power replace dirtier fuels such as kerosene. Its main solar home system includes a solar panel, four LED bulbs, a rechargeable flashlight, a rechargeable radio, and a phone adapter and charger. M-KOPA's advanced solar home system includes a larger panel, a larger battery, and even a 20-inch television, all with a warranty.[56]

What distinguishes M-KOPA from the competition is the flexible financing available for its systems. Because so many of M-KOPA's customers live in poverty, the option to pay a deposit to obtain a system and then pay a daily fee for a year to fully own it makes the product available to customers who would not be able to afford the system outright. M-KOPA also finances the sale of other goods, such as cookstoves and bicycles, to customers who have paid off their solar home systems. (See Box 3.9 to learn more about the difference a clean cookstove can make.) M-KOPA is currently selling 600 solar home systems per day and is focusing on rapid growth.[57] It had provided electricity to 600,000 homes as of early 2018.[58]

Box 3.9: Clean Cookstoves

The Global Alliance for Clean Cookstoves distributed an estimated 37 million stoves in 2016 through partnerships with governments, entrepreneurs, and investors. Leveraging public-private partnerships and providing grants and seed money to startups, the Alliance distributes cookstoves that reduce fuel use by 30–60 percent per household. Household air pollution causes thousands of deaths each year, and millions more are affected. In addition to reducing household air pollution, cookstoves also address issues such as gender parity (women have more time to spend

---

55 Global Off-Grid Lighting Association website, "About Us," https://www.gogla.org/about-us.

56 M-KOPA website, "Products," http://www.m-kopa.com/products/.

57 Kurt Dassel and John Cassidy, June, 2017, "Reaching deep in low-income markets," Deloitte, https://bit.ly/2qo6gVD.

58 M-KOPA, 2018, "Our Impact," M-KOPA, http://solar.m-kopa.com/about/our-impact/.

on pursuits other than gathering fuel and cooking), global warming (solid fuel sources used for traditional cookstoves are much more carbon-intensive), health (cooking is the fourth leading risk factor for disease in developing countries), and other areas.[59]

Box 3.10 details other innovative financing mechanisms that have allowed low-income people to access electricity.

Box 3.10: Flexible Financing

Flexible financing, sometimes known as pay-as-you-go (PAYGO), allows users to prepay for electricity when they have funds available, with no up-front costs. Angaza Design is a startup that offers services similar to that of M-KOPA, also offering an innovative PAYGO system.[60] Customers purchase a solar lantern and panel for a small down payment and then purchase electricity as they need it. The lantern will stay lit only while there is credit remaining in the customer's account. In time, customers will fully pay off the lantern with their electric payments and will have their own solar powered device that is much cleaner and more efficient than kerosene or other traditional fuel sources. PAYGO financing makes this opportunity possible and continues to be a useful financial tool for connecting poor and low-income people to basic goods and services that were previously unobtainable.[61]

Some companies offer energy finance for businesses too. Ilumexico provides loans to install solar powered refrigeration in rural and underserved areas in Mexico. This technology allows entrepreneurs to sell more affordable and safe dairy products and cold drinks. This business model not only provides business opportunities for entrepreneurs but also improves the quality of life for consumers in the region as a more diverse array of higher quality products becomes available to them.[62] Furthermore, the installation of over

---

59   Alliance for Clean Cookstoves, "Impact Areas: Health," Alliance for Clean Cookstoves, http://cleancookstoves.org/impact-areas/health/.

60   Wajiha Ahmed, November 15, 2017, "How fintech is changing lives in the global south," World Economic Forum, https://www.weforum.org/agenda/2017/11/how-fintech-is-changing-lives-in-global-south/.

61   Mike Butcher, October 23, 2015, "Angaza Raises $4M To Make Clean Energy Affordable For World's Poorest," TechCrunch, https://tcrn.ch/2Hhjfme.

62   Beneficial Returns website, "News," http://www.beneficialreturns.com/news.

10,000 systems in rural Mexico has displaced more than 6,000 tons of carbon dioxide.[63]

Some energy solutions focus on innovative products. d.light provides solar powered lanterns and power products such as mobile chargers and personal grid systems that have improved health through lower incidences of fires and burns, increased productivity by extending the workday for income-generating activities, and reduced the financial burden of energy consumption. As of October 2017, d.light has sold more than 12 million solar light and power products in 62 countries.[64]

Water, Sanitation, and Health (WASH)

The global cost of shortcomings in basic water and sanitation services is high—760,000 children die each year, and low-income countries lose around 2 percent of GDP (around $260 billion) annually due to higher health care costs and lower productivity.[65] To achieve the SDGs pertaining to universal water supply, sanitation, and hygiene services by 2030, current capital investment needs to triple.[66] Local and international businesses are finding ways to extend access to underserved communities through private water distribution and sanitation systems. In some cases, these companies provide an opportunity for poor and low-income people to become entrepreneurs.

The lack of access to clean drinking water in villages, slums, schools, and public places is a major problem in India. Sarvajal addresses this problem with "water ATMs." Sarvajal leases its water purification equipment to a franchisee and then helps entrepreneurs mobilize financing from microfinance institutions.[67] More than 330 water ATMs serve 4.3 million people daily across 16 Indian states. This technology also boosts gender equality, as

63   Ilumexico website, "Home," https://ilumexico.mx/home/.

64   D.light website, "About Us," http://www.dlight.com/about-us.

65   Kurt Dassel and John Cassidy, June, 2017, "Reaching deep in low-income markets," Deloitte, https://bit.ly/2qo6gVD.

66   Guy Hutton and Mili Varughese, January, 2016, "The Costs of Meeting the 2030 Sustainable Development Goal Targets on Drinking Water, Sanitation, and Hygiene," World Bank and UNICEF, https://bit.ly/2GOiEVD.

67   Samhita staff, "Sarvajal Case Study," Samhita Better CSR, www.samhita.org/water-for-all/.

water-gathering roles have traditionally fallen on women in India.[68] Companies around the world have seen the value of this business model and have begun employing it elsewhere.

A new type of toilet is providing better, safer, and more sanitary bathrooms in Haiti while also generating positive benefits to households and communities. Sanitary Organic Integrated Livelihoods (SOIL) has installed specially designed toilets that separate liquid and solid waste in hurricane refugee camps housing 20,000 people and in 30 communities in northern Haiti.[69] Better access to sanitary toilets can mitigate the toll taken by crises such as the cholera epidemic, which claimed the lives of 7,500 Haitians.[70] The success of the refugee projects inspired SOIL to manufacture similar toilets for at-home use. This venture is profitable, as the solid waste collected is converted into rich compost and fertilizer.[71] Though SOIL is currently a nonprofit, entrepreneurs in other parts of the world could develop similar methods for turning human waste into profit and increasing the quality and dignity of toilet usage.

Lack of access to safe WASH services has especially adverse impacts for girls and women in developing countries. Many countries still consider menstruation taboo and girls are encouraged to stay home during their monthly menstrual cycle. Even if they want to attend school, they may lack access to safe and private bathrooms that allow them to clean themselves, forcing them to miss school on a regular basis. Several companies have developed innovative products to inexpensively and profitably deal with this problem.

One example is Flo, created by Mariko Higaki Iwai, for girls to wash, dry, and carry reusable sanitary pads.[72] Flo is a discreet kit worn beneath clothing so that girls can carry it to school without detection; the kit also enables girls to safely wash and dry pads to prevent the growth of harmful bacteria. Another company addressing this problem is Aakar Innovations, which started in India

68   Sarvajal website, "Home," www.sarvajal.com/.

69   Christine Dell'Amore, October 28, 2011, "Human Waste to Revive Haitian Farmland?," *National Geographic,* https://bit.ly/2IHZvW1.

70   Jennifer Yang, November 22, 2012, "Why Haiti sees hope in a toilet bowl," *The Star,* Alliance for Clean Cookstoves, "Impact Areas: Health," Alliance for Clean Cookstoves, http://cleancookstoves.org/impact-areas/health/..

71   Christine Dell'Amore, October 28, 2011, "Human Waste to Revive Haitian Farmland?," *National Geographic,* https://bit.ly/2IHZvW1.

72   Mariko Higaki Iwai, Flo website, http://marikoproduct.com/Flo.

and has since expanded to Africa. Aakar's women-led microenterprise model sells "minifactories" to franchisees, who then manufacture inexpensive compostable sanitary pads for sale to the government and local NGOs.[73] Another arm of Aakar, Aakar Social Ventures, raises feminine hygiene awareness and educates consumers on the benefits of Aakar's products. In addition, Aakar focuses its research and development efforts on innovative technology and inputs with the goal of decreasing product prices for low-income customers, which makes it possible for Aakar to reach rural areas and very low-income female customers.[74] Aakar reports a substantial footprint, with more than 40 minifactories operating across India, $15 million in revenue generated by female entrepreneurs, and many thousands of women reached as consumers.[75]

Health care

Sustainable access to health care is critical, yet poor and low-income people in many countries are hard-pressed to find and afford high-quality health care services. Unlicensed health professionals and counterfeit drugs are commonplace in many developing countries. Many health expenditures are out of pocket, making unexpected sickness or injury a significant driver of poverty. While access to health care is increasing globally, an enormous segment of the developing world has yet to participate. Figure 3.12 shows the unmet health needs in nine essential health service areas.[76] The health care arena has an enormous unmet demand for essential services, leaving the door wide open for private sector providers. The private sector is offering services for improved health, better clinics to prevent shoddy and dangerous medical practices, and products that bolster preventative care and improve health at the base of the pyramid.

---

73 Kurt Dassel and John Cassidy, June, 2017, "Reaching deep in low-income markets," Deloitte, https://bit.ly/2qo6gVD.

74 Ibid.

75 Aakar Innovations website, "Impact Measurement," https://aakarinnovations.com/impact-measurement/.

76 Gabriela Flores, Daniel Hogan, Gretchen Stevens, Justine Hsu, Tessa Tan-Torres Edejer, Sarah Thomson, Tamás Evetovits, Agnès Soucat, and John Grove, December, 2017, "Tracking Universal Health Coverage: 2017 Global Monitoring Report," World Health Organization and World Bank, https://bit.ly/2ACuGmb.

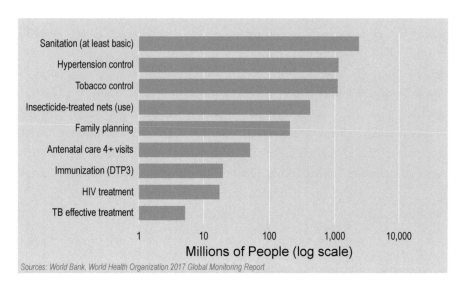

Figure 3.12: Number of People Not Receiving Essential Health Services, 2017

Living Goods is a network of village-based mobile health providers who conduct health education, provide free checkups, and distribute essential health products. Inspired by Avon's distribution model of micro franchising, Living Goods achieves efficiency through scale, standardization, and leverage. It employs 1,300 agents to provide services to roughly 1 million people in Uganda, Kenya, Zambia and Myanmar.[77] This approach reduces wait times, increases product availability at public health centers, and encourages accountability and commitment by requiring workers to invest in the initial products themselves. Similarly, eye clinics across the globe have successfully found return on investment by improving distribution of services through franchising and similar models (see Box 3.11 for examples).

---

77   Living Goods, "Measuring Impact," https://livinggoods.org/what-we-do/measuring-impact/.

Box 3.11: Innovating to Deliver Optometric Health

Micro-entrepreneurs across Bangladesh, El Salvador, India, and South Africa are receiving basic optometry training from social enterprise VisionSpring to diagnose minor eyesight problems in rural communities. The micro-entrepreneurs then sell affordable reading glasses to individuals based on their needs. In general, these patients would otherwise have no access to optometrist services or corrective optic devices. In 2010, VisionSpring generated $228 million in economic growth by selling 600,000 pairs of glasses.[78]

Essilor, a major lens manufacturer, teamed up with two hospitals in India to expand their operations to rural villages. Essilor viewed the villagers as an untapped market but was, in fact, providing them a great service by expanding operations there. Many people in developing countries are unaware that they need eyeglasses, which can be a drain on productivity and reduces life expectancy.[79]

India has the largest blind population in the world. A simple surgery would prevent many cases of blindness. Enter Aravind Eye Hospitals, whose mission is to promote ocular health in India and around the world. Despite only charging those customers able to afford its care and providing services to poor people for little to no cost, Aravind has achieved profitability by focusing on quality to make its brand known and attracting millions of customers at all income levels. Since its inception in 1976, Aravind has treated 29 million people and performed 3.6 million procedures.[80]

Livewell Clinics is a hub and spoke network of independently owned health centers in urban Kenya with an emphasis on efficiency and low-income customers.[81] These centers are a one-stop shop, as each clinic offers both preventative and primary care services in one place. The clinics also provide health consultations and laboratory services, and some even have a pharmacy. Livewell brings in specialists such as obstetricians, gynecologists, and pediatricians on

---

78 VisionSpring, December 20, 2010, "VisionSpring Releases New Research on the Positive Effects of Eyeglasses on Low-Income Consumers in India," VisionSpring, https://bit.ly/2v3Jh7J.

79 Aneel Karnani Aneel Karnani, Bernard Garrette, Jordan Kassalow, & Moses Lee . 2011, "Better Vision for the Poor," *Stanford Social Innovation Review*, https://ssir.org/articles/entry/better_vision_for_the_poor.

80 Naazneen Karmali, March 5, 2010, "Aravind Eye Care's Vision for India," *Forbes*, https://www.forbes.com/global/2010/0315/companies-india-madurai-blindness-nam-familys-vision.html#7b17a0c25c7e.

81 Innovations in Healthcare, "Livewell," https://www.innovationsinhealthcare.org/profile/livewell-(previously-viva-afya)/.

an as-needed basis. Between 2009 and 2017, seven Livewell clinics collectively saw more than 250,000 patients. Livewell's higher-income customers tend to purchase the relatively expensive services, such as radiology, which allows Livewell to provide its inexpensive, low-margin services to poorer Kenyans.[82]

Other niche enterprises are springing up to serve numerous distinct markets. The Life Saving Dot, for example, an iodine-rich bindi used to address iodine deficiencies, has been piloted in India to improve health outcomes for rural women.[83] A packet of 30 bindis costs only 10 rupees (16 cents), making them affordable for most women. Each bindi provides the daily recommended requirement of iodine. Grey for Good, the company that manufactures these bindis, has distributed packets of bindis to more than 30,000 women as of 2015 by collaborating with an Indian NGO.[84] By offering reliable and affordable access to iodine in a culturally appropriate and easily accessible manner, The Life Saving Dot is helping to decrease rates of breast cancer and other serious illnesses associated with iodine deficiency.

Education

The private sector is increasingly offering skills development and training programs for young people in the developing world to position them for better job opportunities, complementing a development sector traditionally reserved for governments, donors, and philanthropists. Private sector firms and employers can extend stretched resources and services, provide more efficient and responsive skills, build opportunities that address immediate and future workforce needs of the private sector, and reduce the costs of on-the-job training needed later on. Research shows that while education matters, skills matter more. In addition, the skills that matter most are changing every day. Box 3.12 highlights one organization that is teaching girls and other young people how to code.

---

82   Kurt Dassel and John Cassidy, June, 2017, "Reaching deep in low-income markets," Deloitte, https://bit.ly/2qo6gVD.

83   Grey Global, "Life Saving Dot Case Study," Grey Global, http://grey.com/global/work/key/singapore-life-saving-dot/id/5623/.

84   Priti Salian, May 19, 2015, "The Little Red Dot Saving Lives in India," *Takepart,* http://www.takepart.com/article/2015/05/19/life-saving-dot-iodine-india.

Box 3.12: Preparing Young Women for the Jobs of Tomorrow

Following an open call for applicants, Laboratoria uses a data-driven process to identify young women who have high potential but are unable to obtain a good education due to economic limitations. They sponsor the selected students' education through a technology bootcamp, which lasts six months, and then find hiring tech companies through an in-house app. Laboratoria's more than 580 alumni report a 75 percent job placement rate and tripled incomes upon graduating. The result is transformative, with young people ready to begin their career in digital technology to improve their future and that of their families.[85]

The gap in education exists at every level; there are nearly 30 million children in Sub-Saharan Africa in need of a primary school education, and new reports state that the investment potential has never been greater in this sector.[86] By targeting this gap between supply and demand in the education market, companies around the world are showing that the private sector can have a significant role to play in delivering education to low-income students.

In Mexico, for example, nearly 80 percent of citizens seeking higher education cannot afford it. It is difficult for these people to find willing funders to provide them with student loans, due to the perceived risk of the would-be students. FINAE is a financial institution and certified B-Corp, created by socially conscious entrepreneurs, that provides student loans to low-income Mexicans seeking higher education. FINAE offers low-interest loans to low-income students and guarantees payments to universities.[87] FINAE's customers can put their loans toward tuition at more than 20 private universities across Mexico. FINAE has provided $55 million in loans to more than 10,000 students.[88]

School systems are beginning to turn more frequently to private schools to solve chronic problems with education, particularly in Sub-Saharan Africa and India. Bridge International Academies opened its first school in a slum outside

---

85   Laboratoria website, "Our Impact," www.laboratoria.la/en.

86   David Ferreira and Scott Featherston, 2017, "The Business of Education in Africa," Caerus Capital, http://edafricareport.caeruscapital.co/thebusinessofeducationinafrica.pdf.

87   SistemaB, September 13, 2017, "FINAE Is Creating New Avenues for First-Generation University Grads in Mexico," B the Change, https://bthechange.com/finae-mexico-on-campus-3160de4e82dd.

88   Kurt Dassel and John Cassidy, June, 2017, "Reaching deep in low-income markets," Deloitte, https://bit.ly/2qo6gVD.

of Nairobi in 2009, and now operates nearly 500 schools.[89] Bridge has educated more than 100,000 pupils, and its goal is to educate 10 million by 2023.[90] Though Bridge is for-profit and charges a monthly fee to each student, it bears noting that many "free" public schools in these regions charge under-the-table fees and bribes, meaning the relative cost for Bridge schooling is not as high as it may seem at first. Bridge uses technology to equip its teachers to engage students and monitor progress, and in Kenya its rate of teacher absenteeism is less than 1 percent, far below the national average.[91] However, for-profit schools do not come without criticism. There are those who criticize Bridge specifically for its "Academy in a Box" approach, describing how teachers give lessons from a canned lesson plan, which some US education experts have dubbed the "McDonaldization" of education.[92] Others have moral concerns about for-profit education more generally. Regardless of these debates, this trend of private-sector expansion into education in the developing world seems likely to continue.

Speaking English can greatly increase the opportunities available to people in the developing world. An innovative company called Urban Planet Mobile (UPM) works with mobile operators to deliver English lessons via phones and other internet connections to more than 750,000 low-income users across 45 countries in East Asia, the Middle East, and Latin America. Urban English is the main product and delivers daily lessons that include quizzes and other exercises. Urban English can be delivered to 95 percent of mobile phones, so even those with basic phones can use this service. The subscription fee is low, around $3 per month, and UPM has agreements with local network operators to deliver the service in exchange for a share of the fee paid.[93] [94]

89   Tina Rosenberg, June 14, 2016, "Liberia, Desperate to Educate, Turns to Charter Schools," *The New York Times*, https://www.nytimes.com/2016/06/14/opinion/liberia-desperate-to-educate-turns-to-charter-schools.html.

90   Global Impact Investing Network, "Bridge International Academies," Global Impact Investing Network, https://thegiin.org/research/profile/bridge-international-academies.

91   The Economist Group, January 18, 2017, "Bridge International Academies gets high marks for ambition but its business model is still unproven," *The Economist*, https://econ.st/2GNJBgy.

92   Eli Wolfe, April 5, 2014, "'Academies-in-a-Box' Are Thriving – But Are They the Best Way to School the World's Poor?," *California Magazine*, https://bit.ly/2GOi3aT.

93   Kurt Dassel and John Cassidy, June, 2017, "Reaching deep in low-income markets," Deloitte, https://bit.ly/2qo6gVD.

94   GSMA, January 1, 2013, "Urban Planet Mobile," GSMA, https://www.gsma.com/mobilefordevelopment/topic/digital-literacy/urban-planet-mobile/.

Agriculture

Agriculture remains one of the principal areas of employment globally, engaging more than one billion people—many of them poor.[95] Agricultural productivity remains low in many high-potential regions due to antiquated technology and practices and lack of investment in or access to irrigation, improved seeds, and other agricultural inputs. Further, inappropriate harvesting techniques combined with lack of storage, transport, processing facilities, and other factors result in post-harvest losses that can exceed 40 percent. The private sector can continue to benefit agricultural workers at the bottom of the economic pyramid by finding ways to leverage new technologies, integrating farmers into supply chains to increase productivity and economies of scale, and employing new methods of financing. Several companies have found ways to address chronic malnutrition, improve crop yields, and develop better tools to improve food storage and transport that are sustainable and profitable.

In Angola, for example, half of households suffer from undernourishment, and protein shortage in particular is a dietary problem. Aldeia Nova's community-based model supports local farmers by providing them with the inputs they need to produce eggs and milk, such as chickens, cages, and feed. Aldeia Nova then purchases what the farmers produce and prepares it for sale across Angola. Egg sales are the main revenue source for Aldeia Nova, though meat and milk are significant contributors to Aldeia Nova's profits as well. The company supports farmers who produce 250,000 eggs each day for 1.7 million customers annually.[96] Even the farmers Aldeia Nova works with are selected with social consciousness in mind. Many of them are former combatants who fought in Angola's civil war; access to agricultural jobs that do not require capital or land provides them with an opportunity to make a living in a time of peace.[97]

Producers in developing economies frequently struggle to keep up with the market's demand for agricultural products. Most Nigerian farmers own

---

95   Catherine Ward, September 3, 2012, "Six Innovations Lifting the World's Agricultural Workers out of Poverty," Worldwatch Institute, https://bit.ly/2EAVeBt.

96   Kurt Dassel and John Cassidy, June, 2017, "Reaching deep in low-income markets," Deloitte, https://bit.ly/2qo6gVD.

97   LR Group website, "Adama Aldeia Nova, Angola," http://lr-group.com/project/adama-aldeia-nova-angola-2/.

less than a hectare of land, and making a decent living can be extremely difficult. Babban Gona is a franchise farming system that aims to help young Nigerians become profitable farmers and stay on their land instead of turning to illegal or dangerous means of earning a living. Babban Gona provides financial services, agricultural inputs, training and development, and even marketing services to its franchisees.[98] Babban Gona has been profitable since its inception, and 99.9 percent of its farmers have repaid the 16,000 loans lent by Babban Gona on time, all while generating crop yields that are 2.3 times the national average.[99] Using market-based solutions to enhance the quality of crop yields results in a win-win for farmers and investors alike.

Today, innovators in the private sector are creating genetically modified, pest-resistant seeds; applying digital tools to extend precision agriculture to smallholders; and developing new technologies to harvest or transport food. For example, the Mazzi container improves the collection, storage, and transportation of milk in developing countries.[100] The Mazzi container is designed to reduce spoilage and minimize the number of contaminants that enter the container while increasing transportability. It has leakproof seals and is stackable, easing the burden of transportation on producers and ensuring more milk makes it to the market, ultimately increasing the amount of milk producers sell. By addressing the needs of the producer, Mazzi is helping to improve the livelihoods of smallholder farmers in Kenya and Ethiopia at a low cost.

In addition to selling services directly to poor and low-income people, some social entrepreneurs have developed business models that benefit poor people by serving clients such as governments, NGOs, or donors. These business models address issues such as citizen voice in government, disaster readiness, and/or anti-corruption. Box 3.13 illustrates the example of disaster readiness.

---

98 Babban Gona, "Our Solution," http://www.babbangona.com/our-solution/.

99 Jonathan Wheatley, November 6, 2017, "Nigeria's 'great farm' model bears fruit in time of high insecurity," *Financial Times*, https://www.ft.com/content/a32b0c58-a75a-11e7-ab66-21cc87a2edde.

100 Mazzi Container website, "Our Container," http://www.mazzican.com/.

Digital platforms that enable real-time data collection on the location, needs, and priorities of a community in the wake of disaster have dramatic lifesaving potential for the world's poor. The information collected can be used to gather insights into a conflict or disaster as it is occurring and to support the allocation of resources and assistance to priority areas. Ushahidi is an open-source software platform originally developed in 2008 to map reports of violence in Kenya after election results there led to civil unrest. Ushahidi is now used worldwide to manage both conflict and natural disasters, and clients include the World Bank, the United Nations, and Al-Jazeera. Ushahidi was used in Honduras to map health care resources through crowdsourcing, as well as to track disease outbreaks, violence, and natural hazards.[101] It was used in Haiti to track the post-earthquake crisis response and recovery efforts.[102] Other crowdsourcing platforms providing critical insight into conflict zones include photo-based apps that track the availability of food in crisis situations. Data can provide real-time insights into local capture and resale of humanitarian aid, track food prices across a country, and monitor disaster areas such as sites of Ebola outbreaks. These results enable the responsible organizations to better track and distribute necessary resources, ensuring they reach the target populations in the quickest and safest means possible.[103]

Economic Opportunity Through Jobs

A good job is the most sustainable pathway out of poverty—especially a job in the formal sector. Employers range in size (microenterprises to large corporations), sector (industry, agriculture, services), sophistication (low skills to high skills), and formality (formal or informal). Figure 3.13 provides a representation of how different firms generally fit the skills spectrum.[104]

---

101 Ushahidi Staff, 2010, "Mapping Honduras Hospitals," Ushahidi, https://www.ushahidi.com/blog/2010/09/27/mapping-honduras-hospitals.

102 Ushahidi Staff, 2010, "Crisis Mapping Haiti: Some Final Reflections," Ushahidi, https://www.ushahidi.com/blog/2010/04/14/crisis-mapping-haiti-some-final-reflections.

103 Aid & International Development Forum, May 8, 2015, "Solutions That Are Saving Lives in Humanitarian Response," Aid & International Development Forum, https://bit.ly/2EBVrnR.

104 Cecilia Chen and Marcus Haymon, 2016, "Realizing the potential of digital job seeking platforms," Brookings Blum Roundtable, https://brook.gs/2bEECiO.

Figure 3.13: The Employer Skill Spectrum

Source: 2016 Brookings Blum Roundtable

Regardless of where firms sit on the spectrum, they all share one character-istic: all companies are part of a value chain. The term value chain refers to the system of firms and their relationships in the processing and delivery of products and services. The value chain breaks down the flow of production and distribution of activities in such a way that the value of each player is identified and potentially maximized. Jobs are created across the value chain. Figure 3.14 illustrates the activities of a generic value chain, where for each activity there could be several companies involved.[105]

---

105 Michael E. Porter, 1985, "Competitive Advantage," The Free Press.

Figure 3.14: The Value Chain

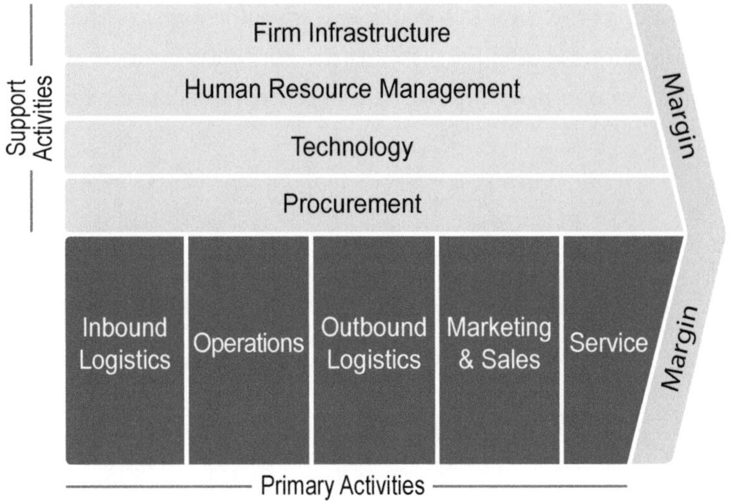

Source: Porter's Generic Value Chain Model

A family-run food shop, for example, sources products from different suppliers whose inputs were in turn grown by farmers and processed by food companies. Suppliers then use distributors and logistics services to get their products to the food shop. The shop uses cleaning services from an outsourced company, pays advertisers to promote its business, and hires an external bookkeeper to keep the finances in shape. This quick run through the value chain of a simple business operation shows the numerous players involved—and each is an employer.

The best-paid and most sustainable jobs in a value chain tend to be the ones that add the most value; namely, those involving more complex processes, a greater degree of sophistication, and more refined skills. This principle applies to individual companies, value chains, and countries, as many value chains are global in scope. Governments try to improve their overall position in the global value chain through policies that nudge companies—and therefore jobs—into higher value-add roles. Ultimately, however, firms will be the ones that decide, based on cost-benefit choices, whether to produce items themselves, outsource to a domestic supplier, or import from an international player.

This section examines three examples of value chains, covering agriculture, industry, and services. For each, it will be possible to see the wide range of jobs and skills required for every activity, as well as some of the complexities involved in the systems. Figure 3.15 provides an overview of job skills required in the coffee, automotive, and call center industries as illustrative examples.

Figure 3.15: Examples of Job Skills in Three Illustrative Value Chains

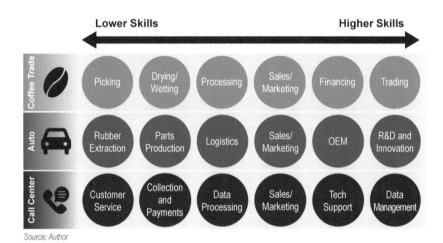

Source: Author

Coffee in Ethiopia

Ethiopia is the birthplace of coffee and produces some of the most desired beans in the world. Coffee plays a central role in Ethiopia's economy, accounting for approximately 35 percent of Ethiopia's total export revenues between 2000 and 2014.[106] Most of the coffee in the country is produced by the roughly 4.2 million smallholder farmers who rely on coffee production as their main source of income.[107] Accounting for those employed in coffee production, transportation, and other supplementary activities, it is estimated that more than 15 million people in Ethiopia are in some way involved in the industry.[108]

---

106 Sara Gustafson and Manuel Hernandez, May 19, 2017, "The Ethiopia Commodity Exchange: A coffee success story?," International Food Policy Research Institute, https://bit.ly/2HfsuDu.

107 Ibid.

108 Chemonics International Inc., 18 June, 2010, "Ethiopia Coffee Industry Value Chain Analysis," USAID, https://bit.ly/2v1T4Ls.

Given its labor-intensive nature, especially in harvesting and processing, coffee is an important source of income for the unskilled and rural poor.

Most coffee value chains are global. Developing countries are the main producers, and developed countries are the main consumers. Most production occurs within 50 or so developing nations, employing roughly 25 million farmers, while most consumption takes place in the United States and Europe.[109] Figure 3.16 provides an overview of the global coffee value chain.[110]

Figure 3.16: Global Coffee Value Chain

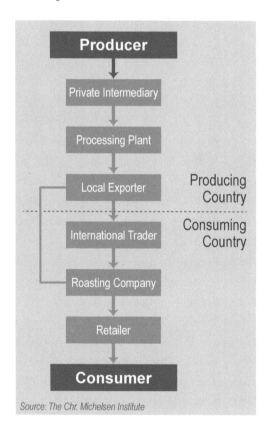

Source: The Chr. Michelsen Institute

---

109 Euromonitor statistics, January 11, 2017, "Caffeine (Coffee) Consumption By Country," *Caffeine Informer*, https://www.caffeineinformer.com/caffeine-what-the-world-drinks.

110 Anna Milford, 2004, "Coffee, Co-operatives and Competition: The Impact of Fair Trade," The Chr. Michelsen Institute, https://www.cmi.no/publications/file/1802-coffee-co-operatives-and-competition.pdf.

Jobs begin at the farm level, including planting, farming, picking grains, and wetting or drying them. In small farms, jobs are often informal and typically performed by farm owners themselves, occasionally with a few additional hires; their salaries are quite low. In medium-sized and large industrial farms, production usually uses more technology (tractors, irrigation machinery, and so forth) and jobs range from low-skilled picking jobs to more-skilled machine operators. Farmers then sell the beans, usually through intermediary companies, to processing plants, where the coffee is further refined.

Coffee often moves to exporters who sell it abroad at internationally established prices. These are higher-paid jobs performed by export companies and/or traders. The coffee then may go through roasting and/or be sold by wholesalers to retailers and then directly to consumers, shops, or restaurants. Figure 3.15 plots some of the jobs on the skills spectrum, with farming work toward the lower end of the range and commerce-related activities toward the higher end.

When it comes to commodities like coffee, enormous gains are obtainable by improving current functions within the domestic value chain. For example, because most farmers in Ethiopia are low-income, small family operations, improving their business practices has a large socioeconomic development impact. Support to such farmers could include helping them access the latest technologies (machines, fertilizers, techniques), financing (microloans), and market information (real-time prices on mobile phones), as well as increasing their collective bargaining power by facilitating the creation of cooperatives and associations. In addition, several improvements in global coffee value chains have followed from the practice of "fair trade" and the expansion of cooperatives.

A key component of the Ethiopian coffee trade system that differentiates it from most other African coffee producers is the Ethiopia Commodity Exchange (ECX). A law created in 2008 mandates that all coffee, except for those crops grown for direct exports, must be traded in the ECX. This means that when farmers sell to local traders and distributors, the latter two must export through the ECX. Cooperatives can also sell directly to the ECX, bypassing intermediaries and allowing farmers to retain higher margins.[111]

The ECX has set a new standard for coffee quality and delivery processes in Ethiopia—as opposed to the classic auction trading system, which is done face

---

111 Chemonics International Inc., 18 June, 2010, "Ethiopia Coffee Industry Value Chain Analysis," USAID, https://bit.ly/2v1T4Ls.

to face in a less efficient, less controlled, and a more time-consuming manner. Quality control through the ECX occurs by weighing and inspecting coffee in ECX-owned warehouses. The electronic database connecting the warehouses works to prevent fraud and loss. This system leads to a much better structured and fairer process, reducing transaction costs and allowing buyers and sellers to fairly receive higher margins. The advent of the ECX has led to better business conditions for cooperative-affiliated and medium-sized farmers, allowing for increased job sustainability, and has created higher-end jobs related to commodity trading and agriculture financing.

Automotive Industry in Mexico

Mexico is the world's seventh largest car manufacturer and the fourth-ranked car exporter, with 72 percent of exports going to the United States. The automotive industry is responsible for 3 percent of Mexico's GDP and 18 percent of total manufacturing production in the country. As of 2015, it employed more than 875,000 people, about 9 percent of these in the terminal industry (assembly of engines and vehicles, stamping, dyeing, and so on) and 81 percent in auto parts manufacturing.[112]

Jobs in the automotive industry require specific skills and constant on-the-job training to keep up with emerging technologies and processes. Given the skills requirements and the economic importance of auto manufacturing, salaries in this industry equal up to three times higher than the average of other manufacturing jobs in the country, and from 2011 to 2014 real wages in auto parts increased 11.7 percent.[113]

Automotive value chains are global, and not all jobs in the chain are created in the same country. Multiple production connections and job opportunities are created throughout the chain. In the case of Volkswagen, a car might have some of its parts produced and assembled in Mexico, other parts imported from Canada and China, and tires sourced from Peru, with most R&D, innovation, and design activities conducted in Germany. In addition, within Mexico, other

---

112 Adriana Barrera Franco and Alejandro Pulido Moran, 2016, "The Mexican Automotive Industry: Current Situation, Challenges, and Opportunities," ProMexico, https://bit.ly/2sdFd1R.

113 National Institute of Statistics and Geography (INEGI) estimates. http://www.beta.inegi.org.mx/app/publicaciones/.

industries can benefit from connecting to the chain; for example, the textile industry provides seat covers, and the electronics industry supplies some of the electronic components. A vibrant and well-functioning value chain creates jobs in several regions and adjacent industries.

Figure 3.15 shows how auto jobs fit on the skill spectrum. The higher the skill requirement, the better paying and usually more stable the jobs. The low-skill end of the spectrum entails extraction of raw materials that are processed and later used in production. An example is extraction of rubber from trees in Peru or Brazil, which requires only a few processes to become tires. At the other extreme is the highly skilled work of researchers and designers, who are responsible for ensuring a company stays ahead of the competition by creating increasingly innovative and high-tech vehicles that outperform the competition.

In addition to dynamic sectors like automotive in Mexico, significant innovation is occurring in the distribution of manufactured goods. Box 3.14 provides an example of a targeted effort to make a value chain more inclusive. The micro-franchising model creates jobs for poor women in the food industry while ensuring high-quality products reach poor consumers in the Dominican Republic.

Box 3.14: Micro-franchising in the Dominican Republic — Nestlé

Nestlé Dominicana partnered with a local bank and the Multilateral Investment Fund to develop Plan Barrio in the Dominican Republic in 2006. This program aimed to elevate women making minimum wage through skills training and the opportunity to sell Nestlé products as franchisees. Low-income women were recruited directly as salespeople and received financial literacy training, cooking classes, and other trainings on top of higher wages. Women also have been recruited as micro-distributors, and this group manages the salespeople while also earning a higher wage than they were previously making. As of 2015, more than 900 women were employed under Plan Barrio, doubling and some even tripling their incomes as a result of participating in the program. Nestlé benefits from the program's contribution to its corporate social responsibility commitment, and the ground-level access franchisees have to Nestlé's customer base provides Nestlé with key business insights.[114]

---

114 SCALA, 2015, "The Power of Downstream," Inter-American Development Bank, https://observatorioscala.uniandes.edu.co/images/The-Power-of-Downstream-SCALA-5.pdf.

Global Call Centers

Beginning in the 1990s, companies in developed countries found it substantially cheaper to outsource call center jobs to countries such as India, Egypt, Morocco, South Africa, and the Philippines. The ICT improvements achieved in the past two decades, such as the growing availability of broadband in developing countries and the falling costs of telecommunications and computing power, have allowed various jobs to be performed remotely. Also, the abundance of low-cost, qualified labor in some countries, combined with welcoming policies that attract foreign direct investment, made business process outsourcing in many service areas an easy choice for western companies.

Call centers can perform two types of services, inbound and outbound. The former are purely cost-management operations, such as call handling and technical support, with no revenue generation capabilities; the second are revenue-focused activities, such as telemarketing and customer retention calling. Call centers have become one of the most emblematic examples of business process outsourcing in global value chains, servicing industries such as health care, telecommunications, tourism, banking, and financial services, to name just a few. Figure 3.15 provides the skills spectrum for some call center job functions.

Call centers tend to improve the dynamics of the local labor market. These enterprises rely on scale to deliver the appropriate cost reduction benefits, so even the smaller operations normally employ 100 people or so, while the largest potentially engage thousands of employees.[115] Not only do call center jobs usually pay better than most local jobs, but the establishment of call centers also propels surrounding industries and businesses that connect to the value chain. For example, a new call center in a small Egyptian city will provide direct employment but also indirectly generate jobs through a range of complementary services, from cleaning to business consulting, and promote sales in adjacent industries for products such as headsets, computers, and office supplies.

In addition to energizing local value chains, call centers have a positive effect on important segments of the labor force. For example, young, single women comprise the majority of call center employees in most countries. In some cul-

---

115 Cornelia Staritz and Jose Guilherme Reis, January, 2013, "Global Value Chains, Economic Upgrading, and Gender," World Bank, https://bit.ly/2JAFG48.

tures, these are among the best jobs a woman can obtain. The industry also lures recent college graduates of all genders, especially as a first job before moving to a job with greater growth prospects. College graduates go for the more technical call center jobs, which require, for example, engineering, systems, linguistic, and financial skills. Call center employees also receive constant on-the-job training in areas such as customer relationship management, marketing, and language skills (sometimes learning a new language, other times learning how to adapt accents to sound more like they are from the client country).

At the same time, traditional players in the business process outsourcing call center industry have faced growing challenges in the past few years. First, poorer countries now compete for market share with the more established countries. Second, service quality is often a problem, especially in the case of fully outsourced enterprises, and many companies have chosen to repatriate their customer service centers despite higher costs. Finally, technology, an enabling factor in the 1990s, can also become a risk when sophisticated software and internet-based applications start to replace the work of more elementary, less-skilled services such as call-answering, automated customer service and satisfaction calls.[116]

Upcoming technologies, such as robotics, artificial intelligence, and blockchain, will further disrupt the dynamics of global value chains, and their impact on jobs in developing countries is yet to be seen. It could be argued that the automation of certain functions may pose a threat to some of the less-skilled jobs normally performed by the poor. At the same time these innovations may present an unparalleled opportunity for the new generations in poor countries to connect to the global economy and leapfrog into the new job market.

---

116 Ibid.

Chapter 4. Meso Level: Ecosystem Enablers

Markets do not always connect poor and low-income people to the services and jobs they need to escape poverty. Services, from the most basic to the state-of-the-art, do not reach all who need them, and job opportunities may be missed by those without relevant tools or information. However, a web of "ecosystem enablers" can improve market functionality and promote economic inclusion.

Ecosystem enablers provide either the supply or the demand side of the market—or both—with services that help these markets function more efficiently. They are particularly important in developing and emerging markets, where it is often difficult for market players seeking to reach poor and low-income people with life-improving products, services, and jobs to do so. Enablers may be private sector companies aiming to capitalize on market opportunities, civil society agents that provide services in not-for-profit endeavors, or government-led interventions. For the purpose of this discussion, they are divided into information champions, business boosters, and job market hackers (Figure 4.1).

Figure 4.1: Ecosystem Enabling Functions

Source: Author

These three groups reflect some of the most innovative and high-impact opportunities for ecosystem enablers to facilitate access to services and jobs. For instance, better information and transparency about the market make it easier for people to access the critical services they need; better support to SMEs and social entrepreneurs improves their ability to offer life-transforming services and create jobs; and digital learning and employment platforms reduce search costs for job seekers and help connect them to better paying jobs. It by no means covers every single player across the ecosystem but rather focuses on those solutions that most directly affect the key market challenges identified for both services and jobs. On the job market side, lack of access to skills and networks forces people into informal and unstable occupations. The players described in this chapter help reduce risks for poor and low-income people, as well as the companies offering services and jobs to them. These players help deliver the right information, capabilities, and digital platforms that connect low-income people to the jobs and services they desire, and in doing so they drive inclusive economic growth.

Information Champions

The free flow of information is key to the provision of services, creation of jobs, and development of entrepreneurial activity at the bottom of the economic pyramid. At least three key dimensions of information and transparency have substantial impact on how economic systems operate and how the poor are empowered: identity, credibility, and digital inclusion.

Identification for Development – ID4D

Many tasks taken for granted by middle income and wealthy people are actually quite difficult for the poor. Trying to sign up for a government assistance program, attempting to get a small loan to start a microenterprise, and looking for a first job are all daunting tasks even with resources. Attempting any of these, but without having any sort of identification to prove who you are, is exceedingly difficult. Unfortunately, this is the reality of one in every five people on the planet. Most government services reach only those that the government can officially identify and include in relevant systems. Investors and financial institutions finance only companies and entrepreneurs that can be identified as creditworthy. Formal employment is available only for people who can verify themselves. Peer-to-peer (P2P) platforms, such as lending and crowdfunding websites, work only for those who have proven identities and, in most cases, a bank account or other institutional affiliation.

Therefore, most service providers cannot easily reach the staggering 1.1 billion people in the world who are unable to prove their identities, 78 percent of whom are in Sub-Saharan Africa and Asia.[1] In poor countries, especially in rural areas, it is common for people to be born into informality. Births in remote hospitals are often not registered (properly) and IDs not issued. Other times, people are born at home and in other nonofficial venues, and no registration occurs. Moreover, even with recent efforts in ID4D, people from previous generations may never have had IDs or may have lost them. In some cases, IDs may simply be outdated and available only in print format and, therefore, not integrated into the most current databases.

---

1   Vyjayanti Desai, Mattias Witt, Kamya Chandra, Jonathan Marskell, June 6, 2017, "Counting the uncounted: 1.1 billion people without IDs," World Bank, http://blogs.worldbank.org/ic4d/counting-uncounted-11-billion-people-without-ids.

Financial services, food vouchers, health insurance, vaccinations, voting rights, and education are just a few of many services and rights people lacking ID are unable to utilize. The government provision of IDs can help their citizens become economically included, which benefits the people as well as society.[2] See Box 4.1 for an example of how India is undertaking a massive project to identify its citizens.

Box 4.1: India's Aadhaar ID Program

An Aadhaar number is a 12-digit unique identity number issued to Indian residents based on their biometric and demographic data. The goal of the project is to get each of India's 1.2 billion residents an ID.[3] Even with India's large rural population, nearly 90 percent of Indian citizens older than 18 have an Aadhaar number as of early 2018, making Aadhaar the world's largest biometric ID system.[4][5]

Aadhaar is used for many purposes, such as digitizing government subsidy flows (government-to-person or "G2P" payments), financial services, recording attendance for government employees in order to reduce absenteeism, and issuance of passports, voter identity cards, and other forms of ID.[6] Aadhaar has direct value in creating digital infrastructure through which social and financial transfers can take place.

Its value as a form of identity implies that those who were marginalized without ID can now be included in a number of welfare and other programs. Aadhaar allows third parties, such as the Income Tax Department and pension distributors, to confirm the identity of a person electronically in real time. This attribute of Aadhaar also enables people access to

2   World Bank, 2017, "Identification for Development (ID4D)," World Bank, http://www.worldbank. org/en/programs/id4d.

3   Reach Project, Mastercard Center for Inclusive Growth, The Munk School of Global Affairs, 2017, "India Case study: Aadhaar – providing proof of identity to one billion," Mastercard Center for Inclusive Growth, https://bit.ly/2MCUjph.

4   Arun Sundararajan, Ravi Bapna, April 24, 2012, "India's Unique Identity (UID) Reaching Underprivileged Households That Have No Existing ID" New York University Stern, http://bit.ly/2Lt79c2.

5   Unique Identification Authority of India, May 31, 2018, "State/UT wise ranking based on Aadhaar saturation as on 31st May, 2018," AADHAAR, https://uidai.gov.in/images/StateWiseAge_AadhaarSat_24082017.pdf.

6   Shweta Banerjee, December 2015, "World Development Report 2016: Aadhaar: Digital Inclusion and Public Services in India," World Bank, https://bit.ly/2lb9rOk.

a range of services online.[7] At the same time, a survey of the existing research suggests at least four problems with the program, related to data privacy concerns, cost-benefit analysis, scaling pains for the direct benefit transfer system, and challenges in completely avoiding leakages in benefit payments.[8]

International organizations and governments have increasingly engaged in ID4D initiatives. A portion of Sustainable Development Goal 16 identifies the need for governments to provide legal identity and birth registrations for all by 2030.[9] SDG 16.9 has not been proposed in a vacuum; it relates to several other SDGs, as shown in Figure 4.2.[10]

Figure 4.2: Identity as an Enabler of the SDGs

Identification contributes to many goals and targets in the SDG agenda. Here are some examples:

Target 1.3 — Implement appropriate social protection systems ... and by 2030 achieve substantial coverage of the poor and vulnerable

Target 1.4 — Ensure that the poor and vulnerable have control over land and other forms of property, including financial assets

Target 5a — Give poor women equal access to economic resources, including finance

Target 5b — Enhance the use of technology, particularly ICT, to promote women's empowerment

Target 12c — Phase out harmful fuel subsidies

Target 16.5 — Reduce corruption

Source: *World Bank Doing Business Indicators*

---

7   Mudit Handa, March 20, 2018, "What are the impacts of linking Aadhaar to personal info?," *E-Startup India*, https://www.e-startupindia.com/blog/what-are-the-impacts-of-linking-aadhaar-to-personal-info/10118.html.

8   Sumit Mishra, July 31, 2017, "The Economics of Aadaar," *Live Mint* https://www.livemint.com/Home-Page/s22gUzxOULwQxqukfcBMiM/The-economics-of-Aadhaar.html.

9   United States Development Programme, 2016, "Goal 16 Targets," United Nations Development Programme, http://bit.ly/2uP7ISX.

10   Mariana Dahan and Alan Gelb, 2015, "The Role of Identification in the Post-2015 Development Agenda," World Bank, https://bit.ly/2JRL9GV.

Two years after SDG 16.9, the *Principles on Identification for Sustainable Development: Towards the Digital Age* were endorsed by several prominent players in the international community, including international organizations such as the UNDP, the World Bank, and private sector players such as the Omidyar Network, GSMA, and MasterCard. Leadership has come from the World Bank's ID4D initiative, as well as ID4DAfrica, a multi-stakeholder initiative, promoting adoption of digital identity systems in Africa. These international efforts help share experiences and institute global best practices for establishing and maintaining identity programs.

ID4D initiatives can have a significant impact on poor people. Identities can be authenticated across government agencies, facilitating access to programs and economic inclusion. The National Database and Registration Authority, for example, an identity database in Pakistan, enabled relief to reach 7.5 million people in the wake of disastrous flooding.[11] In Peru, nearly 99 percent of the population has been identified, and many women, migrants, and other minority groups were successfully targeted under the National Plan Against the Lack of Documentation to address the identification gap.[12]

Several African countries have introduced digital identification programs. South Africa combines biometric identification with smart cards and bank transfers to distribute social transfers. Countries such as Nigeria, Ivory Coast, and Tanzania are using technology to leapfrog traditional paper-based approaches. These countries use mobile devices, biometrics, and SMS messaging to ensure uniqueness and track ID application status. Many have also launched extensive outreach campaigns to rural and underserved populations.[13]

Furthermore, innovative private sector actors are using blockchain to register people and produce an identity in contexts where governments are unlikely to intervene, such as in the case of migrants and displaced populations. These solutions guarantee to charitable donors that only the intended beneficiaries

---

11 World Bank, January 14, 2013, "Pakistan: Uplifting Lives and Livelihoods Through Cash Transfers," World Bank, http://www.worldbank.org/en/results/2013/04/15/pakistan-uplifting-lives-and-livelihoods-through-cash-transfers.

12 William Reuben and Flávia Carbonari, May, 2017, "Identification as a National Priority: The Unique Case of Peru," Center for Global Development, https://www.cgdev.org/sites/default/files/identification-national-priority-unique-case-peru.pdf.

13 Makhtar Diop, May 24, 2017, "Making everyone count: how identification could transform the lives of millions of Africans," World Economic Forum, https://www.weforum.org/agenda/2017/05/making-everyone-count-the-case-for-national-identification-systems/.

receive the transferred resources and eliminate leakage and corruption. Two such examples are Aid-Tech and BanQu, which provide those who own a mobile phone but are economically excluded otherwise with digital identities. Aid-Tech works by giving NGOs and governments a way to create digital identities so that people can receive entitlements digitally, and distributed ledger technology preserves records. This is particularly useful for refugees.[14] BanQu works similarly, allowing the unbanked to engage in transactions on the BanQu blockchain. This allows them to establish a financial history and increases their opportunities for economic participation.[15]

Credibility Mechanisms

In business, credibility is everything. A person with a bad reputation—or someone who is simply unable to prove she has a reputation—has difficulties accessing credit, engaging in fruitful entrepreneurial endeavors, and even getting and keeping a job. A business with a poor financial or governance record likewise struggles to access finance, to grow, and therefore to hire. Consequently, an inclusive economic system relies on credibility mechanisms that allow people and businesses to prove their creditworthiness and performance.

Unlike medium-sized and large companies—which can often attain credit based on collateral and audited balance sheets—micro- and small enterprises and individuals rely on alternative ways to prove creditworthiness. Arguably, the most important player in this respect is the credit bureau. Credit bureaus collect information about the creditworthiness of individuals and businesses and sell it to lending institutions, ensuring creditors have the information they need to make loan decisions. Typical clients for credit bureaus include banks, microfinance lenders, mortgage providers, credit card companies, and other financing institutions. Bureaus look at an individual's borrowing and payments records by acquiring data from creditors, debtors, debt collection agencies, or offices with public records. This information is typically analyzed through algorithms that assess the credit history of the individual or business in question.

---

14 AID: Tech, 2017, "What We Do," AID:Tech, https://tge.aid.technology/welcome/#overview.

15 BanQu App, 2018, "Our Solutions: How It Works," http://www.banquapp.com/our-solutions/how-it-works/.

Historically, the main objective of credit bureaus was to inform financial institutions of bad debtors. Since the 2000s, their role has shifted toward a more holistic approach. Bureaus now provide more broad and valuable credit information about people and businesses—for instance, looking at utility bill payment. Allowing a wider range of information into the credit assessment means that a wider range of people can build their credit record, not just those who already have bank accounts. Financial institutions can then use this information to better assess each individual loan based on data about both bad and good behavior.

Besides lowering credit risk to institutions, credit bureaus also lower the transaction costs of lending by reducing the amount of time financial institutions spend evaluating loan applications. They also contribute to competition among financial service providers as they contend for clients with the best credit histories and raise incentives for borrowers to repay their loans (see Box 4.2 on the impact of bureaus). Those with a poor credit history can be excluded from borrowing again.

Box 4.2: Do Credit Bureaus Work?

The impact of bureaus can be significant for inclusive economies. In Eastern Europe, countries where credit information sharing is available through credit bureaus and/or public credit registries show companies have more success in raising debt.[16] A sample of 5,000 firms in 51 countries shows that the share of SMEs reporting "perceived financial constraints" drops from 49 to 27 percent in countries with a bureau in place.[17] A study of 129 countries shows that the introduction of credit information systems has raised the ratio of private credit to GDP by about 8 percentage points over five years.[18][19]

Credit bureaus also need to offer value-added services like fraud detection, collections, and credit scoring to turn the raw credit data into something useful for consumers and

16 Martin Brown, Tullio Jappelli, and Marco Pagano, 2007, "ECGI Finance Working Paper: Information Sharing and Credit: Firm-Level Evidence from Transition Countries," European Corporate Governance Institute, http://bit.ly/2tCy9vC.

17 Inessa Love and Nataliya Mylenko, October, 2003, "Credit Reporting and Financial Constraints," World Bank http://bit.ly/2tYRial.

18 Simeon Djankov, Oliver Hart, Caralee McLiesh, Andrei Shleifer, 2006, "Debt Enforcement Around the World," National Bureau of Economic Research, http://dx.doi.org/10.3386/w12807.

19 Simeon Djankov, Caralee McLiesh and Andrei Shleifer, January, 2005 "Private Credit in 129 Countries," National Bureau of Economic Research, http://www.nber.org/papers/w11078.pdf.

lenders. One example is the Egyptian Credit Bureau, or I-Score, which was established in 2005 and is currently a private institution. It maintains a database of credit information for consumers and SMEs. Egypt's credit bureau emerged in response to policies established by the Central Bank of Egypt that allowed banks and nonbanks to share data. I-Score gathers and evaluates data on credit card information, ID, and other financial information to create credit score reports.[20] I-Score currently holds almost all credit data on credit consumers from commercial banks, thus providing a clear indicator to the credit and financial community. The number of entities with a credit history registered in its database by the end of October 2015 encompassed 35.8 million individuals and SMEs, compared to 34.2 million in January 2015 and 30.4 million in January 2014. I-Score has facilitated access to finance for millions of people and SMEs.[21] [22]

While proving creditworthiness is a key enabler of financial inclusion and equitable growth, transparency and information are needed on other fronts as well. For example, many impact investors, clients, partners, and employees care about more than the financial strength and commercial success of a company. They also care about its labor practices, governance, and its social, environmental, and economic footprint.

Rating mechanisms such as B-Lab have emerged to fulfill this broader requirement. The nonprofit B-Lab developed an assessment and rating methodology that evaluates and benchmarks companies on their impact and their environmental, social, and governance (ESG) practices (see Box 4.3). Companies that complete the B-Lab assessment can prove their worth by sharing their scores with investors, clients, and partners and find areas for improvement based on industry benchmarks and feedback. They also enter a community of businesses that share common sustainability values, thereby developing relationships and affiliations.

Companies can become B-Certified Corporations, which means they meet B-Lab's highest standards of social and environmental performance, public

---

20 International Finance Corporation, 2006, "Credit Bureau Knowledge Guide," International Finance Corporation, https://bit.ly/2sXPnmJ.

21 Egyptian Banking Institute, "I-Score," http://sme.ebi.gov.eg/supportingactivities/Pages/I-Score.aspx.

22 Hossam Mounir, January 22, 2016, "72m Credit facilities registered in I-Score database as of October 2015," *Daily News Egypt*, https://bit.ly/2l86QV2.

transparency, and legal accountability.[23] As of 2017, B-Lab has certified more than 2,200 companies from 130 industries in more than 50 countries.[24]

Box 4.3: B-Corp and Asilia Africa

Asilia Africa believes that world-class travel must go hand in hand with improving livelihoods and conserving nature. Asilia strives to protect wildlife and their habitats while simultaneously providing job opportunities for local inhabitants. They achieve this by investing in fragile areas with the hope of making them economically sustainable through tourism.[25]

Asilia was one of thousands of companies to take the B Impact Assessment. It had a 137 B Impact Score, compared to an average of 80 for comparable companies. In addition to proving their environmental and community commitment to customers, Asilia executives learned where their success and opportunities stood. Through the B Impact Assessment, Asilia can become even more of a role model in an industry that frequently does not share Asilia's values.[26]

Digital Infrastructure and Inclusion

Systems to verify identity and assess credibility rely on having the fundamental information and communication technologies (ICT) in place. Without essential ICT infrastructure and digital services, such as digital payments (see Box 4.4), ID schemes cannot spread and credit bureaus have limited relevance.

---

23   Certified B Corporation, 2018, "Why B Corps Matter," https://bcorporation.net/about-b-corps

24   Innovation, Science and Economic Development Canada, October 4, 2017, "Minister Bains addresses B Corp community at its annual retreat," *Newswire*, https://bit.ly/2JOjxDc.

25   Asilia Africa, 2011, "About Asilia Africa," https://www.asiliaafrica.com/about-asilia/.

26   B Impact Assessment, June, 2012, "B Impact Report: Jeroen Harderwijk," http://bimpactassessment.net/case-studies/jeroen-harderwijk.

Box 4.4: Digital Payments as Enablers

Digital payment occurs when both sender and receiver execute a payment transaction through a digital platform. No hard cash is involved and the entire transaction occurs digitally. This process enables people to conduct business transactions quickly and effortlessly and allows businesses to operate over a broader geographic area without needing to invest in infrastructure. Without mobile money payments, many services offered online would be accessible only to those who hold a formal bank account.

Digitizing payments has accelerated growth in many countries, and mobile money has shown that access to digital payments can reduce economic inequality gender inequality and provide access to services that would otherwise be unattainable. Digital payments offer immediate gains for senders and receivers, and users of digital payments include utility companies, financial corporations, and bottom-of-the-pyramid people with access to a phone or computer.

Digital payments can increase the financial independence of women by saving them time commuting to make payments, avoiding complicated agent networks, and removing the reliance on remittances that many women have. Mobile payments allow women to access bank accounts, which they can then utilize to give themselves more financial autonomy, whether that means bypassing sexist laws or, more frequently, the whims of oppressive husbands.[27]

Of course, beyond P2P payments, it is necessary for employers to accept electronic payment for the system to work. More than 40 percent of adults globally have a debit card, yet only 23 percent use their cards to make payments to businesses. Barriers to merchant acceptance of electronic payment include the higher cost of acceptance, increased tax liability, and higher financial risks. In order to address this issue, companies and NGOs are working on designing cheaper ways for merchants to accept electronic payments and on strategies to drive a critical mass of consumers to demand acceptance of this form of payment from merchants.[28]

---

27   Leora Klapper, November 27, 2015, "Can digital financial services help close the gender gap?" World Economic Forum, https://www.weforum.org/agenda/2015/11/can-digital-financial-services-help-close-the-gender-gap/.

28   Mastercard, September, 2017, "Building Electronic Payment Acceptance at the Base of the Pyramid to Advance Financial Inclusion," Mastercard, https://mstr.cd/2yyZkMd.

The benefits of digital payments go far beyond their convenience that people in the developed world associate with them. They lower costs, increase security, and increase the ability of low-income people to manage their risk and enhance financial inclusion. The adoption and proliferation of this digital technology has already provided a pathway to prosperity for many in the developing world.[29] [30]

Despite the digital divide between developed and developing nations, and between the rich and poor within countries, digital technologies are spreading more quickly and evenly than any other service before them. For example, while the growth of access to electricity, water, and schooling has been linear, the penetration of mobile phones and internet access has grown exponentially in the past decade (see Figure 4.3).[31] This growth offers hope in terms of faster economic convergence through leapfrogging to state-of-the-art technologies, but digital technology is not a silver bullet for eliminating poverty.

Figure 4.3: The Rapid Pace of Digital Uptake

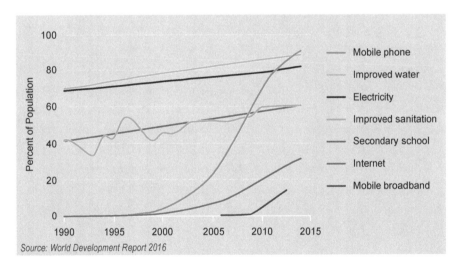

Source: World Development Report 2016

29   World Bank, August 28, 2014, "World Bank Report: Digital Payments Vital to Economic Growth," World Bank, https://bit.ly/Z62dxU.

30   Leora Klapper and Dorothe Singer, August 28, 2014, "The Opportunities of Digitalizing Payments," World Bank, https://bit.ly/2MqMtyR.

31   World Bank, 2016, "World Development Report 2016: Digital Dividends," World Bank, http://bit.ly/2IP3y2m.

Most of today's services, financial or otherwise, as well as knowledge and resources, will reach poor populations only with internet connections, cellular signals, and widespread access to computers and mobile devices. For example, the groundbreaking fintech movement of the past decade, which has provided many solutions to help incorporate poor people into the financial system, has little relevance for people with no or rudimentary access to the internet. Roughly 60 percent of the world's population remains unconnected to the internet, and these people will struggle even more to raise themselves out of poverty if their connectivity issues persist.[32]

This connectivity deficit occurs primarily because in most remote areas, the economics simply do not add up. Companies find that building cellular towers or installing fiber optic cable in remote areas is not a profitable endeavor, as the services this infrastructure provides are unaffordable to the local residents; thus, the profit motive denies these residents the service. Seeking to overcome the profitability challenge, many governments set up a joint fund to which competing telecoms providers contribute equally, and this common fund is used to build shared towers in areas where there is no economic case for a single firm to invest in infrastructure. Often, however, these schemes are not managed adequately, and the intended effect does not materialize.[33]

Digital technologies are ecosystem enablers on many levels. They reduce the cost of acquiring information for people, businesses, and government. Jobseekers can find work more easily (through online job services), improve their productivity (farmers checking commodity prices in real time, for instance), and create opportunities for themselves (entrepreneurs connecting with each other and acquiring skills on the web, for example). Technology facilitates the propagation of innovation and know-how, allowing businesses to become more competitive and productive. It supports governments' ability to deliver services and operate more efficiently and transparently.

---

32 McKinsey & Company, September, 2014, "Offline and falling behind: Barriers to Internet adoption," McKinsey & Company, https://www.mckinsey.com/industries/high-tech/our-insights/offline-and-falling-behind-barriers-to-internet-adoption.

33 Ibid.

Research shows that internet connectivity and digital inclusion more broadly have a positive impact on GDP growth, job creation, and SME development (see Figure 4.4), as well as on social outcomes such as health services and civic engagement.[34]

Figure 4.4: How Internet Access Generates Economic Growth

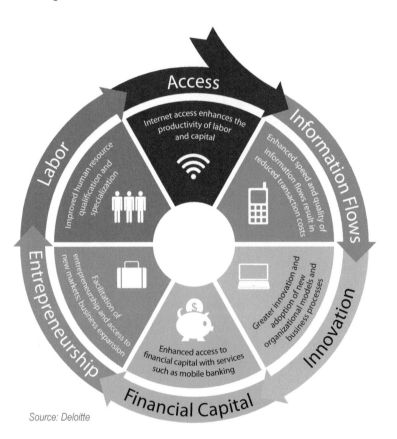

Source: Deloitte

34 Deloitte, 2014, "Value of Connectivity: Economic and social benefits of expanding internet access," Deloitte, https://www2.deloitte.com/content/dam/Deloitte/ie/Documents/TechnologyMediaCommunications/2014_uk_tmt_value_of_connectivity_deloitte_ireland.pdf.

Expanding digital infrastructure to attain these benefits, however, requires a massive effort. In the past two decades, network operators have invested heavily to build out internet infrastructure and extend network access. Fixed-line broadband was the primary driver of internet penetration in developed countries, but it has proved cost prohibitive to build out in many developing markets.[35]

In nations with nascent fixed-line internet infrastructure, consumers access the internet primarily through mobile connections and, in some cases, via satellite networks. Nevertheless, roughly two billion people are not able to get online via mobile networks due to insufficient coverage. Even when mobile networks extend coverage to previously unserved areas, consumers must often navigate a host of other logistical challenges to get online. In rural areas, adjacent infrastructure such as electricity grids and roads can lag internet infrastructure, leaving residents without the basic support and resources that enable internet usage.

The cost of data represents another major obstacle to digital inclusion. In a number of developing countries, households spend around 12 times what consumers in the United States and United Kingdom spend on data (on a per capita basis). Poor people in developing countries often cannot commit to monthly bills or do not have bank accounts to link the bill to, so they end up having prepaid, pay-as-you-go plans. These are more expensive, but they do give users more flexibility and discretion over their spending. In Southeast Asia, 90 percent of users buy prepaid plans.[36]

Given the benefits and challenges of digital inclusion, an ICT for Development movement (ICT4Dev) has emerged among the international development community and governments. The private sector also recognizes the immense market opportunity of transforming the poor into digital consumers. Many emblematic companies, like Facebook and Google, have introduced their own digital inclusion initiatives. Figure 4.5 shows some of the main players and initiatives in the ICT4Dev space.

---

35   McKinsey & Company, September, 2014, "Offline and falling behind: Barriers to Internet adoption," McKinsey & Company, https://www.mckinsey.com/industries/high-tech/our-insights/offline-and-falling-behind-barriers-to-internet-adoption.

36   Catherine Shu, July 30, 2014, "Pricey Data is a Barrier to Internet Access in Developing Countries," *Techcrunch*, https://techcrunch.com/2014/07/30/pricey-data-is-a-barrier-to-internet-access-in-developing-countries/.

Figure 4.5: Key Players in the ICT4Dev Space

International Agencies & DFIs	Independent Global Players & Alliances	Private Sector
Canadian International Development Agency (CIDA), Swedish International Development Cooperation Agency (SIDA), and Swiss Agency for Development and Cooperation (SDC), U.K. Department for International Development (DFID), U.S. Agency for International Development (USAID), World Bank, Inter-American Development Bank (IADB)	International Institute for Communication and Development (IICD), Computer Aid International, ICT4D Collective, TechTribes, SPIDER (Swedish Program for ICT in Developing Regions), NetHope	Samsung, Ericsson, MediaTek, Opera Software, Nokia and Qualcomm, Facebook, Google, Telefonica

Source: Author

Digital inclusion is without a doubt one of the most powerful ecosystem enablers for an inclusive economic system. It boosts information and transparency that supports the provision of services and the creation of economic opportunities for the global poor.

Business Boosters

Companies in developing markets face several challenges when it comes to maintaining and growing their business. These challenges can include a combination of burdensome taxation, labor laws that hinder smooth hiring practices, difficulties in starting and closing down a business, supply chains with weak linkages, government bureaucracy, and/or poor management practices. SMEs and startups, in particular, must deal with a lack of access to financing instruments designed for their particular needs.

Several enablers provide direct support to companies in developing markets. The goal is to help them address critical challenges, which range from policy advocacy to improving management practices to developing innovative business models. They are presented below in three groups: associations and networks, technical assistance and advisory, and incubators and accelerators. The three groups are not mutually exclusive; some associations and networks might provide technical assistance or work with incubators and accelerators.

Associations and Networks

Businesses can find strength in numbers. Business associations and networks are organizations founded and sponsored by businesses from a particular industry or practice (such as biotech, garment manufacturing, or social entrepreneurship) or geography (such as country, state, or municipality). They allow companies to collaborate and to advocate collectively for their interests in terms of policy changes, services, and financing schemes. Associations, which can include chambers of commerce and trade associations, may engage in advertising, education, political donations, lobbying, conferences, networking events, research, and other such activities. They play an important role in building inclusive economic systems and support the ability of firms of all sizes to grow and create jobs.

Ideally, business associations should harness the capacity of the private sector in the national debate and policy making, create business opportunities through networking, promote transparency and stand against corruption, improve the business climate, and promote the adoption of international best practices.[37] The power of business associations can be observed through the efforts of business associations in Thailand to create a certification mechanism that incentivizes companies to employ anti-corruption policies or through the work of several business organizations in the Philippines that have engaged in a group effort to make companies commit to ethical business practices.[38] While accomplishing all these goals may not be possible at all times, the evidence shows associations can contribute to progress in meeting some of these goals (Box 4.5 shows the variety in scale of these organizations).

Associations can promote best practices in terms of ethical conduct, anti-corruption safeguards, industry standards for the quality of products and services, and management practices among its members. In fact, companies are nudged to internalize best practices and behave ethically when others in an association do so, including their competitors.[39] This collective principle also applies to la-

---

37 Mark McCord, "The Business Association Development Guidebook," USAID, http://pdf.usaid.gov/pdf_docs/pnaeb607.pdf.

38 Maira Martini, 2013, "The role of business associations and chambers of commerce in the fight against corruption, U4 Anti-Corruption Research Centre." Transparency International, http://www.u4.no/publications/the-role-of-business-associations-and-chambers-of-commerce-in-the-fight-against-corruption/.

39 Ibid.

bor practices, civil society engagement, and the promotion of environmentally sustainable business practices.

Box 4.5: Business Associations Can Be Local or Global

Some networks are global in nature and support a wide range of businesses under a common umbrella across countries. Such organizations usually lack the depth and reach in advocacy that local associations possess; however, they add unique value in connecting businesses internationally and promoting knowledge transfer. The Aspen Network of Development Entrepreneurs (ANDE) is a global membership network of organizations that promote entrepreneurship in emerging markets. ANDE members provide critical financial, educational, and business support services to small and growing businesses across the developing world.[40]

An interesting example of a successful local organization is the Bangladesh Women Chamber of Commerce & Industry (BWCCI), the first chamber of commerce in Bangladesh exclusively working on women's economic and social empowerment. Established in 2001, its goal is to aid female entrepreneurs by promoting a business environment that is welcoming and tailored to them. BWCCI is a strong collective voice and works by advocating for the economic prospects of Bangladeshi women at the national and international level. BWCCI members hail from across the socioeconomic spectrum.[41]

Globally, companies large and small—and across sectors—work with their associations to tap expertise on sustainable development and corporate citizenship. They offer tailored guidance, tools, and best practices on sustainability issues. Their convening power enables associations to develop technical standards for performance on corporate sustainability that allow benchmarking and data tracking. Associations can engage with policy makers and other stakeholders on behalf of members to advocate for public policy reforms. They raise public and consumer awareness on their sector's contribution to society and the environment.[42]

---

40   Aspen Network of Development Entrepreneurs, 2011, "About ANDE," Aspen Network of Development Entrepreneurs, http://ande.site-ym.com/?page=AboutANDE.

41   Bangladesh Women Chamber of Commerce and Industry, 2018, "BWCCI at a glance," About Us, http://bwcci-bd.org/index.php?option=com_content&view=article&id=46&Itemid=34.

42   Ibid.

Technical Assistance and Advisory Services

To be successful, businesses often rely on having the appropriate technical and strategic support. While access to finance, strong associations, a supportive business climate, and other such recognized factors are key, firms may still underperform or even fail without relevant technical assistance and advisory services.

Large companies in developing countries can count on the support of consulting and advisory firms such as Ernst & Young, McKinsey, Deloitte, and their local counterparts. However, SMEs and startups cannot afford high consulting fees and require services better targeted to their needs. Medium-sized and large companies that care about development impact and inclusive business, in turn, need support in specialized areas that traditional advisory firms may not master.

The range of services offered to SMEs and entrepreneurs varies a great deal. They include financial management, accounting, marketing, legal, export/import, business planning and strategy, logistics, IT, human resources, innovation management, and entrepreneurship. For inclusive businesses, they include advisory services in areas such as shared value, corporate social responsibility (CSR), governance, civil engagement, and environmental sustainability. Service providers, in turn, can be broadly categorized: government agencies, private sector firms, nonprofits, and international programs funded by donors and other global players (see Figure 4.6).

Figure 4.6: Examples of Technical Assistance and Advisory Service Providers

Private Sector	Government Agencies	Nonprofits	International Programs
B-Space (Uganda), Global2020 (Global), Finnpartnership (Global), AV Intellecap (Africa and East Asia), ThinkRoom (South Africa), Genesis Advisory and Consulting (Africa), Open Capital Advisors (Africa), DAI (Global)	SMEDAN (Nigeria), CORFO (Chile), FINEP (Brazil), SEBRAE (Brazil), IamSME (Bangladesh), SME Corporation (Malaysia)	Ashoka (Global), Hystra (Global), SRGB (Bangladesh), RippleWorks (Global), Connect To Grow (South Asia and Africa), Practical Action (Global), Endeavor (Global)	infoDev, DFID's Business Innovation Facility and Connect To Grow Program, IFC Advisory Services, MIF Technical Assistance

Source: Author

Private sector players and nonprofits usually specialize in one or a few sectors (such as agribusiness, ICT4Dev, or energy), region, and/or field (such as social entrepreneurship or shared value). Government agencies and international programs, in turn, often have bigger budgets and broader scopes. For example, SME Corporation in Malaysia provides support on virtually everything an SME needs. The World Bank's infoDev program offers technical assistance and knowledge to more than 2,000 incubators across dozens of developing countries. Box 4.6 elaborates on the case of Brazil's SEBRAE, the world's largest national small business agency.

Box 4.6: Lessons from Brazil's SEBRAE

Brazil has the largest small business administration in the world, SEBRAE, which has a budget equivalent to 0.1 percent of Brazil's entire economy. It utilizes 9,500 consultants who serve more than 1 million small businesses annually. SEBRAE helps business owners at every level of the business lifecycle, including the registration, startup, development, and expansion stages.[43] SEBRAE helps business owners understand and capitalize on opportunities they may not recognize. They also help business owners navigate bureaucracy and reduce their tax burden.[44]

SEBRAE has several key characteristics that distinguish it from other SBAs around the world. Instead of merely providing financing options for small businesses, it provides technical skills to business owners, delivered through consultants that have private sector experience. SEBRAE has capably leveraged various media channels to spread word of their services across the country, and in 2011, more than 500,000 students completed courses offered through SEBRAE. Finally, SEBRAE is a private company that receives public funds. The nature of this public-private partnership means that SEBRAE is not subject to political tides that could hinder other, fully public, SBAs from delivering results.

SEBRAE has positively contributed to the business climate in Brazil. Brazilian small and microenterprises' contribution to GDP increased from 21 percent to 27 percent between 1985 and 2011. These enterprises also saw higher wage growth than larger firms and accounted for 70 percent of all new jobs in 2014.[45]

It is challenging to draw conclusions about the impact of this work at a global level, but an impact evaluation conducted in Puebla, Mexico, on the effects of

---

43 SEBRAE, "700 Service Centers throughout Brazil," *SEBRAE*, http://www.sebrae.com.br/sites/PortalSebrae/canais_adicionais/sebrae_english.

44 Karolina Puin, February 1, 2012, "Introduction to SEBRAE," *The Brazil Business*, http://bit.ly/2tTcDCI.

45 Ricardo Geromel, December 12, 2011, "You must know THIS before investing in Brazil," *Forbes*. http://bit.ly/2O4FLQ3.

consulting on SME performance provides evidence of the importance of technical support, and the results are likely applicable across many regions.[46] Firms in the study were paired with one of nine local consulting firms, and consultants met with businesses for at least four hours a week for one year. The consultants were asked to develop strategies to overcome the obstacles that prevented the firms from growing. More than 400 firms were involved, with 150 randomly selected for the program (treatment group) and the remaining firms serving as the control group. The results were encouraging. Compared to control firms, productivity was significantly higher in the treatment group after one year; sales and number of employees increased in the medium run as well.[47]

The impact of advisory services, however, could be much broader if more SMEs actively looked for support or if support were more widely available through small business administrations. While in markets such as Mexico, Brazil, and India, SMEs actively seek these kinds of services, the market is not as well developed in poorer countries. More work needs to be done to deepen the market for business advisory services that support SMEs and inclusive business models, as well as to promote these services among SMEs so that they know what is available and where to find it.

Finally, a few noteworthy trends have emerged regarding the delivery of consulting and advisory services in the developing world.[48] Perhaps most notable is the value of long-term relationships between support provider and client. Businesses are on a journey, struggling with different needs at different points in time, and are unlikely to succeed based on one-off injections of support. This insight calls for increased collaboration across different types of service providers, whose skills might be complementary both at a certain point in time and at different stages of a business' life.

---

46   Miriam Bruhn, Dean Karlan, and Antoinette Schoar, 2013, "The Impact of Consulting Services on Small and Medium Enterprises: Evidence from a Randomized Trial in Mexico," World Bank, https://siteresources.worldbank.org/EXTGLOBALFINREPORT/Resources/8816096-1361888425203/9062080-1361888442321/sme_consulting_mexico-Paper.pdf

47   Ibid.

48   Aline Menden, May 30, 2017, "More than money: mapping the landscape of advisory support for inclusive business," The Practitioner Hub for Inclusive Business, http://www.inclusivebusinesshub.org/money-mapping-landscape-advisory-support-inclusive-business/.

Incubators and Accelerators

Building an inclusive economic system requires entrepreneurs to access resources and space to develop their ideas into sustainable businesses. Business incubators and accelerators support the birth and nurturing of startups in developing countries, just as they do in developed hubs such as Silicon Valley. They not only help companies start and grow (and even fail properly when things do not work out) but also help promote an entrepreneurial culture that embraces risk-taking and creativity. In this way, incubators help close the "pioneer gap," which refers to the gap in the amount of investment money needed by entrepreneurs in the developing world and the amount of money available to them.[49]

Incubators support the growth of entrepreneurial businesses through resources and services that could include physical space, mentoring, common services (such as legal, accounting, and administrative), networking, and sometimes funding. Private companies, universities, municipal entities, government programs, and international donors can sponsor them. Accelerators, while offering a range of similar support services for startups, tend to be private entities, work with fixed-term cohorts (usually three to six months) and offer more intense mentorship, networking, value chain resources, and funding opportunities. Companies at accelerators are usually more advanced in their businesses (therefore needing "acceleration" not "incubation") and often have higher growth potential than incubated ones. In fact, accelerators usually invest in their startups in exchange for a small (less than 10 percent) equity stake.[50] Figure 4.7 summarizes the main differences and similarities between accelerators and incubators.[51]

49   Sasha Dichter, Robert Katz, Harvey Koh and Ashish Karamchandani, Winter 2013, "Closing the Pioneer Gap," *Stanford Social Innovation Review*, https://ssir.org/articles/entry/closing_the_pioneer_gap.

50   C. Scott Dempwolf, Jennifer Auer and Michellle D'Ippolito, October, 2014, "Innovation Accelerators: Defining Characteristics Among Startup Assistance Organizations," Small Business Administration, https://fr.slideshare.net/eddodds/innovation-accelerators-report.

51   Ian Hathaway, March 1, 2016, "What Startup Accelerators Really Do," *Harvard Business Review*, https://hbr.org/2016/03/what-startup-accelerators-really-do.

Figure 4.7: Comparing Incubators and Accelerators

Incubator	Accelerator
Build Foundation Develop ideas, discovery stage, expose to entrepreneurship	**Accelerate Growth** Mentorship focus, execution stage
Flexible Duration Usually 6 months–2 years	**Definite Amount of Time** Usually 3–4 months
Application Exlusivity Open to specific audiences, accept many applications	**Open Recruitment** Anyone can apply, accept few, competitive
Not Class- or Cohort-Based No set graduation date	**Class- and Cohort-Based** Set graduation/demo day
No Funding Commitment May introduce to outside investors but doesn't usually lead to investment	**Investment Possibility** Normally invests seed capital for 5–8% equity

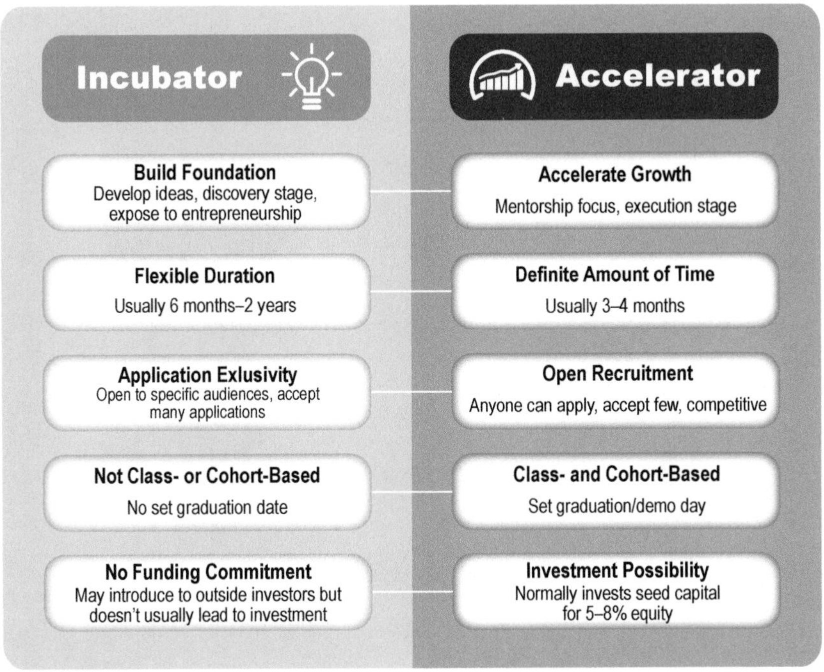

Source: Author

Incubators began to sprout in developing countries in the 1990s and multiplied exponentially in the 2000s and 2010s. Although it is impossible to know the exact number, some estimates suggest that there are between 7,000 and 12,000 incubators worldwide.[52] Accelerators are a more recent phenomenona. Accelerators have started to gain prominence in developing countries in the past 10 years. Some incubators and accelerators active in developing countries are global in reach and often headquartered in developed countries. 1776 Startup Incubator and Agora Partnerships are both based in the United States but work with entrepreneurs across the globe through their networks of mentors, funders, and local partners. Box 4.7 tells the story of a successful international partnership involving Agora, a foundation and group of investors that supports women-led businesses in Latin America.

---

52   Caroline Ashley and Aline Menden, November 15, 2015, "Business Incubation FAQs," International Business Innovation Association, https://web.archive.org/web/20151115190341/https://inbia.org/resources/business-incubation-faq.

Box 4.7: A Partnership for Impact

Agora Partnerships is a nonprofit headquartered in Washington, DC, and Managua, Nicaragua. They aim to accelerate the growth of companies with a focus on social impact in Latin America.[53] The Eleos Foundation is an investment firm that invests primarily in social entrepreneurs.[54] In 2012, the two organizations collaborated to create the Agora-Eleos LatAM Women's fund to provide opportunities for impact investors to support social enterprises led by women in Latin America.

Agora Partnerships uses its abilities as an accelerator to find entrepreneurs and provide them with the tools they need to succeed. If the entrepreneur meets Eleos' standards, Eleos will become a lead investor and provide opportunities for coinvestors to fund the entrepreneur as well.

In one example, Agora found a company called Maya Mountain Cacao (MMC), which Eleos then successfully vetted. Eleos subsequently found twenty investors to contribute $10,000 each to an investment fund for MMC, which allowed MMC to prosper and grow. As a result, MMC was able to shorten its supply chain and to give its low-income farmers in Belize premium prices, as well as plant more cacao trees and expand operations into Guatemala.[55]

Although there are no definitive answers as to the impact of incubators and accelerators in the developing world, there are some important lessons learned. The benefits of incubators in emerging economies are:

- Provision of support beyond technical services such as the formation of business relationship and exchange of ideas.
- Reduction of expenses through economies of scale, like tenants in a business incubator sharing overhead costs.
- Help with noncore activities, such as market research, obtaining licenses, and accounting.

---

53   Nicholas Fitzgerald, October 11, 2012, "Women Entrepreneurs Focus of New Collaboration Between Agora Partnerships and the Eleos Foundation," Accelerate the Shift, http://bit.ly/2INHBB0.

54   Devex, June 13, 2018, "The Eleos Foundation," Devex, https://www.devex.com/organizations/the-eleos-foundation-23546.

55   Aspen Network of Development Entrepreneurs, November 21, 2014, "Measuring Value Created: By Impact Incubators & Accelerators," Aspen Network of Development Entrepreneurs, https://bit.ly/2lbqZd9.

- Legitimacy that comes from belonging to an incubator allows for access to early-stage capital that emerging companies may not otherwise find.[56]

At the same time, there are some challenges that have limited the impact of incubators. Most developing countries suffer from limited sources of finance for early-stage companies, which leads to the premature death of otherwise promising businesses. In addition, unlike incubators in developed markets, which are often run by successful entrepreneurs and business consultants, staff at incubators in less mature markets often lack the experience and expertise to mentor their entrepreneurs effectively. Finally, especially in poorer countries, incubators sometimes lack the basic IT infrastructure, such as broadband Wi-Fi and computers, to provide the right connectivity and opportunities for their entrepreneurs. Figure 4.8 summarizes the key findings regarding success factors and challenges for accelerators.[57]

Figure 4.8: Impact Accelerators in Developing Countries

Finding	Explanation
Partnerships with local investors increase the chance of enterprise success.	Domestic commercial investors offered the best funding partnerships for accelerator graduates, but did not necessarily identify as impact investors.
Selectivity matters.	Accelerators with a more rigorous selection process produced enterprises with a higher degree of success.
Accelerators currently require grants to remain viable, meaning philanthropy is still a necessary component.	75% of accelerators rely on philanthropy to survive, and more than half of all accelerator budgets rely on grants. Unfortunately, revenue streams are not yet strong enough for accelerators to survive without charitable funding.
Most impact investors are looking to accelerators for investment opportunities but are not finding them.	While 60% of impact investors report that they have a partnership with an accelerator, 47 say that nothing in their portfolio was sourced from an accelerator. This implies that there is a problem with matching in the marketplace.
There is a lack of data on accelerators' performance.	We need more data on incubator and accelerator effectiveness to assess the sources of success. Many accelerators do not even collect their own data.

Source: Aspen Network of Development Entrepreneurs and Village Capital

---

56   infoDEV, 2015, "Business Incubation Basics" https://www.infodev.org/infodev-files/m1_traineemanual_20101029.pdf.

57   Ross Baird, Lily Bowles, Saurabh Lall, June 2013, "Bridging the 'Pioneer Gap': The Role of Accelerators in Launching High-Impact Enterprises," Aspen Network of Development Entrepreneurs and Village Capital, https://bit.ly/2LRtzA2.

Job Market Hackers

The job market today is more dynamic than ever before. New technologies improve labor productivity and facilitate the free flow of knowledge and information. While the current market offers opportunities, the rapidly changing job market poses a challenge to people with skills perceived as less relevant and people unable to adapt quickly. This problem is particularly acute in developing countries.

Several players are dedicated to helping people acquire new skills quickly, find the right jobs, and launch their own enterprises, particularly online. The platforms and skills presented in this section are certainly not the only ones that will be necessary to improve the lives of workers in developing and emerging markets. Poorer and less educated people, for example, or those living in isolated rural areas require support systems. For this discussion, however, we have chosen to highlight some of the latest and most promising trends that help connect the youth in developing countries to some of the most exciting parts of the new economy.

The digital revolution has decreased the costs and frictions of outsourcing across borders and allowed several jobs to be performed remotely, such as common jobs in IT, design, and marketing. Increased availability of knowledge online means that almost anyone with access to the internet can acquire the skills needed to perform certain jobs. A person in India or Kenya can learn how to code for little or no cost by taking online courses or MOOCs (massive open online courses) and offer her services to a firm in the United States or Europe through one of the many online job matching platforms available.

e-Learning

Some workers in developing countries lose their "routine jobs" to emerging technologies that perform their task faster, more efficiently, and at a lower cost. This technology-driven effect can happen both directly at the companies where people work and in firms in developed countries that previously outsourced their work to offshore firms, in a movement called "reshoring."[58][59] Searching for similar jobs

---

58   Luc Christiaensen, Siddhartha Raja, and Esteve Sala, June 1, 2017, "Can technology reshape the world of work for developing countries?," World Bank, http://bit.ly/2u86gLp.

59   Carl Benedikt Frey and Ebrahim Rahbari, July 20, 2016, "Do labor-saving technologies spell the death of jobs in the developing world?," Brookings Blum Roundtable, https://brook.gs/2tRSqgD.

elsewhere might not be fruitful because people's skills may have become obsolete and unmarketable. At the same time, other workers are not able to improve their job situation—for example, from a low-paid, informal activity such as street vending to a more knowledge-based, formal position such as guiding tourists—due to limited options to upgrade and diversify their skills.

Acquiring new, relevant skills quickly and inexpensively is important for survival in the marketplace. It allows people not only to get new jobs but also to keep their current job by staying up to date and relevant. A number of solutions that meet these needs fall under the "e-Learning" umbrella. In its broadest definition, e-learning represents all educational content delivered through digital media.

E-Learning courses can complement classroom learning or come as standalone solutions for remote students. Some are as short as a few hours (a "how to" course on plumbing, for example); others can last years (such as online undergraduate degrees). While e-training may be limited to simple slideshows delivered online, other e-courses may feature videos, live broadcasting, and interactive chatrooms. Some charge a fee; some are free, such as so-called MOOCs (massive open online courses), which can be taken by anyone, anywhere, and almost at any time. Box 4.8 compares traditional e-Learning courses to MOOCs.

Box 4.8: Differences Between e-Learning Courses and MOOCs

Traditional e-Learning courses have several advantages. Evaluation and accreditation often give these courses more legitimacy, as does the support from teaching staff. Group work is a factor, and communication with teachers and other students through online forums can enhance the quality of the course. However, this comes at a cost, as traditional e-Learning courses are not free.

MOOCs are free to access and have community support due to a higher number of users. There is an emphasis on the learning process and not on grades, which can create a better learning environment but may not be as impressive to employers. MOOC content is not static, and MOOCs can be accessed all year around, not just during the academic year.[60][61]

---

60 Sahana Chattopadhyay, June 26, 2014, "11 Differences between a MOOC and an Online course," *ID and Other Reflections*, http://idreflections.blogspot.com/2014/06/11-differences-between-mooc-and-online.html.

61 Universitat Autonóma de Barcelona, 2017, "Differences between a MOOC and an online course," Universitat Autonóma de Barcelona, http://www.uab.cat/web/study-abroad/mooc/differences-between-a-mooc-and-an-onlinecourse-1345668290741.html.

E-learning cuts down on infrastructure costs and logistical barriers. It also reduces the commuting challenges associated with poor public transportation or the large distances between urban and rural areas. e-Learning courses tend to cost the student less than brick-and-mortar education and are sometimes even free, which allows people to explore different subjects with little or no exit or transition costs. Finally, e-Learning offers flexibility, so students can take courses when their work schedules allow.[62] Even the poor, who might not own a computer or have personal access to the internet, are often able to access this technology through enablers such as NGOs or government programs that promote digital inclusion.

E-Learning usage rates are expected to grow by more than 14 percent annually in many countries in Asia and Africa, including Nepal, Sri Lanka, Ethiopia, and Uganda. e-Learning courses are designed for both individuals hoping to obtain a better job and for college students trying to obtain their first quality job. In all of Africa and Asia, around 4.5 million students students have taken at least one course online, a number estimated to exceed 18 million by 2021. Mobile learning will be the next step in e-Learning, with double-digit growth rates projected over 5 years. [63] [64] [65]

However, developing country contexts pose several challenges for the expansion of e-Learning. In Africa, these challenges include internet connectivity, availability of country or region-specific content, and training and professional capacity. Although countries such as South Africa, Tunisia, and Kenya enjoy high levels of internet penetration, some Sub-Saharan countries have penetration rates of less than 5 percent.[66] In addition, English remains the predominant language for e-Learning, yet English proficiency is limited in Africa, Asia, and Latin America, especially in rural areas.

---

62   Lily Wilson, July 8, 2015, "Utilizing eLearning In Developing Countries: eLearning Breakthroughs In 2015," eLearning Industry, https://elearningindustry.com/utilizing-elearning-in-developing-countries-elearning-breakthroughs-2015.

63   Sam S. Adkins, August 2016, "The 2016-2021 Worldwide Self-paced eLearning Market: Global eLearning Market in Steep Decline," Ambient Insight, http://bit.ly/2KIzISq.

64   Rishabh Saxena, May 2, 2017, "E-learning challenges and trends in developing regions," Totara, https://www.totaralms.com/blog/e-learning-challenges-and-trends-developing-regions.

65   Karla Gutierrez, November 29, 2012, "18 Mind-Blowing eLearning Statistics You Need To Know," Shift Learning, https://www.shiftelearning.com/blog/bid/247473/18-Mind-Blowing-eLearning-Statistics-You-Need-To-Know.

66   Internet World Stats, December 31, 2017, "Internet Usage Statistics," https://www.internetworldstats.com/stats.htm.

Companies such as Coursera, Udacity, Khan Academy, and edX drive rapid growth in MOOCs. Leading universities also participate. Examples include the Massachusetts Institute of Technology, Harvard University, University of California, Berkeley, and the University of Queensland in Australia, all of which contribute a range of free courses to edX. Box 4.9 illustrates India's passion for MOOCs.

Box 4.9: India Loves MOOCs

It is very difficult for most Indian students to gain entry into elite Indian universities due to overwhelming demand. Through MOOCs, young Indians are equipping themselves with skill sets that qualify them for jobs such as outsourced workers. By enrolling in online courses through platforms like Coursera, intelligent individuals can become noticed by larger companies without having to go through the university process. Indian enrollments account for about 8 percent of worldwide activity in Coursera and 12 percent in edX, the two leading providers of MOOCs. India's universities have taken notice and are publishing video content to put would-be students in contact with professors. MOOCs are an equalizing force in Indian society.[67]

While it is still too soon to measure the long-term impact of e-Learning on the creation and maintenance of jobs in developing countries, there is little doubt that increasing access to education and training, whichever form it takes, improves qualifications, makes employees more productive, and enhances their chances of landing the next job. Access to the right skills and knowledge also boosts people's ability to become entrepreneurs and freelancers, as well as improves their self-esteem and connectivity to the world.[68] [69] [70]

---

67   George Anders, 2015, "India Loves MOOCs," July 27, 2015, *Technology Review*, https://www.technologyreview.com/s/539131/india-loves-moocs/.

68   Adaiah Lilenstein, June 7, 2016, "In West Africa, education = jobs and jobs = development," World Bank, http://blogs.worldbank.org/jobs/psd/west-africa-education-jobs-and-jobs-development.

69   Theo Sparreboom and Anita Staneva, December, 2014, "Is education the solution to decent work for youth in developing economies?," United Nations, http://www.un.org/youthenvoy/wp-content/uploads/2014/10/Work4Youth-Publication.pdf.

70   Lucy Goodchild van Hilten, July 27, 2015, "Higher education is key to economic development (but it's not as simple as you think)," Elsevier, https://www.elsevier.com/atlas/story/people/higher-education-is-key-to-economic-development.

Finding the Best Jobs

Finding the right job is as important as having the right skills. Digital job seeking platforms present the most promising trend in this respect. Offline options such as newspaper advertisements, employment agencies, and cold calling are costly, slow, and not always effective. With increasing numbers of people digitally included, even relatively poor people can use the internet to look for jobs. These job platforms accumulate large databases of seeker profiles, open opportunities, and employers that connect talent with jobs. They open new opportunities to create work for the unemployed through access to the internet. It is estimated that digital platforms can benefit up to 540 million people by 2025. Countries with a history of high unemployment rates stand to benefit the most, especially those with high youth unemployment rates. Companies as well as workers will benefit, saving up to 7 percent in recruiting costs.[71] [72] [73]

In recent years, various digital platforms have emerged to combat unemployment and underemployment in developing countries. These platforms target both low-skilled job seekers suitable for MSMEs and the informal sector and higher-skilled workers demanded by larger domestic and international companies (see Box 4.10 for a discussion on their impact).

Kenya's Lynk platform, for example, is designed for the large informal economy that exists in emerging markets. The application makes it easy for customers to find, screen, and book reliable workers across a variety of blue-collar categories and provides career development and personal growth for the workers.[74] Shortlist is a job search tool with a focus on finding higher-end talent in developing countries in areas such as marketing, finance and engineering, and matching them with the best employers and opportunities.[75]

---

71   Laurence Chandy, January 31, 2017, "The Future of Work in the Developing World," Brookings Institute, https://brook.gs/2IMLnus.

72   Global Opportunity Network, July 8, 2016, "The Digital Labour Market," Global Opportunity Network, http://bit.ly/2KERkhY.

73   James Manyika, Susan Lund, Kelsey Robinson, John Valentino, Richard Dobbs, June 2015, "Connecting talent with opportunity in the digital age," McKinsey & Company, https://www.mckinsey.com/global-themes/employment-and-growth/connecting-talent-with-opportunity-in-the-digital-age.

74   Lynk, "About Us. https://lynk.global/aboutus.

75   Shortlist, "About Us," https://shortlist.net/about-us/.

Box 4.10: Do Digital Job Search Tools Work in Developing Countries?

Of course, for job search tools to be useful, workers in developing countries need to be aware of them and have the opportunity to use them effectively. Souktel is a service based in six countries in Africa and Asia, but primarily in Palestine, that matches job seekers with development and aid projects. Souktel not only matches job seekers to employers but also provides advice on resume preparation and offers other career building tools.[76]

An analysis of Souktel's impact in the countries in which it operates yielded encouraging results. Of the 15,000 registered users in the West Bank and Gaza, 35 percent are female, a far higher proportion than the 19 percent of the labor force as a whole that is female. This indicates that Souktel frees women in the region from constraints that the traditional labor market imposes on them. Half of the men surveyed reported earning less than $500 a month before using Souktel. After finding a job through this service, only 30 percent of the men reported earnings of $500 a month (or less), meaning Souktel was finding quality jobs and not just the first job that appeared. Finally, employers enjoyed using Souktel's services, reporting that the high-quality candidates and time saved through the service had reduced their recruiting costs by 20 percent.[77]

Young people in Palestine frequently count on family connections or good luck to find quality employment. Services like Souktel are part of the future of employment in the developing world due to their wide scope and ease of access.[78]

Another vibrant area of the digital job search space is the evolving business practice of impact sourcing. Impact sourcing is an approach to outsourcing that intentionally employs people at the base of the pyramid. It focuses on upskilling and employing socioeconomically disadvantaged individuals to work for both local and international companies performing low-skill functions such as data entry or video tagging. A company in the United States or Europe may hire and train unemployed youth in Asia or Africa to become remote employees—a win-win situation that creates jobs for people with limited opportunities while

---

76 Souktel, January 20, 2016, "World Bank: Souktel's Job-Find Solution Boosts Wages, Closes Gender Gaps," *Souktel,* http://www.souktel.org/media/news/world-bank-souktel%E2%80%99s-job-find-solution-boosts-wages-closes-gender-gaps.

77 World Bank, 2016, "World Development Report 2016: Digital Dividends," World Bank, http://bit.ly/2IP3y2m.

78 Rory McCarthy, September 21, 2009, "Text messaging helps young palestinians find work," *The Guardian,* https://www.theguardian.com/world/2009/sep/21/souktel-jobs-west-bank.

training workers according to the company's needs.[79] Microsoft, Bloomberg, Nielsen, and many others have benefited from impact sourcing through efficiency gains, cost savings, and access to new and diversified talent.[80] Box 4.11 presents the case of an impact sourcing platform, Cloud Factory.

Box 4.11: Impact Outsourcing with Cloud Factory

Cloud Factory was founded in 2008 and works by breaking its clients' projects down into smaller tasks that can then be outsourced to a global community of workers. Cloud Factory's innovative approach to outsourcing uses an assembly line method of task completion, so their workers can contribute as much or as little as they want to. The company currently employs 3,000 data operators known "cloud workers." Cloud Factory's goal is to connect one million people in the developing world to basic computer work and thereby raise them up to address poverty in their own communities. Its core mission is to deliver business processes through the lens of social impact. Cloud Factory claims that its business model offers a flexible, cost-effective alternative to traditional business process outsourcing, savings of up to 50 percent in labor costs, and turnaround times that are three times faster than traditional outsourcing methods.[81] The company has improved circumstances for people such as single mothers, who take advantage of online outsourcing to remove the constraint of rigid timeframes that traditional jobs impose.[82]

The benefits of impact sourcing are remarkable. Research shows impact sourcing increases workers' individual income by 40 to 200 percent, in addition to enhancing their professional development and confidence levels, reducing their tendency to migrate, and improving overall stress levels.[83] The increase in individual income strengthens communities by growing local economies and im-

---

79   Rockefeller Foundation, June, 2011, "Job Creation Through Building the Field of Impact Sourcing," World Bank, https://olc.worldbank.org/sites/default/files/Impact%20Sourcing_0.pdf.

80   Global Impact Sourcing Coalition, "What is the Global Impact Sourcing Coalition," BSR Collaboration, https://gisc.bsr.org/files/BSR_GISC_Factsheet.pdf.

81   Pumela Salela, June 23, 2014, "The Business Case for Impact Sourcing," Global Sourcing Council, https://www.gscouncil.org/the-business-case-for-impact-sourcing/.

82   Siou Chew Kuek, Cecilia Paradi-Guilford, Toks Fayomi, Saori Imaizumi, Panos Ipeirotis, Patricia Pina, and Manpreet Singh, June, 2015, "The Global Opportunity in Online Outsourcing," World Bank, https://bit.ly/2HOQzgE.

83   Rockefeller Foundation, June, 2011, "Job Creation Through Building the Field of Impact Sourcing," World Bank, https://olc.worldbank.org/sites/default/files/Impact%20Sourcing_0.pdf.

proving the future employability of disadvantaged individuals. Finally, impact sourcing is especially empowering for women, who benefit from flexible hours and the ability to work from home. The impact sourcing market is growing fast. As of 2017, this market was believed to account for roughly 240,000 workers or about 12 percent of the business process outsourcing market globally.[84]

Online Outsourcing

In the modern job market, many people choose to create their own occupations by working as freelancers or online outsourcers. Online outsourcing can be defined as contracting third-party professionals, often overseas, to supply services or tasks remotely via the internet. Examples of online outsourcing include data entry and treatment for low-skilled workers but can also include graphic design and other tasks that require a more complex skillset. While classic job seeking platforms normally aim at finding people jobs with one specific employer, online outsourcing tools are task oriented and workers are autonomous in nature. These workers are freelancers looking to land several clients, either to generate complementary income or build a career as an independent worker with a portfolio of clients.

Companies and individuals use online platforms to outsource work to a large and widely spread network of remote workers. These platforms enable companies to reach a large pool of remote workers and allow them to coordinate and pay these workers online. All that these freelancers need to participate is a computer with an internet connection.[85]

One popular online outsourcing platform is Fiverr, an Israeli startup that is a global online marketplace where freelancers (mostly from developing countries) offer services to people and companies worldwide. As of 2017, Fiverr claims more than 10 million services available, encompassing services such as logo design, text editing and translation, voiceover services, and software coding. Jobs range between $5 and $500, and more established freelancers typically take on dozens of tasks a week, which allow many of them to live off the

---

84 Aditya Verma, September 18, 2014, "Impact Sourcing 101: The Fundamentals of a Powerful Global Sourcing Model," Everest Group, http://www.everestgrp.com/2014-09-impact-sourcing-101-the-fundamentals-of-a-powerful-globalsourcing-model-sherpas-in-blue-shirts-15558.html/.

85 Toks Fayomi, March 3, 2015, "Online outsourcing is creating opportunities for job seekers and job creators," World Bank, http://blogs.worldbank.org/ic4d/online-outsourcing-creating-opportunities-job-seekers-and-job-creators.

platform.[86] Other such platforms include Upwork, Microworkers, Freelancer, Samasource, and Crowdflower.[87] The top three advantages and disadvantages of online work over traditional work, as reported by surveyed workers from microworkers.com, are shown in Figure 4.9.[88] Others reported the top advantage to be the ability to receive on-the-job training and access to a job market that was previously unavailable. Other reported top disadvantages include a requirement to have internet access and lack of social benefits.[89]

Figure 4.9: Pros and Cons of Online Work

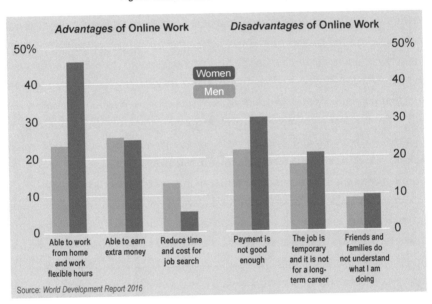

Online outsourcing is expected to sustain its growth, due to increased demand from private sector employers, trends such as the expansion of big data and open data use, and demographic shifts. It is estimated that by 2020, the size of the

86   Shoshanna Solomon, September 7, 2017, "Israeli startup Fiverr sees Amazon as model for growth," *The Times of Israel*, https://www.timesofisrael.com/israeli-startup-fiverr-sees-amazon-as-model-for-growth/.

87   Toks Fayomi, March 3, 2015, "Online outsourcing is creating opportunities for job seekers and job creators," World Bank, http://blogs.worldbank.org/ic4d/online-outsourcing-creating-opportunities-job-seekers-and-job-creators.

88   World Bank, 2016, "World Development Report 2016: Digital Dividends," World Bank, http://bit.ly/2IP3y2m.

89   Ibid.

online outsourcing industry will be $15 to $25 billion. As of 2015, there were 48 million workers registered on websites like Zhubajie and Upwork, which connect workers to employers. It is feasible that with enough growth in developing countries, this number could top 100 million by 2025. Figure 4.10 shows common types of online jobs according to different levels of complexity.[90]

Figure 4.10: The Complexity Spectrum of Online Jobs

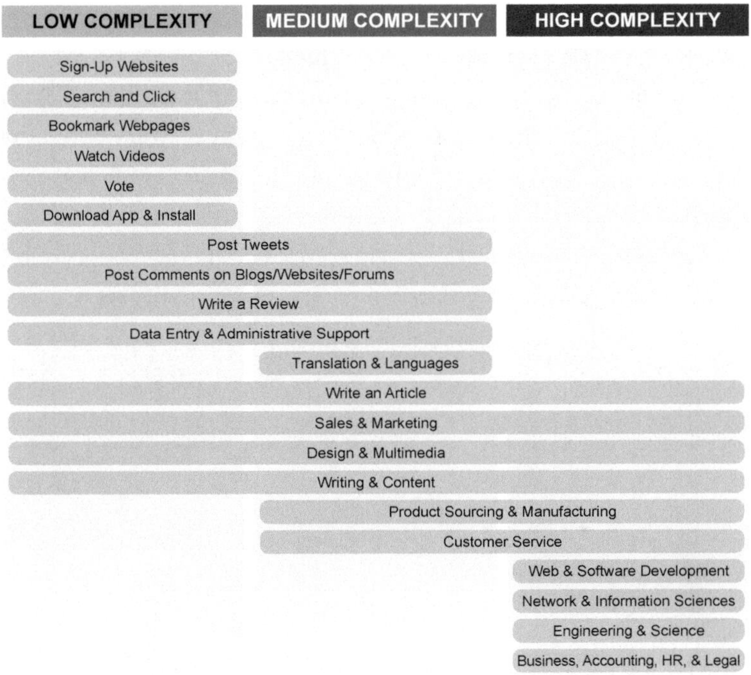

Source: World Bank

Online outsourcing is particularly attractive to female workers. For example, in India, female workers take advantage of online work to earn money without leaving their homes, so they can look after their children while working. Women from conservative areas use freelance work as a way to circumvent

---

90   Siou Chew Kuek, Cecilia Paradi-Guilford, Toks Fayomi, Saori Imaizumi, Panos Ipeirotis, Patricia Pina, and Manpreet Singh, June, 2015, "The Global Opportunity in Online Outsourcing," World Bank, https://bit.ly/2HOQzgE

male-dominated workplaces where they may face discrimination. Furthermore, this work does not necessarily come with lower wages; online workers in Kenya, Nigeria, and India earn salaries similar to that of their peers in traditional work. It is no surprise that most online outsourcing workers are millennials, and given that this demographic will comprise 75 percent of the global workforce by 2025, the demand for workers involved in online outsourcing will likely to continue to grow.[91]

Freelance and outsourced work is a global trend that is bound to continue to leapfrog into the more entrepreneurial and higher-qualified strata of the developing world's labor force. People are realizing that often it is more convenient, productive, and empowering to work on their own or within small online enterprises for many clients than it is to find a traditional job with one employer. It often pays better too. It is a highly inclusive method of employment since the barrier to entry is relatively low: besides a computer, internet connection, and a set of skills, it requires only a proactive attitude to attain success.

---

91   World Bank, June 2, 2015, "Jobs Without Borders," World Bank, http://www.worldbank.org/en/news/feature/2015/06/02/jobs-without-borders.

Chapter 5. Macro Level: Government

The role governments play in spurring inclusive economic growth ranges from minimal involvement—creating the right conditions for private investment—to directly delivering products and services to poor and low-income people (see Figure 5.1).

Figure 5.1: The Spectrum of Government Roles in Inclusive Economies

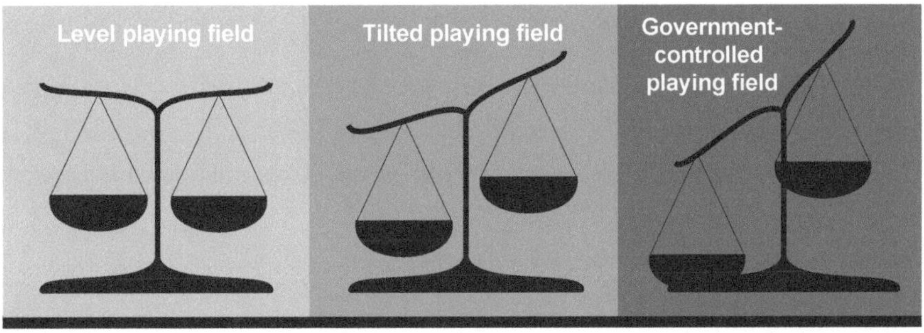

Source: Author

- On the **level playing field** end of the spectrum, governments can enable inclusive economies by creating regulatory frameworks that equally affect all businesses and specifically make it easier for smaller businesses to operate.

- Some governments choose to promote certain sectors or industries by implementing policies or regulations that create a **tilted playing field**, strongly

149

encouraging or even forcing the private sector to invest, offer services to, or buy from specific market segments (e.g., low-income) or sectors (e.g., light manufacturing).

- Finally, a more activist approach means that the government chooses to **control the playing field** completely by delivering services directly (for instance, by offering subsidized credit to agriculture).

This chapter examines these three general approaches, highlighting select examples and considering the pros and cons of different models. The policies and frameworks adopted by governments constitute one piece of a broader economic policy puzzle necessary for social inclusion and are primarily concerned with the supply side of the market. This chapter focuses mostly on policies targeted toward the micro players, with the recognition that macro-economic policies related to increasing real wages, expanding the consumer market, and other demand-side components are necessary complements.

Another way of looking at these three approaches relates to their principal function: enablers (level playing field), promoters (tilted playing field), and preventers (government-controlled playing field).[1] While not all government-controlled actions inhibit the private sector, this "crowding out" effect can often be the ultimate result, especially in countries with relatively weak governance. Rising economic nationalism is partly responsible for an upsurge in countries choosing to intervene more strenuously in their economies, as discussed in Box 5.1.

Box 5.1: Economic Nationalism Fuels Activist Governments

Economic nationalism is on the rise in both developed and developing countries, due in part to rising income inequality, shifting labor markets, and dependence on volatile commodity markets. Countries are looking inward, imposing tariffs or other barriers to trade and investment, and in some cases seeking to renegotiate trade agreements. These actions threaten the export market, research and development efforts, and foreign direct investment.

---

1   Liliana Rojas-Suarez and Lucía Pacheco, "An Index of Regulatory Practices for Financial Inclusion in Latin America: Enablers, Promoters, and Preventers," Center for Global Development, https://www.cgdev.org/sites/default/files/index-regulatory-practices-financial-inclusion-latin-america_0.pdf.

Key factors in the rise of nationalism are poverty and inequality. As incomes stagnate and economic growth flags, it becomes easy for politicians to blame other groups for perceived failures.[2] Information technology and globalization mean that this "us vs. them" mentality can spread more quickly than ever before.

Level Playing Field

Governments can choose to create policy and regulatory environments conducive to economic inclusion. Eliminating the requirement for a business to obtain a government seal, creating a database to facilitate land titling for farmers, or making it easier for microlenders to extend credit are examples of policies that enable economic inclusion. The World Bank's *Doing Business* indicators offer a useful framework for evaluating policies that help businesses to open and operate. *Doing Business* ranks countries on 10 indicators, shown in Figure 5.2. In this section, we drill down on those areas most relevant for economic inclusion: getting credit, registering property, starting a business, paying taxes, and obtaining decent work.

---

2   Robert J. Shiller, October 14, 2016, "What's Behind a Rise in Ethnic Nationalism? Maybe the Economy," *The New York Times*, https://www.nytimes.com/2016/10/16/upshot/whats-behind-a-rise-in-ethnic-nationalism-maybe-the-economy.html.

Figure 5.2: Doing Business Indicators

Source: World Bank Doing Business Indicators

Getting Credit

Access to credit and other financial services is essential for entrepreneurs and SMEs to succeed and grow. Governments can build economies that are more inclusive by promoting efficient capital markets, making bank accounts easier to open, and establishing functional credit bureaus.

Capital Markets Policies

Businesses in the developing world often identify access to finance as their largest barrier to success, outweighing corruption, access to electricity, and tax rates.[3] Capital markets allow for the availability of long-term financing, as well as a chance for businesses to save money on traditionally expensive loans from banks by issuing bonds or equity directly. In Asia's emerging markets, for example, deeper and better-developed capital markets could free up $800 billion in funding, potentially lifting millions out of poverty.[4] A global trend in the promotion of capital markets entails tailoring regulations that allow SMEs to list on stock exchanges.[5] SMEs usually choose to list to enhance growth prospects, diversify investor bases, or obtain capital at a lower cost.[6] See Figure 5.3 for a list of reasons why firms in Jamaica chose to list.[7]

---

3   John Schellhase, Moutusi Sau, and Apanard Prabha, June 2014, "Capital Markets in Developing Coutnries: The State of Play" Milken Institute: Center For Financial Markets, https://bit.ly/2taZ2X9.

4   McKinsey & Company, April 2017, "Deepening capital markets in emerging economies," McKinsey & Company, https://mck.co/2tazr0t.

5   Alison Harwood and Tanya Konidaris, January, 2015, "SME Exchanges in Emerging Market Economies: A Stocktaking of Development Practices," World Bank, https://bit.ly/2K2MCao.

6   Siobhan Cleary, Stefano Alderighi, Jacqueline Irving and Jim Woodsome, July 18, 2017, "Small and Medium-Sized Enterprises and SME Exchanges," World Federation of Exchanges and Milken Institute, https://bit.ly/2I1H5Pm.

7   Jacqueline Irving, John Schellhase, and Jim Woodsome, July 13, 2017, "Can Stock Exchanges support the Growth of Small and Medium-Sized Enterprises?" Milken Institute. https://bit.ly/2t9pCzX.

Figure 5.3: Why Jamaican SMEs Chose to List

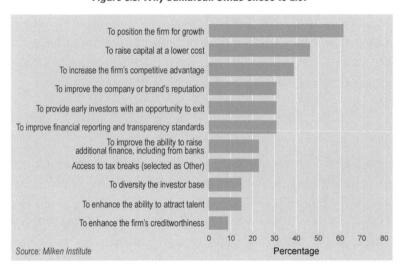

Source: Milken Institute

Governments can support the listing process by reducing fees for entry and maintaining a robust regulatory structure that prevents lower quality companies from tarnishing an emerging exchange's reputation. The Polish government, through the NewConnect platform within the Warsaw Stock Exchange, reduced entry requirements, established rules revoking regulators' licenses if they allowed too many failed enterprises to list, and implemented other reforms to assure investors that backing SMEs was not too risky.[8] Governments can also reduce the frequency of required financial disclosure and/or allow for online reporting, saving SMEs time and money. India reduced the cost of ongoing compliance and dropped the requirement for SMEs to distribute paper copies of annual reports.[9] Finally, tax incentives for SMEs encourage companies to list. The Jamaican Junior Market originally offered companies that listed on the junior exchange a five-year tax income holiday. The chairperson of this exchange estimated that the Jamaican government collected $13 million in additional tax revenue due to increased growth of the SME sector through listing, despite foregoing the corporate profit tax.[10]

8   Alison Harwood and Tanya Konidaris, January, 2015, "SME Exchanges in Emerging Market Economies: A Stocktaking of Development Practices," World Bank, https://bit.ly/2K2MCao.

9   Jacqueline Irving, John Schellhase, and Jim Woodsome, July 13, 2017, "Can Stock Exchanges support the Growth of Small and Medium-Sized Enterprises?" Milken Institute. https://bit.ly/2t9pCzX.

10   Ibid.

Facilitating Bank Accounts

To comply with international standards, banks all over the world implement know-your-customer rules and anti-money laundering/combating the financing of terrorism (AML/CFT) regulations to confirm the identity of those seeking to open bank accounts. These AML/CFT requirements can pose a problem for low-income people who lack official identification, proof of address, or income and can even prohibit them from accessing financial services. Some countries have relaxed know-your-customer requirements to facilitate bank account access for individuals who do not have the documentation to obtain a formal account. These accounts have limits on balances and transactions so as not to facilitate suspicious activity. Customers can open this type of account without formal, legal identification materials.[11] For example, South African law allows customers to open restricted accounts with a maximum balance limit of approximately $1,500 and a daily transaction limit of about $315—adequate to suit the needs of most poor and low-income people. Less onerous regulations on accounts and the removal of face-to-face account opening requirements can also enhance access to branchless banking.

Governments can also scale know-your-customer requirements through tiered systems, taking a risk-based approach. The riskier the customer, the more requirements needed to open a bank account. These systems increase regulatory and customer information requirements as transaction sizes increase. Financial sector authorities in Mexico successfully implemented this type of account structure in 2011 (see Box 5.2). Furthermore, these types of accounts actually mitigate AML/CFT risk, as more money in the banking system means that more money is subject to government oversight.[12]

---

11   Liliana Rojas-Suarez and Lucía Pacheco, June 2017, "An Index of Regulatory Practices for Financial Inclusion in Latin America: Enablers, Promoters and Preventers," BBVA Research, https://bit.ly/2tm1zNp.

12   Xavier Faz, Denise Dias, Carlos Lopez-Moctezuma and Brenda Samaniego, May 19, 2011, "A Bold Move Toward Simplifying AML/CFT: Lessons from Mexico," CGAP, http://www.cgap.org/blog/bold-move-toward-simplifying-amlcft-lessons-mexico.

> ## Box 5.2: Tiered Bank Accounts in Mexico
>
> Mexico implemented its tiered scheme for opening bank accounts based on risk in 2011. The different "levels" of accounts make it easier for low-income people to open accounts without compromising security.
>
> The first tier does not require any customer information to open but allows only $300 in transactions per month and only a debit card can be used to access funds.
>
> The second tier requires basic customer information, but customers have a higher maximum monthly transaction and can transact with mobile phones, as well as debit cards.
>
> The third tier requires complete customer information and customers must open the account in person, but the monthly transaction limit is increased to $3,700.
>
> The fourth tier requires complete customer information but customers do not have limits on how they can transact.
>
> 9.1 million new accounts—representing a 14 percent increase in total deposit accounts—had been opened in the tiered system's first two years, most of them tier one or tier two accounts, with more than 4.5 million of them tier one accounts.[13] Though account ownership cannot be correlated directly with the advent of tiered accounts, the percentage of Mexicans with an account at a financial institution increased from 27 percent in 2011 to 37 percent in 2017.[14] The data suggest that a tiered system can be an efficient way to increase financial inclusion without taking unnecessary risks.

Financial and regulatory technologies are evolving rapidly to assist with governments' need to keep up with AML/CFT regulations. Figure 5.4 shows investment trends in this area. However, even with better and better technology at their disposal, it can be difficult for regulators to keep up, particularly in the developing world. High velocity, highly diverse, and big volumes of data characterize the financial technology or fintech revolution. Despite the benefits of fintech related to increasing access to services, concerns over data protection, bank secrecy, and cybersecurity abound, as many mobile money platforms and other forms of fintech have vulnerabilities.[15]

---

13 Xavier Faz, June 25, 2013, "Mexico's Tiered KYC: An Update on Market Response," CGAP, http://www.cgap.org/blog/mexicos-tiered-kyc-update-market-response.

14 Asli Demirgüç-Kunt, Leora Klapper, Dorothe Singer, Saniya Ansar, and Jake Hess, 2018, "The Global Findex Database 2017: Measuring Financial Inclusion and the Fintech Revolution," World Bank, https://globalfindex.worldbank.org/#data_sec_focus.

15 FinTech Global, 2017, "London Leads Growth in Regtech Investments as Sector set to Soar in 2017," FinTech Global, https://bit.ly/2xRB4Dc.

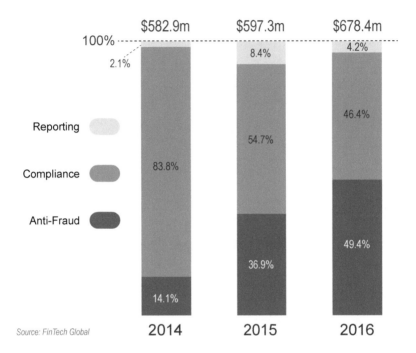

Figure 5.4: Regtech Investment

Reporting

Compliance

Anti-Fraud

$582.9m — 2014: 2.1% / 83.8% / 14.1%

$597.3m — 2015: 8.4% / 54.7% / 36.9%

$678.4m — 2016: 4.2% / 46.4% / 49.4%

Source: FinTech Global

Governments and central banks have a role to play in regulating this market, and some are leapfrogging classic regulatory systems to take advantage of regulatory technology (regtech) and supervisory technology (suptech). Regtech and suptech allow regulators to tackle regulatory and compliance problems more efficiently and transparently.[16] Regulators can streamline reporting processes, flag transactions that could be related to AML/CFT regulations, or improve risk management with regtech.[17] Suptech allows regulators to collect better data more frequently. Because data is so central to regulation, governments that wish to monitor their financial systems more efficiently should adopt processes that automate data collection and minimize manual procedures to facilitate and expedite transfers of information.

---

16 Denise Dias, August, 2017, "FinTech, Regtech and Suptech: What They Mean for Financial Supervision," Toronto Centre, https://bit.ly/2JP4fOT.

17 Catherine Cheney, May 23, 2016, "Filling the gaps between financial access and financial inclusion," Devex, https://www.devex.com/news/filling-the-gaps-between-financial-access-and-financial-inclusion-88036.

Examples of regtech products include Sybenetix, which monitors bank activity to flag unusual or suspicious behavior, or Suade, which helps banks sort data and generate regulatory reports. These technologies are particularly useful in developing countries that lack strong regulatory infrastructure.

Credit Bureau Legal Frameworks

A credit bureau is an agency that provides an accurate history of players in the economy to banks and creditors so that these lenders can determine the riskiness of lending them money. A simple example: if an entrepreneur requests a loan from a bank, that bank can request information about the entrepreneur from a credit bureau to see if that person has defaulted on loans in the past. A credit bureau relies on the interplay between borrowers, lenders, credit reporting service providers, data providers—such as banks, utility companies, retailers, and other entities that have a history with a subject and in turn supply information to the credit reporting service provider—and the regulators who oversee this exchange process.

The ultimate goal of a credit bureau is to reduce the risk of financial transactions. Credit bureaus can enable access to financial services, but certain regulatory frameworks are not conducive to efficient and holistic credit reporting. Credit bureaus face challenges including cultural skepticism surrounding information protection, insufficient enforcement of contracts, issues pertaining to data sharing among financial entities, and insufficient data.[18] Customer confidentiality laws and banks' unwillingness to provide information about customers to their peer institutions impede credit reporting and weaken incentives for banks to lend to potential clients. Furthermore, due to the high administrative and technical cost of establishing a comprehensive bureau, many microfinance institutions develop their own credit rating systems for the clients they regularly serve at a local level.[19]

---

18 Tobias Baer, Massimo Carassinu, Andrea Del Miglio, Claudio Fabiani, and Edoardo Ginevra, December 2009, "The national credit bureau: A key enabler of fionancial infrastructure and lending in developing economies," McKinsey & Company, https://mck.co/2ynUcuK.

19 Timothy Lyman, Tony Lythgoe, Margaret Miller, Xavier Reille, and Shalini Sankaranarayan, September, 2011, "Credit Reporting at the Base of the Pyramid Key Issues and Success Factors," CGAP, http://bit.ly/2KJdMqb.

Despite these challenges, many developing countries have established effective credit bureaus by combining proper government guidance of the private sector with a robust regulatory environment. One of the hallmarks of a successful credit bureau is the willingness of financial institutions to share positive information (such as on-time bill payment by the customer), which can be accomplished either by fostering cultural acceptance of this practice or through government mandate. The sharing of utility payment information or mobile phone bill payment, for example, creates a clearer picture of a customer's true credit history. Having this information allows lenders to understand a customer's true creditworthiness more holistically. Figure 5.5 shows how the sharing of positive information could lead to a decrease in loan default rates in Argentina and Brazil.[20]

Figure 5.5: The Effect of Positive Information Sharing

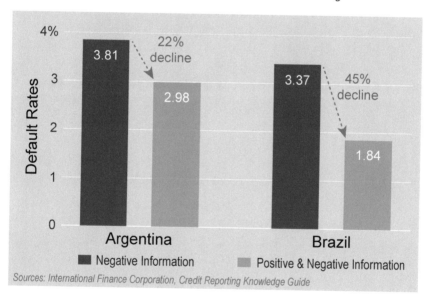

Sources: International Finance Corporation, Credit Reporting Knowledge Guide

Governments establishing credit bureaus first need to address the skepticism that often surrounds the sharing of financial information. In Tajikistan, for instance, banks and microfinance institutions typically distrusted each other. The Tajik government worked with the International Finance Corporation (IFC) to train

---

20   IFC's Global Credit Reporting Team, 2012, "Credit Reporting Knowledge Guide," International Finance Corporation, https://bit.ly/2JReSQW.

representatives from banks, microfinance institutions, and members of parliament to change the culture around the exchange of credit information. These stakeholders quickly came to understand the advantages of a credit bureau and within a year, the project had established the Credit Information Bureau of Tajikistan. This institution now houses credit information on more than 600,000 clients, mostly individuals and SMEs. This entity boosts the competitiveness of Tajikistan's financial institutions and expands access to credit for Tajik entrepreneurs. [21] [22]

Another issue is the lack of awareness about credit bureaus. For example, even though Nigeria has three functioning bureaus, only 15 percent of MSMEs were aware that a credit reporting system existed. Many businesses would indeed qualify for a loan, but because they had never seen their credit reports, they may think themselves unqualified and thus do not apply.[23] Box 5.3 describes how Nigeria implemented a credit registry to help overcome this problem.

Box 5.3: Credit Registries in Nigeria

Would-be borrowers in Nigeria commonly cite collateral as a barrier to getting the loans they need. Most MSMEs would rather use less liquid assets, such as cars and machinery, as loan collateral, whereas banks prefer land or other fixed assets. This mismatch led to a problem where even if firms have sufficient collateral in the form of fixed assets, they may be unable to show lenders collateral in liquid terms and thus they cannot get loans. The government established a new collateral registry enabling financial institutions to register livestock, machinery, and other assets, which in turn enables MSMEs to prove their creditworthiness more easily. This collateral registry has helped remove a barrier to finance for small enterprises, and surveys show that MSMEs and the financial institutions are both benefiting from the reform.[24]

---

21 Azerbaijan-Central Asia Financial Markets Infrastructure Advisory Services Project, August, 2010, "Development of the First Private Credit Information Bureau," IFC Central Asia – Azerbaijan Financial Markets Infrastructure Project, https://bit.ly/2MCkLiU.

22 World Bank, April 28, 2015, "Tajikistan's First Credit Bureau Contributes to Private Sector Development," World Bank, http://www.worldbank.org/en/results/2015/04/28/tajikistans-first-credit-bureau-for-private-sector-development.

23 The Central Bank of Nigeria, IFC, February 28, 2017, "The Credit Crunch: How the use of movable collateral and credit reporting can help finance inclusive economic growth in Nigeria." World Bank, https://bit.ly/2K5vmUQ.

24 Ibid.

e-Government

Governments around the world are going online to deliver public services more efficiently. For example, El Salvador's government implemented the Tax Administration Strengthening Program, increasing tax revenue by 1 percent of GDP by 2021 through reducing tax code violations and noncompliance. The project created an online platform for tax payment, as well as a system for delivering invoices electronically.[25] Electronic tax payments are part of a larger trend toward e-Government, which spans various functions. Governments can save their citizens time and money by establishing an online presence and thus enabling their citizens to register property, start a business, and pay taxes without having to commute, which greatly reduces costs and increases efficiency.

India is undertaking perhaps the most ambitious digital project to address economic inclusion, the India Stack. The India Stack connects individuals to the government, businesses, and each other through an integrated ID, documentation, and payment system (see Figure 5.6).

Figure 5.6: The India Stack

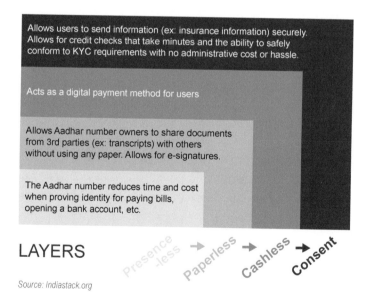

Allows users to send information (ex: insurance information) securely. Allows for credit checks that take minutes and the ability to safely conform to KYC requirements with no administrative cost or hassle.

Acts as a digital payment method for users

Allows Aadhar number owners to share documents from 3rd parties (ex: transcripts) with others without using any paper. Allows for e-signatures.

The Aadhar number reduces time and cost when proving identity for paying bills, opening a bank account, etc.

LAYERS

Presence-less → Paperless → Cashless → Consent

Source: Indiastack.org

---

25   Carola Pessino, December 7, 2016, "El Salvador will improve tax and customs management with IDB support," Inter-American Development Bank, https://bit.ly/2M5xMQK.

The base of the stack, the presence-less layer, refers to India's biometric ID number, the Aadhar number. This layer eliminates much of the time and cost of proving identity for paying bills, opening a bank account, and accessing other services. The paperless layer allows each Aadhar number owner to share third-party documents, such as college transcripts or hospital records, with third parties without using any paper. This layer also allows for e-signatures. The next layer up acts as a digital payment method for users. The final layer, the consent layer, allows users to send information such as bank documents or insurance information securely. This capability allows for credit checks that take mere minutes and facilitates compliance with know-your-customer requirements without any administrative costs.[26] [27] Though some observers have raised concerns about privacy implications, the India Stack may well be a harbinger of a growing market for easy and secure digital transaction methods that make economic integration possible for everyone.

Registering Property

Many people in the developing world lack legal title to their land; only 30 percent of the world's landholders have property that is legally recognized.[28] As a result, poor and low-income families and businesses are less productive and less food secure and invest less in their properties. Lack of land title bars people from using their assets as collateral to obtain a loan. The most common strategies employed by developing and emerging economy governments to encourage land titling include allowing the free transfer of property, building more efficient and transparent systems, fostering community engagement, and cutting "red tape" to make it easier for low-income people to obtain titles.[29] Many governments have also created publicly accessible land registration databases, which limit the confusion and adverse consequences that stem from a lack of title and provide citizens with security in knowing they have a legal claim to their property. Box 5.4 shows examples of how these databases are created.

26   Sasi Desai and Nipun Jasuja, October 27, 2016, "India Stack: The Bedrock of a Digital India," Wharton FinTech, https://medium.com/wharton-fintech/the-bedrock-of-a-digital-india-3e96240b3718.

27   Jayadevan PK, September 5, 2017, "Consent, the final layer in India's ambitious data regime, falling in place," *Factory Daily*, https://factordaily.com/consent-architecture-indiastack/.

28   World Bank, March 24, 2017, "Why Secure Land Rights Matter," World Bank, http://bit.ly/2KMiD6D.

29   The Economist, August 24, 2006, "Of property and poverty," *The Economist*, http://www.economist.com/node/7830252.

Box 5.4: Cross-Cutting Land Titling Initiatives

A DAI project funded through USAID called the Feed the Future Tanzania Land Tenure Assistance activity works to register smallholders in Tanzania. DAI is utilizing a low-cost app-based tool, Mobile Application to Secure Tenure (MAST), to map villages and prevent tension between farmers and their neighbors, as well as between farmers and the government. DAI expects this project to benefit more than 14,000 villagers across 41 villages, representing 50,000 plots of land, by the end of 2019. More than 50 percent of these plots belong to women.[30]

Technology has also enhanced land rights in Cape Verde. Residents once hesitated to use their land to start a business. Transaction costs pertaining to confusion over ownership and registration were so high that they hindered foreign investment and thus economic growth. The government worked with DAI and the Millennium Challenge Corporation to geomap and survey parcels of land, establish ownership rights, and set up a property database. The government also enacted a law that made land registration compulsory. The digital registration of thousands of parcels of land, including all units of property on some of the islands, has allowed developers to use their land confidently to build apartments and condominiums and makes the country much more attractive for foreign investment and tourism, a mainstay of Cape Verde's economy.[31] [32]

The Vietnamese government is undertaking a project to develop a publicly available National Land Database. By increasing land surveying efforts and investing in technology to create this database, the Vietnamese government increases the validity of the land claims of small and medium-sized landowners who comprise the majority of poor households in Vietnam. This added stability will stimulate investment in the land. In addition to securing rights for Vietnamese citizens, the database will allow Vietnam to meet environmental and climate change goals more easily, as well as improve natural disaster responsiveness.[33] [34]

---

30   Thomas Donigan, June 2017, "Rural Tanzanians Map Their Country's Future," Frontlines, USAID, https://bit.ly/2ll6rio

31   DAI, 2016, "The Capo Verde Land Project," *DAI*, https://bit.ly/2lkBqe8.

32   Preston Winter, Januaray 9, 2018, "Land Rights Open Economic Opportunities in Cabo Verde," Millennium Challenge Corporation, https://www.mcc.gov/blog/entry/blog-010918-land-rights-cabo-verde.

33   World Bank, July 5, 2016, "Vietnam: Improving Efficiency and Transparency in Land Administration Services," World Bank, https://bit.ly/29l8DhS.

34   World Bank, June 12, 2016, "Vietnam: Impoved Land Governance and Database Project," World Bank, https://bit.ly/2MCBEty.

Starting a Business

Entrepreneurs often face serious obstacles in starting a business. In some cases, it can take months and even a year or more to become legitimate. These obstacles explain why so many enterprises remain in the informal sector. Governments can fix this problem by easing the regulatory burdens on businesses and facilitating easy startup procedures. The *Doing Business* report identifies five policies and services governments can provide to make it easier for entrepreneurs to formalize their business: simplify registration formalities, simplify post-registration procedures, improve online procedures, create "one-stop shops," and abolish or reduce minimum capital requirements.[35]

Macedonia's business reforms between 2004 and 2017 have drastically reduced the time and fees necessary to start and register a business, making the country a model in this regard. Starting a business in Macedonia in 2004 entailed 13 procedures, took 48 days, and cost 12.1 percent of per capita income. After Macedonia implemented its online one-stop shop for business creation and incorporation, simplified the process to obtain a company seal, and made online registration free between 2010 and 2017, it now takes two business days and .1 percent of income per capita to incorporate. The only processes involved entail a few hours registering at the online one-stop shop and filling out short, free forms to open a bank account and register to pay taxes.[36] [37] [38]

Chile, too, is delivering on promises to become more business friendly through a new law that lets entrepreneurs incorporate their businesses in one day at no cost. Chile's online platform, developed by the Ministry of Economy, allows entrepreneurs to fill out a form on the website that will then translate the information into a formal document. Previously, registration took about eight days and cost between $500 and $700, which discouraged entrepreneurs

---

35   World Bank, June, 2017, "Starting a Business: Reforms," World Bank, http://www.doingbusiness.org/data/exploretopics/starting-a-business/reforms.

36   World Bank, 2012, "Doing Business 2012: Economy Profile: Macedonia, FYR," World Bank, https://bit.ly/2JMajaC.

37   World Bank, 2015, "Doing Business 2015: Economy Profile: Macedonia, FYR," World Bank, https://bit.ly/2M65yW9.

38   World Bank, 2017, "Doing Business 2017: Economy Profile: Macedonia, FYR," World Bank, https://bit.ly/2tmoIPE.

from formally registering.[39] The Ministry hopes that this new law will enable a potential 370,000 entrepreneurs in Chile's informal economy to reap the benefits of formality.[40]

Paying Taxes

Well-structured, transparent, consistent, and user-friendly tax policies that make it easy for citizens and companies to file are necessary for a functioning society. Increasingly, the availability and reliability of electronic filing systems make it much easier for filers and reviewers to pay taxes correctly. The developing world is undertaking projects that enable electronic filing and payment more frequently, especially in central Asia, and electronic systems are beginning to gain in popularity in Sub-Saharan Africa. Seventeen economies in frontier markets introduced or enhanced online platforms for tax payments in 2017, which has led to significant efficiency gains.[41] These e-filing systems have reduced filing time by up to 25 percent within five years of being implemented and have the additional benefit of reducing tax evasion and other forms of fraud.[42] Serbia has made paying taxes easier by creating an online portal that consolidates all communications between a given taxpayer and the government, and through which taxpayers can file and pay their taxes as well. This innovation, in conjunction with the abolishment of a land usage fee that had to be paid in person each month, has reduced the time it takes to fulfill tax obligations by nearly 35 hours per person every year.[43] The benefits of online filing include a reduction in fraud, reduced compliance fees, less tax evasion, saved time, easier auditing, and more, but obviously such approaches risk leaving out those who do not have access to online technology.

---

39   Start-Up Chile, May 5, 2013, "Chile's new law: incorporate your business in just one day, in one step, and for free," Start-Up Chile, https://bit.ly/2I0Nbzy.

40   Shonika Proctor, May 3, 2013, "Chile launches one day business incorporation online portal," *AndesBeat*, http://andesbeat.com/2013/05/03/chile-one-day-business-incorporation-online-now-possibl/.

41   World Bank, 2018, "Doing Business 2018: Reforming to Crate Jobs," World Bank, http://www.doingbusiness.org/-/media/WBG/DoingBusiness/Documents/Annual-Reports/English/DB2018-Full-Report.pdf.

42   International Monetary Fund, April, 2018, "Fiscal Monitor" International Monetary Fund, https://www.imf.org/-/media/Files/Publications/fiscal-monitor/2018/April/pdf/fm1801.ashx?la=en.

43   Andrew Packman and Augusto Lopez-Claros, 2016, "Paying Taxes 2016," PricewaterhouseCoopers, https://www.pwc.com/gx/en/paying-taxes-2016/paying-taxes-2016.pdf.

Decent Work and Labor Standards

A high degree of informality, low levels of union membership, and minimal social insurance coverage characterize labor markets in the frontier countries. These labor market traits pose challenges to long-term socioeconomic development, such as a loss of tax income for the government, poor or substandard working conditions, avoidance of regulations, and lower levels of worker happiness.[44] [45] Labor protection is essential for protecting workers in developing countries, especially groups that are particularly vulnerable to abuse, discrimination, and unfair labor practices. Examples of worker exploitation are withholding documents, verbal and physical abuse, sexual harassment, excessive overtime, gender pay gaps, and other forms of mistreatment. Box 5.5 explains how the Better Work initiative helps protect workers in the garment industry.

Box 5.5: Better Work and the Garment Industry

Better Work, a nonprofit collaboration between the International Labor Organization (ILO) and the International Finance Corporation (IFC), works with apparel companies and factories in the developing world to prove that improved working conditions can actually make businesses more competitive. Evidence from Better Work's Vietnam project shows that factories with improved working conditions met daily production targets 40 minutes faster, and these factories experienced a 22 percent increase in productivity. Better Work helps factories achieve these results by using training programs to empower women; reducing coerced or excessive overtime; preventing sexual, verbal, and physical abuse through harassment prevention training; and reducing the frequency of the business getting audited, all of which lead to fewer accidents, happier and more productive workers, and higher profitability. Though not always beneficial for a factory from a "bottom line" perspective, the spillover effects of Better Work's intervention yield positive social returns to the country's economy, such as higher educational attainment for children of employees.[46]

---

44   Carl Frey, Ebrahim Rahbari, Harry Patrinos, Cecilia Chen, Marcus Haymon, Louise Fox, Eric Simonson, Michael Grimm, August 1, 2016, "2016 Brookings Blum Roundtable: The future of work in the developing world," Brookings Institute, https://www.brookings.edu/multi-chapter-report/the-future-of-work-in-the-developing-world/.

45   Benjamin Temkin, January, 2016, "The impact of labor informality on subjective well-being," *Global Labour Journal*, https://bit.ly/2JZPeWi.

46   Drusilla Brown, September, 2016, "Highlights: Progress and Potential – Findings from an independent impact assessment," Better Work Global Programme, https://betterwork.org/dev/wp-content/uploads/2016/09/BW-ProgressAndPotential-Highlights.pdf.

Furthermore, Better Work maintains a database of apparel factories' compliance with international and national labor standards in the six countries in which it operates. Better Work records reported issues and factories' responses so that observers can verify whether a factory has responded. For example, the database shows that when the PT Dragon Forever factory in Indonesia received a complaint that its fire detection and alarm system was not up to standard, the firm responded by removing fabrics from the unloading area and installing fire safety equipment.[47]

These forms of exploitation also extend to segments of society where conditions are not socially optimal, as is the case with "trash pickers." Brazil has recognized this form of work as legitimate, and these independent "catadores" are now engaged in an official occupation. With an investment of more than $6 million from the government, government-owned recycling warehouses remove the need for middlemen, improve working conditions, and increase productivity. Similarly, in Pune, India, trash pickers have been given legal recognition, and even health insurance, from the city.[48]

The regulatory challenge for governments is to design labor standards that advance social and economic goals without inhibiting business growth. New trends in labor policies relevant for economic inclusion cover areas such as social protection and high youth unemployment.

Tilted Playing Field

Governments often take a more active role in enticing the private sector to expand access to services and jobs. Policies in the tilted playing field give preference to certain sectors or segments, often focusing on domestic companies and altering the nature of markets. Tilted playing field policies that affect inclusive economies in frontier markets include a renewed interest in industrial policy, import substitution, local content laws, free trade zones, the subsidization of jobs, and partnering with the private sector to form public-private partnerships.

---

47 BetterWork, May 28, 2018, "Compliance Data," BetterWork, https://portal.betterwork.org/transparency/compliance#.

48 Robert Thornett, October 14, 2015, "In Brazil, a City's Waste Pickers Find Hope in a Pioneering Program," Yale School of Forestry & Environmental Studies, http://bit.ly/2MJSS7T.

Industrial Policy

Industrial policy refers to public policies intended to create growth in selected sectors, usually industrial and high-value services sectors. This strategy worked well for some emerging Asian economies, the "Asian Tigers" of the 1970s and 1980s, as they became exported-oriented economies. Many South and Latin American countries, including Brazil, Argentina, and Mexico, also adopted this strategy before the 1950s and 1960s but did not find sustained success due to macroeconomic and structural factors such as high inflation, a dearth of investment, and high levels of debt.[49] Today, industrial policy often carries a negative connotation, particularly in the developing world. Governments have not always been successful at picking winners and have often ended up saving losers instead. Governments often heavily subsidized or otherwise protected industries or companies that wound up failing anyway and pushed out successful would-be competitors in the process.[50]

Notwithstanding these mixed results, industrial policy is making a resurgence. More data now exists in developing countries, providing governments with crucial information necessary for making evidence-based industrial policy.[51] Private sector inclusion in the policy formulation process, realistic goals, and accountability of all parties characterize well-crafted industrial policies.[52] Advances in the technology and green energy sectors could provide good opportunities for governments to assist fledgling industries. This assistance can come through direct investment or the creation of policies friendly to the industry.

Many developing countries want to get ahead of the competition when it comes to specializing in green energy technologies such as solar, wind, or hydropower. This development is reminiscent of the way countries first invested in fossil fuel industries, but renewables do not have the same negative externalities. Green energy technology carries with it the opportunity for skills de-

---

49 Gary Gereffi, 1990, "Manufacturing Miracles: Path of industrialization in Latin America and East Asia," Princeton University Press, https://press.princeton.edu/titles/4840.html

50 The Economist, August 5, 2010, "The global revival of industrial policy: Picking winners, saving losers," *The Economist*, http://www.economist.com/node/16741043.

51 Dirk Pilat, 2012, "Resurrecting industrial policy," Organisation for Economic Co-operation and Development, http://oecdobserver.org/news/fullstory.php/aid/3814/Resurrecting_industrial_policy.html.

52 Dani Rodrik, January 6, 2011, "The Return of Industrial Policy," Ethos Insights, https://www.project-syndicate.org/commentary/the-return-of-industrial-policy?barrier=accesspaylog

velopment, improved health effects, and the delivery of high social returns.[53] As of 2013, more than 50 developing countries have policies in place that aim to develop their green energy sectors. Policy tools commonly employed by governments are renewable portfolio standards (which mandate that a certain percentage of energy production comes from renewable sources), subsidies for renewables research and development, accelerated depreciation for certain assets, and strict regulation of source-point greenhouse gas emissions (though this tends to occur more in middle-income countries).

Numerous benefits come from nurturing a sustainable energy sector. For countries that rely on the fossil fuel industry, diversifying their energy mix can protect against the economic disruption associated with price shocks. Unclean fuels lead to detrimental health outcomes, so preempting the growth of fossil fuel industries by investing in sustainable energy has numerous long- and short-run benefits. These benefits also include creating low-cost energy for low-income consumers, creating a competitive advantage with regard to emerging technology (as China has with solar panels, which it was able to do through tax incentives for solar companies), and creating the jobs and wealth that accompany new industries.[54] [55]

The two major criticisms of industrial policy are that the government is not always skilled at picking winners and that once an industry becomes favored, government involvement invites political manipulation and corruption. Countries designing industrial policy for renewable energy should be wary of falling into the historical pitfalls.[56]

Import Substitution

Import substitution is a policy tool used to implement industrial policy by protecting domestic producers of a given good from import competition. Typical

53 Dani Rodrik, 2014, "Green industrial policy," *Oxford Review of Economic Policy*, https://drodrik. scholar.harvard.edu/files/dani-rodrik/files/green_industrial_policy.pdf.

54 John Fialka, December 19, 2016, "Why China Is Dominating the Solar Industry," *Scientific American*, http://bit.ly/2tZV2bv.

55 Tilman Altenburg and Claudia Assmann, 2017, "Green Industrial Policy: Concept, Policies, Country Experiences," Partnership for Action on Green Economy, http://www.un-page.org/files/public/green_ industrial_policy_book_aw_web.pdf.

56 Dani Rodrik, 2014, "Green industrial policy," *Oxford Review of Economic Policy*, https://drodrik.scholar. harvard.edu/files/dani-rodrik/files/green_industrial_policy.pdf.

policy measures include import quotas, high tariffs on imports of a specific good, or the subsidization of domestic producers to render foreign companies uncompetitive. Countries may also manipulate exchange rates to bolster exports. Many newly independent developing nations looked inward to develop industry in the 1950s and 1960s. Import substitution was a popular strategy but rarely succeeded because domestic production often became inefficient, leading most countries to adopt an export-oriented approach.[57] [58]

Many developing countries, particularly in Africa, are dealing with uncertainty regarding foreign aid. Many of them are simultaneously coping with commodity price instability, which has led to larger trade deficits and foreign exchange shortages. Due to these factors, import substitution policies began to make a resurgence in the mid-2010s.[59] More recently, depressed commodity prices have led many emerging and frontier nations to adopt import substitution strategies, often branded as domestic market recapture.

For example, in 2016 the Algerian government—under pressure to support domestic industries and diversify Algeria's economy in the wake of depressed oil prices—focused on bolstering the automotive sector.[60] The import of foreign cars was limited to 152,000 in 2016, about half the number imported in 2015.[61] Algeria has also imposed import restrictions on cement and concrete, which has supported the local industry as well. Other countries in Africa are following suit: Tanzania, for example, banned secondhand clothing imports, while Nigeria is using a strategy of backwards integration with foreign cement customers to build

---

57   Avik Basu, April 15, 2005, "Urban & Regional Planning Economic Development Handbook: Import substitution as economic development," Taubman College of Architecture and Regional Planning.

58   Gary Gereffi, 1990, "Manufacturing Miracles: Path of industrialization in Latin America and East Asia," Princeton University Press, https://press.princeton.edu/titles/4840.html.

59   Pritish Behuria, June 12, 2017, "The Cautious Return of Import Substitution in Africa," London School of Economics, http://blogs.lse.ac.uk/africaatlse/2017/06/12/the-cautious-return-of-import-substitution-in-africa/.

60   Henry Smith, August 8, 2017, "Algeria: Regulatory changes in automotive sector to favour domestic production over imports," Control Risks, https://www.controlrisks.com/our-thinking/insights/automotive-algeria.

61   The Skuld P&I Club, January 19, 2016, "Algeria: Restriction on import of vehicles, cement and steel debars," The Skuld P&I Club, https://safety4sea.com/algeria-restriction-on-import-of-vehicles-cement-and-steel-debars/.

an in-country industry.[62] Ethiopia's strategy of offering tax incentives to foreign companies to partner with domestic manufacturers of steel, pharmaceuticals, electronics, and other products to develop these industries within Ethiopian borders has seen success as well.[63] However, it can lead to counterproductive long-term effects, as it reduces trade and does not allow companies to leverage comparative advantages in manufacturing.

Free Trade Zones

The United Arab Emirates wanted to double the number of pharmaceutical factories in its free trade zone, the Jebel Ali Free Zone (Jazfa), by working with multinational companies to build their factories within the UAE and thereby create added value within the Emirates' borders.[64] The UAE and many other countries are turning away from protectionist policies like import substitution in favor of developing an export market for their industries and integrating more with the global economy by creating special economic zones with regulations and tax structures that differ from the rest of the country's.[65]

These so-called Special Economic Zones (SEZ) vary from country to country but generally the term refers to an area where tax, labor, and investment laws differ from the rest of the country as a way to promote exports and foreign direct investment. SEZs include industrial parks, urban enterprise zones, and export processing zones. Arguably, the best-known type of SEZ is a free trade zone (FTZ), which refers to a geographic area where goods can be handled, manufactured, or re-exported without being subject to customs or duties. FTZs can be powerful tools for stimulating foreign direct investment, creating local jobs and industries, and raising government revenue. Successful FTZs are situated at strategic geographic locations, have strong government support,

---

62 Pritish Behuria, June 12, 2017, "The Cautious Return of Import Substitution in Africa," London School of Economics, http://blogs.lse.ac.uk/africaatlse/2017/06/12/the-cautious-return-of-import-substitution-in-africa/.

63 Maritz Africa Intelligence, August 30, 2016, "Ethiopia: Import substitution likely to be a growing theme," *East Africa Consumer Industries Quarterly*, https://www.howwemadeitinafrica.com/ethiopia-import-substitution-likely-growing-theme/55584/.

64 Mohamed Elsayed, October 16, 2017, "New import substitution initiatives in the Middle East – 2017, the year of new policies," *IHS Markit*, https://bit.ly/2JXX0Qp.

65 Thomas Farole, September 2011, "Special Economic Zones: What Have We Learned?," *Economic Premise*, http://siteresources.worldbank.org/INTPREMNET/Resources/EP64.pdf.

and are governed by regulatory frameworks conducive to business.[66] FTZs are an expensive undertaking, but the rewards can be immense. Jazfa is one of 22 free zones in Dubai, and most of these are based around particular industries. Because of government support, Jazfa is on track to become the world's largest container port by 2030, and all of Dubai's zones are seeing a growth in companies and investment, which translates to economic growth.[67]

China has stimulated economic growth through FTZs and other SEZs since the 1970s. In 2017, China announced the opening of seven new FTZs to bring the countrywide total to 11. Companies that register in these zones are subject to less stringent regulation and a reduction in import/export taxes, with a primary goal of increasing China's competitiveness in logistics and other high-end industries. As of 2017, investment in the existing four FTZs was more than $50 billion. These FTZs have been crucial to the rise of China's middle class, particularly in coastal regions.[68] [69]

The Dominican Republic has shown that SEZs are a viable policy option even for small countries. The DR has found success with SEZs by ensuring that it has a strong regulator (which attracts foreign investment by reducing risk), a government that is active in negotiating favorable trade agreements, and productive collaboration with the private sector. Figure 5.7 shows the jobs created directly by SEZs in the DR, illustrating how they can create high-value technical jobs over time (not just low-level jobs). However, the DR is facing an emerging skills mismatch as the demand for skilled labor increases. The government could address this latter problem through training and job search assistance.[70] [71]

---

66   Douglas Zhihua Zeng, May 5, 2015, "Why are more countries embracing industrial zones?," World Bank, http://blogs.worldbank.org/trade/why-are-more-countries-embracing-industrial-zones-video.

67   The Economist, June 4, 2015, "Dubai's Economy: Growing up," *The Economist*, https://www.economist.com/middle-east-and-africa/2015/06/04/growing-up.

68   Gaby Smeenk, Yi Duan and Dulijon Veldhoen, July 24, 2017, "China's Free Trade Zones – Overview Of 2017 Developments," Mondaq, https://bit.ly/2I1jRZK.

69   John Whalley, February 24, 2015, "The impact of China's new free trade zone," World Economic Forum, https://www.weforum.org/agenda/2015/02/the-impact-of-chinas-new-free-trade-zone/.

70   World Bank, February 22, 2017, "Free-Trade Zones in the Dominican Republic, an Engine for Competitiveness and Jobs: World Bank," World Bank, http://www.worldbank.org/en/news/press-release/2017/02/21/zonas-francas-republica-dominicana-competitividad-empleos.

71   Joes-Daniel Reyes and Miguel Eduardo Sanchez, November 2016, "Special Economic Zones in the Dominican Republic: Policy Consideration for a More Competitive and Inclusive Sector," World Bank, https://bit.ly/2tk7J0x.

Figure 5.7: Direct Jobs Created by SEZs in the Dominican Republic

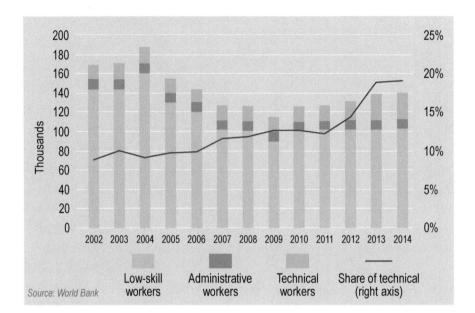

Source: World Bank

Unfortunately, SEZs often lack strict environmental standards or regulation, which brings them into conflict with the sustainable development goals. As a result, some countries are starting to create Sustainable Economic Zones, which are likely the next iteration of SEZ development.[72] The number of SEZs increased from 176 in 1986 to 4,500 in 2015, and they are becoming increasingly competitive with each other. Because there are now so many SEZs globally, racing to the bottom—in terms of offering tax breaks and other cost savings to multinationals—may not be as effective as pivoting strategy and becoming sustainability champions. Countries can attract investment through SEZs by adopting a framework that ensures quality and aligns with corporate social responsibility standards by offering sustainable solutions, such as using green energy or limiting GHG emissions. Furthermore, looser regulations can result in poorer labor conditions within SEZs. Sustainable economic zones can also address these labor and health concerns.

---

72 James Zhan, February 21, 2018, "Growing popularity of SEZs demonstrates the raft of benefits they offer," *World Finance*, https://www.worldfinance.com/markets/growing-popularity-of-sezs-demonstrates-the-raft-of-benefits-they-offer.

Adapting to regulations consistent with the SDGs could give early adopters an edge over rest of the market as even more SEZs become established.[73]

Local Content

Many resource-rich countries have historically not reaped the rewards of their natural endowment, particularly those with resources such as oil, gas, and other extractives. Corrupt governments squander the revenue from these resources, foreign companies exploit weak states to obtain resources without paying sufficient royalties, or ineffective rulers do not attempt economic diversification and stymie economic growth. Recently, many countries have developed legislation, known as local content laws, to capture more of the wealth inherent in their natural resources. Local content refers to the requirement that foreign companies employ a certain amount of local labor, source a certain amount of local product, and/or create a certain amount of value within the country. A local content measure might dictate that for an electronics manufacturer, 50 percent of a device's components must be produced within that country's borders. Local content policies have been around for a long time but are becoming increasingly popular in the developing world; between 2008 and 2016, more than 140 local content measures were implemented globally.[74] Figure 5.8 illustrates the geographical distribution of local content measures.[75]

73   Dennis Görlich, March, 2016, "Growth and Jobs by investing in Sustainable Special Economic Zones," Council of Global Problem-Solving, https://bit.ly/2tacyKI.

74   Organisation For Economic Co-Operation and Development, February, 2016, "The economic impact of local content requirements," Organisation for Economic Co-operation and Development, https://www.oecd.org/tad/policynotes/economic-impact-local-content-requirements.pdf.

75   Hanna Deringer, Fredrik Erixon, Philipp Lamprecht and Erik van der Marel, January, 2018, "The Economic Impact of Local Content Requirements: A Case Study of Heavy Vehicles," European Centre For International Political Economy, http://ecipe.org//app/uploads/2018/01/LCR-Paper-final-2-KL.pdf.

Figure 5.8: Local Content Measures Passed Between 2008 and 2016 by Sector

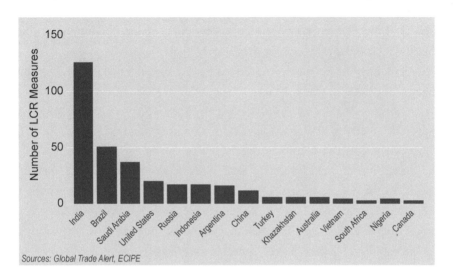

Sources: Global Trade Alert, ECIPE

Local content policies have had mixed results. In some cases, they have discouraged investment, created inefficiencies, and even fostered corruption. More than 80 percent of the Nigerian governments revenue comes from the oil industry. The Nigerian government passed a local content measure in 2010 that attempted to spread oil wealth among everyone in the country. The bill came with requirements that all concrete barges and floating platforms for offshore drilling be fabricated in the country, all line-pipes and heat exchangers must be sourced from Nigerian companies, and other rules on inputs in the same vein. While the bill was noble in intention, Nigerian companies simply did not have the sourcing capacity to meet these requirements. There was only one Nigerian line-pipe manufacturer, and there were not nearly enough trained Nigerian welders to meet the labor standards.[76] Thus, while the bill was successful in providing gainful employment in some sectors of the Nigerian economy, it was destined to fail in others, which led to divestment by firms such as Shell and Conoco Phillips.[77] Another unintended consequence of local content laws can be foreign firms' use

---

76   Joseph Nna Emeka Nwaokoro, April, 2011, "Nigeria's National Content Bill: The Hype, the Hope and the Reality," *Journal of African Law*. http://bit.ly/2KWReyX.

77   Benoit Faucon and Sarah Kent, July 30, 2014, "ConocoPhillips Sells Nigerian Oil Assets to Oando," *The Wall Street Journal*, https://www.wsj.com/articles/conocophillips-sells-nigerian-oil-assets-to-oando-1406741704.

of local citizens to front for them; the companies work with national residents to set up shell companies that import foreign parts and then pass them off as locally sourced. This phenomenon has been observed in Ghana, for instance, which passed a substantial local content measure in 2013.[78]

Some countries are starting to adapt local content policies to get around some of the adverse consequences of the older models. Writing legislation to avoid problems such as an insufficient specialized labor pool or lack of a local supply chain has made local content an economic boon to Oman. In 2013, Oman unveiled its in-country value (ICV) Blueprint Strategy, which emphasized spending on skill building for Omanis and does not dictate spending thresholds for specific inputs. In this way, foreign companies can leverage the comparative strengths Oman has, identify areas where investment can create long-term value through the development of new industrial activity, and use foreign suppliers for areas where Oman is comparatively weak.[79]

Public-Private Partnerships (PPPs)

Since the 1980s, PPPs have become an increasingly popular option for governments to deliver services, build infrastructure, and accomplish policy objectives. PPPs seek to combine the resources of the government with the efficiency and innovative mindset of the private sector, with the goal of a mutually beneficial relationship. PPPs allow the private sector to pass some of their risk to the government, while the public sector can guard against budgetary overruns and incentivize the private partners to meet deadlines and other benchmarks. This results in ambitious projects that neither party may have taken on by itself.[80] PPPs tend to be successful if the government's objectives are in line with those of the private entity and if there is open and honest communication between the parties.

Infrastructure has seen the most frequent application of PPPs in recent years. Regionally, the EAP region overtook LAC as the region with the most PPP infra-

---

78   Peter Arthur and Emmanuel Arthur, Winter, 2014, "Local Content and Private Sector Participation in Ghana's Oil Industry: An Economic and Strategic Imperative," *Africa Today,* http://bit.ly/2uaKciV.

79   Oxford Business Group, 2016, "Oman's in-country value scheme expected to broaden domestic industry," Oxford Business Group, https://oxfordbusinessgroup.com/analysis/adding-value-country-value-icv-scheme-expected-broaden-domestic-industry.

80   World Bank, October 10, 2016, "Government Objectives: Benefits and Risks of PPPs," World Bank, https://ppp.worldbank.org/public-private-partnership/overview/ppp-objectives.

structure investment in 2017, with Indonesia taking on the most projects, primarily within the energy and infrastructure sectors. Interestingly, renewables projects dominate in the energy space, comprising 68 of 82 projects in 2017. Governments are working with the private sector to create infrastructure that is viable in the long term, especially in commodity-rich countries.[81] Within the infrastructure space, one of the more popular models, called Build-Operate-Transfer, accounts for a sizable number of projects. With this style of PPP, the private sector receives government money to construct a project, operates it for a given amount of time (often around 30 years), then hands it over to the government. This approach allows for efficient design and construction with risk shared between the two parties.[82]

Social impact bonds represent another new development in the PPP space. Social impact bonds reflect the intersection of PPPs with impact investing and results-based financing. Investors provide money to a service provider, the service provider delivers the social outcome desired by government (such as job placement or educational retention), and then an outcome funder—often the government—repays the investor its initial investment plus an additional rate of return if the service provider delivers the desired outcome. Other parties, such as evaluators or data collectors, may also be involved.

Social impact bonds are quite popular in the United Kingdom, the United States, and Australia and typically focus on domestic issues such as homelessness or prison recidivism. Development impact bonds have the same basic structure as social impact bonds, but the outcome payers tend to be international donors instead of governments, and the service delivery focuses on services traditionally provided by international aid or the public sector. Currently, 28 impact bonds deliver services in middle- or low-income countries, with Brazil, Cameroon, India, Palestine, Peru, South Africa, and Uganda experimenting with more than one development impact bond each. See Figure 5.9 for sector distribution.[83]

---

81 Paul Da Rita, May 4, 2017, "What are the new trends driving private infrastructure investment in emerging markets?," World Bank, http://blogs.worldbank.org/ppps/what-are-new-trends-driving-private-infrastructure-investment-emerging-markets.

82 Deblina Saha, June, 2017, "Private Participation in Infrastructure (PPI): Half Year Update: January-June 2017," World Bank, https://ppi.worldbank.org/-/media/GIAWB/PPI/Documents/Global-Notes/PPI2017_HalfYear_Update.pdf.

83 Emily Gustafsson-Wright, Izzy Boggild-Jones, Dean Segell and Justice Durland, September, 2017, "Impact Bonds in Developing Countries: Early Learnings from the Field," Brookings Institute and Convergence, https://www.brookings.edu/wp-content/uploads/2017/09/impact-bonds-in-developing-countries_web.pdf.

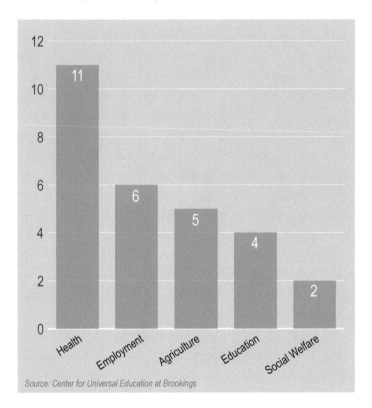

Figure 5.9: Development Impact Bonds by Sector

Source: Center for Universal Education at Brookings

Development impact bonds are a promising way for governments to partner with the private sector and NGOs to deliver services to vulnerable populations and for last-mile service delivery.[84] Impact bonds can result in more efficient service provision compared to the traditional government model—a model where no party directly loses money if service providers fail to meet outcome objectives.[85] See Box 5.6 for a case study on what a development impact bond looks like in practice.

---

84 Owen Barder, June 11, 2012, "What If You Could Invest in Development?," Center for Global Development, https://www.cgdev.org/blog/what-if-you-could-invest-development.

85 Owen Barder, Toby Eccles, Elizabth Littlefield, October 2013, "Investing in Social Outcomes: Development Impact Bonds The Report of the Development Impact Bond Working Group," Center for Global Development, https://www.cgdev.org/sites/default/files/investing-in-social-outcomes-development-impact-bonds.pdf.

Box 5.6: A Development Impact Bond in India

The Utkrisht impact bond aims to promote maternal and newborn health in Rajasthan, India. UBS Optimum Foundation provides the initial capital and raises additional funding from other private investors. Two Indian NGOs, PSI and HLFPPT, act as the service providers and make sure that health clinics meet governmental standards of quality to reduce newborn and maternal death, both of which are far above the national average. The Indian government, USAID, and MSD for Mothers (another NGO) act as outcome funders and pay investors back if providers meet predetermined targets. Mathematica, a third party, acts as an evaluator to ensure the service provider achieves the bond's goals. Organizations have committed more than $10 million to bond outcomes, a cost-effective way of deploying this capital compared to public sector spending.[86] It is projected that the Utkrisht bonds can help up to 600,000 pregnant women and save the lives of more than 2,000 newborns and mothers every year.[87]

Though some observers are critical of PPPs for a variety of reasons, chief among them that the private sector will always place profit above people, they are often an effective solution to policy problems. Whatever the criticisms may be, PPP relationships are definitively on the rise.

Government-Controlled Playing Field

Governments frequently wish to play a bigger role in directing the market. In many countries, there is broad agreement that government should provide security, education, health, and economic stability and interfere directly in the economy only when it does more good than harm. Still, governments sometimes feel that they are better equipped to solve certain problems than the invisible hand of the market.

There are many forms of government intervention. Banking sector interventions—including conditional cash transfers (CCTs), lending to high-priority sectors, and interest rate ceilings—serve to direct investment toward certain

---

86   Sean, Newhouse, April 3, 2018, "Utkrisht Bond Aims to Prevent Maternal Mortality in India," The Borgen Project, https://borgenproject.org/utkrisht-bond-maternal-mortality-india/.

87   USAID, November, 2017, "The Utkrisht Impact Bond – Improving Maternal and Newborn Health Care in Rajasthan, India," USAID, https://www.usaid.gov/sites/default/files/documents/1864/Utkrish-Impact-Bond-Brochure-November-2017.pdf.

people or sectors in an attempt to lift citizens out of poverty. While sometimes these policies do result in more financial inclusion, they can have detrimental economic impacts as well.

Technical and vocational education and training (TVET) programs and public works programs are government attempts to stimulate labor markets. They can match people with jobs they might not otherwise be able to obtain, either because they did not have the right skillset or because the job would not have existed without government action.

One thing is certain: when political considerations drive these actions as much as or more than economic logic does, government intervention can hinder local markets. Box 5.7 contains an example of crowding out in Myanmar.

Box 5.7: Crowding Out in Myanmar

Brighterlite is a home solar system company that aims to leapfrog traditional energy sources by providing low-cost systems to low-income people. After finding success with its PAYGO model in Pakistan, Brighterlite in 2015 entered the market in Myanmar, a country where only 34 percent of the population was connected to the electricity grid, through a partnership with GSMA and two other NGOs. The company established a partnership with the leading mobile operator in Myanmar to help capture customers who would benefit from clean, affordable energy. Though it seemed likely that Brighterlite would become profitable by operating in the country's main corridor, in January 2017 the Department of Rural Development began distributing home solar systems for close to nothing under the country's National Electrification Plan. The World Bank assisted the government with its plan for electrification, heavily subsidizing the solar systems to make them so affordable. Despite meeting its sales targets, Brighterlite was forced to exit Myanmar in 2017 as it could not compete with the NEP systems. This example shows how noble actions can crowd out commercially viable businesses that are sustainable and provide jobs. Foreign aid organizations should strive to avoid programs that divert business from commercial activity.[88] [89]

---

88   Jørund Buen, January 8, 2018, "The Danger of Subsidized Solar: How government and Donors Unwittingly Hobbled Our Business," Next Billion, https://nextbillion.net/danger-subsidized-solar-government-donors-unwittingly-hobbled-business/.

89   Arianna Freschi, November 27, 2017, "Trialling mobile-enabled PAYG energy in a greenfield market: lessons from Brighterlite in Myanmar," Global System for Mobile Communications, https://bit.ly/2MBlNeO.

Resource Transfers and Banking

Access to finance, including access to credit, and functional credit markets are key to both lifting people out of poverty and providing them with jobs. When the private sector is unable to serve poor and low-income clients because of perceived risk, costs, or lack of information, governments sometimes provide access to finance directly. While these policies can have the intended effect of connecting the poor to credit and cash, they often distort markets and can sometimes do more harm than good. This section will examine experiences with direct cash transfers, mandatory savings accounts, and priority sector lending.

Direct Transfers/CCT

Direct cash transfers from governments to citizens are growing in importance for poverty alleviation. Conditional cash transfers are direct transfers of money from the government to low-income citizens, provided they meet certain targets such as sending their children to school. This policy instrument began in Latin America, but many developing countries have since adopted direct transfer programs. Brazil has made progress in poverty alleviation through its Bolsa Familia conditional cash transfer program. Bolsa Familia gives a monthly payment of $22 with the proviso that the household's children must get regular checkups and attend school. The handout is quite small but still serves to keep many children in school at a time when their parents might prefer to have them work. The dual benefit of families receiving more income plus incentives for parents to ensure their children attend school and get checkups has resulted in Bolsa Familia lifting 36 million Brazilians out of extreme poverty.[90]

Some governments use CCT programs to encourage adults to join the private sector. Uganda has developed a program that gives money to young adults to use for vocational training and starting a business. The Youth Opportunities Program helped to dispel notions that the poor will misuse cash transfers (by spending it on alcohol or other nonproductive products). Upon receiving funding from the government, these young people spent their allocated $382 to

---

90   Jennifer Guay, June 10, 2017, "Brazil lifts millions out of poverty with direct cash transfer scheme," *Apolitical*, https://apolitical.co/solution_article/brazil-lifts-millions-poverty-direct-cash-transfer-scheme/.

improve their earnings by 38 percent and elevated their hours worked per week by 17 percent. [91]

While CCTs can be an impactful short-term solution to alleviating poverty, they are not long-term drivers of economic growth. The programs are not self-funding or self-sustaining, and so without other policies for labor market integration, dependents may not have access to jobs and will come to rely on the program in perpetuity. These programs are also subject to the whims of the government, so in times of budget crises or simply changing administrations, programs can be scaled back or eliminated.

Mandatory Savings Accounts

Because it can be difficult for low-income people to get access to bank accounts, some governments require banks to offer accounts that cater to the bottom of the pyramid in an attempt to force financial inclusion. South Africa undertook a noteworthy experiment in this area with Mzansi accounts. The pro-inclusion Financial Sector Charter in South Africa dictated that the largest banks create a product that would not charge a monthly fee and eschew the administrative requirements that typically prevented low-income people from opening bank accounts. While 6 million accounts were opened between 2004 and 2008, 30 percent were inactive or closed by the end of 2008, and even more had very low usage and balances. The transaction costs for the banks exceeded the benefits for them, and so they did not market this product. Ultimately, the Mzansi project has been deemed a failure. Most banks offered Mzansi accounts only because the Financial Sector Charter forced them to. These accounts never made financial sense and could not become part of their core business. It was an expensive exercise performed out of social obligation, not a viable strategy for providing services for low-income people. [92] [93]

---

91   Christopher Blattman, Natrhan Fiala, and Sebastian Martinez, 2013, "Generating Skilled Self-Employment In Developing Countries: Experimental Evidence from Uganda," Oxford University Press, https://chrisblattman.com/documents/research/2014.GeneratingSkilledEmployment.QJE.pdf.

92   Maya Fisher-French, February 17, 2012, "Mzansi accounts reach dead end," *Mail & Guardian*, https://mg.co.za/article/2012-02-17-mzansi-accounts-reach-dead-end.

93   Michel Hanouch, October 19, 2012, "Beyond the Mzansi Account in South Africa – Targeting Usage," CGAP, http://www.cgap.org/blog/beyond-mzansi-account-south-africa-%E2%80%93-targeting-usage.

Priority Sector Lending

Some governments opt to mandate that banks lend a certain amount of capital to SMEs, specified sectors, or minority-owned enterprises, often at a lower interest rate than market loans. This practice is known as priority sector lending or directed lending. South Africa's first Financial Sector Charter stipulated that banks must lend $400 million to black-owned or -run SMEs between 2004 and 2008, which banks easily surpassed. A renewed agreement that ran between 2012 and 2017 set the new lending target at $4 billion for priority sectors, including black-owned SMEs, black farmers, affordable housing, and infrastructure. The amount of these loans is small compared to the amount lent to SMEs more generally, but governments can implement and expand similar lending policies in years to come to encourage banks and SMEs to become stronger partners.[94]

Many Asian governments also use priority sector lending to direct investment. India, Indonesia, the Philippines, and Thailand dictate that banks must direct a certain percentage (7.5 percent, 20 percent, 8 percent, and 6 percent, respectively) of their loans to SMEs. While this policy guarantees that these sectors will have access to a certain amount of credit, priority lending can pose a problem for the lenders. For example, while SMEs comprised just 9 percent of loans for banks in India between 2001 and 2013, they made up 15.1 percent of Indian banks' nonperforming loans. This disparity indicates that priority lending can force banks to make risky loans they may not make without the policy.[95] [96]

India has a rich history with priority sector lending to small businesses and other socially excluded sectors. However, this mandate can cause a variety of problems for banks. These loans are not as profitable, carry a relatively high risk of non-repayment, and impose high transaction costs. Both public and private banks have struggled to meet lending targets. One solution to help banks become compliant and allow priority sectors to gain better access to credit is the

---

94 Stephen Timm, July 20, 2015, "Is forcing banks to lend to SMEs a good idea?," *Ventureburn*, http://ventureburn.com/2015/07/forcing-banks-to-lend-to-smes-a-good-idea/.

95 Sean Creehan, September 2014, "Asia Focus: Priority Sector Lending in Asia," Federal Reserve Bank of San Francisco, https://www.frbsf.org/banking/files/Asia-Focus-Priority-Sector-Lending-in-Asia-September-2014.pdf.

96 Reserve Bank of India, April 18, 2018, "Frequently Asked Questions," Reserve Bank of India, https://www.rbi.org.in/scripts/FAQView.aspx?Id=87.

introduction of lending certificates, which will allow banks that have surpassed their targets to sell the debt to their peers that are lagging.[97][98]

In addition to the high rate of nonperforming loans for priority sectors, there is still some question about whether loan mandates truly increase access to finance. The relationship between large and rigidly structured banks (the lenders) and the rural or small-scale farmers or entrepreneurs (the borrowers) can be difficult to navigate, often leaving the former unable to meet the demand from the latter. Thus, banks do not meet their targets and pay a price fiscally, and people operating in the priority sector are not necessarily better off.[99]

Interest Rate Ceilings

Malaysia and Vietnam dictate that banks cannot charge 2 percent more than their country's deposit rate to certain sectors—in the case of these two countries, agriculture and SMEs.[100] This interest rate ceiling is another policy tool governments use to try to direct credit to underserved segments. The use of interest rate ceilings as a policy instrument has been on the decline for several years in most developed parts of the world, but they remain a popular policy in many countries, particularly in Sub-Saharan Africa and LAC (see Figure 5.10).[101]

---

97   Stephen Timm, July 20, 2015, "Is forcing banks to lend to SMEs a good idea?," Ventureburn, http://ventureburn.com/2015/07/forcing-banks-to-lend-to-smes-a-good-idea/.

98   Shilpa Rani and Diksha Garg, January, 2015, "Priority Sector Lending: Trends, Issues and Strategies," *International Journal of Management and Social Sciences Research*, http://www.irjcjournals.org/ijmssr/Jan2015/4.pdf.

99   Muneesh Kumar, Neetika Batra, and Florent Deisting, 2016, "Determinants of Priority Sector Lending: Evidence From Bank Lendiong Patterns in India," *International Journal of Business and Finance Research*, ftp://ftp.repec.org/opt/ReDIF/RePEc/ibf/ijbfre/ijbfr-v10n2-2016/IJBFR-V10N2-2016-5.pdf.

100 Sean Creehan, September 2014, "Asia Focus: Priority Sector Lending in Asia," Federal Reserve Bank of San Francisco, https://www.frbsf.org/banking/files/Asia-Focus-Priority-Sector-Lending-in-Asia-September-2014.pdf.

101 Samuel Munzele Maimbo and Claudia Alejandra Henriquez Gallegos, October 2014, "Interest Rate Caps Around the World: Still Popular, but a Blunt Instrument" World Bank, http://bit.ly/2MH1dJg.

Figure 5.10: Interest Rate Ceilings by Region

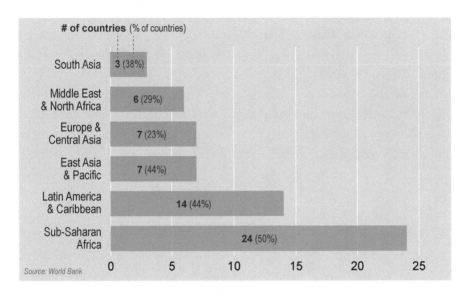

Source: World Bank

Banks and central governments implement interest rate ceilings to protect consumers from usurious interest rates, make markets more accessible for the poor, fix a perceived market failure, or promote lending to a specific sector.[102] However, these ceilings can actually pose a barrier to financial inclusion. Because operating expenses are the primary driver of the interest rates banks charge, when a government or central bank implements a cap on how much lenders can charge for capital, the lender may be unable to cover its costs and thus not make the loan. [103] A mismatch between risk and return may also occur, and the bank will exit the market, leaving low-income borrowers to turn to riskier, more expensive informal means.

In Nicaragua, the application of a rate ceiling reduced microlending and forced some microfinance institutions to leave rural areas due to borrowers being too expensive and risky to lend to at the ceiling rate. Lending growth from MFIs in Nicaragua dropped from 30 percent a year to only 2 percent a year

---

102 Ibid.

103 Djibril Maguette Mbengue, November 11, 2013, "The Worrying Trend of Interest Rate Caps in Africa," CGAP, http://www.cgap.org/blog/worrying-trend-interest-rate-caps-africa.

after the imposition of the cap.[104] Additionally, to circumvent the cap, some of these organizations imposed fees and charges to help cover their costs.[105] These fees reverse the intent of the regulator by causing prices to be essentially the same for consumers while reducing transparency. The good news is that due to reduced lending, the door is open for nonbank entities to step in and meet the unmet demand for credit.[106]

Credit bureaus, stable capital markets, and robust competition policies that put downward pressure on interest rates are among the best policy options for countries to use in lieu of interest rate ceilings. These policies are conducive to information transparency and competitive financial markets.[107]

TVET

Policies that provide training and job matching opportunities are essential to help people access jobs and escape poverty by earning higher incomes. Figure 5.11 details the key features of successful labor market intervention programs.[108]

104 The Economist, September 8, 2016, "Interest-rate caps: Cut-price logic," *The Economist*, https://www.economist.com/news/leaders/21706528-bad-idea-remarkably-common-cut-price-logic.

105 Samuel Munzele Maimbo and Claudia Alejandra Henriquez Gallegos, October 2014, "Interest Rate Caps around the World: Still Popular, but a Blunt Instrument" World Bank, http://bit.ly/2MH1dJg.

106 Danielle Piskadlo, May 21, 2018, "The Politics (and Varied Experiences) of Interest Rate Caps," Center for Financial Inclusion, Client Focus, Governance, Policy, https://cfi-blog.org/2018/05/21/the-politics-and-varied-experiences-of-interest-rate-caps/.

107 Liliana Rojas-Suarez and Lucía Pacheco, "An Index of Regulatory Practices for Financial Inclusion in Latin America: Enablers, Promoters, and Preventers," Center for Global Development, https://www.cgdev.org/sites/default/files/index-regulatory-practices-financial-inclusion-latin-america_0.pdf.

108 Jochen Kluve, March, 2016, "A review of the effectiveness of Active Labour Market Programmes with a focus on Latin America and the Caribbean," International Labour Office, https://bit.ly/2taxAbT.

Figure 5.11: Key Features and Effects of Active Labor Market Programs

	Job Search Assistance	Training	Private-Sector Incentives	Public Employment
Government cost	Low	Medium/High	High	High
Short-run effect	Positive	Negative	Positive	Positive
Long-run effect (best case)	Small Positive	Large Positive	Small Positive	Zero-to-small Positive
Long-run effect (worst case)	Small Negative	Small Negative	Negative	Large Negative
Displacement	Medium	Low	High	High

Source: International Labor Organization

In Latin America, these kinds of programs are well known and frequently referred to as Jóvenes programs. Each country in the region has had mixed results (naturally), but Jovenes programs generally tend to have a modestly positive effect on employment outcomes for young people, especially young women. These programs typically fall into one of two categories: "work first" job search assistance (which usually has a more beneficial impact in the short run) or "human capital" training (which builds skills first and typically has a more beneficial medium- and long-run impact). Most modern programs are of the latter variety.[109] Governments will need to continue to use these programs, as youth unemployment remains a concern, and bear in mind that the data show that positive results can take years to materialize. Also, assistance in finding a job must complement job training to help young people succeed.[110] Youth unemployment stymies economic growth. Without jobs, young people are susceptible to living in poverty and may turn to violent or illegal means to do so. Box 5.8 looks at how skills training programs may help fight terrorism.

---

109 Ibid.

110 Ibid.

Box 5.8: TVET and Preventing Terrorism

In response to the growing influence of terrorist groups influencing the Punjab region of Pakistan, the government of Punjab leveraged foreign aid to launch the Punjab Skills Development Fund in 2011.[111] The goal of the program is to train 145,000 young people from low-income groups by leaning on the private sector to provide effective skills training to increase incomes. This program has been largely successful; it exceeded its training target by 2016, and nearly 38 percent of the trainees were women. This project also used the private sector to provide monitoring and evaluation services. As a result, the Punjab government learned that in-village training, rather than simply providing information or encouraging young people to come to their courses, has a much stronger impact on employment outcomes. This insight has led to improvements in the design of the program, particularly in those aspects pertaining to program access for women.[112]

Vocational education is one of the more complicated aspects of the education system in any country. Government-run TVET systems do not always provide perfect results. Often, governments provide training that is antiquated, or they equip people for jobs that do not exist. In developing countries, this is an especially difficult problem because the hopes and expectations of trainees too often go unmet. The Ghanaian government has run a TVET program for many years to try to address Ghana's chronic youth unemployment problem, but surveys regarding the effectiveness of the program yield less than desirable results. Many program participants were still unemployed after completing the program, citing a lack of technical expertise on the part of teachers, large class sizes that hinder education, a mismatch between skills taught and job market needs, and—perhaps most important—a sense that the jobs they are being trained for simply do not exist in the marketplace.[113] Supply-side TVET programs may not be enough if openings on the demand side are not there.

---

111 Government of Punjab, March 2015, "Punjab Skills Development Sector Plan 2018: Providing skills for productive employment," Planning & Development Department, http://bit.ly/2KvIvb2.

112 Ijaz Nabi, January 11, 2017, "Course correcting learning in the provision of skills," Brookings Institute, https://www.brookings.edu/blog/future-development/2017/01/11/course-correcting-learning-in-the-provision-of-skills/.

113 Adam Dasmani, 2011, "Challenges facing technical institute graduates in practical skills acquisition in the Upper East Region of Ghana," *Asia-Pacific Journal of Cooperative Education*, https://www.ijwil.org/files/APJCE_12_2_67_77.pdf.

Demand concerns hinder youth employment prospects as well. Countries such as Tanzania form partnerships with the private sector to create integrated pipelines that match unemployed youth to employers that are hiring. Through the Youth Economic Empowerment Activity, the Tanzanian government works with local organizations to create curricula and education tailored to specific job openings. This program also serves to create long-term soft skills such as leadership and health education.[114] In this way, the government avoids wasting time and money training people for jobs that are not there.

Public Works and Employment-Intensive Investment

As of 2015, 94 developing countries were using public works programs, which are particularly prevalent in post-conflict countries. Countries have introduced public works programs primarily to protect their citizens from events such as natural disasters, economic crises, or seasonal labor demand shortfalls. Governments might also establish public works programs to shield households from temporary job losses, fight poverty, generate long-term employment, or help poor people gain temporary employment. Post-conflict countries are well suited for public works programs, as combatants need new livelihoods if they are to maintain peace.[115] Another way governments use employment-intensive investment, with mixed results, is in the wake of natural disasters.

A typical labor-intensive public works program might look like a project implemented in Comoros in 2017. The Comoros Social Safety Net Project provided short-term jobs building sustainable infrastructure, such as water terraces, to 4,000 villagers for a three-year period. Villagers in the bottom income bracket were targeted for this project.[116] Figure 5.12 provides more descriptions of typical public works programs.[117]

---

114 DAI, 2017, "Tanzania – Advancing Youth Activity," DAI, https://www.dai.com/our-work/projects/tanzania-youth-economic-empowerment-activity.

115 Carlo del Ninno, Kalanidhi Subbarao and Annamaria Milazzo, May, 2009, "How to Make Public Works Work: A Review of the Experiences," World Bank, http://bit.ly/2z8QEwE.

116 World Bank, March, 2017, "Public Works and Welfare: A Randomized Control Trial of a Cash for Work Program Targeting the Poor in a Lower Income Country," Impact Evaluation to Development Impact.

117 Kalandihi Subbarao, Carlo del Ninno, Colin Andrews, and Claudia Rodríguez-Alas, 2013, "Public Works as a Safety Net: Design, Evidence, and Implementation," World Bank, https://bit.ly/2MDGy9T.

Figure 5.12: Projects Initiated Under Public Works Programs

Projects and Activities	
Economic Infrastructure	**Transport sector:** rural/urban roads, feeder roads, pedestrian bridges, bus stops, sidewalks, culverts **Marketplace:** public marketplaces including facilities, parking lots, latrines, helipads, market yards **Gas/electricity:** installation of electricity cables, gas network systems **Irrigation:** irrigation canals and drains
Sanitary Infrastructure	**Drinking water:** community water supply networks **Storm water:** erosion control structures, infiltration pits **Wastewater & solid waste:** sewage networks, latrines, disposal pits
Social Infrastructure	**Health:** community clinics, hospitals **Education:** schools, libraries, training facilities **Recreation:** theaters, parks, playgrounds **Other services:** public showers, housing
Land Management	**Land productivity/availability/restoration:** gully control, hillside terracing, harmful tree removal **Soil & water:** afforestation, tree nurseries, flood control structures **Fodder availability:** vegetative fencing and fodder belts, fodder seed collection
Social Services	Operation of child care centers and nursing homes, training, garbage collection, street sweeping

Source: World Bank

Public works programs for low-income individuals can provide a social safety net in the wake of crises, resulting in good short-term outcomes, but they are not typically long-term solutions. Studies show that the lowest-income people benefit the most in the medium term. However, there can be long-term payoffs in the form of infrastructure, which has an important impact on access to basic services such as education, health, clean water, sanitation, and transportation. These permanent installations continue to pay dividends in terms of access to jobs, improved health, and other economic activities.[118] See Box 5.9 for a case study about a public works program in post-war Sierra Leone.

Box 5.9: Sierra Leone's Cash for Work Program

The Government of Sierra Leone launched the Cash for Work public works program in 2010. This program targeted vulnerable youth between the ages of 15 and 35. Program participants, once selected, were entitled to a minimum of 50 days or maximum of 75 days of work for $1.80 a day. A notable feature of this design is that this rate is below the market rate, which discouraged non-vulnerable citizens from registering. The projects that participants could work on were mostly agricultural, such as building roads that made farms more accessible or toiling in rice farms.

Another key feature of this program is the rotation of participants. Because there were more poor people seeking jobs than available spots, the program sought to give the most opportunity to the most people, which necessarily came at the expense of depth. This feature was especially relevant in the wake of the civil war, as any job at all could make a huge difference in a post-combatant's life.

Overall, the program seems to be a success. Participant household incomes rose by 29 percent, and these households spent most of this income on goods such as medicine, clothing, health care, and durable goods. Additionally, this program increased the likelihood of participants using their income to start a business. The use of income to boost long-term earnings signals that public works programs do have the potential to sustain long-term economic growth through better jobs for participants.[119]

The Playing Field in Practice—the Case of Rwanda

Rwanda has taken a comprehensive approach to policy reform. Implementing policies that leveled the playing field, shrewdly tilting the playing field in a

---

118 International Labor Organization, 2018, "Employment Intensive Investment Programme: Creating jobs through public investment," International Labor Organization, http://bit.ly/2KDvtHz.

119 Nina Rosas and Shwetlena Sabarwal, February, 2016, "Can You Work it?: Evidence on the Productive Potential of Public Works from a Youth Employment Program in Sierra Leone," World Bank, http://documents.worldbank.org/curated/en/105531467996736274/pdf/WPS7580.pdf.

desired direction, and even occasionally taking control of key economic functions allowed Rwanda to jump more than 100 places in the World Bank's
Doing Business rankings between 2008 and 2015. The Government of Rwanda
released a set of national priorities in 2000 dubbed "Vision 2020," aimed at
transforming Rwanda into a middle-income country by the year 2020. Rwanda
is on its way to delivering on this vision, more than tripling GDP from $216
person in 2000 to $703 per person in 2016.[120]

Figure 5.13 shows the policy tools that the Rwandan government used to
grow its economy and make Rwanda a better place to do business.

Figure 5.13: Strategies for Growth in Rwanda

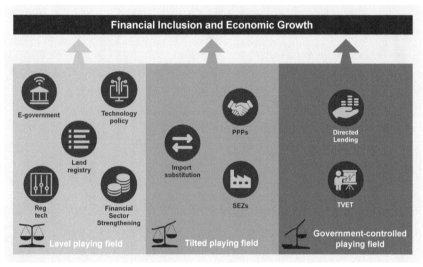

Source: Author

---

120 Google Public Data, April 24, 2018, "GDP per capita (current US$) 1960-2016," http://bit.
ly/2lNOklo.

Rwanda implemented several level playing field reforms. As of 2017, the World Bank ranked Rwanda as tied for sixth in the world in the ease of getting credit because of its government-approved rating agencies, strong legal protections for borrowers and lenders, and policies that have developed the capital and stock markets, such as making trade data electronically available and training exchange staff.[121] Rwanda also increased its e-government presence with the web-based Land Administration Information System, which made registering property easy and transparent.[122]

Another part of Vision 2020 is the adoption of regtech. The National Bank of Rwanda (BNR) collaborated with Sunoida Solutions to develop a database that automates and streamlines reporting processes to improve the quality and frequency of reported data. BNR is now much more effective at monitoring the entities it supervises in real time.[123]

The government pursued a number of other pro-financial inclusion policies. For instance, Rwanda has a high percentage of the population (87 percent) with the requisite IDs to open an account, encourages MNOs to provide interoperability of all payment services, and legitimizes savings and credit cooperatives via a National Bank of Rwanda rating system.[124] [125] These policies culminated in a financial inclusion rate of 89 percent in 2016, within striking distance of Vision 2020's goal of 90 percent. Most of this growth is due to the increase in usage of nonbank formal accounts, such as mobile money (see Figure 5.14 for details).[126]

---

121 John Schellhase, Eric Bundugu and Jim Woodsome, December, 2015, "Capital Markets in Rwanda: Assessment and Aspirations," Milken Institute, https://bit.ly/2K13Ftl.

122 World Bank, 2017, "Doing Business 2017: Equal Opportunity for All – Economy Profile 2017: Rwanda," World Bank, https://bit.ly/2ta61Qe.

123 Wilson Kamali and Douglas Randall, August 6, 2017, "Leveraging 'suptech' for financial inclusion in Rwanda," World Bank, http://blogs.worldbank.org/psd/leveraging-suptech-financial-inclusion-rwanda.

124 Jonathan Argent, James A. Hanson and Maria Paula Gomez, August, 2013, "The Regulation of Mobile Money in Rwanda," International Growth Centre, https://www.theigc.org/wp-content/uploads/2014/09/Argent-Et-Al-2013-Working-Paper.pdf.

125 National Bank of Rwanda, July, 2014, "Rwanda's Financial Inclusion Success Story: Umurenge SACCOs," Alliance for Financial Inclusion, https://www.microfinancegateway.org/library/rwanda%E2%80%99s-financial-inclusion-success-story-umurenge-saccos.

126 Access to Finance Rwanda, March 2016, "FinScope Rwanda 2016," National Institute of Statistics of Rwanda, http://www.statistics.gov.rw/publication/finscope-rwanda-2016.

Figure 5.14: Change in Financial Inclusion Between 2008 and 2016

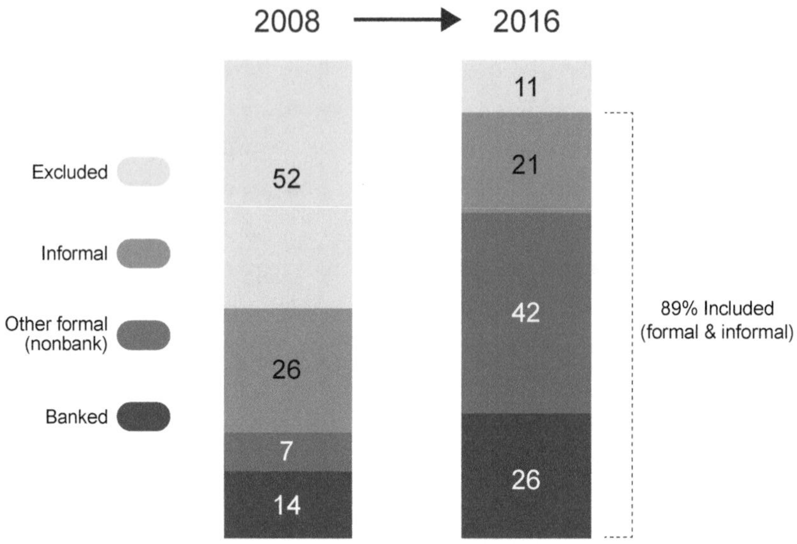

2008 ⟶ 2016

Excluded

Informal

Other formal
(nonbank)

Banked

2008	2016
52	11
	21
26	42
7	26
14	

89% Included
(formal & informal)

Sources: FinScope, Access to Finance Rwanda

As shown in Box 5.10, in addition to these "bread and butter" reforms, the Rwandan government has also made it easier to innovate.

Box 5.10: Regulating Innovation

Rwanda became the first country to adopt performance standards for drones in 2018. The Rwandan government collaborated with a Silicon Valley startup to deliver blood to patients in need via drone, allowing the government to collect data on the blood supply chain and drone use.[127] The regulatory infrastructure Rwanda established to foster the deployment of new technologies could serve as a model for other countries that wish to take the lead in the innovation space. Tackling emerging challenges and implementing policy that can keep up with technology is essential for countries to break from the status quo and provide opportunities for new entrepreneurs to lift themselves out of poverty in emerging fields.

---

127 Catherine Cheney, January 23, 2018, "Rwanda could become a model for drone regulation," Devex, https://bit.ly/2yoI8sX.

Using the tilted playing field approach, Rwanda's industrial policy, called the Domestic Market Recapturing Strategy (DMRS), aimed to reduce its trade deficit. The DMRS covers a variety of industries and works in concert with a private sector development plan to achieve the goal of a robust domestic market through limiting imports and bolstering exports.[128] The DMRS plans to strengthen industries in which Rwanda has some advantage but that require investment, such as pharmaceuticals and building materials. Tariffs have been levied on goods that pose a threat to fledgling industries in Rwanda, and the government is working to strengthen its domestic procurement processes—essentially adopting the motto "Buy Rwandan." In this way, the DMRS aims to create long-term structural change as a complement to increases in domestic consumption and a better environment for domestic industries to operate.[129]

In 2013, Rwanda opened the Kigali Special Economic Zone, an industrial park with light and heavy manufacturing. The KSEZ offers easier export regulations compared to the rest of the country and is equipped with good roads and reliable electricity and internet, which make it an attractive place to establish a factory. Between 2013 and 2016, the KSEZ grew from 4.5 to 10 percent of all Rwandan exports, and the government continues to expand the KSEZ to bolster sales of domestic firms.[130]

Finally, Rwanda also controlled the playing field as part of its strategy. The agricultural sector accounts for 70 percent of employment and has seen year-over-year growth of 5 percent between 2010 and 2018. Many banks perceive enterprises and entrepreneurs in this sector as risky, and thus credit can be difficult to obtain. In response, the government mandated that banks loan a certain amount of their book to agricultural enterprises, making agriculture a priority sector. This policy has had mixed success, as priority lending exposes banks to default risk, but Rwanda also saw increased output of rice, beans, wheat, cassa-

---

128 Ibid.

129 Republic of Rwanda, March, 2015, "Domestic Market Recapturing Strategy," Ministry of Trade and Industry, http://www.minicom.gov.rw/fileadmin/minicom_publications/Planning_documents/Domestic_Market_Recapturing_Strategy.pdf.

130 Victor Steenbergen and Beata Javorcik, August, 2017, "Analysing the impact of the Kigali Special Economic Zone on firm behavior," International Growth Center, https://www.theigc.org/wp-content/uploads/2017/10/Steenbergen-and-Javorcik-working-paper-2017_1.pdf.

va, bananas, and other crops in the intervening years.[131] [132]

Like many countries, Rwanda struggles with youth unemployment. In response, the country launched several TVET programs in 2008. The Akilah Institute for women, funded by the Ministry of Education, has taken an intelligent approach that has resulted in a 95 percent placement rate for graduates. This program's design is demand-driven, and Akilah collaborates with private sector partners to develop its curriculum to ensure that training matches the needs of employers.[133] The lessons learned from former TVET programs were implemented well here; instead of training women for jobs that did not exist in the market, Akilah's curriculum uses its private sector connection to ensure the jobs for which they provide training are relevant.

---

131 Eugène Kwibuka, April 4, 2018, "Agric will remain a priority sector – Premier," *The New Times*, http://www.newtimes.co.rw/rwanda/agric-will-remain-priority-sector-premier.

132 Jaya Shukla, March 21, 2017, "Embrace priority sector lending to enhance financing of the agric sector," *The New Times*, http://www.newtimes.co.rw/section/read/209279.

133 Junior Sabena Mutabazi, September 3, 2014, "TVET schooling the answer to youth unemployment?," *The New Times*, http://www.newtimes.co.rw/section/read/380.

Chapter 6. Funders

The funding landscape for economic inclusion has undergone significant change in the past few years. And that trend will have to continue if we intend to meet global development aspirations. In considering the costs entailed in meeting the Sustainable Development Goals (SDGs), for example, analysts have identified a funding gap of $2.5 trillion per year. Governments and traditional bilateral and multilateral donors cannot close this gap on their own—private funding is required. At the same time, new business models and a recognition of the economic opportunities at the base of the pyramid have increasingly attracted commercial funders such as institutional investors and private wealth managers. The UN identified opportunities worth $12 trillion by 2030 in four SDG-related sectors: agriculture and land use, health and well-being, renewable energy, and education.

This chapter examines the range of funders of initiatives that expand access to services and/or jobs for poor and low-income people in emerging and frontier economies. Most funding focuses on the micro level (SMEs, social entrepreneurs). However, some funders pursue opportunities to support the meso level (ecosystem enablers such as digital platforms, business support services, and jobs platforms) or the macro level (legal and regulatory framework reform). Individuals, public donors, philanthropic foundations, venture capital funds, pension funds, and other entities are all getting involved. They use a variety of instruments, from grants to loans to equity, and increasingly seek innovative funding mechanisms that "blend" concessional with commercial funds to crowd in the latter.

A key distinction between funders is whether they take an "impact first" versus a "returns first" approach. As shown in Figure 6.1, concessional funders such as government agencies offering overseas development assistance (ODA) and philanthropic foundations tend to emphasize impact, whereas commercial funders (such as banks, private equity and venture capital funds, or corporations) tend to look for returns first. Impact-oriented investors, including public sector development finance institutions or other self-proclaimed impact investors, attempt to optimize both impact and returns.

Figure 6.1: The Funding Map: Impact and Returns

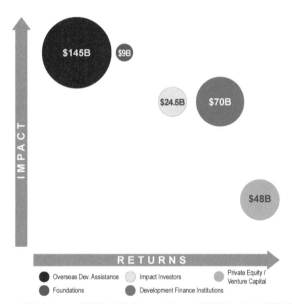

Sources: OECD aid at a glance, OECD Private Philanthropy for Development, OPIC 2017 Annual Report, EDFI, IFC 2016 Highlights Brochure, AfDB Annual Report 2016, ADB Development Effectiveness Report 2017, EIB 2016 Activity Report, The EIB Outside the EU 2016 Report, IDB Invest Annual Report 2016, EBRD Annual Report 2016, 2018 GIIN Annual Impact Investor Survey, EMPEA Industry Statistics Year-end 2017

When considering the overall flow of funds into emerging and frontier markets, however, commercial sources and remittances dwarf traditional donor flows. As Figure 6.2 indicates, in 1990, donor flows were the largest portion of foreign financial flows. Today, foreign direct investments (FDI) and remittances (transfers of money from migrants to people in their home countries) have become much more important sources of capital.

Figure 6.2: The Evolution of Capital Flows to Developing Countries

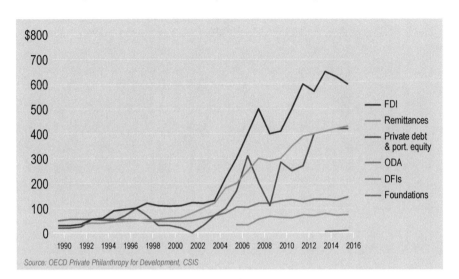

Remittances are an important source of capitals flows to developing countries. They offer a number of benefits when it comes to investing in companies that offer services and jobs to poor and low-income people. Box 6.1 highlights the impact of remittances on economic growth in recipient countries.

Box 6.1: The Impact of Remittances

Remittances are an enormous source of multinational financial flows, equal to more than three times the amount of ODA annually at around $450 billion in 2017.[1, 2] For some countries, particularly those with small populations and large diasporas, such as Nepal and Armenia, remittances can be one-fifth or more of GDP. The amount of global remittances nearly tripled between 2000 and 2015, reflecting the increased number of emigrants, with an increasing share of money flowing from middle-income country to middle-income country, as opposed to the (previously) typical pattern of high-income country to low-income country.

1   Drew DeSilver, January 29, 2018, "Remittances from abroad are major economic assets for some developing countries," Pew Research Center, http://www.pewresearch.org/fact-tank/2018/01/29/remittances-from-abroad-are-major-economic-assets-for-some-developing-countries/.

2   World Bank, October 3, 2017, "Remittances to Recover Modestly after Two Years of Decline," World Bank, http://www.worldbank.org/en/news/press-release/2017/10/03/remittances-to-recover-modestly-after-two-years-of-decline.

Remittances have numerous microeconomic and macroeconomic effects. Evidence suggests that remittances help families meet their basic needs (the primary purpose of remittances), and they can also reduce GDP volatility by stabilizing consumer demand.[3] Often, however, remittances can have adverse effects, such as when recipients work less, knowing that they have a regular remittance income. Dependence on remittances can be problematic as well. When remittances dwindle, as they did in the wake of the 2008 financial crisis, the negative economic effects are amplified.[4] Additionally, recipients do not always spend their remittances on investment or education, instead spending on shelter and basic consumption. The good news is that while remittances may not be strong drivers of economic growth, their contribution to stabilizing household income and contributing to macroeconomic stability means that remittances help create the conditions for economic growth.[5]

While this chapter focuses on international funding flows, it is important to remember that domestic resource mobilization (DRM) and strengthening local capital markets are also critical. International sources should complement and encourage, rather than displace, domestic funding. DRM refers to countries raising and spending their own funds to provide services for their citizens and is another important component of building inclusive economies. DRM can come from higher taxes or more sophisticated tax collection systems, both of which provide governments with more revenue. ODA to bolster DRM efforts can produce enormous returns. For example, through $6 million in USAID support and a matching amount from the government, El Salvador enjoyed a $1.5 billion increase in revenue between 2005 and 2010 without raising the tax rate.[6] Excitement about the potential of DRM led to an agreement among donor countries called the Addis Tax Initiative, which aims to double ODA for DRM from $223.7 million in 2015 to $447.5 million by 2020.

Local capital markets are an important source of funding as well. Nigeria's Sovereign Wealth Fund's portfolio grew to $2 billion in 2017 and has helped

3   Connel Fullenkamp, February 10, 2015, "Do remittances drive economic growth?," World Economic Forum, https://www.weforum.org/agenda/2015/02/do-remittances-drive-economic-growth/.

4   Ralph Chami, Dalia Hakura, and Peter Montiel, April 2009, "Remittances: An Automatic Output Stabilizer," International Monetary Fund, http://www.imf.org/external/pubs/ft/wp/2009/wp0991.pdf.

5   Connel Fullenkamp, February 10, 2015, "Do remittances drive economic growth?," World Economic Forum, https://www.weforum.org/agenda/2015/02/do-remittances-drive-economic-growth/.

6   USAID, 2014, "Domestic Resource Mobilzation: El Salvador Tax Reform Boosts Revenues for Development," USAID, https://bit.ly/2cQ2ErI.

the economy revitalize fertilizer plants, boosting the local agriculture industry.[7] South Africa's Industrial Development Corporation is an important source of finance for multiple sectors and countries across Sub-Saharan Africa and often takes on investments that others deem too risky.[8] Issuing bonds in local currencies is another important step toward developing local capital markets; private sector financing for infrastructure could be double its current level if countries could fully harness the potential of their markets.[9] The African Local Currency Bond Fund was set up to allow African companies to issue bonds in local currency, which will crowd in local investors.[10]

Funding Instruments

Funders across the impact/return spectrum use various financial instruments to nurture inclusive economic opportunities. Five of the most commonly deployed instruments are grants, technical assistance, guarantees, loans, and equity investments.

Grants entail funding to an entity (a government or a business, for example) to achieve a certain outcome. A grant can be provided as cash or in-kind. Grants are not expected to be paid back; however, some are conditional upon the grantee fulfilling all commitments laid down by the grant-making organization. They can be structured in a variety of ways to fit specific development objectives. For example, the Alliance for a Green Revolution in Africa (AGRA) is an organization dedicated to increasing the productivity of small farms in Africa. AGRA operates in 16 countries, working on diverse projects from creating high-yield crops and improving women's participation in agriculture to

---

7   Nariman Gizitdinov and David Malngha Doya, September 7, 2017, "Nigerian Soveraign Welath Fund Grows to $2 Billion, CEO Says," *Bloomberg*, https://www.bloomberg.com/news/articles/2017-09-06/nigerian-sovereign-wealth-fund-now-at-2-billion-ceo-orji-says.

8   IDC website, "Africa Unit," https://www.idc.co.za/africa-strategic-business-unit.html.

9   Ceyla Pazarbasioglu, May 2, 2017, "Developing local capital markets to fund domestic long-term financing needs," World Bank, http://blogs.worldbank.org/voices/developing-local-capital-markets-fund-domestic-long-term-financing-needs.

10   Olvia Ndong-Obiang, May 2, 2018, "African Development Bank approves ZAR 140-million loan to support African Local Currency Bond Fund," African Development Bank Group, https://www.afdb.org/en/news-and-events/african-development-bank-approves-zar-140-million-loan-to-support-african-local-currency-bond-fund-17813/.

protecting biodiversity. AGRA takes many risks in its projects, but through $380 million in grants from the Bill & Melinda Gates Foundation, it has been able to scale its work.[11]

Technical Assistance refers to specialized services (training, consulting, twinning, and so forth) provided to an organization to improve that organization's capacity, commitment, or connections in a given domain. For example, through the Technical Assistance Program for Rural Microfinance (PATMIR), DAI has helped tens of thousands of Mexicans access basic financial services. By improving mediation between banks and regulators, building government capacity, promoting technology and low-cost delivery channels, and other methods, PATMIR's experts enabled rural bank cooperatives to recruit 180,000 new customers and provided credit products to 23,000 members.[12]

Guarantees, such as USAID's Development Credit Authority (DCA), mitigate the risk of lenders or investors so they will not lose all their capital in the case of borrower default. They typically cover assets such as loans, leases, and lines of credit to businesses or sectors that are underserved and carry a higher risk. Through more than 500 guarantees, the DCA has unlocked as much as $4.8 billion in private financing for 245,000 entrepreneurs around the world. For example, USAID developed a DCA with The First Microfinance Bank—Afghanistan, through which the bank was able to provide $6 million in collateral-free loans to entrepreneurial Afghans.[13]

Loans are funds lent to entities with the expectation of repayment with interest. An example of a loan for development is the Asian Development Bank's (ADB) $200 million Green Transport Finance project in China. In 2017, ADB loaned the sum to Minsheng Financial Leasing Co. to support its new "green"

---

11   Bill & Melinda Gates Foundation, "Alliance For A Green Revolution," Bill & Melinda Gates *Foundation*, https://www.gatesfoundation.org/How-We-Work/Resources/Grantee-Profiles/Grantee-Profile-Alliance-for-a-Green-Revolution-in-Africa-AGRA.

12   DAI, 2016, "Mexico – Technical assistance Perogram for Rural Microfinance (PATMIR)," DAI, https://www.dai.com/our-work/projects/mexico-technical-assistance-program-rural-microfinance-patmir.

13   USAID Development Credit Authority, September 30, 2017, "Empowering Returning Afghans and Internally Displaced Persons," USAID, https://usaid-credit.exposure.co/empowering-returning-afghans-and-internally-displaced-persons.

business model. With the loan, Minsheng could acquire green vehicles, such as buses and passenger cars, and batteries and charging stations for them. All vehicles must meet Euro V-equivalent emission standards and either are energy efficient or run on cleaner fuel such as compressed natural gas. ADB expects to be repaid with interest in up to eight years.[14]

Equity-based instruments entail the exchange of money for an ownership stake in a company. They are often accompanied by technical and business support on the part of the investor to improve business operations. The IFC invests $500 million each year in private equity funds and is often the first equity investor in new infrastructure projects. Impact investors often use equity to lead their investments. In 2017, Acumen invested $13.5 million in PEG, a Ghana-based company that loans solar home systems to off-grid low-income people in West Africa. PEG offers customers an innovative pay-as-you-go system that allows them to own the solar systems in 12 months and saves them more than a thousand dollars compared to what they would otherwise spend on batteries, kerosene, and other traditional energy sources. With its equity investment, Acumen became a partner in the business and will profit only when (or if) it can sell its shares to a larger investor or an acquiring company.[15]

Funders often specialize in one or two instruments, although there are important exceptions. Concessional funders concentrate mainly on grants but often have more flexibility and opportunity to use a range of instruments to meet the needs of partners. Impact-oriented investors deploy a variety of instruments, but loans and equity dominate in this space. Commercial players tend to be more constrained in terms of the instruments they can use, often limited to commercially priced loans or equity investments. Figure 6.3 illustrates the relative intensity of instrument use among concessional, impact-oriented, and commercial funders.

14   Huang Biao, August 7, 2017, "China, People's Republic of: Green Transport Finance." Asian Development Bank, https://www.adb.org/projects/51056-001/main#project-overview.

15   Acumen, "Our Portfolio: Our Companies Create Sustainable Solutions That Enable the Poor to Transform Their Lives," Acumen, https://acumen.org/companies/.

Figure 6.3: Funders and Instruments

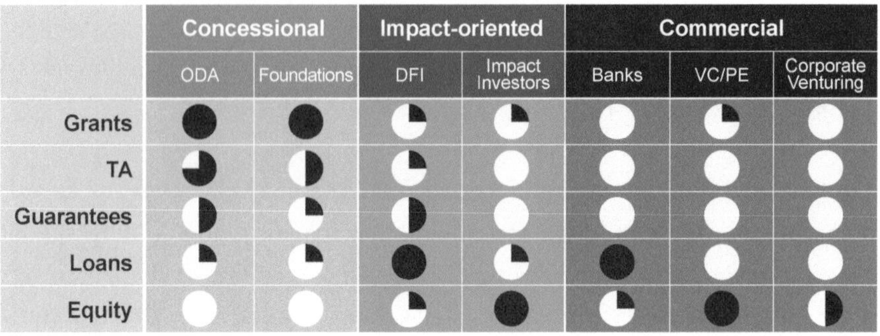

	Concessional		Impact-oriented		Commercial		
	ODA	Foundations	DFI	Impact Investors	Banks	VC/PE	Corporate Venturing
Grants	●	●	◖	◕	○	◖	○
TA	◕	◗	◖	○	○	○	○
Guarantees	◗	◕	◗	○	○	○	○
Loans	◖	◕	●	◕	●	○	○
Equity	○	○	◖	●	◖	●	◗

Source: Author

Complementing these five basic instruments, recent innovations either make funding more streamlined or combine features of different instruments to ensure that funding is relevant and effective for the situation at hand. For instance, crowdfunding enables everyday citizens to participate in funding social or environmental solutions in developing countries. Kiva recently surpassed $1 billion in loans to 2.5 million people in developing countries.[16] Crowdfunding platforms are proliferating at a rapid pace, with more than 1,250 in use today.[17] Most are quite small, but the market is estimated to reach $93 billion by 2025.[18] Figure 6.4 provides examples of other innovations.

---

16   Elizabeth MacBride, July 31, 2017, "Kiva Hits $1B In Loans, $25 At A Time. Here's One Of The Hidden Keys To Its success," *Forbes*, https://www.forbes.com/sites/elizabethmacbride/2017/07/31/can-online-lenders-assess-your-character-to-a-certain-extent-yes/#7a8c28cb1b2f.

17   CrowdExpert, February 29, 2016, "Crowdfunding Industry Statistics 2015-2016" CrowdExpert. http://crowdexpert.com/crowdfunding-industry-statistics/.

18   Richard Swart, December, 2013, "World Bank: Crowdfunding Investment Market to Hit $93 Billion by 2025," *Media Shift*, http://mediashift.org/2013/12/world-bank-crowdfunding-investment-market-to-hit-93-billion-by-2025/.

Figure 6.4: Financial Tool Innovations

Innovation	Description	Example
Returnable Capital	Grant mechanisms with some expectation that the grantee will return the base grant funding provided (or a portion of it) after achieving certain outcomes. Returnable capital is typically given to a private sector entity that intends to make a profit in time but requires the grant to jumpstart activities.	The DFID Impact Fund, a returnable capital mechanism launched in 2012 and managed by CDC, scaled up to $400 million in 2016 and committed $64 million as of the end of 2016. By that time, 26 portfolio companies had reached 3.7 million low-income people. The Impact Fund's use of "patient capital" provided these low-income people greater access to affordable goods and services, generating more income opportunities.
Impact Bonds	Also referred to as social impact bonds or development impact bonds, these are part of a family of outcomes-based financing. They are not really bonds in the capital markets sense, but rather mechanisms where investors provide upfront funding to service providers, and are repaid by governments or non-profits if and when certain outcomes are achieved. Most impact bonds are implemented in developed countries and cover such issues as jail recidivism and school attendance. Some impact bonds are beginning to appear in emerging and frontier markets as well.	The Peru Sustainable Cocoa and Coffee Production development impact bond helps the Ashaninka people in the Kemito Ene producers' association improve farming techniques and restore some of their land. A private U.S. foundation was the investor, the Rainforest Foundation UK was the service provider, and the Common Fund for Commodities was the NGO that would repay the investor. The success metrics were (A) members improving their yield to 600kg per hectare, and (B) an increased supply of coffee and cocoa to the association by its members. The return to the investor was capped at 25 percent. Kemito Ene had met most of its targets by the project's completion.
Challenge Funds	A challenge fund is a competitive financing facility that uses public sector or private foundation funds for market-based solutions that focus on impact. Donors use challenge fund mechanisms to invest in promising sectors or businesses to develop, expand, and/or scale new solutions. Challenge funds aim to minimize their financial contribution to projects while maximizing social return, making the project less risky while maintaining commercial viability.	The Africa Enterprise Challenge Fund (AECF) was launched at the World Economic Forum Africa in 2008 to respond to the need for an Africa-based fund that would support African business, particularly in finance and agriculture. The AECF began with start-up capital from the U.K. and Dutch Governments, CGAP, and the International Fund for Agricultural Development (IFAD). Since its inception, the AECF has mobilized more than $310 million, leveraging more than $580 million in matching capital from other funders and improving the lives of more than 13 million people in 2016 alone through jobs and increased household incomes. AECF has supported 257 companies in 24 countries in Sub-Saharan Africa across 40 value chains in agribusiness and renewable energy.
Revenue Participation	Revenue participation models allow investors to receive a share of future revenue instead of an equity stake or interest income from traditional debt instruments. These instruments, sometimes called revenue-based loans or royalty-based loans, reduce investor risk and align incentives between the entrepreneur and the investor.	Business Partners Limited charges clients a base interest rate plus a royalty for its loans. For SMEs, such loans are more viable from a cash flow perspective than bank loans, since they are tied to projected sales growth. They are also more attractive than equity investments as entrepreneurs do not have to give up ownership control. From the investors' perspective, these instruments offer a steady flow of repayments, which help overcome exit barriers that typically present problems for private equity investors. Business Partners Limited has provided 70,688 investments to SMEs since its founding in 1981.
Program Related Investments (PRI)	A PRI is a loan, equity investment, or guarantee given by a foundation to support its mission but without demanding a high (or sometimes any) rate of return. Unlike grants, however, a PRI implies that the foundation will get its initial investment back. This makes PRIs an attractive option in developing countries, as philanthropic organizations can recoup the money they lend, and the recipient does not have to pay high interest rates.	The Bill and Melinda Gates Foundation made a PRI to bKash, a mobile money service operated by BRAC Bank. The BMGF identified bKash as a strong, albeit slightly risky and certainly capital-intensive model for providing mobile finance to Bangladeshis who were financially excluded. bKash needed $15 million to become commercially viable; a loan would burden the young bKash with too much debt, but a grant for the full $15 million would have been too risky. In 2009, the BMGF offered a $4 million grant and an $11 million equity investment to help scale up operations. This PRI paid off, as bKash was serving 4.2 million customers by July of 2013, and was able to purchase the BMGF's equity back by early 2014.

Sources: DFID, Center for Universal Education at Brookings, ODI, AECF, USAID, Business Partners, Forbes, Stanford Social Innovation Review

Concessional Funders

Responding to insecure, undeveloped, or simply unknown market conditions, concessional funders play an important role in supporting inclusive economies. Generally, concessional funders can be broken down into two types: development agencies (ODA) and private foundations. They do not typically seek financial returns, although they may support financial returns for partner institutions (such as banks) or drive investment into sectors with potential returns (such as small and growing businesses). Concessional funders can also engage in activities that produce financial returns or at a minimum get their initial capital back, but in these cases the returns are redirected to further promote development objectives rather than reward shareholders or boost government coffers.

Because they do not require financial returns on their "investments," these funders enjoy a great deal of flexibility. They can support organizations and initiatives at all levels of the economic system—micro, meso, or macro. A concessional funder can provide a seed grant to a social enterprise that helps it get started and raise more capital, for example, or offer technical advice to a firm trying to partner with the government to establish a private credit bureau. Finally, this type of funder can support governments interested in improving the business environment by reforming the processes for starting a business. These are just a few illustrative examples of the range of opportunities these funders seek to support.

Concessional funders—both ODA and private foundations—leverage many of the same tools to address the myriad private sector development challenges facing their countries of focus. Concessional funders usually employ grants, guarantees, and technical assistance. Concessional funders also use the tools in stages and/or in combination to create bespoke financing and investment solutions. For instance, they may start with grants and then move to reimbursable instruments or combine technical assistance with funding. Box 6.2 describes how USAID's East Africa Trade and Investment Hub combines different approaches to expand economic opportunities in that region.

Box 6.2: The East Africa Trade and Investment Hub

The USAID East Africa Trade and Investment Hub, implemented by DAI, works with East African and US businesses to bring investment to the East African private sector. The Hub aims to increase the competitiveness and economic diversification of businesses in the region. The Hub, through partnerships with advisors Cross Boundary and Open Capital Advisors, offers advisory services and facilitates regional relationship support to reduce the risk, cost, and deal time of transactions. The Hub channels investment to the region's agribusiness sector in collaboration with the impact investor, GroFin, and provides customized technical assistance and training to government agencies.[19, 20] During its first four years, the Hub facilitated more than $100 million in private sector investment, multiplying its technical assistance investment of around $4 million by a factor of 25.[21]

Notwithstanding their commonalities, many differences exist between ODA and foundations and within their respective ranks (for instance, in terms of size, geographic focus, development focus areas, and partnerships). ODA, which is tied to national spending budgets, far outweighs spending by private foundations on development initiatives, which rely on the contributions of individuals or corporations. Foundations also often support initiatives within their own countries alongside programs in emerging and frontier markets.

ODA spending has a higher concentration in least-developed country contexts, which is likely the result of the on-the-ground infrastructure (USAID Missions, World Bank Representative Offices, DFID Offices, and so on) they can leverage as well as the geopolitical imperatives of responding to pandemic threats, emergencies such as earthquakes and hurricanes, and conflict. Philanthropic organizations, by contrast, typically have a more limited geographic scope, especially those based outside of Europe or the United States (such as the Tata Foundation in India), which tend to focus on domestic initiatives.

19 USAID, February, 2018, "USAID East Africa Trade and Investment Hub," USAID, https://bit.ly/2ttG3XQ.

20 DAI, June 30, 2016, "USAID East Africa Trade and Investment Hub: Quarterly Report," DAI, https://dai0.sharepoint.com/Projects/ProjectDocuments/EATIH%20FY2016%20Q3_DEC.pdf.

21 Brigit Helms and Kanini Mutooni, Summer 2018, "Blended Finance in Action - How USAID Leveraged $100 Million in East Africa," DAI, http://dai-global-developments.com/articles/blended-finance-in-actionhow-usaid-leveraged-100-million-in-east-africa/.

ODA focuses a greater proportion of funding on economic infrastructure and services and productive sectors than foundations (30 percent and 15 percent, respectively, as shown in Figure 6.5). However, social infrastructure and service initiatives—which include education, WASH, transport, and production—represent the largest percentage of overall spend by each institutional type.

Figure 6.5: Funding Priorities for ODA and Foundations

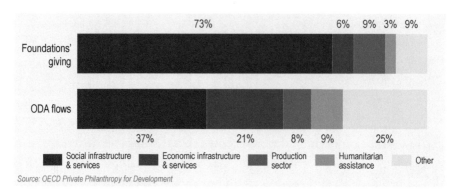

Official Development Assistance

Bilateral and multilateral development agencies—such as USAID, DFID, the Swedish International Development Cooperation Agency (SIDA), the European Commission (EC), and the UN—spend public resources to pursue development objectives through projects in recipient countries. The funding includes support for economic growth, private sector development, and enabling environment programs. Figure 6.6 shows the major providers of ODA.

Figure 6.6: Principal Sources of ODA

Institution	Year Established	Geographic Focus	Sector Focus	Sample Impact Data
USAID	1961 United States	Global	Health, education, environment, democracy, economic growth	Saved 3 million lives every year through immunization, enabled 50 million couples to use family planning, helped build a $50 billion market for private power.
DFID	1997 United Kingdom	Global, with focus on Sub-Saharan Africa, MENA	Poverty reduction	Helped 7.1 million children get an education, reached 26.3 million children under 5 with nutrition programs, helped 27.2 million people better access WASH services.
GIZ	1974 Germany	Global	Environment, civil society, agriculture	Enabled 162,000 refugees to attend school, protected forest areas equal to 17 times Germany's entire forest area, enabled 34 million people to vote through GIZ-supported programs.
JICA	2003 Japan	Global, with focus on Africa, Asia, Oceania, Latin America	Education, health, water resources, governance	Trained 80,000 teachers annually in math and science education, distributed 8 million copies of the maternal and child health handbook, provided 59 million people with access to safe water between 2002 and 2016.
AFD	1998 France	Global, with focus on former French colonies, Africa	Infrastructure, production, energy	Installed 665 MW of renewable energy, provided 730,000 small farms with better irrigation systems and training, made 636,000 homes safer.
European Union	1959	Africa, the Caribbean, Oceania	Achieving the SDGs	Provided legal aid to 923,000 people, benefitted 314,000 through conflict prevention and peacebuilding.
UNDP	1965	Global	Sustainable development, governance, climate and disaster resilience	Registered 170 million new voters across 52 countries, vaccinated 2 million people with antiretroviral treatment, provided legal aid to more than 2 million women.

Sources: USAID, DFID Annual Report, GIZ Integrated Company Report 2016, JICA 2017 Annual Report, AFD 2016 Annual Report, European Development Fund 2017 Annual Report, UNDP Results at a Glance

Meeting the SDGs requires significant funding, which is motivating ODA agencies to undertake process and tool innovation to better engage and leverage private sector resources. See Box 6.3 about how USAID uses blended finance to close the SDG financing gap.

Box 6.3: Mobilizing Private Capital for Development

ODA providers are testing various approaches to crowd in more commercial finance. Here are three examples:

Insurance for microfinance customers in disaster-prone areas of Africa: Microfinance can help households become more resilient to natural disasters and can also help households after disasters. However, microfinance institutions rarely operate in disaster-prone areas due to the higher risk. The ARC Company, with support from KfW and DFID, has stepped in to provide insurance through a risk-pooling model for African Union states, which reduces the cost of providing disaster relief funds for these governments. This finance instrument has connected 2.1 million people in Malawi, Mauritania, Niger, and Senegal with insurance instruments, and the ARC Company aims to channel an additional $500 million in climate change adaptation investment by 2020.

De-risking water investments in the Philippines: Water service providers in the Philippines could not rely on government financing for their projects, and the private sector did not lend to them at affordable rates due to their lack of familiarity with this sector. The Philippines Water Revolving Fund (PWRF) was set up to mix concessional funding with private capital investment in WASH services in the Philippines. DAI worked to facilitate a relationship between banks that saw water services as a risky investment and water utilities that were starved for investment. DAI allowed USAID, with help from the Japan International Cooperation Agency, to share some of the banks' investment risk through default guarantees, which made these utilities a much better investment prospect. The PWRF has unlocked $234 million in investment for water service providers. This has resulted in the construction of bulk water projects, newer sewage systems, and cleaner water infrastructure across the Philippines, allowing 6 million people to enjoy new or improved water services.

Blended Finance: Launched in 2017, the INVEST project is a USAID program designed to use blended finance to solve development challenges. The blended finance tools used by INVEST can make high-impact projects commercially viable, improve USAID's procurement process, allow USAID to work with new partners, and help direct more private investment toward enterprise-led development outcomes.[22]

---

22   USAID, May, 2018, "INVEST Project: Mobilizing Private Investment for Development Overview Presentation." USAID.

Figure 6.7 shows the principal sources of ODA, the top recipients of ODA, and the sectoral breakdown of ODA dollars based on average amounts for 2015 and 2016.[23]

Figure 6.7: ODA Snapshot

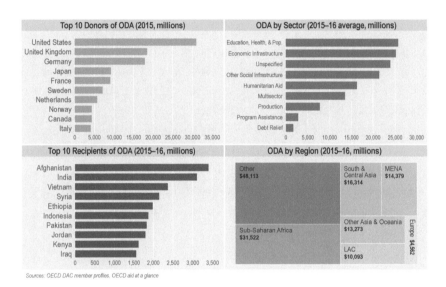

Sources: OECD DAC member profiles, OECD aid at a glance

ODA equaled $131.5 billion in 2015, increased to $145 billion in 2016, and then increased slightly, by 1.1 percent, to $146.6 billion in 2017.[24] ODA dollars support a wide range of projects, including health, education, and infrastructure. A significant portion of ODA, 11.7 percent in 2016, contributes to helping refugees and other forms of humanitarian aid.[25][26] A higher percentage of ODA is being directed toward humanitarian aid each year; while ODA grew by 41 percent between 2007 and 2016, humanitarian assistance as a percentage of ODA has grown by 124 percent.[27]

23   Tableau, December 2, 2017, "Gross bilateral ODA, 2015-2016 average," Organisation for Economic Co-operation and Development, https://tabsoft.co/2KD3E28.

24   Rob Tew, April 20, 2018, "Aid spending by DAC donors in 2017," Development Initiatives, http://devinit.org/post/oda-data-2017/.

25   Ibid.

26   Organisation for Economic Co-operation and Development Data, "ODA by sector," Organisation for Economic Co-Operation and Development, https://data.oecd.org/oda/oda-by-sector.htm.

27   Angus Urquhart and Luminita Tuchel, 2018, "Global Humanitarian Assistance Report 2018," *Development Initiatives*, http://devinit.org/wp-content/uploads/2018/06/GHA-Report-2018.pdf.

ODA is particularly well suited to finance Global Public Goods (GPGs). GPGs include clean air, climate change mitigation, disease prevention, and other endeavors that solve problems that afflict many (or all) countries. Estimates vary on how much of ODA goes toward GPG initiatives, ranging from 2 to 10 percent; some development experts agree that donors spend too much of their funds on politically motivated country specific projects and not enough on GPGs.[28] [29] Institutions like the World Bank are under pressure to use their resources to develop more cross-border initiatives. Projects like the Pandemic Emergency Facility, which acts as an insurance policy of sorts against communicable disease outbreak, are key to cross-border development.[30]

The top providers of ODA are the United States and Western Europe, with Japan as the principal Asian donor. While Western nations have historically been the leading providers of ODA, other countries are increasingly active in this space, with China, the United Arab Emirates, and Turkey particularly notable. Figure 6.8 shows the flows from middle-income bilateral donors.

---

28   Nancy Birdsall and Anna Diofasi, May 18, 2015, "Global Public Goods for Development: How Much and What For," Center for Global Development, https://www.cgdev.org/publication/global-public-goods-development-how-much-and-what.

29   Duncan Knox, July 13, 2016, "Measuring aid to global public goods (GPGs)," Development Initiatives, http://devinit.org/post/measuring-aid-to-global-public-goods-gpgs/.

30   Jeff Tyson, May 23, 2016, "Inside the World Bank's Pandemic Emergency Facility," Devex, https://www.devex.com/news/inside-the-world-bank-s-pandemic-emergency-facility-88195.

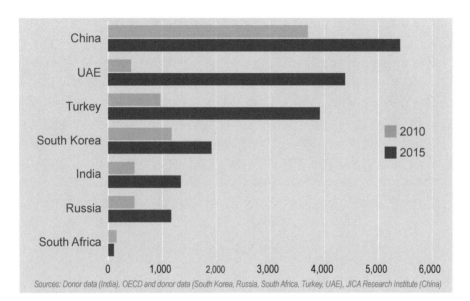

Figure 6.8: Aid Flows from Emerging Bilateral Donors, 2010 vs. 2015

Foreign aid from emerging markets increased by $2.7 billion between 2010 and 2015, reflecting a 47 percent increase. These countries are also looking farther afield and not giving only to their geographical neighbors, as the case typically has been. India is shifting some its focus from South Asia to Africa, and China is aggressively pursuing infrastructure projects, such as railways, roads, and ports, that will connect China with Western Asia and parts of Africa.[31] Box 6.4 describes the important case of China's Belt and Road Action Plan.

---

31 Devex, "Emerging Donors 2.0," Devex, https://pgs.devex.com/emerging-donors-report/.

> ## Box 6.4: New Sources of ODA
>
> China is the largest provider of ODA outside of the Development Assistance Committee. Since 2005, China's foreign aid donations have grown at a rate of 21.8 percent annually. China directs the majority of its aid to African countries, primarily for infrastructure projects.[32] However, China's ODA is by no means limited to the African continent. A $900 billion initiative, the Belt and Road Action Plan, aims to connect China with trading partners in Western and Central Asia, Europe, and the Middle East. It will make land and sea infrastructure investments to boost its domestic economy while also helping the countries affected by the Plan. One of the largest infrastructure projects in history, it could have an impact on 65 percent of the world's population.[33]
>
> The geopolitical implications of this project are complex, but they signal Chinese money and ambition will increasingly shape investment and trade relationships in the future.

Private Foundations

Private philanthropic flows for development originate from foundations' own sources, notably endowments; donations from companies and individuals (including high net worth individuals and crowdfunding); and income from royalties, investments (including government securities), dividends, lotteries, and similar.[34] Massive increases in global wealth and significant changes in viewpoints and policies regarding the role of private foundations have led to a significant increase in the number of philanthropies, in their assets under their management, and in the proliferation of philanthropies beyond the United States and Europe. The Gates-Buffett Giving Pledge, which encourages the world's wealthiest people to donate most of their wealth to philanthropy, has gone a long way to promote philanthropic activities among the world's largest wealth-holders. Figure 6.9 shows some of the major philanthropic foundations that fund development.

---

32   Junyi Zhang, July 19, 2016, "Order from Chaos: Chinese foreign assistance, explained," Brookings Institute, https://www.brookings.edu/blog/order-from-chaos/2016/07/19/chinese-foreign-assistance-explained/.

33   Anne Bruce-Lockhart, June 26, 2017, "China;s $900 billion New Silk Road. What you need to know," World Economic Forum, https://www.weforum.org/agenda/2017/06/china-new-silk-road-explainer/.

34   Organisation for Economic Co-operation and Development, March 23, 2018, "Private Philanthropy for Development," Organisation for Economic Co-operation and Development, https://read.oecd-ilibrary.org/development/private-philanthropy-for-development_9789264085190-en#page39.

Figure 6.9: Selected Private Foundations

Institution	Year Established	Geographic Focus	Sector Focus	Sample Impact Data
Bill & Melinda Gates Foundation	2000	Africa, China, India, MENA	Polio/other vaccine delivery, infectious disease control, ag. development, education, family planning	Afforded 7.3 million people access to HIV treatment, helped to nearly eradicate guinea worm disease, vaccinated 500 million children.
Children's Investment Fund Foundation	2002	Global, with focus on Africa, India	Family health, HIV/AIDS, stunting, malnutrition, neglected tropical diseases, other issues affecting children	Treated 110 million children suffering from parasitic worms in India, Ethiopia, and Kenya; saved 203,000 Nigerian children from starving.
Dutch Postcode Lottery	1989	Global, with focus on Africa	Environment, wildlife, youth development	Donated more than $400 million to 112 charities in 2017.
MasterCard Foundation	2006	Global, with focus on Africa	Financial inclusion, education, youth livelihoods	Provided employment opportunities for 15,000 Moroccan youth and devised a program that provided secondary education opportunities for 5,000 Kenyan students.
Bloomberg Philanthropies	2006	Global	Environment, public health, art, education, government innovation	Invested $702 million in nearly 480 cities across 120 countries in 2017.
Slim Foundation	1986	Mexico, Latin America	Education, health, employment, infrastructure, economic development	Created Acceso Latino, a website designed to help Latinos succeed in the United States through increased access to economic opportunities, English lessons, and skills training; benefitted 46,178 women and their children through investment in primary care hospitals in Mexico.
Tata Trusts	1932	India	Health care, education, WASH, general poverty relief	Provided 3,000 villages with safe drinking water; plans to provide internet access to 1,000 villages, primarily to empower women.

Sources: BMGF, CIFF, Novamedia, Bloomberg Philanthropies 2018 Annual Report, Carlos Slim Foundation, Tata Trusts Annual Report 2016–2017

Philanthropic giving for development initiatives is largely concentrated in a few large foundations and regions. Twenty foundations provided 81 percent of total philanthropic giving in developing countries from 2013 to 2015, mainly foundations in America and Europe.[35] The Bill and Melinda Gates Foundation outweighs all other philanthropic donor giving. Figure 6.10 shows the principal philanthropic donors, the top beneficiaries of foundation giving, and the sectoral breakdown of philanthropic dollars, based on estimates from 2015.[36] [37]

---

35   Ibid.

36   Ibid.

37   Organisation for Economic Co-operation and Development, 2018. "Private Philanthropy for Development, 2013-15." Tableau. https://tabsoft.co/2IosTAh.

Figure 6.10: Foundations Snapshot

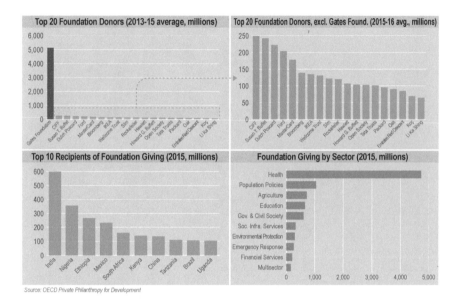

Source: OECD Private Philanthropy for Development

Private foundations spent $9.619 billion on initiatives in the developing world. Countries and regions benefiting from foundations' philanthropic funding are quite diverse—with India and Sub-Saharan countries being the largest targets. Turkey, Mexico, and Brazil are also top beneficiary countries, due in part to the relatively large amount of domestic philanthropy in those countries.

Philanthropic support is highly concentrated in the health sector, even when disregarding Gates Foundation funding, which largely targets global health challenges. Foundations increasingly use new financial tools and are changing their internal processes due to improved technology and access to data. Big data allows foundations to set better benchmarks, measure output more effectively, and better collaborate with each other and external partners.[38] However-er, these innovations are still far from being the norm across organizations that typically employ "traditional philanthropy" (short-term project engagements, for example, or untargeted giving).

---

38 Lucy Bernholz, Edward Skloot and Barry Varela, May, 2010, "Disrupting Philanthropy: Technology and the Future of the Social Sector," Duke University, http://cspcs.sanford.duke.edu/sites/default/files/DisruptingPhil_online_FINAL.pdf.

Recent Trends and Strategies in Concessional Funding

Concessional funders typically use their resources to tackle four overarching challenges that relate to building inclusive economic systems.

In many countries where concessional funders focus, markets are nascent, rebuilding after long periods of neglect or conflict, or moving from command to market-based systems. In these situations, private sector or market-led investments are minimal and funders need to demonstrate the case that market-based solutions can work. Potential investors face very real risks in such markets, including country, borrower, lender, and transaction risks. In addition, there are also many perceived risks borne by potential investors, including local banks. These perceived risks particularly affect underserved sectors such as agriculture or small and medium-sized enterprises. Concessional funders can identify promising markets, assemble more compelling market information, and develop convincing investment strategies. In this way, they create a demonstration effect that gives comfort for other funders to follow suit. Funders can also de-risk investments, helping to draw in more commercially minded investors in high-risk or new and innovative sectors.

Concessional funders often lead other stakeholders in terms of access to best practices and convening power among local, regional, and international stakeholders. For this reason, they are well positioned to encourage and stimulate new approaches and market tools. They can support novel business solutions or startups without a validated product or service and little to no revenue when other sources of startup capital are scarce, insufficient, or inaccessible.

Concessional funders play an important role in providing resources for infrastructure and ecosystem enablers by establishing or expanding market infrastructure at the meso level. These investments are often critical to inclusive market development goals. Hard infrastructure includes bridges, roads, storage, communications and technology networks, water infrastructure, and electricity grids. These kinds of investments can be large and do not always fall within the domain or ability of a single funder or funding type. Soft infrastructure includes ecosystem enablers such as associations or industry groups, credit bureaus, or universal identification providers.

Given their global role and convening power, concessional funders often play an important role in setting standards or providing funding for entities that develop best practices. The multidonor-funded Consultative Group to Assist the Poor (CGAP), for instance, sets standards for financial inclusion, both for institutions and donors. A range of donors support the UN's Better Than Cash Alliance to promote best practices in digital payments. Donors also provide capital for associations or member networks—such as the Global Impact Investing Network (GIIN)—on standards and measurement guidelines for impact investing.

Impact-Oriented Funders

Impact-oriented funders invest not only to generate a monetary return but also to create positive social or environmental benefits. These investors "seek to do good while doing well."[39] This style of investment challenges the notion that charities and nonprofits solve social problems while the private sector generates financial returns on investments. Unlike donors of ODA or philanthropic funders, impact investors demand an explicit financial return but do not necessarily expect government assistance or donations to accomplish goals. Unlike purely commercial investment, projects are expected to generate positive social and/or environmental outcomes.[40] Together, development finance institutions and impact investors form the core of impact-oriented investment.

Development Finance Institutions (DFIs)

DFIs are banks operating in developing and emerging economies that provide financing and other services, such as technical assistance, to the private sector. They engage across a range of sectors, from infrastructure projects and corporate loans to financial support to SMEs. Their funders and shareholders are mainly member governments, but DFIs also source funds from capital markets.

---

39   Paul Brest and Kelly Born, August 14, 2013, "Unpacking the Impact in Impact Investing," *Stanford Social Innovation Review*, https://ssir.org/articles/entry/unpacking_the_impact_in_impact_investing.

40   Jenna Balkus, Maria Luque, and Trent Van Alfen, January, 2014, "The Intersection of Impact Investing and International Development: A Primer," Accelerating Market-Driven Partnerships, https://bit.ly/2tq3iCo.

Most DFIs are either bilateral or multilateral in nature. Other DFIs include national development banks that finance projects or companies in their own countries, such as Brazil's BNDES and the Development Bank of Kenya. Bilateral institutions are established and funded by one country (Germany's DEG Development Bank, for example, and the United States' Overseas Private Investment Corporation [OPIC]), and follow the regional and sectoral priorities of the government in question. Multilateral Development Banks (MDBs), on the other hand, have several countries as shareholders (for example, The World Bank and the African Development Bank) and therefore more diverse board and governance structures.

Some MDBs, such as the World Bank and the Inter-American Development Bank (IDB), have separate DFI entities as part of their larger group of institutions (the International Finance Corporation [IFC] and IDB Invest, respectively, in this case). Others, such as the African Development Bank (AfDB), and the Asian Development Bank (ADB), conduct private sector operations (also often classified as "non-sovereign guaranteed" operations) within their institutions. Box 6.5 discusses the public sector or "sovereign" side of MDBs, much of which is relevant for building inclusive economic systems.

Box 6.5: The Core Business of MDBs

Most of the financial and nonfinancial support provided by MDBs goes to governments, mostly at the federal level. MDBs work with governments on projects in policy reform, infrastructure, health, education, social safety nets, macroeconomic stability, political strengthening (often in fragile states), science and technology, entrepreneurship, and innovation.

MDBs' core business is to provide large loans to federal governments, often accompanied by economic policy prescriptions and support to reforms. One example is the World Bank's $500 million loan to Tunisia in 2013. The Governance, Opportunity, and Jobs Development Policy Project promoted Tunisia's postrevolution economic recovery by offering assistance for much-needed reforms in the areas of the business climate, the financial sector, social services, and government transparency. World Bank economists worked closely with government officials to design and implement those reforms, and funds have been released as the government meets reform targets.[41]

MDBs also finance large public works projects, such as roads and ports, increasingly under public-private partnership frameworks but also under government-only schemes. For example, in early 2018 the Asian Development Bank signed the first $250 million tranche of a $500 million loan with the Government of India to finance the improvement of 12,000 kilometers of roads in five Indian states. Expected to enhance connectivity and improve social and economic conditions for rural communities, the project will generate hundreds of jobs and train 2,000 people on road safety and maintenance practices.[42]

The original argument for DFIs was that they should step in where markets are not working properly, a phenomenon often referred to as market failure. They provide financing (mostly loans) where other investors are not willing or able to operate, especially for projects that take a long time to pay off, rendering the investment risky and difficult to predict, such as ports, roads, power plants, and other large infrastructure projects. Over time, DFIs have diversified their offerings to include mechanisms such as grants, equity, technical assistance, and knowledge development and dissemination. They have also expanded support to almost every sector, from health and education to ICT and financial intermediaries, mostly through private sector transactions directly with companies and banks.

Figure 6.11 presents the basic characteristics of the key DFIs. OPIC's portfolio is the largest of the bilaterals, though investment is certainly not sluggish from its European counterparts. All of these organizations emphasize their commitment to sustainability and civil rights issues, such as gender inclusion. The IFC and the comparatively smaller continental DFIs are investing heavily in energy and infrastructure and funding a plethora of projects that emphasize service delivery.

41　World Bank, November 27, 2012, "World Bank approves $500 million to accelerate Tunisia's economic recovery, pave way for more inclusive growth," World Bank, http://www.worldbank.org/en/news/press-release/2012/11/27/world-bank-approves-fiv-million-accelerate-tunisias-economic-recovery-pave-way-more-inclusive-growth.

42　Asian Development Bank, January 30, 2018, "ADB, India Sign $250 Million Loan to Improve Rural Connectivity in 5 States," Asian Development Bank, https://www.adb.org/news/adb-india-sign-250-million-loan-improve-rural-connectivity-5-states.

Figure 6.11: Principal Development Finance Institutions

	DFI	Year Established	Geographic Focus	Sector Focus	Sample Impact Data
Bilaterals	OPIC	1971, United States	Sub-Saharan Africa, Latin America, Global	Energy, health care, technology, education, other	Supported projects providing education to 100,000 students, supported 105,000 jobs through its lending, and committed one-third of portfolio to conflict-affected regions.
	Commonwealth Development Corporation	1948, United Kingdom	Sub-Saharan Africa, South Asia	Manufacturing, agribusiness, infrastructure, finance, construction	Created 44,000 jobs directly, CDC-backed businesses paid $4.1 billion in local taxes; infrastructure generated 69,000 GWh of energy in 2016.
	DEG (Deutsche Investitions)	1962, Germany	Asia, Latin America, Sub-Saharan Africa, Global	Finance, industry, manufacturing, infrastructure	Plans 1,850 GWh serving 5 million people from 2016 investments; 600,000 MSMEs financed by DEG-supported enterprises.
	FMO	1970, the Netherlands	Africa, Asia, Global	Finance, energy, infrastructure and manufacturing, green energy	Supported 900,000 jobs, avoided 1.6 million tons of greenhouse gas emissions, and served 33 million people with power generation.
Multilaterals	International Finance Corporation	1956	Global	Many	Provided 21 million phone connections in MENA and $8 billion in loans to MSMEs in Sub-Saharan Africa; supplied 3.5 million customers with water in Latin America and the Caribbean.
	African Development Bank	1964	Africa	Transport, water supply and sanitation, finance	Created 630,000 jobs, directly served 16 million farmers, and provided 112,000 hectares of land with access to water management resources.
	Asian Development Bank	1966	Asia	Energy, transport, finance	Through investments made in 2017, will help generate 1,557 MW of capacity through renewable sources, save 738 GWh each year, and avoid 11.8 million tons of GHGs each year.
	EIB	1958	EU countries, some non-EU Europe, Asia, Africa	SMEs, infrastructure, environment, technology	Improved rice irrigation techniques to feed 160,000, saved 51 million journey hours annually from transportation investment, and enrolled 37,100 students in higher education.
	IDB Invest	1959	South America, Central America, the Caribbean	Finance, energy	Benefitted 4.5 million people through access to health care and equipped 300,000 homes with access to sanitation.
	EBRD	1991	Former Soviet bloc	Finance, industry, agribusiness, energy	Reduced industrial emissions by 1.15 million tons of CO2 equivalent each year through investment in sustainable processes, improved travel conditions for 312 million passengers annually, and created 24,512 jobs by improving SMEs.

Sources: OPIC 2017 Annual Report, CDC Annual Report 2016, DEG Annual Report 2016, FMO Annual Report 2017, IFC 2016 Highlights Brochure, AfDB Annual Report 2016, ADB Development Effectiveness Report 2017, EIB 2016 Activity Report, The EIB Outside the EU 2016 Report, IDB Invest Annual Report 2016, EBRD Annual Report 2016

The impact DFIs can have is significant. For instance, the IFC's 2016 operations helped create 305,000 new jobs, supported another 1.1 million jobs (185,000 of which were women-specific occupations), and financed almost 1,000 SMEs. Through its Asset Management Company (AMC), a private equity fund specialized in emerging markets, the IFC has invested almost $6 billion in 95 companies and funds since 2009. An example of an AMC investment is Bandhan Bank in India, which offers financial services to millions of underserved, low-income people. Another example from AMC is the Women Entrepreneurs Debt Fund, which finances thousands of women-owned SMEs in emerging markets.[43]

The CDC Group, the United Kingdom's bilateral DFI, provides private equity, venture capital, debt, and guarantees both directly and through funds and intermediaries, especially in South Asia and Africa. For instance, CDC invested $15 million in Miro, a sustainable timber business that employs about 1,000 people in Sierra Leone and Ghana. Besides helping the company grow and generate jobs, the investment helped Sierra Leone's economy start bouncing back from the Ebola crisis, which had reduced formal employment by 50 percent in the country. Figure 6.12 offers insight into the size, target markets, and sectors where DFIs are investing.

---

43   IFC Asset Management Company, December 31, 2016, "Emerging Markets, established expertise: 2016 Review," International Finance Corporation, https://bit.ly/2IpzhqO.

Figure 6.12: DFI Snapshot

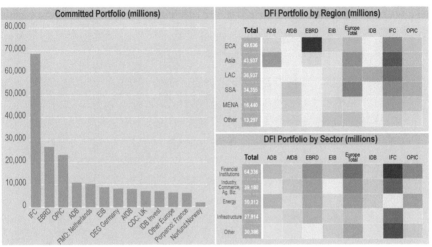

Source: OPIC 2017 Annual Report, EDFI, IFC 2016 Highlights Brochure, AfDB Annual Report 2016, ADB Development Effectiveness Report 2017, EIB 2016 Activity Report, The EIB Outside the EU 2016 Report, IDB Invest Annual Report 2016, EBRD Annual Report 2016

DFIs make new commitments of some $70 billion each year. The largest DFIs are the IFC, the European Bank for Reconstruction and Development (EBRD), and OPIC. Projects cover a range of sectors but are concentrated in financial services, industry, and energy. The EBRD, to take one example, focuses almost exclusively on projects in these three sectors. Its investment goes toward projects such as building wind farms in Georgia, providing finance to female entrepreneurs in Kazakhstan, and financing Romanian aerospace companies.

One of the main trends of the past 15 years has been the growth of private sector operations led by development institutions. Private sector commitments in the outstanding portfolio of DFIs have skyrocketed to more than $200 billion in 2016.[44] IFC investments alone account for nearly $70 billion of this figure, with new commitments of $18 billion in 2016, which means that it remains the largest DFI player. This overall growth in DFI investments reflects a realization that long-term, sustainable economic growth must be led by a dynamic and inclusive private sector. While development banks continue to work

44 Conor M. Savoy, Paddy Carter, and Alberto Lemma, October, 2016, "Development Finance Institutions Come of Age: Development Finance Institutions Come of Age Policy Engagement, Impact, and New Directions," Center for Strategic and International Studies, https://csis-prod.s3.amazonaws.com/s3fs-public/publication/161021_Savoy_DFI_Web_Rev.pdf.

with governments through loans and technical assistance, the parallel effort of energizing the private sector is key to creating jobs and offering essential services complementary to those provided by governments. Large developing countries such as China and India are catching on and raising their profile in the DFI business. Box 6.6 discusses these newer entrants.

Box 6.6: New Banks on the Block

The past few years have witnessed the creation of new DFIs, most notably the Asian Infrastructure Investment Bank (AIIB) and the New Development Bank (NDB). Both emerged in response to two gaps: the need for additional investment, especially in infrastructure, in the target countries; and the need for stronger developing country representation in the global development finance arena.

The AIIB was created in 2016 in an effort led by China to address the urgent need for infrastructure development in Asia. According to some estimates, Asia would require investments of more than $8 trillion over 10 years to close the so-called "infrastructure gap." [45] Pundits also claim that the AIIB is China's response to its so-far relatively small participation in the MDB world (China's influence among the current major MDBs, such as the World Bank, is limited).[46] [47] The AIIB currently has 84 member countries, although China dominates the Board with 29 percent of the voting shares, with India occupying a distant second place with 8 percent. One of the first projects approved by the AIIB was the National Motorway M4—funded by a loan of $100 million out of a total project cost of more than $270 million—which also received funding from the Asian Development Bank. The project connects key areas of Pakistan, facilitating regional trade. As of January 2017, the AIIB has approved nine major projects, investing $1.7 billion.

The leaders of Brazil, Russia, India, China, and South Africa created the NDB in 2014 at the sixth BRICS Summit. Known colloquially as the BRICS Bank, its primary goal is to support infrastructure and sustainable projects in the BRICS countries and complement

---

45   Asian Development Bank, September 30, 2013, "Who Will Pay for Asia's $8 Trillion Infrastructure Gap?," Asian Development Bank, http://www.adb.org/news/infographics/who-will-pay-asias-8-trillion-infrastructure-gap.

46   Daniel C.K Chow, February 25, 2016, "Why China Established the Asia Infrastructure Investment Bank," *Vanderbilt Journal of Transnational Law*, https://www.vanderbilt.edu/jotl/wp-content/uploads/sites/78/7.-Chow_Paginated.pdf.

47   Martin A. Weiss, February 3, 2017, "Asian Infrastructure Investment Bank (AIIB)," Congressional Research Service, https://fas.org/sgp/crs/row/R44754.pdf.

the work of other multilateral and regional financial institutions.[48] NDB is also perceived as a response to an underrepresentation of these developing nations in the more established DFIs. A growing sentiment holds that developing countries need DFIs that not only work for them but are run by them. In the case of NDB, shares and voting powers are equally distributed, with each country owning a 20 percent participation. In 2016, NDB approved more than $1.5 billion of investments in seven projects across all BRICS—six in renewable energy, including wind, solar and hydropower, and one major road in India.[49]

In addition to investments, some DFIs engage in regulatory and policy work, supporting governments to apply international best practices that are pro-poor and pro-market at the same time and improve conditions for private sector development. Moreover, DFIs increasingly appreciate the need for innovation and completely new ways of working with the private sector to maximize their effectiveness. Box 6.7 tells the story of a unique innovation lab set up by the Inter-American Development Bank (IDB) and the Global Innovation Fund (GIF).

Box 6.7: An Innovation Lab within a DFI: IDB's Multilateral Investment Fund (MIF)

Launched in 1993, the MIF serves as the innovation lab of the IDB, supporting, testing, and piloting innovative private sector solutions that promote poverty alleviation and inclusion. It has approved nearly $2 billion for roughly 2,300 projects throughout Latin America and the Caribbean. Since 2016, the MIF has refined its strategic focus around three themes: climate-smart agriculture, inclusive cities, and the knowledge economy. In supporting these three areas, the MIF also ensures that projects maximize their impact on poor and vulnerable populations, climate change, gender, and diversity.

A recent example of a MIF project is the $500,000 NXTP fintech and agtech Startups Acceleration Program. Its goal is to support startups in the fintech and agtech spaces in Argentina, Chile, Colombia, and Uruguay. The expected impact is to accelerate more than 80 startups and finance approximately 60 of them, which in turn will offer products and services to more than 126,000 customers. Another emblematic project is the Sustainable Agriculture & Food Enterprises (SAFE) platform that promotes sustainable coffee and cocoa farming, especially in Mexico, Central America, and the Andean region. The platform brings together donors, NGOs, and private

---

48   New Development Bank, 2017, "History," New Development Bank, https://www.ndb.int/about-us/essence/history/.

49   Raj Desai and James Vreeland, July 17, 2014, "What the new bank of BRICS is all about," *The Washington Post*, https://wapo.st/2lyOgFQ.

sector players such as Starbucks, Keurig, and EComm, all interested in supporting projects with the potential to scale innovative business models in climate-smart value chain improvements, access to finance, and women and youth inclusion. To date, SAFE projects have supported more than 120,000 farmers.[50]

Other investors, such as the Global Innovation Fund (GIF), have also stepped in to provide investment to those at the early stage of enterprise creation. The GIF operates using a venture capital approach and aims to help organizations scale up regardless of their size. It is a hybrid investment fund, funded from both public and private sources, that uses evidence-based investments to improve the lives of the world's poorest. Because their equity investments can be as low as $50,000, the GIF is nimbler than larger funders and can take on riskier projects.[51]

Some are critical of DFIs, arguing that they do not take on as much risk as they should and do not invest enough in very low-income countries. Institutions do not want to jeopardize their sterling credit ratings by directing investment to riskier projects, which are often the projects most critical to meeting the SDGs. The IFC, to take one example, shifted most of its investment from lower-middle income countries in the early 2000s to upper-middle income countries like Turkey and Brazil by 2015.[52]

DFIs and MDBs also could crowd in more private finance through their operations. More than 90 percent of the $59.4 billion in long-term cofinancing mobilized by DFIs and MDBs in low-income and middle-income countries went to the better-off middle-income countries. An even larger amount was mobilized in high-income countries. This reflects the lack of willingness to take risk in the most vulnerable countries and indicates that changes to the current business model may be necessary.[53] One possible strategy is to use special purpose investment vehicles (SPVs) to channel funds to high-risk and early-stage investment opportunities. These SPVs would catalyze capital off the DFIs balance sheets, allowing them to avoid jeopardizing their high credit ratings. Another attractive feature of SPVs is the

---

50   Fomin website, https://www.fomin.org/en-us/.

51   Global Innovation Fund, "Stages of funding," https://globalinnovation.fund/what-we-do/stages-of-funding/.

52   Vijaya Ramachandran and Charles Kenny, January 17, 2018, "The International Finance Corporation's Mission is Facilitating Risky Investments – So Why Is It Taking on Less and Less Risk?" Center for Global Development, https://www.cgdev.org/blog/international-finance-corporation-mission-facilitating-risky-investments-so-why-it-taking.

53   Multilateral Development Banks, June, 2018, Mobilization of Private Finance 2017: By Multilateral Development Banks and Development Finance Institutions, https://www.edfi.eu/wp/wp-content/uploads/2018/06/201806_Mobilization-of-Private-Finance_v2.pdf.

small amount of initial capital needed relative to senior and growth projects. In this way, SPVs could allow MDBs to mobilize capital while expanding their portfolios and help solve the twin problems of a lack of early-stage capital and a lack of capital in the lowest-income countries.[54]

Impact Investors

Impact investors intentionally invest to generate both a financial return and positive social or environmental impact. They seek opportunities that provide, in addition to a social or environmental return, at least a return of capital and preferably a return on capital.[55] They report on and are held accountable for key impact indicators, such as jobs created, GHG reductions generated, and number of poor people benefited. Impact investing is a relatively new phenomenon, the term coined as recently as 2007. This style of investment challenges the traditional notion that only governments, DFIs, and charities can finance initiatives with a social or environmental mission.

Impact investing evolved from the microfinance industry, which paved the way for commercially viable businesses serving poor and low-income people. Other market-based initiatives grew from there, including base-of-the-pyramid businesses, social entrepreneurship, the ICT4Dev movement, and agritech, cleantech, and fintech innovations. Countless exciting new businesses have emerged, all demanding capital to prove concept and achieve scale.

Impact investing responds to the needs of these new business models, which largely remain outside the reach of commercial funders because they cannot accommodate the risks, uncertainties, and sometimes lower financial returns involved. Governments, DFIs, and foundations often lack the agility or appropriate instruments to support these new models. A new class of investor emerged to capitalize on this new source of deal-flow, and now hundreds of impact investing funds operate across the globe. Figure 6.13 shows some of the largest.[56]

---

54   Charles Kenny, Jared Kalow, and Vijaya Ramachandran, January 17, 2018, "Inside the Portfolio of the International Finance Corporation: Does IFC Do Enough in Low-Income Countries?" Center for Global Development, https://www.cgdev.org/publication/inside-portfolio-international-finance-corporation-does-ifc-do-enough-low-income.

55   Sean Greene, September 2014, "A Short Guide to Impact Investing," The Case Foundation, https://bit.ly/2MlFztR.

56   Though Acumen is a 501c-3 and thus not for profit, it is still a significant player in the impact investing space.

Figure 6.13: Largest Impact Investing Fund Managers ($100+ Million in Assets)

Fund Name	Year Established	Geographic Focus	Sector Focus	Sample Impact Data
MicroVest Capital Management	2003	Asia, Africa, South America	Small/medium-sized business development, microfinance, low-income financial services, micro-insurance	MicroVest's Investment in Annapurna Microfinance offers skills training and technical assistance that reaches hundreds of thousands of Indian entrepreneurs through its 264 branches.
Vital Capital Fund	2011	Africa	Diversified	Vital's largest investment, Kora Housing, has provided low-income housing designed by a renowned architect for more than 240,000 Angolans.
LeapFrog Investments	2009	Asia, Africa	Microfinance, low-income financial services, micro-insurance, global health	Investments reach 97 million people globally, allowing them to access insurance, pensions, and health care for the first time.
Accion	1951	Asia, Africa, South America	Media, technology and mobile, small/medium-sized business development, micro-finance, low-income financial services, micro-insurance	Serves India's "missing middle" by providing $20 million in funding to an MSME lender, which in turn provides loans to borrowers who have trouble obtaining them from mainstream institutions. Incubated investment fund Quona provides capital to startups that help with financial inclusion.
Elevar Equity	2006	Asia, Latin America	Education and charter schools, small/medium-sized business development, micro-finance, low-income financial services, micro-insurance	Elevar's investments in 31 early stage companies have in turn served more than 20 million clients, often from underserved populations. An example is their investment in Afluenta, a platform that connects borrowers to reliable lenders, and has originated more than $19 million in loans.
Mirova-Althelia	2014	Asia, Africa, Latin America	Clean technology, natural resources/conservation, sustainable agriculture	Loans enable a partner in Rwanda, Inyenyeri, to leverage finance to provide 150,000 households with a clean cookstove by 2020.
Sarona Asset Management	2010	Asia, Africa, Latin America	Diversified	One of its holdings, Progresemos, has provided more than $40 million in loans to poor, rural Mexican women to help with their businesses.
ProFund	1995	Africa, Latin America	Microfinance	Serviced roughly 900,000 microentrepreneurs and inspired the creation of 20 similar funds.
Acumen Fund	2001	America, East and West Africa, India, Latin America, Pakistan	Poverty alleviation, diversified	Benefited 230 million people through financing innovation and invested in 102 companies that cater to low-income consumers.

Sources: MicroVest Social Impact Report 2017, Vital Capiral Fund Overview, Impact Assets Overviews, Calmeadow, Acumen approach

Impact investing has four core characteristics:

- **Intention** to have a positive social or environmental impact
- Expectation of generating a **financial return**
- **Instruments** that range from a combination of concessional grants to equity investments, loans, and guarantees
- Commitment to **measure and report the performance** and progress of investments. [57]

Impact investing has become widespread, with funds operating out of developed and developing countries (see Box 6.8 for the case of Brazil's Vox Capital). In fact, about half of impact investment is allocated in developed countries, with the other half targeting developing and emerging markets such as Sub-Saharan Africa and Latin America.[58]

Box 6.8: Vox Capital, Brazil's First Impact Investing Fund

Vox Capital is Brazil's first impact investing fund. Founded in 2009, Vox provides early-stage equity funding (acquiring 20 to 35 percent of a company's shares) for businesses offering innovative, market-based, and scalable solutions with the potential to improve lives for the population at the base of the economic pyramid. Vox focuses on financial services, education, and health care. It takes an "ecosystems approach" to supporting investee companies, based on three key bottlenecks that otherwise hinder businesses from reaching the base of the pyramid: distribution channels, access to finance, and market intelligence.[59]

Avante, a financial services company, received a $12 million Series C investment from Vox in 2017. Vox's continuing support has allowed Avante to offer "humanized financial services" to micro- and small entrepreneurs, such as specialized face-to-face and online advice. Avante helps promote entrepreneurship in poor communities and works with

---

57 Global Impact Investing Network, 2018, "What You Need To Know About Impact Investing," Global Impact Investing Network, https://thegiin.org/impact-investing/need-to-know/#s2.

58 Abhilash Mudaliar, Hannah Schiff, Rachel Bass and Hannah Dithrich, May 2017, "Annual Impact Investor Survey 2017," Global Impact Investing Network, https://thegiin.org/assets/GIIN_AnnualImpactInvestorSurvey_2017_Web_Final.pdf.

59 Impact Assessments, "ImpactAssets 50: An Annual Showcase of Impact Investment Fund Managers – Vox Capital," Impact Assesments, http://www.impactassets.org/ia50_new/fund.php?id=a01E000000TzYWrIAN.

microenterprises in shantytowns where traditional banking institutions do not normally go. As of May 2018, Avante had 16 branches covering more than 100 cities across four Brazilian states. It has provided roughly $50 million in microloans, benefiting more than 35,000 families.[60][61]

See Figure 6.14 for key characteristics of the impact investors that responded to a Global Impact Investing Network (GIIN) survey.

Figure 6.14: 2017 Impact Investor Snapshot

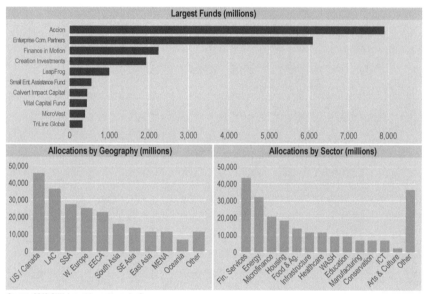

Source: 2018 GIIN Annual Impact Investor Survey

The field has grown substantially in the past decade and has begun to converge on standards and best practices led by industry organizations such as the GIIN. In 2018, GIIN respondents reported doubling their impact investment portfolios, reaching $228.1 billion in assets under management. Investors seem satisfied, too, given that a majority of them said their investments met or exceeded expectations for both impact (97 percent) and financial performance

---

60   Vox Capital website, "Portfolio," Vox Capital, http://www.voxcapital.com.br/new-gallery-1/p6k9hvkzgt3i46rxk0g8mdjto4u3al.

61   Crunchbase, April 6, 2018, "Overview of Vox Capital," *Crunchbase*, https://www.crunchbase.com/organization/vox-capital-llc#section-overview.

(91 percent). Globally, including developed markets, financial services receive most impact investment funding, followed closely by energy projects, with microfinance operations coming in third. Impact investors also invest in sectors such as housing, health care, food security, education, digital inclusion, and youth workforce development.[62]

Recent Trends and Strategies in Impact-Oriented Investment

DFIs face serious hurdles working directly with small companies in client countries, including high transaction costs and lack of staff and know-how to work closely with the businesses. DFIs most frequently support SMEs indirectly by providing financing and technical support to financial intermediaries that in turn offer targeted products and services to SMEs. However, some DFIs support SMEs directly, as well, especially through technical assistance and knowledge dissemination. For example, the G20's SME Finance Forum supports SMEs by bringing together companies, financial institutions, and DFIs to share knowledge, spark innovation, and promote investments.[63]

While serving the private sector, DFIs increasingly apply the concept of additionality as an important investment criterion. Additionality dictates that DFIs should finance only projects that would not otherwise be funded by the private sector on its own, to avoid distorting local markets. This principle means that DFIs should operate under market conditions, offering commercial terms that do not crowd out other financial institutions that cannot compete. From a nonfinancial perspective, additionality means that the DFI would seek to add value through know-how transfer (for example, in terms of environmental and social best practices, risk mitigation, training, and other nonfinancial benefits).

A related concern is that DFIs' private sector operations not only show additionality but also actively crowd in other investors and help develop local financial markets. Private sector loans from by DFIs are often packaged togeth-

---

62 Abhilash Mudaliar, Rachel Bass, Hannah Dithrich, June 2018, " Annual Impact investor Survey 2018," Global Impact Investing Network, https://thegiin.org/assets/2018_GIIN_Annual_Impact_Investor_Survey_webfile.pdf.

63 SME Finance Forum, 2018, "About: What We Do," SME Finance Forum, http://www.smefinanceforum.org/about/what-we-do.

er with resources from other funders, from local commercial banks to equity investors and concessional funds. Figure 6.15 shows the amounts of private sector resources mobilized by DFIs from 2012 to 2015 in the form of guarantees, loans, and equity. Given the importance of this so-called syndication effort—and expectations of the international community regarding it—DFIs frequently report not only the amount of funds they have invested themselves but the total amount of funds they mobilize from others. OPIC, for example, in 2017 made $3.8 billion in investments and mobilized an additional $6.8 billion from other private sources.[64] The Netherlands' FMO, in turn, reported a more modest mobilization, with 1.1 billion out of the 3.1 billion it invested in 2017 being leveraged from other investors.[65]

Figure 6.15: Crowding In Private Sector Investments

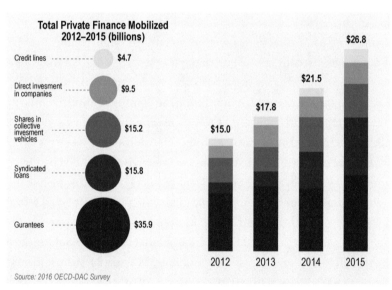

Source: 2016 OECD-DAC Survey

When concessional funding is involved, transactions are often considered as blended finance operations. Blended finance refers to the use of concessional funding to mobilize commercial funding to finance projects that market

---

64   Overseas Private Investment Corporation, February 22, 2018, "Investment As A Stabilizing Force: Highlights From OPIC's 2017 Annual Report," Overseas Private Investment Corporation, https://www. opic.gov/blog/opic-action/investment-stabilizing-force-highlights-opics-2017-annual-report.

65   FMO, March 27, 2018, "Major Development impact and profitability FMO in 2017," FMO, https:// bit.ly/2lw023P.

players would not have entered alone. For example, in a blended deal, a concessional fund, philanthropic institution, or donor agency might offer a grant to a project that mitigates the overall risk of the transaction, stimulating commercial lenders to join in. Box 6.9 gives an example of blended finance.

Box 6.9: Blending Is Trending: The Case of the Clean Technology Fund (CTF)

The Clean Technology Fund is a $5.8 billion fund that operates in partnership with MDBs in developing and emerging markets, providing concessional funding to renewable energy, energy efficiency, and clean transportation projects. It is expected to leverage, or crowd in, another $50 billion in resources from coinvestors. The CTF provides companies, governments, and investors with incentives to scale technologies that will help green their economies by reducing GHGs. CTF projects are tailored to each country's environmental policy and broader development goals.

In Turkey, for example, the European Bank for Reconstruction and Development, the World Bank, and the IFC are channeling $270 million from the CTF to promote investments in renewable energy and energy efficiency alongside local financial intermediaries. Through its first phase, which ended in 2012, $172 million from the CTF helped raise another $1.8 billion from other banks, financing 430 subprojects and saving more than 900,000 tons of carbon dioxide equivalent emissions.

Financing such energy projects in Turkey was virtually unheard of until the CTF and its partner MDBs stepped in. Today, this market not only is booming but such deals can be financed under commercial terms. It can therefore be claimed that blended finance played its role of crowding in local players and building local markets. The next move for the CTF in Turkey is to work with MDBs and local banks to expand Turkey's geothermal capacity from 600 MW to 1 GW by 2030 in deals that are structured in such way that CTF funds are exposed to the highest risks, making the deals more attractive to coinvestors.[66]

Blended finance is bound to play an increasingly important role in international development finance. Its role as first-loss capital is key in attracting other investors, from DFIs to commercial banks and private equity funds, to deals that would otherwise not materialize due to their perceived high risk. Blended finance is therefore critical to the dissemination and scaling

---

66 Clean Technology Fund, December 14, 2017, "Scaling Up: Low Carbon Technologies," Climate Investment Funds, http://www.climateinvestmentfunds.org/sites/default/files/knowledge-documents/ctf_factsheet.pdf.

of innovations and new technologies needed to expand inclusive economies across emerging and frontier countries.

DFIs have also realized that SMEs are essential drivers of job creation and growth in developing markets and they need better services, both financial and technical. Formal sector SMEs contribute up to 60 percent of total employment and up to 40 percent of GDP in emerging economies.[67] In the Asia-Pacific region, SMEs constitute more than 90 percent of total companies, and they provide between 60 and 80 percent of total jobs. These numbers would be even higher if we consider the informal sector, to which a large share of SMEs in these countries still belong.

Many DFIs are impact investors themselves, as the nature of their funds is to generate social good, whether for climate change mitigation, gender equality, or other impacts that generate a nonfinancial return. DFIs frequently invest directly in impact investment funds. OPIC is a partner of MicroVest, providing MicroVest with legitimacy and a way to scale its funds and thus its impact.[68] Similarly, FMO and the IFC invest heavily in the Accion Frontier Inclusion Fund, which allows them to finance ventures such as India's CreditMantri for improved credit reporting in India and Invoinet for improved SME invoice management in Argentina.[69]

Streamlining and standardizing environmental and social requirements across DFI operations ensure that they only approve projects with neutral or positive impact on the environment and communities. For example, most DFIs have adhered to the Equator Principles, a framework for assessing and managing the environmental and social risks of development projects. Originally based on IFC's standards and periodically revised to incorporate emerging global needs, the Equator Principles serve as a benchmark for sound risk assessments and have now been adopted by 92 institutions.[70]

However, DFIs recognize that screening and compliance is not enough to ensure positive environmental impact. They have turned their attention

---

67 World Bank, Small and Medium Enterprises (SMEs) Finance," World Bank, http://www.worldbank. org/en/topic/smefinance.

68 Overseas Private Investment Corporation, March 24, 2016, "Partner Spotlight: How microvest Combines a Commercial and Social Approach to Microfinance Investing," OPIC, https://bit.ly/2lvZFpX.

69 Accion website, "What We Do: Investments," https://www.accion.org/frontier.

70 Equator Principles website, http://equator-principles.com/.

to supporting projects whose main objectives are to encourage positive out-comes on climate change mitigation and adaptation. Multilateral DFIs have committed to channel 25 to 40 percent of their business to climate financing by 2020. Indeed, the amount invested in climate finance by multilateral DFIs increased from $11 billion in 2015 to $15.6 billion in 2016. Newcomers AIIB and NDB alone contributed to $2.5 billion in new investments in 2016.[71] The recent focus on climate investments has already put multilateral DFIs more than 75 percent of the way to reaching their 2020 targets.[72] For impact investors, green and clean energy projects also capture a large proportion of investment. Energy was the second-most targeted sector for impact investment funds in 2017. Instruments in the sustainability space issued by major financial institutions, such as Green Bonds, are gaining in popularity because they can be easily replicated and come with reliable performance measurement.[73] These funds provide an accessible way for investors (especially individuals) to break into impact investing.

Some impact investment dollars come from for-profit funds that want to be socially or environmentally conscious, but much of the funding comes from those seeking impact above all else. Investors include high-net-worth individuals, family offices, foundations, DFIs, and a wide range of institutional asset owners, such as insurance companies, pension funds, endowments, and retail investors. Capital raised from high-net-worth individuals and family offices represents the bulk of impact funds, followed by foundations and financial institutions (see Figure 6.16).[74] Box 6.10 discusses the role of high-net-worth individuals, including millennials.

71   Barbara Buchner, Padraig Oliver, Xueying Wang, Cameron Carswell, Chavi Meattle, and Federico Mazza, October, 2017, "Global Landscape of Climate Finance 2017," Climate Policy Initiative, https://climatepolicyinitiative.org/wp-content/uploads/2017/10/2017-Global-Landscape-of-Climate-Finance.pdf.

72   Ibid.

73   Goldman Sachs, 2018, "Environmental Market Opportunities: Green Bonds and Impact Investing," Goldman Sachs, http://www.goldmansachs.com/citizenship/environmental-stewardship/market-opportunities/green-bonds-impact-investing/.

74   Abhilash Mudaliar, Hannah Schiff, Rachel Bass and Hannah Dithrich, May 2017, "Annual Impact Investor Survey 2017," Global Impact Investing Network, https://thegiin.org/assets/GIIN_AnnualImpactInvestorSurvey_2017_Web_Final.pdf.

Box 6.10: Investing (Fortunes) With Purpose

Interest in impact investing among high-net-worth individuals and family offices has continued to grow in recent years. Socially and environmentally sound private sector enterprises have been increasingly recognized as the most effective mechanism to foster economic opportunity and impact. Forty-five percent of high-net-worth investors in the United States own or are interested in owning impact investments, and more than half of those who already invested stated that it is "the right thing to do as a responsible citizen and investor."[75]

This morally charged investment rationale is particularly prevalent among millennials who are inheriting their family fortunes. Millennials are not only twice as likely to invest in companies targeting social or environmental goals but are far more interested in pursuing this category of investment overall.[76] For example, from 2015 to 2017, the percentage of millennial investors who claimed to be "very interested" in impact investment grew by 10 percent, compared to the general investment community that demonstrated a mere 4 percent expansion of interest over the same period. Also, while women exhibit a higher interest in impact investment than men, both groups have acted on this desire to the same extent.

In 2015, Facebook founder Mark Zuckerberg and his wife, Priscilla Chan, established the Chan Zuckerberg Initiative (CZI), LLC. CZI combines impact investing, grant making, and technical assistance to support bold and scalable initiatives in the areas of education, science, justice, and opportunity.[77] Zuckerberg is one of many wealthy individuals who have found impact investing a way to do good while continuing to do well.

---

75   U.S. Trust, 2017, "U.S. Trust Insights on Wealth and Worth: Annual survey of high-net-worth and ultra-high-net-worth Americans - 2017 The Generational Collide," U.S. Trust, http://preview. ustrust.com/publish/content/application/pdf/GWMOL/USTp_Detailed_Findings_Deck_Final_ARWW6GXM_9_2017.pdf.

76   Ibid.

77   Chan Zuckerberg Initiative, 2018, "About," Chan Zuckerberg Initiative, https://www.chanzuckerberg.com/about.

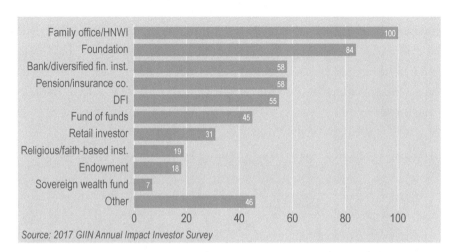

Figure 6.16: Impact Fund Managers' Sources of Capital

Source: 2017 GIIN Annual Impact Investor Survey

The landscape of impact investment is diverse. The GIIN 2018 survey responders include fund managers, foundations, banks, pension funds, insurance companies, and family offices. Respondents invested in companies at every stage of the growth cycle, and nearly as many invested in developed markets as in emerging markets. Roughly 66 percent made exclusively impact-oriented investments. No single region accounted for more than 20 percent of total assets under management, nor did any single sector. With the exception of Oceania, each region received upwards of $10 billion. However, more than 75 percent of investors are headquartered in the United States, Canada, or Western Europe. Most respondents also agreed that political changes and country-specific phenomena affect the way investors choose to allocate funds.[78] Although growing fast, the impact investing market is still maturing.

Many investors find impact investing difficult to navigate due to a lack of consensus surrounding product definition and underdeveloped performance indicators.[79] Box 6.11 explains how the impact management process can help guide investors toward a credible impact determination. One of the most difficult aspects of investing in a social enterprise is measuring its impact on lives, communities, and the

---

78   Abhilash Mudaliar, Rachel Bass, Hannah Dithrich, June 2018, " Annual Impact investor Survey 2018," Global Impact Investing Network, https://thegiin.org/assets/2018_GIIN_Annual_Impact_Investor_Survey_webfile.pdf.

79   Cathy Clark and Ben Thornley July 5, 2016, "Cracking the Code of Impact Investing," *Stanford Social Innovation Review*, https://ssir.org/articles/entry/cracking_the_code_of_impact_investing.

environment. Measuring and proving this type of impact can be resource heavy and expensive. While data on business operations is plentiful, data on companies' real-world impact remains poor, incomplete, unstandardized, or inaccessible. Despite the efforts of institutions like the GIIN, which promotes its standardized set of performance metrics called IRIS, and of B-Lab, an organization that assigns impact and governance ratings and issues impact (B-Corp) certifications to companies that demonstrate positive environmental and social practices, the impact investing sector still lacks the clarity and consensus of more mature industries.

Box 6.11: Impact Management

Impact investors are taking a harder look at impact management, a holistic view of how investment affects people and the planet, both the good and the bad. Impact investing still does not have a concrete definition, but through using a set of guidelines called IMPACT Principles, investors can determine the impact of their investment for themselves. IMPACT stands for integration, materiality, pragmatism, authenticity, commitment, and transparency. Integration encourages investors to weigh social and financial impact at every step of their investment. The concept of materiality encourages companies to invest where they have demonstrated strength before and truly have an ability to make positive change. The pragmatism aspect of impact management means that investments should be feasible, cost-effective, and in line with investor expectations. Authenticity means that investors should be transparent about what roles they are playing and to what degree their investment is oriented to social or financial returns. The commitment dimension encourages investors to determine to what degree the people managing their fund are committed to impact outcomes. Finally, transparency means investors should be aware of what is happening during the entire impact management process.[80]

Commercial Funders

Concessional and impact-oriented funding alone is not sufficient to achieve inclusive economies across emerging and frontier markets. Commercial-grade money will be required to fill the gap needed to meet the SDGs. This gap, together with the amounts necessary to reach carbon goals prescribed by the Paris

---

80 Ben Thornley and Brian Locasio, June 18, 2018, "Best Practices in Impact Management Begin to Take Hold," *Stanford Social Innovation Review*, https://bit.ly/2yyjXIH.

Climate Accords, can be measured in the tens of trillions of dollars, compared to the several hundred billion currently spent by government ODA agencies, foundations, DFIs, and impact investors. The Business and Sustainable Development Commission estimates that the SDGs open up $12 trillion in market opportunities in four sectors alone: food and agriculture, cities, energy, and health.[81]

Commercial funders are increasingly interested in emerging and frontier markets. Untapped investment opportunities—especially in fast-growing markets in Africa, Asia, and Latin America—are attracting private investors from across the globe. These newer funders include commercial banks, private equity (PE) and venture capital (VC) firms, institutional investors such as pension funds and endowments, and corporations. Because developing countries have historically suffered from low levels of commercial investment, regardless of "impact intent," the increase in overall private investments invariably promotes growth and tends to benefit the poor. Examples include banks funding fintech services through mobile platforms, corporates investing in essential infrastructure such as water distribution and affordable housing, and PE funds investing in agritech solutions that improve farm productivity and food security.

Although commercial investors started to become more socially and environmentally conscious in the 1990s, this imperative manifested itself mostly in terms of compliance or "do no harm" measures. The objective has been to neutralize the potential adverse effects of traditional investments by adopting solid environmental, social, and governance (ESG) practices and mitigating social and environmental risks. ESG standards filter and shape investment decisions, but commercial players have been slower to see the value in incorporating a purposeful, impact-driven approach (sometimes referred to as double or triple bottom line). Beyond compliance with ESG standards, some companies adopted corporate social responsibility (CSR) practices, which finance social and environmental initiatives, often in partnership with foundations, nonprofits, and governments. However, the amounts invested were typically small and most programs local in scale with limited impact.

---

81 Business & Sustainable Development Commission, January, 2017, "Better Business Better World," Business & Sustainable Development Commission, http://report.businesscommission.org/report.

Today, the private sector has embraced the SDGs and in many cases firms have aligned their business plans with SDG or other impact metrics. Commercial players now realize that the long-term profitability of companies, banks, and funds relies on the sustainability of the planet and the growth of consumer markets. Lifting people out of poverty is good business, as the poor become customers as well as productive workers and citizens. Shareholders have also become less nearsighted in terms of their expectations of short-term financial results versus the longer-term impact and returns on their investments.

Investment mogul Larry Fink, founder of $6.3 trillion fund manager Blackrock, wrote an open letter to CEOs that emphasized the importance of purpose for companies to achieve their full potential. He urged companies not to focus only on financial performance but also to show how they make a positive contribution to society—if they want to prosper in the long run. They need to benefit all their stakeholders, not just shareholders but also employees, customers, and communities.[82] His statement resonates not only from a CSR angle but also when it comes to designing business solutions to world problems.

Continuing this pull of commercial money into investments that pave the pathways out of poverty through access to services and jobs requires new and innovative approaches. It also means working in tandem with local governments and regulators to bring successful investment practices and time-tested financial instruments into their markets. In addition, commercial sources of funding are found both in international markets and local pools of capital, which can be unlocked, matched, and blended with international resources. It is also about overcoming structural risks in the market and finding new financing tools to channel money to developing economies. See Box 6.12 for how investors are mitigating foreign exchange risk. This section focuses mostly on international sources of funding from commercial banks, PE and VC funds, and corporations.

---

82 Matt Turner, January 26, 2018, " Everyone at Davos is talking about 'Larry's letter'," *Business Insider*, http://www.businessinsider.com/everyone-at-davos-is-talking-about-larry-finks-letter-to-ceos-2018-1.

Box 6.12: Foreign Exchange Risk as a Barrier to Investment

In developing countries with weak capital markets, foreign debt or equity can be an important source of funding for large infrastructure projects and other opportunities. The problem is that while the borrower will earn revenue in the local currency, their debt obligations will be denominated in foreign currency. This subjects both parties to a large amount of risk if the exchange rate becomes volatile or if the local government limits currency flows out of the country.[83] Nearly half of the debt raised in emerging markets for infrastructure projects in 2016 was denominated in dollars, and almost all equity flows are exposed to foreign exchange (FX) risk. Because so little financing is available in local currency markets, many worthwhile projects are unable to take off.

Many tools and best practices have been adopted to help mitigate FX risk, but they have not all reached scale in many markets. Forward contracts (which essentially fix future currency prices), guarantee instruments (such as services offered by a third party to whom the lenders pay a premium in return for accepting the FX risk), and other financial instruments are some ways to circumvent this risk. Using a third proxy currency, such as financing a project in Columbia in Chilean pesos rather than dollars, is another.[84] [85] Though these hedging instruments can be expensive, they are necessary to attract capital flows to emerging markets. Finally, governments can develop capital markets and create an environment of stability that makes investors more willing to take on local currency projects in their countries.

Commercial Banks

Several leading financial institutions have turned their attention—and deep pockets—to impact-driven endeavors in recent years, either through creating specialized business units, supporting strategic initiatives, or structuring investment platforms dedicated to impact financing. Citigroup announced its

---

83   Kay Parplies, Y. Ehlert, A. Efiong, P. Horrocks, J. Sedemund, and W. Bartz, S. Andreasen, C. Clubb, J. Durland, and H. Hirschhofer, February 1, 2017, "The Need to Reduce FX Risk in Development Countries by Scaling Blended Finance Solutions," European Commission, OECD, EDFI, Convergence, and TCX, https://assets.ctfassets.net/bbfdx7vx8x8r/3UYrVVpyqckCsw802wWoOi/e5ca01a8c2109991e15a0c950906 7e0c/FX_Risk_in_Development_Primer.pdf.

84   Julie Monaco, July 18, 2017, "Why addressing FX risk could hold the key to infrastructure investment," World Bank, http://blogs.worldbank.org/ppps/why-addressing-fx-risk-could-hold-key-infrastructure-investment.

85   Tomoko Matsukawa, Robert Sheppard, and Joseph Wright, December, 2003, "Foreign Exchange Risk Mitigation for Power and Water Projects in Developing Countries," World Bank, http://documents.worldbank.org/curated/en/433171468779677009/pdf/280940Energy0Exchange0EMS0no-09.pdf.

10-year, $100 billion commitment to finance sustainable growth in 2015.[86] Later that year, Bank of America declared it would increase its environmental business initiative from $50 billion to $125 billion by 2025.[87] In 2018, BBVA announced it will invest $122 billion in green finance, sustainable infrastructure, social entrepreneurship, and financial inclusion by 2025.[88]

The entry of multinational banks and other large financial institutions into the impact investing space will increase the size and robustness of the market, but their arrival carries certain risks as well. On the one hand, some believe banks and other major asset management firms will professionalize the market and that this enormous injection of capital will result in impact investing becoming more prominent. On the other hand, some are concerned that these banks will favor financial returns over social benefits, distorting market statistics and performance in a phenomenon dubbed impact washing.[89]

Large banks generate impact not just by investing directly in companies or through funds but also by working closely with smaller, local financial institutions and investors. In 2016, Citi partnered with the Asian Development Bank to provide $100 million in financing to microfinance institutions that deliver loans to poor families and SMEs in rural and remote areas in Asia and the Pacific.[90] Box 6.13 discusses the entrance of so-called "super platforms" in financial services.

In Brazil, Itau bank teamed up with early-stage investor Redpoint to launch the Cubo tech co-working space. Already the largest entrepreneurship hub in Latin America, Cubo owns a 12-story building in Sao Paulo, where it supports startups by connecting them to investors, large corporations, academia, and fellow startups, thereby promoting innovation, technological advancement, and disruptive

---

86   Citigroup, February 18, 2015, "Citi Announces $100 Billion, 10-Year Commitment to Finance Sustainable Growth," Citigroup, http://www.citigroup.com/citi/news/2015/150218a.htm.

87   Bank of America, July 27, 2015, "Bank of America Announces Industry-leading $125 Billion Environmental Business Initiative," Bank of America, https://bit.ly/2MVOVhe.

88   Banco Bilbao Vizcaya Argentaria, February 28, 2018, "BBVA to mobilize €100 billion by 2025 to fight climate change and drive sustainable development," BBVA, https://bbva.info/2tA0AcA.

89   Abhilash Mudaliar, Hannah Schiff, Rachel Bass and Hannah Dithrich, May 2017, "Annual Impact Investor Survey 2017," Global Impact Investing Network, https://thegiin.org/assets/GIIN_AnnualImpactInvestorSurvey_2017_Web_Final.pdf.

90   Asian Development Bank, October 7, 2016, "ADB and Citi Partner to Provide $100 Million for Microfinance in Asia," Asian Development Bank, https://www.adb.org/news/adb-and-citi-partner-provide-100-million-microfinance-asia.

business models.[91] Cubo has supported startups in various sectors, including fintech, business intelligence, big data, education, and energy. At any point in time, Cubo hosts on average 200 companies, with about 1,250 employees, and receives more than 2,000 visitors every day.[92]

Box 6.13: Super-Disruptors in Global Banking

Fintech startups are responsible for some of the most exciting and disruptive innovations, and for that reason many are acquired and even bred from seed by larger banks. However, the list of the largest banking groups in 2018—headed by the likes of JP Morgan, Bank of America, and HSBC—includes at the number 10 spot a less familiar name: Ant Financial.[93] Ant Financial belongs to one of the world's biggest e-commerce platforms, China's Alibaba.

Alibaba is not an outlier. Many internet giants—such as Amazon, Facebook, Apple, and Google—are becoming major players in financial services, including in developing and emerging markets. These so-called super-platforms differ significantly from traditional banks that have been around for centuries providing essentially the same services. These new financial service providers are only around a decade old, born in the era of social media, e-commerce, big data, crowdsourcing, and mobile servicing. They benefit from scale and scope and can innovate more freely, facilitating financial inclusion by reaching the excluded more efficiently and cost effectively.

Ant Financial, which started as Alipay in 2004 to enable escrow and payments for Alibaba's e-commerce, now offers services from wealth management to insurance, loans, and even credit scoring. Rakuten, Japan's largest online retail marketplace and messaging app, with 800 million users globally, already issues credit cards and provides financial services such as mortgages and securities. Amazon started offering loans to SMEs and Apple is integrating iMessage with cash-transferring capabilities.[94]

This disruption means that traditional banks must innovate to remain competitive—or die. This dynamic is good news for consumers, including the poor, who can expect a wider range of services targeted at them at increasingly affordable rates.

---

91 Cubo website, https://cubo.network/en.

92 Anderson Thees, September 15, 2017, "Corporate venture in Brazil gains steam as giants amp up startup investments," *Techcrunch*, https://tcrn.ch/2xp1hZW.

93 Huy Nguyen Trieu, May 26, 2018, "Alibaba Becomes Top 10 Global Bank," *Disruptive Finance*, http://www.disruptivefinance.co.uk/2018/05/26/alibaba-becomes-top-10-global-bank/.

94 John Detrixhe, October 26, 2017, "Big tech firms like Amazon are eager to eat the banking industry's lunch," *Quartz*, https://bit.ly/2xqbzGr.

Private Equity and Venture Capital Funds

PE and VC funds make equity investments in privately held companies with high growth potential. VCs invest more in early-stage ventures, usually between proof-of-concept and break-even, whereas PEs make larger investments in businesses that have proven concepts and are ready to scale. Both types of investors realize returns by selling their shares in invested companies four to seven years after investment for a multiple of the initial valuation. Private capital investors are key funders for any economy that aspires to generate growth through innovation, technology, and competitiveness.

Total private equity investments by global players (including credit to private companies and investments in private infrastructure) have increased in emerging markets, from $29 billion in 2013 to $49 billion in 2017, primarily through loans and equity. Asia attracts most of the investments, mainly because of China and India. In 2017, the region received $38 billion in private equity investments, with Latin America a distant second at $5.3 billion, led by Brazil and Mexico. The smaller numbers in the remaining regions reflect in part smaller markets but also more challenging environments for global capital, including higher costs of doing business, poor business environments, and higher macro and political risks. About a third of private investment goes to companies in consumer services, which have a direct impact in people's lives, including the poor. Investments in technology, a fundamental enabler of the economy and often a tool of empowerment for the poor (think mobile banking or agritech) ranks second, representing 17 percent of total allocation.[95] Figure 6.17 provides a snapshot of current commercial private equity portfolios.

---

95 Emerging Market Private Equity Association, 2018, "Industry Statistics: Year-end 2017," EMPEA, https://www.empea.org/app/uploads/2018/02/EMPEA-Industry-Statistics-YE-2017-Official-Member.pdf.

Figure 6.17: Private Equity/Venture Capital Snapshot

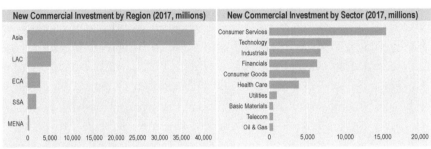

Sources: EMPEA, Industry Statistics Year-end 2017

PE and VC managers have also gone beyond traditional targets and ramped up their investments in impact-oriented companies. KKR, one of the world's largest PE firms, recently launched its own $1 billion Global Impact Fund with the goal of making 12 to 15 investments in sustainable businesses, clean energy, agriculture, and other areas aligned with the SDGs. Another PE giant, TPG, raised $2 billion, creating The Rise Fund, in partnership with Elevar Equity and The Bridgespan Group, to invest in seven sectors, including education, health, infrastructure, and financial services.[96] TPG expects high financial returns on its investments without compromising on social returns.[97]

PEs and VCs with impact funds are also increasingly working together to share best practices and learn from each other in terms of measurement, investment criteria for impact with high financial returns, and due diligence procedures. Impact Capital Managers (ICM) was launched in 2018 as a network of fund managers—also called general partners (GPs)—from across the United States and Canada that are committed to impact and financial returns. Together, these GPs manage more than $8 billion in impact-focused capital. ICM members work together to set common standards and goals and to share knowledge and experiences.[98]

---

96   Melissa Mittelman, October 3, 2017, "TPG Seals Record $2 Billion for Fund Co-Led by Bono," *Bloomberg,* https://www.bloomberg.com/news/articles/2017-10-03/tpg-seals-record-2-billion-for-rise-impact-fund-co-led-by-bono.

97   David Bank, April 23, 2018, "Rise Fund's Impact Multiple of Money: A conversation with TPG's Bill McGlashan," *ImpactAlpha,* https://impactalpha.com/the-rise-funds-impact-multiple-of-money/.

98   Impact Capital Managers website, https://www.impactcapitalmanagers.com/.

But investing with purpose is not just a trend among the largest PEs and VCs. Firms of all sizes and regions are launching their own funds—with resources from limited partners that range from institutional investors to DFIs, private sector players, and government agencies—which in most cases are run in parallel to their traditional equity funds. In developing and emerging markets, this movement is led mostly by VCs, given the smaller size of the companies and often of the markets themselves. Companies focused on social and environmental impact are usually in relatively early stages of development and are not yet within the investment range of PE firms.

PEs and VCs operating in developing markets face significant challenges inherent to those markets. For one, it is harder for invested companies to get other sources of financing that are essential for survival, such as working capital loans from commercial banks. The cost of doing business in these countries is also much higher, due to excessive bureaucracy, deficient infrastructure, and inadequate labor laws, to name a few factors. In this context, turning an impact-oriented company—or any company, for that matter—into a profitable and scalable business can be a challenge.

Funds also struggle with exit options for getting their money out of their investments. PEs and VCs invest in a company to improve its management, support its growth, and sell its shares for a profit years later. In developed markets, companies are either sold to a later-stage fund, acquired by a larger company, or listed in an initial public offering (IPO) in the stock market. In emerging economies, all three exit options are significantly more limited, which challenges the long-term survival of funds and the equity impact ecosystem more broadly.

That said, success stories allow for an optimistic view of the future. Emerging Capital Partners is a PE firm focused on and based in Africa. In its 17 years of existence, it has raised more than $3 billion and invested in approximately 60 businesses, including 40 exits.[99] Its focus on key sectors—such as telecommunications, water, and financial services—and its commitment to sustainable practices, job creation, and fighting corruption show it is possible to make an impact and generate high market returns. Also, the budding involvement of traditionally conservative institutional investors, such as pension

---

99   Emerging Capital Partners website, http://www.ecpinvestments.com/.

246

funds and endowments in impact investing, shows that private capital believes in the proposition that solving social and environmental problems through market-based solutions can be good business (see Box 6.14 for more on institutional investors).

Box 6.14: Institutional Investors Wake Up to Impact

Institutional investors include endowments, insurance, pension plans, and sovereign wealth funds that invest on behalf of their individual members or customers. These investors typically hold extremely large sums in long-term assets and invest conservatively, given their need for predictability and their responsibility to investors such as retirees.

Recently, inspired by the SDGs and by the actions of other commercial players, institutional investors have turned their attention to impact. Many have become funders (limited partners) in impact investing funds. The New York State's $184 billion Common Retirement Fund committed $2 billion to a low-carbon index fund, for example, which aims to reduce carbon emissions by 70 percent while performing as well as market benchmarks."[100]

The think-tank New America lists the *25 Most Responsible Asset Allocators*, detailing institutional investors selected by independent reviewers for their sustainable and ethically responsible positions. The list, called the Bretton Woods II Leaders List, was selected from a larger group of more than 500 entities and represents almost $5 trillion in assets under management. Each of the 25 institutions has allocated part of its funds to investment initiatives that comply with robust ESG standards. At the top of the list are the Government Pension Fund of Norway (with $981 billion in assets under management), APG Groep in the Netherlands ($532 billion), and the National Pension Service in South Korea ($522 billion).[101]

---

100 David Bank, October 30, 2017, "Universal Ownership: The supertankers of global finance are shifting course," *ImpactAlpha*, https://bit.ly/2ImeTa9.

101 Tomicah Tillemann and Scott Kalb, October 13, 2017, "Bretton Woods II Responsible Asset Allocator Initiative: Bretton Woods II Leaders List," *New America*, https://www.newamerica.org/in-depth/bwii-responsible-asset-allocator/bretton-woods-ii-leaders-list/.

Corporate Venturing

Corporate venturing refers to large corporations engaging with strategic startup companies in search of synergies and new technologies. In most cases, corporate venturing occurs through equity investments by so-called corporate venture capital (CVC) funds. CVC funds are created by established companies to invest in innovative businesses complementary to their own. Unlike VC funds, however, CVCs look beyond financial returns to the long-term strategic benefits from these investments. Corporate venturing has been used as an investing strategy since at least the 1990s, but it has made a resurgence in the 2010s. From 2013 to 2017, global CVC investments rose from $9.9 billion to $31.2 billion, deployed in roughly 1,800 deals. In the second quarter of 2016, CVC funds took part in 19 percent of all VC deals and accounted for 27 percent of total VC investments.[102]

Many of the world's largest companies have embraced CVC, and several large corporations in developing countries have also launched their own CVCs in the past decade or so, including Tata in India and Votorantim in Brazil.[103]

Established companies also benefit from breeding synergic startups through incubators and accelerators. Shell Global, one of the first to adopt the corporate incubator model, launched its GameChanger program in the mid-1990s. It incubates both internal projects (about one-quarter) and external startups (three-quarters), focused on energy solutions. Shell accepts roughly 30 companies per year, invests an average of $500,000 in each, and is ready to accept a success rate of 10 to 20 percent. Other companies such as PayPal, Nike, Qualcomm, and Microsoft have incubation or acceleration initiatives as well. Large banks such as Barclays, Deutsche, JP Morgan Chase, and Wells Fargo have launched fintech corporate accelerator initiatives to find the "next big thing" and stay ahead of the curve.[104]

While corporate venturing has focused so far on bringing strategic technologies closer to the investing company, the past few years have seen many corporations launching CVC funds and incubators focused on impact as well.

---

102 CB Insights, 2018, "The 2017 Global CVC Report," CB Insights, https://www.cbinsights.com/research/report/corporate-venture-capital-trends-2017/.

103 CB Insights, March 13, 2018, "Hungry for Investment: Big Food Races Toward Startups," CB Insights, https://bit.ly/2KmwPU1.

104 Entrepreneur Staff, February 15, 2017, "What Corporate Incubators and Accelerators Can Mean for Your Business," *Entrepreneur*, https://www.entrepreneur.com/article/287495.

The impact wave has spilled over to the corporate venturing world with the growth of corporate impact venturing (CIV). Much like financial institutions, corporations want to make an impact and turn a profit. So in addition to more traditional approaches—such as CSR—some have also adapted the corporate venturing approach to impact investing. Figure 6.18 shows how CIV draws from corporate venturing and impact investing.

Figure 6.18: Corporate Impact Venturing: Between CVC and Impact Investing

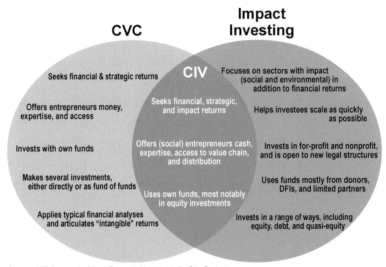

Sources: MIF, Beyond the Binary: Corporate Venturing in the 21st Century

Salesforce has launched the Sales Force Impact Fund. With $50 million committed, the fund focuses on companies that use Salesforce technology to generate impact in workforce development, equality, sustainability, and the social sectors. One of its latest investments is Ellevest, an investment platform whose goal is to solve the gender investment gap. Another company in its portfolio is Andela, which builds and connects developers and engineering teams from Africa with companies across the world.[105]

The Turkish Economy Bank started a corporate venturing initiative called the TEB Incubation and Acceleration Center in 2013. Headquartered in Is-

---

105 Salesforce, October 3, 2017, "Salesforce Ventures Introduces New $50 Million Impact Investment Fund," Salesforce, https://www.salesforce.com/company/news-press/press-releases/2017/10/171003/.

tanbul, it has programs outside of the city to make it more accessible to entrepreneurs from other parts of the country. The center revolves around five
complementary programs tailored to the maturity of the venture: education,
preincubation, incubation, acceleration, and growth. Entrepreneurs are placed
according to their level and move along the spectrum as their ideas mature into
companies. Approximately 4,000 applications to join the center have been sub-
mitted from a variety of sectors, from tech to services and education. Roughly
300 have been accepted and about 50 ventures have graduated. Of these, a doz-
en received funding from the TEB Private Banking Angel Investment Platform
to accelerate the development of their businesses.[106]

The SDG financing gap, which is a hurdle for access to services and pro-
poor job creation, is simply too large to be filled by mission-driven institutions
alone. At the same time, commercial funders such as banks, PE firms, and large
corporations cannot be expected to invest substantial amounts in ventures that
do not provide a market-competitive return. Encouragingly, the private sector
is increasingly aware that solving social and environmental challenges is also
good business, as reflected in the increasing amounts of funds being channeled
to profit and purpose. The challenge for the next decade is for this awareness—
and funding—to continue to grow exponentially, so that SDG targets are met
in a collaborative effort between governments, philanthropists, DFIs, impact
funds, and the private sector.

---

106 Florian Heinemann, January 14, 2016, "Focus areas of Corporate Accelerators," Corporate Accelerator
DB, https://www.corporate-accelerators.net/database/focus-areas.html.

Chapter 7. Frontier and Cross-Cutting Challenges

The economic system encompasses a range of actors. These include poor and low-income people, many of whom are currently excluded; micro-level market players that deliver life-improving services and jobs; meso-level ecosystem enablers that grease the wheels to better connect demand with supply; macro-level government entities that can enable, promote, or prevent inclusive economic activity; and funders that deliver capital to fuel opportunities across the system. Previous chapters have addressed the latest and greatest knowledge about these players and their prospects and challenges.

This chapter looks at a number of frontier issues and cross-cutting challenges that affect inclusive economic systems. In some cases, these issues are so new—like the impact of new technologies, urbanization, or climate change—that knowledge is scarce when it comes to the implications for developing and emerging markets. In other cases, the topic cuts across all the levels of the economic system—such as women's economic empowerment or consumer protection—and deserve dedicated treatment.

Although numerous issues could be considered frontier or cross-cutting, the following were selected for this chapter:

Ensuring gender equity: What are the best strategies for supporting women's economic empowerment, both through improved products and services tailored to their needs and through effective job insertion?

251

Supporting refugees: How can refugees obtain access to needed services and jobs, especially given their tenuous legal status and fragile situation?

Protecting consumers and workers: How can consumers and workers cope with the challenges posed by a shift to digital payments and delivery of services, as well as the workforce requirements of the new economy?

Optimizing new technologies: What could be the impact of new technologies like robotics, artificial intelligence, and virtual reality on the development and delivery of services, as well as the future of work for poor and low-income people?

Embracing urbanization: What solutions will make cities are more livable, sustainable, and inclusive?

Coping with climate change: How can poor and low-income people become more resilient in the face of shifting weather patterns that affect their livelihoods and mobility?

Ensuring Gender Equity

Closing the gender gap and empowering women would benefit all countries, morally and economically. The UN Secretary General's High Level Panel on Women's Economic Empowerment and the *Leave No One Behind* report in 2016 are representative of the growing interest in women's incomes and economic roles. These two initiatives identified seven drivers of women's economic empowerment, highlighted in Figure 7.1.[1] Many of them reflect the two main pathways out of poverty: access to services and jobs.

---

1   United Nations Women's Economic Empowerment, "Leave no One Behind: A Call To Action For Gender Equality And Women's Economic Empowerment," United Nations Women's Economic Empowerment, https://bit.ly/2KtcTBR.

Figure 7.1: Seven Drivers of Women's Economic Empowerment

Source: UN Women

Women's Access to Services

Inequality between men and women is measured by the global gender gap index. This index includes measures of economic participation and opportunity, educational attainment, health, and political empowerment and provides a good indication of women's relative lack of access to services.[2] Of the 142 countries covered by the index in 2016, 68 had larger gender gaps than the previous year. Overall, there is limited evidence of progress.[3]

In the list of top 10 performing countries, only Rwanda represented the African continent (at number four). Women's political participation in Rwanda is the highest in the world, as 64 percent of parliamentarians are female, compared to the global average of 23 percent. Rwanda is one of only two countries where women outnumber men in parliament (the other is Bolivia).[4] Access

---

2 World Economic Forum, 2017, "Worlds Apart: Global Gender Gap Report 2017," World Economic Forum, http://reports.weforum.org/global-gender-gap-report-2017/key-findings/.

3 United Nations Population Fund, 2017, "State of the World's Population 2017," United Nations Population Fund, https://www.unfpa.org/swop.

4 Sarah Jane Cooper-Knock, February 26, 2016, "Gender, politics, and parliament in Rwanda," openDemocracy, https://www.opendemocracy.net/westminster/sarah-jane-cooper-knock/gender-politics-and-parliament-in-rwanda.

to—and the ability to make decisions about—health care and family planning is a key indicator of women's access to services because it speaks to their decision-making power, the availability and quality of the service, and the degree of control women have over their own bodies. Rwanda has seen significant progress and less inequality of access over the past 10 years.[5]

Especially in the arena of maternal health, lack of access to services can have a devastating effect on women's lives, resulting in multiple pregnancies, debilitating injuries from childbirth, or unsafe abortions due to a lack of skilled care. Between 2012 and 2017, only half of live births in Sub-Saharan Africa benefited from skilled care during delivery.[6] A rapid succession of pregnancies can also prevent a woman from entering or remaining in the paid labor force or undermine her long-term prospects for securing a high-paying job.[7] See Box 7.1 for an example of a Mexican nonprofit attempting to improve health services for women.

Box 7.1: Offering Affordable Health Care to Mexican Families

Guimedic, a nonprofit in Mexico, is tackling the health challenges faced by women and their families by bringing mobile clinics to remote or vulnerable communities. Guimedic not only provides immediate health care but also invests in tools to help communities stay healthy over the long term, (for example, through family planning education).[8][9] In 2016, Guimedic treated 126,000 indigenous people, 53 percent of them female. Additionally, Guimedic runs monthly health education clinics where 71 percent of attendees are women.[10]

---

5   World Economic Forum, 2017, "Worlds Apart: Global Gender Gap Report 2017," World Economic Forum, http://reports.weforum.org/global-gender-gap-report-2017/key-findings/.

6   World Health Organization, "Global Health Observatory (GHO) data," World Health Organization, http://www.who.int/gho/maternal_health/skilled_care/skilled_birth_attendance_text/en/.

7   Edilberto Loaiza and Mengjia Liang, January, 2016, "Universal Access to Reproductive Health: Progress and Challenges," United Nations Population Fund, https://www.unfpa.org/sites/default/files/pub-pdf/UNFPA_Reproductive_Paper_20160120_online.pdf.

8   International Youth Foundation, February 18, 2016 At Work in Rural Communities to Prevent the Spread of the Zika Virus," International Youth Foundation, https://www.iyfnet.org/blog/work-rural-communities-prevent-spread-zika-virus.

9   Harry Moxley, Febrary 24, 2016, "At Work in Rural Communities to Prevent the Spread of the Zika Virus," Youtube, https://www.youtube.com/watch?v=gTksWjbUVoE.

10   Grupo Antolin, 2016, "Informe Anual 2016," Guimedic, http://www.grupoantolin.com/sites/default/files/informe_anual_2016_es_0.pdf.

At the same time, equality between girls and boys in education continues to improve, and girls' participation in education at the primary and lower secondary level is reaching parity in many countries. Yet higher secondary and tertiary education remains unattainable for many girls. Variable school attendance and performance can reflect discrimination against girls in school due to limited or inadequate accommodations for girls. For example, most schools in Sub-Saharan Africa do not have separate sanitation facilities for boys and girls.[11]

Access to financial services is unequal between men and women, and while overall access increased over the past few years, the gender gap remains at 9 percent for developing countries. In countries such as India, the gender gap in access to finance dropped from 20 percent to 6 percent between 2014 and 2017, largely due to the Aadhaar ID program. Globally, 81 percent of women own a mobile phone, so mobile money platforms will likely continue to drive increased access to financial services for women.[12]

Even when women-owned businesses have excellent growth potential, it can be hard to find investment and financial services to support them. Gender lens impact investment is an emerging source of finance that could enhance the potential of women's entrepreneurial activities. This type of investment aims either to influence gender equality within organizations or promote products and services that improve the economic and social well-being of women and girls. It also has the potential to inject private sector energy and innovation into the delivery of services, infrastructure, and labor-saving technology for women, which the public sector in low-income countries often lacks.

Over the past two years, gender lens impact investing increased dramatically and is estimated to have reached $2 billion in 2017, funding products and services such as reproductive and maternal health innovations, daycare services, water wheels, and financial literacy.[13, 14] Box 7.2 illustrates some examples of gender lens impact investing.

---

11 United Nations Department of Economic and Social Affairs, 2017, "Goal 4: Ensure inclusive and equitable quality education and promote lifelong learning opportunities for all," United Nations, https://unstats.un.org/sdgs/report/2017/goal-04/.

12 Max Mattern, June 21, 2018, "How Ghana Becaem One of Africa's Top Mobile Money Markets," CGAP, http://www.cgap.org/blog/measuring-women's-financial-inclusion-2017-findex-story.

13 Suzanne Biegel, Sandra M. Hunt and Sherryl Kuhlman, October 2017, "Project Sage –Tracking Venture Capital with a Gender Lens," Social Impact Initiative, https://whr.tn/2N5ni5n

14 Women Effect, "Women Effect: What is Gender Lens Investing," www.womeneffect.com.

> ## Box 7.2: Gender Lens Impact Investment in Practice
>
> National Australia Bank raised 500 million Australian dollars (US$384 million) from investors keen to promote gender equality. It became the country's first gender bond. Multilateral organizations have since picked up the mantle; the IFC began issuing a women's bond in 2013. Through the Banking on Women Program, the IFC is helping partners and financial institutions profitably and sustainably invest in women-owned businesses.[15]
>
> Another example is Women's World Banking Asset Management, launched in 2012 and the only microfinance equity fund that is both managed by women and invests with women in mind. Its mission is to prove that providing women with access to finance is profitable and contributes to economic growth.[16] One of its implementing partners in Peru, Caja Arequipa, provides clients—45 percent of whom are women—with comprehensive and flexible financial products for MSMEs.[17]
>
> Other examples include Pax Global Women's Equality Fund and State Street Global Advisors' SHE Fund. These funds work only with companies that demonstrate a commitment to gender equity in the workplace. Organizations such as Zevin Asset Management help clients use their power as shareholders to advocate for gender equality and gender-equitable practices in the companies in which they invest.[18]

Women and Work

Over the past few years, international donors launched a flurry of initiatives to address women's economic exclusion and better understand economic dynamics at household and community levels. Across countries, low levels of female workforce participation are linked to both lower levels of economic growth and human development (the latter is illustrated in Figure 7.2).[19] If all countries had matched the rate of gender inclusion of the most progressive country in their region in 2015, global GDP could be $12 trillion dollars higher than it

---

15 International Finance Corporation, "Banking on Women," International Finance Corporation, https://bit.ly/2tCiexi.

16 Women's World Banking, "Women's World Banking Capital Partners, LP," Women's World Banking https://www.womensworldbanking.org/about-us/capital-partners-gender-lens-investing/.

17 Ramiro Postigo Castro "Caja Arequipa," Women's World Banking, https://bit.ly/2KsWRIu.

18 Zevin Asset Management LLC, "Investors 'Take the Lead' on Advocating for Gender Equality," Zevin Asset Management LLC https://www.zevin.com/documents/Take%20The%20Lead%20Article%20Final%20Draft%2017-1103.pdf.

19 World Economic Forum, 2016, "The Global Gender Gap Report 2016," World Economic Forum, http://www3.weforum.org/docs/GGGR16/WEF_Global_Gender_Gap_Report_2016.pdf.

would be in the business-as-usual scenario. If women participated economical-ly in the same way men do globally, global GDP between 2015 and 2025 could be $28 trillion more than if the current trend remains unaltered.[20]

Figure 7.2: Gender Equity and Human Development

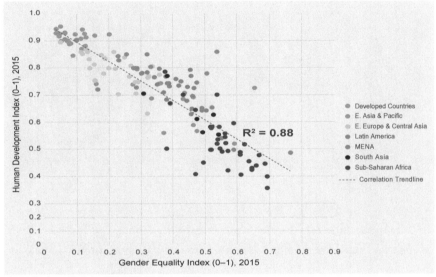

Source: Development Indicators 2015, IMF Staff Estimates, UNDP

Despite the clear benefit of reducing gender inequities and the fact that many countries have committed to implementing the Beijing Platform for Action, which protects women from discrimination, many countries do not guaran-tee women equal treatment under the law. Therefore, many challenges remain in applying the principles of nondiscrimination in the workplace.[21] Figure 7.3 shows the global snapshot of gender-based discrimination in the workplace.

20   McKinsey & Company, September 2015, "The Power of Parity: How Advancing Women's Equality Can Add $12 Trillion to Global Growth," McKinsey & Company, https://mck.co/2twK4Kq.

21   United Nations Women, "Commission on the Status of Women," United Nations Women, http://www.unwomen.org/en/csw.

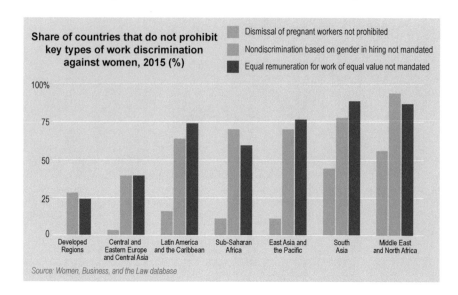

Figure 7.3: Global View of Nondiscrimination in Hiring

To fully understand how women contribute to the economy, it is critical to focus on two features of women's lives: their concentration in informal work and the systematic undervaluing of unpaid care and household work.

Informal Work

Most poor women who are economically engaged work in the informal sector. In Sub-Saharan Africa, 74 percent of women who work do so in the informal sector, compared to 61 percent of men. Working in the informal sector poses several challenges, especially for women, such as low and inconsistent incomes, poor working conditions, and legal and physical risks.[22] Wages in the informal sector tend to be lower than wages in the formal sector, which is why poverty rates tend to be higher among informal workers. Women's earnings in the informal sector tend to be concentrated in the most vulnerable activities, such as

---

22   Martha Chen and Jenna Harvey, January 23, 2017, "The Informal economy in Arab Nations: A Comparative Perspective," Women in Informal Employment: Globalizing and Organizing, http://www.wiego.org/sites/default/files/resources/files/Informal-Economy-Arab-Countries-2017.pdf

street trading, waste picking, domestic work, and small-scale agriculture.[23] In each of these settings, women are more vulnerable to harassment or workplace injury. Women in the informal sector also have limited access to social protection. Close to 60 percent of women workers, or around 750 million women worldwide, do not benefit from a statutory right to maternity leave.[24]

In many countries, severe shortages of health workers offer an opportunity for women to fill these roles in the formal sector. Yet limited science education for girls and inadequate investment in health personnel by governments remain a challenge. Organizations such as mothers2mothers offer a model of positive change. mothers2mothers bolsters national health care systems by empowering HIV-positive women to become paid community health care workers—providing services at the household level, supporting understaffed community health care facilities, and ensuring that women receive high-quality health education and connect to the right clinical services for their treatment.[25]

Gender-based violence poses another challenge for women in the workplace. As many as 35 percent of women over the age of 15 experience sexual or physical violence, which can affect their ability to earn an income and retain employment, as well as hamper their productivity.[26] In some countries, such as Bangladesh, women who work are more likely to endure abuse from their husbands than women who do not work.[27]

Unpaid Work

Women invest much more of their income into families, health care, and education than men do. This disparity is likely due to gender roles and social

23   Donald Brown, April 2016, "The urban informal economy, local inclusion and achieving a global green transformation," Habitat International, https://bit.ly/2KhW0qv.

24   Laura Addati, Florence Bonnet, Ekkehard Ernst, Rossana Merola and Pei Man Jessica Wan, 2016, "Women at Work: Trends 2016," International Labor Organization, http://www.ilo.org/wcmsp5/groups/public/---dgreports/---dcomm/---publ/documents/publication/wcms_457317.pdf.

25   Skoll, 2018, "Mothers2Mothers," Skoll, http://skoll.org/organization/mothers2mothers/.

26   United Nationals Population Fund, September 18, 2017, "Gender-based violence: Overview," United Nationals Population Fund, https://www.unfpa.org/gender-based-violence.

27   Meera Senthilingam, November 29, 2017, "Sexual harassment: How it stands around the globe," CNN, https://www.cnn.com/2017/11/25/health/sexual-harassment-violence-abuse-global-levels/index.html.

norms around household responsibilities, as reflected in the fact that women are typically responsible for most of the unpaid care and household work. Across all regions of the world, women spend on average three to six hours a day performing unpaid care activities, while men spend half an hour to two hours a day.[28] Figure 7.4 illustrates this divide.

Figure 7.4: Time Spent on Unpaid Care Work by Gender and Region

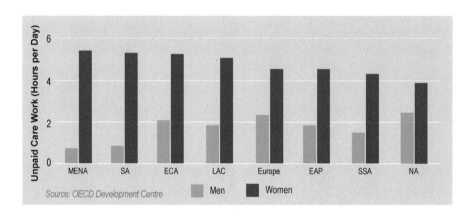

Source: OECD Development Centre

Furthermore, the value of unpaid care is estimated to reach between 20 percent and 60 percent of GDP.[29] This unpaid work by women can be considered a subsidy to economies and communities—a safety net of last resort—because families, especially the elderly and children, are cared for without remuneration for the care provider.[30] [31] Initiatives such as the Gender Action Learning System (GALS), a community-led empowerment methodology, show

---

28   Gaëlle Ferrant, Luca Maria Pesando and Keiko Nowacka, December 2014, "Unpaid Care Work: The missing link in the analysis of gender gaps in labour outcomes," OECD Development Centre, https://bit.ly/2ICWUw6.

29   Laura Addati, Florence Bonnet, Ekkehard Ernst, Rossana Merola and Pei Man Jessica Wan, 2016, "Women at Work: Trends 2016," International Labor Organization, http://www.ilo.org/wcmsp5/groups/public/---dgreports/---dcomm/---publ/documents/publication/wcms_457317.pdf.

30   Commission on the Status of Women [Fifty-fourth session], March 8, 2010, "Interactive expert panel on 'Women's economic empowerment in the context of the global economic and financial crisis'," United Nations, https://bit.ly/2KenO33.

31   Human Development Report Office Research Team, March 2016 "Valuing Care Work," United Nations Development Programme, http://hdr.undp.org/en/content/valuing-care-work.

some promise in refashioning traditional relationships and divisions of labor between men and women.[32] [33] Box 7.3 elaborates on this approach.

Box 7.3: The Gender Action Learning System (GALS)
The GALS program uses training and visual diagrams to increase the incomes and production of small farmers by getting women more involved outside their households.[34] GALS strengthens the decision-making ability of households and communities and benefits both men and women by promoting a more equitable division of labor and by removing other barriers to gender equality. In Uganda, GALS improved incomes by increasing the quality and quantity of harvests and by improving the relationship between participating farmers and other people in the supply chain.[35] GALS has also been implemented in India, South Africa, and South Sudan. In those countries, 70 percent of both male and female participants reported changes in attitude and behavior related to gender roles.[36]

Supporting Refugees

The number of refugees (people forced from their homes due to violence or disaster and who have taken residence in another country), asylum seekers (people seeking sanctuary who have not yet been recognized as refugees), and internally displaced persons (people who have been forced from their homes but have not crossed international borders) has risen dramatically in the past 40 years, as shown in Figure 7.5. At the end of 2017, that number stood at 71.44 million people worldwide—an unprecedented

32 Cathy Rozel Farnworth, Clare M. Stirlinga, Amon Chinyophiroc, Andrew Namakhomac, Rebecca Morahand February 2018, "Exploring the potential of household methodologies to strengthen gender equality and improve smallholder livelihoods: Research in Malawi in maizebased systems," *Journal of Arid Environments*, https://bit.ly/2yNdJ85.

33 Gender Action Learning for Sustainability at Scale, "GALS at scale website," http://www.galsatscale.net.

34 Women Watch, "IFAD: Good Practice Example: Household-based Approaches to Training and Extension," United Nations, http://www.un.org/womenwatch/feature/ruralwomen/ifad-good-practice.html.

35 Linda Mayoux, September, 2014, "Gender Action Learning System (GALS)," GALS at Scale, https://bit.ly/2lF5nG4.

36 Gender at Work, "Gender Action Learning: Gender at Work Action Learning Program as an Approach to Furthering Gender Equality," Gender at Work, http://genderatwork.org/gender-action-learning/.

level. Of those, nearly 20 million are refugees.[37] For some, displacement is temporary; for others, it can last generations.

Figure 7.5: The Growth of the Refugee Crisis

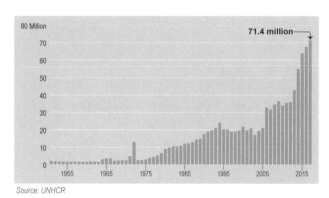

Source: UNHCR

More than 169 countries host refugees, including 23 countries that individually host more than 200,000 refugees each (see Figure 7.6).[38] [39]

Figure 7.6: Refugees by Country

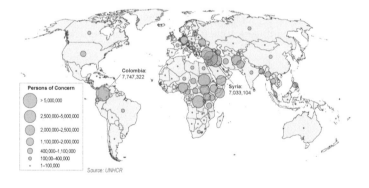

Source: UNHCR

---

37   United Nations High Commissioner for Refugees, June 19, 2018, "Figures at a Glance," United Nations, http://www.unhcr.org/en-us/figures-at-a-glance.html.

38   Roger Zetter and Héloïse Ruaudel, Septemeber 2016, "Refugees' Right to Work and Access to Labor Markets – An Assessment (Part 1: Synthesis), Global Knowledge Partnership on Migration and Development. https://www.knomad.org/sites/default/files/2017-03/KNOMAD%20Study%201%20 Part%20I-%20Assessing%20Refugees'%20Rights%20to%20Work_final.pdf.

39   United Nations High Commissioner for Refugees, "UNHCR Statistics Population Statistics Database," United Nations High Commissioner for Refugees, http://popstats.unhcr.org/en/overview#_ ga=2.71656465.344681890.1525814728-24605281.1523638495.

The challenge of meeting the humanitarian and economic needs of displaced people and resettling them has captured media attention over the past five years, particularly in Europe and the Middle East where countries continue to grapple with the inflow of Syrian refugees. However, as challenging as the Syria crisis is, nine of the world's 12 most populated refugee camps are in Africa, due largely to prolonged crises in Burundi, the Democratic Republic of the Congo (DRC), Somalia, and South Sudan.[40][41] Most refugees do not flee to wealthy countries but instead to the nearest stable country, which is often another poor or middle-income state struggling to feed and care for new arrivals.[42] These arrivals place immense economic and financial pressure on host governments, which leads to reduced access to needed services and jobs.

Services for Refugees

Gaining access to services is highly challenging for displaced people and refugees. The United Nations High Commission for Refugees (UNHCR) is the largest humanitarian organization charged with delivering such services, often in collaboration with bilateral, multilateral, and private donors or NGOs.[43]

Humanitarian Aid and Identity

In the Zaatari refugee camp in Jordan, the World Food Programme (WFP) adopted a number of innovations to deliver food aid to refugees. For instance, the Building Blocks program utilizes blockchain technology to manage a cash-for-food program serving more than 100,000 refugees. By the end of 2018, the program is expected to cover half a million food aid recipients. Working with shops such as the Tazweed Supermarket, located on the periphery of Zaatari, Building Blocks also employs a unique technology called EyePay, which uses retinal scanning to validate a person's identity and complete transactions.

---

40 United Nations High Commissioner for Refugees, 2016, "Story Maps: Refugee Camps," United Nations High Commissioner for Refugees, https://storymaps.esri.com/stories/2016/refugee-camps/#.

41 Refugee Council, November 13, 2016, "The 7 Largest Refugees Camps in the World," Refugee Council, http://www.refugeecouncilusa.org/the-7-largest-refugee-camps-in-the-world/.

42 Beauchamp, Zach, January 30, 2017, "9 Maps and Charts that Explain the Global Refugee Crisis," *Vox*, https://www.vox.com/world/2017/1/30/14432500/refugee-crisis-trump-muslim-ban-maps-charts.

43 United Nations High Commissioner for Refugees, "What We Do," United Nations High Commissioner for Refugees, http://www.unhcr.org/en-us/what-we-do.html.

Blockchain technology enables WFP to streamline its operations by reducing transaction costs and leakage. Additionally, the system captures vital information about people who fled their home countries without identification documents, which can in turn help them set up a bank account or get a job.[44] WFP believes it can use the same system to capture and store information about a person's employment or financial history, much like a credit information bureau. This information would then be transferrable if a person or family moved back to their home country or to a different country for resettlement, allowing them to maintain important records through periods of instability.

Blockchain-based programs for refugees are being used in other countries as well. The Finnish Immigration Service, for example, collaborated with a blockchain startup called MONI to give every refugee arriving in Finland a prepaid Mastercard tied to a digital identity number stored on a blockchain. The program not only provides refugees access to government services but also enables refugees to open bank accounts even if they lack a passport or other identification documents.[45] Similarly, in Kenya, the private company BanQu developed a digital identity platform for refugees and individuals living in extreme poverty zones, with the aim of creating long-term, secure economic profiles that can be used to access financial and government services.[46]

Education

More than half of all refugees are under the age of 18. Therefore, addressing the education shortfall for these children is critical in both the short and long term. The longer a child is not in school, the bleaker his or her future employment prospects become; the longer a child remains illiterate or innumerate, the more challenging his or her social and economic integration. In 2016, more than 3.5 million refugee children did not go to school. Figure 7.7 illustrates the dramatic differences between school attendance for refugee children compared to global youth.[47]

44   Russ Juskalian, April 12, 2018, "Inside the Jordan refugee camp that runs on blockchain," *MIT Technology Review*, https://www.technologyreview.com/s/610806/inside-the-jordan-refugee-camp-that-runs-on-blockchain/.

45   Ibid.

46   BanQu, "Current BanQu Case Studies," BanQu App, http://www.banquapp.com/our-solutions/pilots/.

47   United Nations High Commissioner on Refugees, 2017, "Left Behind: Refugee Education In Crisis," United Nations, http://www.unhcr.org/59b696f44.pdf.

Figure 7.7: Refugee Versus Global Youth Education Rates

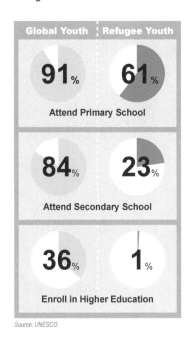

Source: UNESCO

Unfortunately, many barriers remain between children and the classroom. Some are political: approximately 20 percent of refugee host countries legally restrict refugee children from attending national schools.[48] The main barrier, however, is financial. Only 2 percent of humanitarian aid goes toward funding refugees' education, not nearly enough to meet the growing needs.[49] Other challenges include getting children who have missed many school cycles back to grade-level standards, addressing illiteracy, and providing vocational training to older students. Box 7.4 highlights an innovative partnership between the Vodafone Foundation and UNHCR to address this problem.

---

48   United Nations High Commissioner on Refugees, September 2016, "Missing Out: Refugee Education In Crisis," United Nations, http://www.unhcr.org/57d9d01d0.pdf.

49   Charlotte Alfred, April 17, 2017, "The Future of Refugee Education: A Roundup," *NewsDeeply*, https://bit.ly/2pctO1v.

> ### Box 7.4: A Partnership to Address Education Challenges in Kenyan Refugee Camps
>
> In 2014, the Vodafone Foundation and UNHCR provided "digital boxes" to selected schools and community centers in refugee camps in Kenya's Daadab complex, reaching approximately 18,000 students. These boxes included computer tablets, online learning materials, and other digital tools. Teachers received IT support and training.[50] The popular tablet-based program increased student attendance by 15 percent. Given its success, the program has been replicated in 31 refugee centers for approximately 15,000 students in three other countries: Tanzania, South Sudan, and the DRC.[51]

Financial Services

As with other poor and vulnerable populations, refugees need access to financial services, particularly to start or fund entrepreneurial endeavors. NGOs and donors have long provided microfinance options to refugees and migrants in resettlement situations and upon returning to their home countries. However, the results of these financing programs are mixed. Some programs enabled refugees to raise their incomes or assets and contributed to building sustainable businesses. Others failed due to repayment problems, high arrears, and institutional inefficiencies.[52] As a result, and to create more consistent outcomes, UNHCR and other donors identified best practices for providing financial services to refugees and migrants. These include providing access to credit jointly with other services such as financial literacy or business skills training, ensuring clients are well screened and monitored, branding loans differently from other relief services (which are often free), and utilizing group accountability models such as self-help and savings groups.[53]

Social Entrepreneurship

Over the past decade, support to refugees shifted from purely humanitarian aid for basic needs to supporting economic development, entrepreneurship, and job

---

50 Catherine Wachiaya, March 14, 2017, "Innovation transforms education for refugee students in Africa," United Nations High Commissioner on Refugees, https://bit.ly/2yPPHJz.

51 Kate Collins, March 1, 2015, "Vodafone 'Instant Classroom' is digital school in a box for refugees," *Wired Magazine*, http://www.wired.co.uk/article/vodafone-instant-classroom.

52 Timothy H. Nourse, November 2003, "Microfinance for Refugees: Emerging Principles for Effective Implementation," United Nations High Commissioner on Refugees, http://www.unhcr.org/3fc47f78d.pdf.

53 Ibid.

creation. More recently, a wave of innovation is leveraging new technologies to create new avenues to access services. Additionally, there are several refugee-led social entrepreneurship models that help refugees integrate economically in new countries.

In Germany, refugees launched the "Arriving in Berlin" project to help new arrivals access services such as medical attention, legal advice, counseling services, and housing. To complement the program, the project organizers developed an app that shows a map of all services available to refugees across the city, updated by crowdsourcing the knowledge and experiences of the users themselves.[54] Another example is the Young Africa Refugees for Integral Development (YARID),[55] a nonprofit founded by a Congolese refugee to help refugees access employment, health services, and education.[56] The organization provides English classes, skills training, empowerment programming, and community building through sports.[57]

Private Sector Engagement

Several corporations are seeking new ways to work with refugees. Chobani Yogurt's Tent Foundation mobilizes companies' resources and innovations to create solutions for refugee aid. Recognizing that refugees have the potential to be productive contributors to the economy, Tent aims to incentivize companies to hire refugees, invest in refugee businesses, and integrate them into supply chains.[58]

In 2016, then-US President Barack Obama led a call to action, asking firms to help refugees.[59] More than 50 US companies answered the call. Google, for example, collaborated with Mercy Corps and the International Rescue Committee to develop the Refugee Info Hub, hosting critical information for refugees arriv-

---

54   Haus Leo and Haus der Kulturen der Welt, "Arriving In Berlin," https://arriving-in-berlin.de.

55   Hannah Darnton, June 20, 2016, "Promising Innovations for Tackling the Refugee Crisis," Skoll Foundation, http://skoll.org/2016/06/20/promising-innovations-for-tackling-the-refugee-crisis/.

56   Ibid.

57   Young African Refugees for Integral Development, "Young African Refugees For Integral Development," Young African Refugees for Integral Development, http://www.yarid.org/index.php.

58   Tent Partnership for Refugees, "About," Tent, https://www.tent.org/about/.

59   John Kluge, Septemeber 20, 2016, "Over 50 U.S. Businesses Step Up For Refugees," *Forbes*, https://www.forbes.com/sites/johnkluge/2016/09/20/u-s-businesses-step-up-for-refugees/#532a9b8b3a9e.

ing in Greece. Coursera, an online education provider, created Coursera for Refugees, through which refugees can access more than 1,000 online courses offered by international universities, allowing them to build career skills through certifications.[60] Microsoft made its Arabic-to-German language training program available to 30,000 refugee children in Greece, Jordan, Lebanon, and Turkey and launched a technology lab for adults at a refugee camp in Jordan.[61]

Jobs and Self-Employment

The 1951 Convention Relating to the Status of Refugees establishes that refugees have the right to opportunities for paid employment and self-employment. Although 145 countries signed this convention, in practice refugees struggle to work or set up their own business due to legal, bureaucratic, status, and discriminatory barriers—even in signatory countries. Other obstacles to obtaining work permits include confusing bureaucratic processes or high costs.[62] Where legal limitations are not imposed on the right to work, countries instead limit the sectors in which refugees can work or otherwise restrict their ability to become economically and financially included in their new societies. Often, host countries impose constraints due to fears that a job for a refugee is a job taken away from a local, concerns that hiring migrants will drive down wages, or outright xenophobia.[63] Finally, many countries that host refugees, particularly in Africa, simply lack the resources to ensure jobs for their own populations, let alone refugees, which further fuels marginalization. Some countries are beginning to recognize the entrepreneurial power often associated with overcoming adversity; see, for example, the refugee compact model discussed in Box 7.5.

---

60   The White House, June 30, 2016, "Fact Sheet: White House Launches a Call to Action for Private Sector Engagement on the Global Refugee Crisis," The White House, https://bit.ly/2yN3dOg.

61   Ibid.

62   Kirsten Schuettler, November 9, 2017, "Refugees' right to work: Necessary but insufficient for formal employment of refugees," World Bank, https://bit.ly/2KvD2Qy.

63   Roger Zetter and Héloïse Ruaudel, Septemeber 2016, "Refugees' Right to Work and Access to Labor Markets – An Assessment (Part 1: Synthesis), Global Knowledge Partnership on Migration and Development. https://bit.ly/2lHK9HQ.

Box 7.5: The Refugee Compact Model

In February 2016, Jordan negotiated the Jordan Compact with Germany, Kuwait, Norway, the United Kingdom, and the UN. The Compact consolidates international and humanitarian funding through grants and concessional loans totaling $2.6 billion. It also offers tariff-free trade in the European market, conditional on Jordan's fulfillment of targets including the issuance of 200,000 work permits for Syrian refugees; access for refugees to work in special economic zones; business enabling environment reforms; and places for Syrian children in Jordanian schools and vocational training institutes. Jordan, which hosts more than 1.5 million refugees, has issued work permits and increased school enrollment, yet progress is slower than anticipated, with key sectors closed off to Syrian employment and self-employment.[64][65]

In 2016, the European Commission also negotiated a compact with Lebanon, providing $400 million to provide a safe environment for refugees and displaced persons; fund education, health, and job creation initiatives; and support infrastructure and investments in job-creating projects. Lebanon hosts more than 450,000 Palestinian refugees.[66]

The compact model shows promise as a means of integrating refugees more effectively in host communities. It is also being discussed for Bangladesh, which now hosts Rohingya refugees from Myanmar, and for Ethiopia.[67]

Other countries such as Uganda are forging a new path on their own, simply enabling freedom of movement and employment with the aim of tapping refugees to drive business and economic growth, as described in Box 7.6.

---

64   Veronique Barbelet, Jessica Hagen-Zanker and Dina Mansour-Ille, February 2018, "The Jordan Compact: lessons learnt and implications for future refugee compacts," Overseas Development Institute Policy Brief, https://bit.ly/2Mwf0Cq.

65   Apolitical, April 20, 2017, "Case Study: Can Jordan's special economic zones give jobs to Syrian refugees?" *Apolitical*, https://apolitical.co/solution_article/can-jordans-special-economic-zones-gives-jobs-syrian-refugees/.

66   United Nations Relief and Works Agency, July 1, 2014, "Where We Work: Lebanon," United Nations Relief and Works Agency, https://www.unrwa.org/where-we-work/lebanon.

67   Cindy Huang, February 7, 2018, "New Opportunities for Bangladeshi Citizens and Rohingya Refugees: A Refugee Compact for Bangladesh," Center for Global Development. https://bit.ly/2tDgiV4.

Box 7.6: Uganda's Progressive Approach to Managing Refugees

Home to almost 1 million refugees, Uganda is exceptional in its approach. The country affords refugees the right to work and freedom of movement, which has benefited both the country and the refugees living there. Nearly 80 percent of refugees in rural settlements are engaged in agriculture, and 43 percent are engaged in the labor market, with 12 percent in the formal sector and 31 percent self-employed.[68] In the capital, Kampala, 21 percent of refugee-owned businesses generate employment beyond themselves and their families, hiring Ugandan nationals as staff. Donors and social investors have built on Uganda's openness by setting up other enabling infrastructure to foster greater employment and self-employment. This infrastructure includes Community Technology Access Centers, which provide computer classes, grant funds to support startups, and backing for refugee-led community organizations.[69]

Investors are also looking at how to support refugee integration, employment, and entrepreneurship. For example, the Alight Fund mobilizes capital to empower refugee entrepreneurs to live self-reliant and dignified lives. It partners with organizations such as Kiva, BCG, and the Global Development Incubator to leverage finance for refugee-owned businesses, using a blended approach that brings together impact, institutional, and philanthropic investors. The offerings range from non-interest-bearing loans to market-rate opportunities for SMEs and larger companies that work with refugees.

Another example is Convergence, a blended finance institution that encourages private sector investment in emerging markets. Convergence helped structure and launch a development impact bond aimed at funding organizations that provide job service programs to Syrian refugees in the Middle East. This bond hopes to raise $10–30 million from social investors to fund skills and entrepreneurship training from NGOs. If these NGOs successfully secure gainful employment with good benefits for graduates, outcome funders such as

---

68 World Bank, August 31, 2016, "Uganda's Progressive Approach to Refugee Management," World Bank, http://www.worldbank.org/en/topic/fragilityconflictviolence/brief/ugandas-progressive-approach-refugee-management.

69 The White House, June 30, 2016, "Fact Sheet: White House Launches a Call to Action for Private Sector Engagement on the Global Refugee Crisis," The White House, https://bit.ly/2yN3dOg.

foundations and aid agencies will repay the original investors, with a financial return commensurate with performance.[70]

Protecting Consumers and Workers

The two main pathways out of poverty—services and jobs—are not always in line with broadly accepted principles of fairness and efficiency. Providing financial services can shade into predatory lending in the hands of unscrupulous vendors; easily accessible mobile banking can lead the poor into unwise financial commitments. Needing a job to make a living, poor people often have little choice but to work in terrible and unfair conditions, with inadequate wages and dangerous work environments.

Financial consumer protection is of special importance given the fast pace of technical and product innovation in the field, especially now that fintech services are reaching the poor for the first time. Some countries have regulatory provisions that restrict predatory lending (59 percent of countries), bundling of services in an opaque way (49 percent), and abusive collections (45 percent).[71] Abuses in this arena can lead to millions of financially uneducated people taking on loans they cannot pay back, resulting in economic costs, social shaming, and even violence. When it comes to labor conditions, work-related health problems represent a cost of 4 to 6 percent of GDP in developing countries, as well as an enormous human cost.[72]

In developing and emerging markets, financial consumer protection and the protection of workers are increasingly mainstream priorities for financial service providers, businesses, and governments aiming to meet global social and environmental standards. Robust consumer protection laws enable people to make informed decisions about the products they use, know their rights and prohibitions, and ensure that they are protected when service providers engage in illegal or unscrupulous practices. Similarly, strong worker protections guard employees from health risks and ensure they are treated fairly.

70   Convergence, October 12, 2017, "Impact Bond For Syrian Refugee Livelihoods Recieves Funding For Structuring and Launch," Convergence, https://www.convergence.finance/news-and-events/news/9JWH3yAel2Gekq0MqEoy6/view

71   World Bank, 2014, "Global Survey on Consumer Protection and Financial Literacy: Oversight Frameworks and Practices in 114 Economies," World Bank, https://bit.ly/2KeRjlf.

72   World Health Organization, November 30, 2017, "Protecting workers' health," World Health Organization, https://bit.ly/2lDEr9C.

Financial Consumer Protection

Since the 2008 financial crisis, consumer protection has become a policy priority among regulators and governments worldwide. The crisis highlighted the weaknesses of the global financial system in protecting clients from predatory service providers that offer high-risk products inappropriate for some clients and income segments. These lending practices often lead to household overindebtedness, mislead clients about pricing and terms for financial products through deceptive advertising or other disclosures, fail to protect the privacy of client data, and do not offer mechanisms for recourse. Some countries, including some in the developing world, are legislating to protect consumers. See Figure 7.8 for an overview of global regulations in the e-commerce sector.

Figure 7.8: Global E-Commerce Legislation

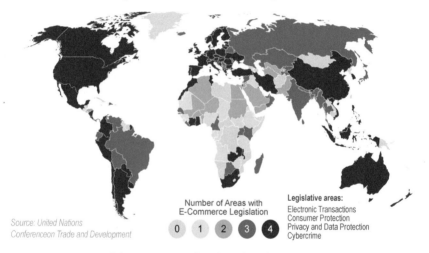

Source: United Nations Conferenceon Trade and Development

Number of Areas with E-Commerce Legislation
0 1 2 3 4

Legislative areas:
Electronic Transactions
Consumer Protection
Privacy and Data Protection
Cybercrime

Even prior to 2008, debtor crises in developed and emerging markets highlighted these weaknesses, particularly for poorer, marginalized clients. For example, debtor revolts in Latin America in the late 1990s to early 2000s emphasized the pressure of overindebtedness that arose with the increase of consumer lenders that spun off from microfinance lending but without strong credit information systems. Similarly, the suicides of indebted farmers in 2010 in Andhra Pradesh, India, showed the need for stricter regulation including disclosure rules, collection practices, tightening credit, and financial literacy.[73]

---

73 Hugh Sinclair, October 8, 2014, "Does microfinance really help poor people?" *The Guardian*, https://bit.ly/2d5LNR8.

Despite the high profile of cases such as Andhra Pradesh, abusive practices around collections remain commonplace. For example, in Uganda it was not uncommon to place defaulting debtors in jail.[74] Social humiliation has also long been utilized by financial institutions, including in microfinance.[75] In numerous countries, lenders have sent texts threatening violence to borrowers as a tactic to collect loans or promised to embarrass people within their social circles or on social media if they fail to repay, even for the smallest loans.

With increased access to the internet, more financial services are being provided online, making it easier and quicker for clients to obtain finance. However, this ease of access raises concerns about clients' ability to repay loans, data privacy, and security. Regulators are also rethinking their approaches. For example, in Kenya, more than 20 companies provide digital credit. If there were a credit crisis in Kenya, many people would suffer financial blows with little opportunity for remuneration due to a lack of protective infrastructure. Financial consumer protection aims to establish a clear code of conduct for financial institutions as they engage with customers. At a minimum, these guidelines aim to ensure that consumers:

- receive accurate, transparent information about financial products and services to enable informed decision making (**disclosure and transparency**);
- are not subject to unfair, deceptive, or fraudulent practices (**fair treatment and business conduct**);
- have access to a unit that will hear and address any complaints (**dispute resolution mechanism**); and
- have their information protected and the collection, usage, and sharing of that data done lawfully with the full knowledge of the client (**data protection and privacy**).[76]

Most countries seek to complement financial consumer protection with access to consumer education or financial literacy information and tools. Transparent

---

74   Jami Solli, January, 2015, "What Happens to Microfinance Clients who Default," Smart Campaign, https://bit.ly/1nvqx8l.

75   Ibid.

76   World Bank, 2017, "Good Practices for Financial Consumer Protection, 2017 Edition," World Bank, https://bit.ly/2Kj1dlS.

rules of behavior for financial institutions, combined with financial literacy programs aimed at consumers, are shown to increase trust in financial markets and, in turn, encourage market development.[77] Secondary school students in Ukraine and Brazil have benefited from a financial education curriculum. Governments are increasingly leveraging new techniques too, including behavioral science, to improve consumer literacy and protection (see Box 7.7).

Box 7.7: Using Behavioral Research to Improve Financial Consumer Protection

Regulators are increasingly using behavioral research to improve consumer protection policies. Although the practice is driven largely by more developed countries, emerging markets can learn from the trend. Evidence suggests that understanding consumer behavior can improve products, services, and outcomes for consumers. For example, research is showing how scarcity plays into people's financial decisions; how simplified information can improve a consumer's ability to compare, select, and use different financial products; and how aligning information to a consumer's personal context can improve decision making (while at the same time recognizing that better information does not always enable better decisions). In such cases, default options (nudges) can be designed to influence and prod consumer behavior. Similarly, researchers are analyzing the factors and incentives that drive financial service provider behaviors—behaviors that can also be shaped to benefit both consumers and providers in the long term.[78]

When financial consumer issues arise, people should have a mechanism to address their complaints. If a consumer is not satisfied with an outcome, alternative dispute resolution mechanisms provide additional recourse, particularly in countries where judicial fairness may be questionable due to corruption. At least 92 countries have adopted alternative dispute resolution mechanisms that include standards for resolving issues, such as specifying a maximum time to respond to a complaint and naming a regulator to receive the complaint. Eighty countries designate an out-of-court entity, such as a financial ombudsman, that is legally allowed to handle consumer complaints. In some instances, the financial institutions themselves attempt to define the parameters by which they operate. Several initiatives have sprung up to self-regulate, vet, and certify

---

77   Ibid.

78   Rafe Mazer, Katharine McKee and Alexandra Fiorillo, June 2014, "Applying Behavioral Insights in Consumer Protection Policy," CGAP, https://bit.ly/2MuZLtu.

financial institutions. Examples include FinCoNet, an international organization of supervisory authorities, and The SMART Campaign, a network of more than 100 microfinance providers in 42 low-income countries.[79][80]

Governments, regulators, financial service providers, and consumer-focused NGOs are looking for new ways to build creative financial capability programs that involve schools, add-ons to government programs, apps, entertainment vehicles, and new business models. For example, in Guinea, Liberia, and Sierra Leone, governments have built financial education programs for recipients of transfer payments that strengthen these people's ability to manage their money. These programs teach people who receive cash transfers how to better manage their households, deal with income shocks, and invest wisely.[81]

Privacy is also a big issue. Financial service providers must collect personal information from potential clients to evaluate them for new products and services. This information may include contact details, consumer agreements, transaction logs, and passwords. Providers should be allowed to collect, hold, and use personal data after receiving informed and legal consent from clients. However, they must recognize that what constitutes consent may be a gray area, particularly when alternatives do not exist or when consumers are illiterate, uneducated, and do not have the time to read or understand dense and opaque privacy notices (see Box 7.8). Institutions should also be held accountable for data confidentiality and security, and regulations should specify how data can be used.[82]

Box 7.8: Data Privacy and Informed Consent in India

In 2017, CGAP, Dalberg, and the Future of Finance Initiative at Dvara (India) conducted research on what Indian citizens think about data privacy. Indians care deeply about their personal information, including photographs and messages. If they are to share this information, they expect certain conditions to be in place, including consent and a guarantee that it will not be used unscrupulously. However, the research found that people often did not understand what they were consenting to, a factor related to levels of literacy. Finally,

---

79 FinCoNet, "About us," FinCoNet, http://www.finconet.org/about/.

80 The Smart Campaign, http://www.smartcampaign.org/.

81 World Bank, June 2018, "Financial Education Program (FEP)—Ghana: Needs Assessment Report," World Bank, http://documents.worldbank.org/curated/en/331891528817424815/pdf/127119-WP-P155002-PUBLIC.pdf.

82 World Bank, 2017, "Good Practices for Financial Consumer Protection, 2017 Edition," World Bank, https://bit.ly/2Kj1dlS.

most people interviewed had been the victim of fraud but did not know what channels of redress were open to them or how to protect themselves. Women were more exposed to fraud, particularly where they feared reputational harm, and to protect themselves they often opted out of providing personal data such as phone numbers.[83]

Worker Protection

Hundreds of millions suffer from work-related health issues, both physical and mental (Figure 7.9 shows critical statistics).[84][85] Not surprisingly, many of the 3.2 billion workers worldwide are not content in their jobs. The situation is particularly alarming in developing countries, where work conditions are worse on average, oversight is poor, and employers tend to be more predatory (Box 7.9 discusses modern slavery). These hazardous environments have major human and economic cost implications for workers, their families, and for employers themselves. Employers have to manage early retirements, loss of staff, and absenteeism resulting from substandard conditions.

Figure 7.9: The Importance of Worker Protections

4–6% of global GDP is lost to occupational accidents and diseases

people die annually from work-related accidents and diseases **2 million**

137 million people suffer from work-related diseases

people suffer nonfatal, work-related accidents **330 million**

70% of workers lack insurance to compensate them in case of occupational diseases and injuries

Sources: World Health Organization, International Labour Organization

83   Dalberg, November 2017, "Privacy On the Line," https://bit.ly/2D72w3U.

84   World Health Organization, November 30, 2017, "Protecting workers' health," World Health Organization, https://bit.ly/2lDEr9C.

85   International Labor Organization, April 12, 1999, "ILO Estimates Over 1 Million Work-Related Fatalities Each Year," International Labor Organization, http://www.ilo.org/global/about-the-ilo/newsroom/news/WCMS_007969/lang--en/index.htm.

Many of these losses are preventable through the use of reporting and inspection practices and by promoting a culture of accident prevention and safety. The International Labor Organization's global strategy lays out an approach for countries to adopt preventive safety and a healthy work culture.[86] In addition, Sustainable Development Goal 8 makes worker rights and protection a global imperative. The goal, which promotes decent work, aims to engage both government and employers more effectively, including setting targets for businesses.

The UN and others are working with the private sector directly in programs that create new, fair employment, especially for youth. Sustaining Competitive and Responsible Enterprises (SCORE), a training and workplace improvement program, aims to increase the productivity of SMEs while promoting better working conditions. By integrating SCORE into their corporate social responsibility or supplier support programs, companies help smaller businesses participate in supply chains and improve conditions for workers.

Box 7.9: Slavery—A Ghost from the Present

Slavery, assumed by many to be a thing of the past, is sadly a current issue touching the lives of more than 40 million people and their families. Of modern slaves, 71 percent are women and 25 percent children. Modern slavery can be divided into forced labor and forced marriage. More than 25 million people are stuck in forced labor, 11.7 million in Asia-Pacific alone, followed by Africa (3.7 million) and Latin America (1.8 million). Forced labor represents a global industry of $150 billion and is imposed by both the private sector (in 50 percent of cases due to debt bondage) and oppressive state governments, in varied sectors including construction, domestic work, manufacturing, agriculture, and tourism.[87] Forced marriage afflicts 15 million people, mostly in Africa and the Middle East.[88] [89]

Multinational companies are also being held accountable and taking more responsibility for work practices in their supply chains. Instead of simply buying

---

86   International Labor Organization, "International Labour Standards on Occupational Safety and Health," International Labor Organization https://bit.ly/1LQ4e2H.

87   International Labor Organization, 2017, "Global Estimates of Modern Slavery: Forced Labour and Forced Marriage," International Labor Organization, https://www.ilo.org/global/publications/books/WCMS_575479/lang--en/index.htm.

88   International Labor Organization, "Statistics on forced labor, modern slavery and human trafficking," International Labor Organization, https://bit.ly/1MRrt2y.

89   International Labor Organization, 2017, "Global Estimates of Modern Slavery: Forced Labour and Forced Marriage," https://bit.ly/2HNLLfC.

from the cheapest supplier, they increasingly take into consideration work conditions and strive to make a positive impact. In China, companies such as the Gap, Metro Group, and COOP Switzerland use SCORE to complement their supplier monitoring activities, which has resulted in less absenteeism, reduced employee turnover, and improved product quality.[90] Similarly, the ILO and the IFC are implementing the Better Work Program to improve working conditions and business competitiveness in the global garment and footwear industries. Committed global brands and retailers can enter a public-private partnership with the program to make sector-wide improvements, sharing lessons learned and best practices. The program includes work at the enterprise level to identify and report companies that fail to comply with national labor laws and international standards, then provide workplace tools and training.[91]

Despite the protocols and initiatives in place to move these standards forward, significant worker protection gaps remain, especially for migrant and foreign domestic workers. Foreign domestic workers tend to be young women sent abroad to work as maids or child care providers, who can be a significant source of income for their families at home. In fact, some governments, such as the Philippines, justify this practice by the vast amount of remittances coming in each year.[92] However, these women can end up in financially precarious jobs without work permits and are targeted for sexual abuse and other exploitations by their employers and supervisors.[93] Some of the same issues affect farm workers and other low-skill laborers such as janitors.

In 2017, the ILO estimated that there are approximately 232 million international migrants, of whom 206.6 million are older than 15 years old. Of this working-age migrant population, 150 million are workers and 40 percent of them are women. Some migrant-receiving countries and regions have begun to institute better labor governance practices. For example, Singapore requires all

---

90   International Labor Organization, 2017, "SDG NOTE: Engaging The Private Sector On Decent Work – Business Operation And Investments," International Labor Organization, https://bit.ly/2KyCOYS.

91   Ibid.

92   Teresita Cruz del Rosario, February 19, 2018, "Abuse of foreign domestic workers must end now," *Aljazeera*, https://www.aljazeera.com/indepth/opinion/abuse-foreign-domestic-workers-180219082433652.html.

93   Bernice Yeung, March 13, 2018, "How the most vulnerable workers are targeted for sexual abuse," *The Guardian*, https://www.theguardian.com/news/2018/mar/13/how-the-most-vulnerable-workers-are-targeted-for-sexual-abuse.

employers to provide health insurance for migrant workers and provides special protections for these workers, such as mandatory rest days, required health checkups, and safety agreements.[94] All domestic migrant employers have to take an online program before they can hire such workers, so that the employers can understand their responsibilities.[95] [96] In 2017, ASEAN countries came together to sign the Consensus for the Protection and Promotion of the Rights and Welfare of Migrant Workers. The document reflects their collective promise to strengthen social protection, access to justice, humane and fair treatment, and access to health services for the region's migrant workers.[97]

Optimizing New Technologies

Emerging technologies such as artificial intelligence, advanced robotics, virtual reality, blockchain, and aerial drones offer a new way to reach remote populations and empower low-income individuals. It is too soon to predict the exact impact of these technologies, especially in emerging and frontier markets. Nonetheless, some current examples demonstrate how they might facilitate access to services and jobs.

Services and Technology

Technology has the potential to expand access to affordable and high-quality services. To achieve this goal, however, government institutions must be effective and the technologies in question need to be made widely available and packaged into business models tailored for low-income people.[98]

94   Ministry of Manpower, April 15, 2016, "Medical insurance requirements for foreign worker," Ministry of Manpower, http://www.mom.gov.sg/passes-and-permits/work-permit-for-foreign-worker/sector-specific-rules/medical-insurance.

95   Ministry of Manpower, June 21, 2018, "Employers' Orientation Programme (EOP)," Ministry of Manpower, https://bit.ly/2mh91aB.

96   Teresita Cruz del Rosario, February 19, 2018, "Abuse of foreign domestic workers must end now," Aljazeera, https://www.aljazeera.com/indepth/opinion/abuse-foreign-domestic-workers-180219082433652.html.

97   Association of Southeast Asian Nations, November 2017, "ASEAN Consensus On The Protection And Promotion Of The Rights Of Migrant Workers," Association of Southeast Asian Nations, https://bit.ly/2KqPh0J.

98   World Bank, 2016, "World Development Report 2016: Digital Dividends," World Bank, http://documents.worldbank.org/curated/en/896971468194972881/pdf/102725-PUB-Replacement-PUBLIC.pdf.

Mobile and Digital Technologies

Mobile and digital technologies already reach many of the excluded and un-banked. The most well-known example is the Kenyan mobile payment plat-form M-Pesa, which radically reduced the transaction cost of transferring mon-ey in Kenya and has spread to many other countries. A massive expansion of access to financial services followed in Kenya and elsewhere, as described in Box 7.10.[99]

Providing access to banking is not the only way mobile and digital technologies promote financial inclusion at scale. Limited knowledge of banks is also targeted through digital initiatives focused on financial literacy. Fundación Capital launched a pilot program with Citi Foundation in Colombia to develop an alternative to in-person financial learning. They offered unbanked communities a tech-based offline program through a shared tablet. Thus far, the program has trained more than 200,000 people with 1,000 tablets rotating in the field. [100] Preliminary results of the pilot program indicate that participating individuals benefit from a better understanding of basic finance concepts, such as savings and debt.[101]

Box 7.10: Impact of Mobile Money

Launched in 2007 by Safaricom, M-Pesa, a mobile money platform, has revolutionized the Kenyan economy. Today, it is the dominant mobile money platform in Kenya (although not the only one), and in 96 percent of households in Kenya, at least one person now has a mobile money account. Access to M-Pesa helped lift 194,000 Kenyan households out of poverty.[102] Simultaneously, it created additional income for more than 80,000 agents working for the M-Pesa network.[103]

---

99   Claudia McKay and Rafe Mazer, October 1, 2014, "10 Myths About M-Pesa: 2014 Update," CGAP, https://bit.ly/2KsLEYo.

100 Fundacíon Capital, 2017 "LISTA Initiative," Fundacíon Capital, https://fundacioncapital.org/our-work/lista-initiative/.

101 Orazio Attanasio, Matthew Bird, and Pablo Lavado, 2017, "Tablet-based financial education in technology," Innovations for Poverty Action, https://www.poverty-action.org/study/tablet-based-financial-education.

102 Tavneet Suri and William Jack, December 8, 2016, "The Long-Run Poverty and Gender Impacts of Mobile Money, *Science Magazine*, http://www.microfinancegateway.org/sites/default/files/publication_files/new_jack_and_suri_paper_1.pdf.

103 World Bank, 2016, "World Development Report 2016: Digital Dividends," World Bank, http://documents.worldbank.org/curated/en/896971468194972881/pdf/102725-PUB-Replacement-PUBLIC.pdf.

Globally, about 1.7 billion people lack access to financial services, which leads many of these individuals to rely on costly and inefficient informal financial services.[104] Digital technology, through mobile money, helps overcome these challenges. For the 80 percent of poor adults estimated to be excluded from the financial sector, mobile money helps provide access to these services in an efficient way. In addition, it helps businesses be more productive and streamlines delivery of public sector services. [105]

Governments also use technology to distribute social safety net programs, such as cash transfers, more efficiently by decreasing costs, improving transparency and reducing leakage. In Brazil, the Bolsa Familia conditional cash transfer program reaches nearly 12 million households through an electronic benefit card.[106] In India, electronic transfers could save the government $22 billion each year.[107]

Health services are also changing due to mobile and digital technologies. For rural communities, distance to the nearest hospital is a major inhibitor for getting high-quality health care. A mobile app named First Derm allows rural doctors in Tanzania to upload an image, get a second opinion on the medical condition, and then decide whether a hospital visit is necessary for their patient.[108]

Blockchain

Although blockchain technology has not yet broadly diffused into the global market, understanding what blockchain is and how it could be used to increase access to services has significant development implications. Blockchain is a decentralized ledger of digital transactions that are recorded and confirmed anonymously and cannot be changed. More simply put, blockchains are like

104 Asli Demirgüç-Kunt, Leora Klapper, Dorothe Singer, Saniya Ansar and Jake Hess, 2017, "The Global Findex Database," World Bank, https://globalfindex.worldbank.org.

105 World Bank, 2016, "World Development Report 2016: Digital Dividends," World Bank, http://documents.worldbank.org/curated/en/896971468194972881/pdf/102725-PUB-Replacement-PUBLIC.pdf.

106 Gary Duffy, May 25, 2010, "Family Friendly: Brazil's scheme to tackle poverty," BBC, https://www.bbc.com/news/10122754.

107 World Bank, 2016, "World Development Report 2016: Digital Dividends," World Bank, http://documents.worldbank.org/curated/en/896971468194972881/pdf/102725-PUB-Replacement-PUBLIC.pdf.

108 Jonathan Mayes and Andrew White, November 1, 2016, "How Smartphone Technology Is Changing Healthcare In Developing Countries," *Journal of Global Health*, http://www.ghjournal.org/how-smartphone-technology-is-changing-healthcare-in-developing-countries/.

an Excel spreadsheet that many have access to, but none can change the information once it is entered. Transactions are recorded as encrypted "blocks" of information and are added to the "chain" database once both parties have fulfilled their obligations. This greatly reduces transaction costs and does not require the reconciliation of different ledgers maintained by different parties.[109]

In many developing countries, the lack of reliable land registration data poses several challenges, including limited foreign investment. Through blockchain, any country could create an immutable database of land ownership and through a self-improving algorithm check who owns what land prior to sale or construction. Bitland, a nonprofit, is trying to do exactly this in a pilot with 28 communities across Kumasi, Ghana.[110] Should the pilot succeed, Bitland hopes to expand its operations to the entire African continent.[111]

Remittance payments are another service that blockchains can make more transparent, efficient, and affordable. The current system for sending remittances is based on wire transfers, which take time and can be quite costly for those depending on limited funds, with the total fees amounting to 7 percent of the transaction on average. With blockchain technology, those sending remittances can circumvent the existing process to get their money where it needs to go more securely, more quickly, and less expensively than ever before.[112]

Drones and Innovative Engineering

Advances in robotics and drone technology are also helping deliver vital services. Zipline, a US-based company, is partnering with the Ethiopian and Tanzanian governments to deliver on-demand medical supplies to hospitals via drone. Given the poor road infrastructure in these countries, drones dramatically reduce the time it takes for blood to be delivered to a hospital.[113] Other

---

109 Paul Dughi, February 3, 2018, "A simple explanation of how blockchain works," *Medium*, https://bit. ly/2xGMICL.

110 Jane Thomason, August 11, 2017, "7 ways to use blockchain for international development," Devex, https://bit.ly/2KipXe8.

111 Ibid.

112 Kevin Rands, November 14, 2017, "How blockchain technology is disrupting the remittance industry," *CIO Magazine*, https://bit.ly/2KsyeLW.

113 Aryn Baker, 2017, "The American Drones Saving Lives in Rwanda," *Time Magazine*, https:// ti.me/2yQME3O.

drone companies, such as SenseFly, provide mapping services that offer a way to create digital terrain models for developing countries to manage water or infrastructure projects more effectively.[114] [115]

Medical devices represent another area where people in developing countries lack affordable access. D-Rev, a nonprofit, uses innovative engineering to design affordable, high-quality medical devices, such as prosthetic limbs, for low-income individuals around the world.[116] Currently, D-Rev has fitted almost 500 patients with prosthetic limbs, 274 of whom would not have had access to a prosthetic limb without D-Rev's affordable product.[117] Similarly, Embrace, another nonprofit, developed Embrace Warmers to provide a cost-effective wrap that maintains the body temperature of premature and low-birth-weight babies at risk of dying from hypothermia in many developing countries. Currently, these warmers have been used to care for over 200,000 infants in over 20 countries.[118]

Virtual Reality

Virtual reality (VR) offers new ways to deliver services. In the health sector, VR is being used to train medical staff to perform surgeries. For example, HelpMeSee, a nonprofit committed to fighting cataract blindness, hopes to use VR technology to train 30,000 medical practitioners to treat cataracts using a virtual human eye to recreate the feel of performing surgery (see Box 7.11).[119] VR can also expand access to education for vulnerable populations. In Nigeria, ongoing discussions consider how VR can help internally displaced children by transporting them into any classroom, destination, or learning environment of their choice.[120] Examples include learning about marine life by virtually diving

114 SenseFly, "The professionals drone mapping choice, "https://www.sensefly.com.

115 Drones For Development, "The Dr.One Concept," https://www.dronesfordevelopment.org.

116 D-Rev, "Mobility Impact Dashboard," http://d-rev.org/impact/remotion/.

117 Ibid.

118 Embrace, "Our Story," http://embraceglobal.org/about-us/.

119 Sheila Jagannathan, March 7, 2017, "Virtual Reality: The Future of Immersive Learning for Development," World Bank, https://blogs.worldbank.org/publicsphere/virtual-reality-future-immersive-learning-development.

120 Judith Okonkow, June, 20, 2017, "An immersive and accessible tool for education," TED Archive, https://www.youtube.com/watch?v=5-KWeRmdklY.

into the ocean, projecting 3D holograms to study organisms in a biology lab, or virtually traveling into space to learn about the solar system, regardless of a person's native tongue.[121] But these technologies become useful only when they are built to meet the realities of different populations.

Box 7.11: Virtual Reality in Action

Globally, cataracts accounts for 51 percent of blindness cases.[122] Though cataract surgery is commonplace in the developed world, in many developing countries, access to adequate medical treatment is limited largely by the lack of surgeons qualified to perform cataract procedures. HelpMeSee, a nonprofit, is using VR technology to address this problem. Basing its approach on the simulation training used for aircraft pilots, HelpMeSee developed a technology to train local surgeons to perform cataract surgery in a sustainable and safe way.[123] VR enables trainees to learn from their mistakes and achieve greater proficiency without putting any real patients at risk. Furthermore, these programs can scale: more than 300 surgeons have been trained through the HelpMeSee program, and 256,265 sight-restoring procedures were completed in China, Gambia, India, Madagascar, Myanmar, Nepal, and Peru.[124]

Internet of Things

The internet of things (IoT) enables advances in services by connecting electronic devices and other elements of the physical world to intelligent networks.[125] The growing ubiquity of interconnected devices should enable providers to deliver more tailored and individualized services. Figure 7.10 illustrates the variety of industries where IoT has an impact.[126]

---

121 Eyitayo Alimi, February 21, 2018, "A practical look at virtual reality in Nigerian education," TEDxGbagadaSalon, https://www.youtube.com/watch?v=40gesn6Sgec.

122 World Health Organization, "Blindness and Vision Impairment Prevention," https://bit.ly/1rTbp2S.

123 HelpMeSee, "Simulation-Based Training Program," https://helpmesee.org.in/OurTechnology#anchorCollapse.

124 HelpMeSee, "Our Progress," https://helpmesee.org.in/Home.

125 International Telecommunication Union, 2016, "Harnessing the Internet of Things for Global Development," https://bit.ly/23wI5nN.

126 Al-Fuqaha Ala, 2015, "Internet of Things: A Survey of Enabling Technologies, Protocols and Applications, Communications Surveys & Tutorials," Institute of Electrical and Electronic Engineers, https://ieeexplore.ieee.org/document/7123563/.

Figure 7.10: IoT Uses Across Industries

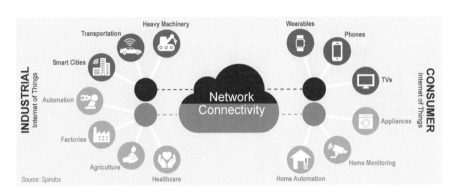

The internet of things has an array of applicable sectors; farmers can use remote sensors to keep track of the moisture levels of their crops, governments can use this technology to keep track of movement during crises, and utilities can monitor water pump usage rates and performance.[127] IoT also has applications in health care. Keeping vaccines cold remains a challenge in many countries. The 200,000 vaccine refrigerators across developing countries are particularly vulnerable to breaking down given their often harsh climates, increasing the risk that vaccines will become unusable. The nonprofit Nexleaf is using IoT technology to prevent this outcome by installing sensors in refrigerators to monitor changes in temperature. If an adverse change occurs, a health care professional in that facility is notified through a connected device, ensuring that the refrigerators are fixed in a timely manner to prevent spoilage. [128]

Jobs and Technology

Artificial intelligence (AI) is already reshaping the global job market, and the debate rages as to whether AI will replace or augment human labor. Fundamentally, the debate centers on whether AI will be able to automate nonroutine tasks at the same level it automates routine tasks. Historically, technologies such as computeri-

---

127 Rob Goodier, July 1, 2016, "How the Internet of Things Is Improving Lives and Livelihoods in Developing Countries," Engineering for Change, https://bit.ly/2KeqH3T.

128 NexLeaf Analytics, "Coldtrace helps health workers get safe vaccines to kids," NexLeaf Analytics http://nexleaf.org/vaccines/.

zation have replaced routine jobs. The share of routine jobs fell by nearly 8 percent between 1995 and 2012 in most developing countries, with China as a notable exception.[129] As AI becomes more sophisticated, examples of AI technology automating nonroutine tasks, such as driving a car, are becoming more frequent.[130]

Automation affects jobs in manufacturing and agriculture more than jobs in the service sector.[131] Today, agriculture makes up roughly 70 percent of employment in low-income countries and 30 to 40 percent in lower-middle- and middle-income countries.[132] Automation may disrupt these markets, hinder developing countries in leveraging their labor-cost advantages, and potentially exacerbate inequality. [133] [134] It has been estimated that 375 million workers may need to switch occupational categories between now and 2030 as a result of displacement by intelligent machines. China, in absolute terms, faces the largest number of workers susceptible to automation if firms embrace these technologies rapidly.[135] Figure 7.11 illustrates the varying potential for automation of the workforce around the world, based on currently existing technologies.[136]

129 Carl Benedikt Frey and Ebrahim Rahbari, August 2016, "The Future of Work in the Developing World: Do labor-saving technologies spell the death of jobs in the developing world?" Brookings Institute, https://brook.gs/2tJ8z7p.

130 Erik Brynjolfson and Andrew McAfee, 2016, "The Second Machine Age: Work, Progress and Prosperity in a time of Brilliant Technologies," WW. Norton and Company.

131 Ljubica Nedelkoska and Glenda Quintini, March 2018, "Automation, skills use and training," Organisation for Economic Co-operation and Development, https://bit.ly/2N1xNXr.

132 World Bank, 2017, "Employment in agriculture (% of employment) (modeled ILO estimate)," https://bit.ly/2KvPw7w.

133 Citi GPS, 2016, "Technology at Work v2.0, The Future Is Not What It Used to Be," https://bit.ly/2KhYfyg.

134 Harry Anthony Patrinos, August 2016, "The skills that matter in the race between education and technology" Brookings Institute, https://www.brookings.edu/wp-content/uploads/2017/01/global_20170131_future-of-work.pdf.

135 James Manyika, Susan Lund, Michael Chui, Jacques Bughin, Jonathan Woetzel, Parul Batra, Ryan Ko, and Saurabh Sanghvi, November 2017, "Jobs lost, jobs gained: What the future of work will mean for jobs, skills, and wages," McKinsey Global Institute, https://mck.co/2ig4Ufo.

136 Ibid.

Figure 7.11: Potential for Automation by Country

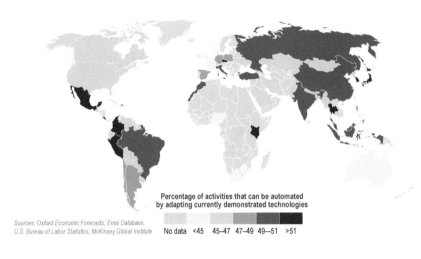

Percentage of activities that can be automated
by adapting currently demonstrated technologies

Sources: Oxford Economic Forecasts, Emsi Database,
U.S. Bureau of Labor Statistics, McKinsey Global Institute   No data   <45   45–47   47–49   49–51   >51

Breakthroughs in 3D printing, robotics, and other technologies increase the likelihood of game-changing disruption of global supply chains. Previously, cheap labor incentivized multinational corporations to go offshore, but new technology may make it more cost effective to re-shore production to automated factories in the developed world.[137] The rate at which these potential changes occur will be different from country to country, depending on social preferences, regulations, and labor costs.[138]

The fast-paced nature of changing technologies, markets, and business models makes it hard to predict the demands of the labor market of the future. Continuous learning and re-skilling is likely to be critical. These skills do not necessarily require long and costly commitments. They can be self-taught, informal, and short term through MOOCs, e-learning, online courses, and technical courses. Coding bootcamps offer another way to re-skill workers. Andela, for example, pays individuals in Africa to learn coding. The vision is to develop the continent's next generation of software developers. In three years of operations, Andela trained 20,000 programmers across Africa and has an ambitious

---

137 Carl Benedikt Frey and Ebrahim Rahbari, August 2016, "The Future of Work in the Developing World: Do labor-saving technologies spell the death of jobs in the developing world?" Brookings Institute, https://brook.gs/2tJ8z7p.

138 Melanie Arntz, Terry Gregory, and Ulrich Zierahn, 2016, "The Risk of Automation for Jobs in OECD Countries: A Comparative Analysis," Organisation for Economic Co-operation and Development Social, https://bit.ly/2aL60tC.

goal to reach 100,000 individuals by 2024.[139] Badging, a common online skills validation practice, is one way for people to earn recognition for skills. Those searching for jobs can display a badge indicating their mastery of, say, Java-Script or Python, to strengthen an online job-matching profile. Mozilla Open Badges is one company offering these certification programs.[140]

Embracing Urbanization

By 2050, two out of every three people in the world will live in an urban area, compared to just 30 percent of people in 1950 (see Figure 7.12).[141] The world's population will grow by 2.5 billion people in the next 30 years, while the world's rural population will decrease to just 3.2 billion.[142] Migration patterns, advances in technology, and economic shifts all contribute to and stem from urbanization, making it one of the defining trends of the 21st century. Global poverty, also, will increasingly be urban. Today, 1 billion people live in urban slums—a number expected to reach 1.5 billion by 2020.[143] The pathways out of poverty for developing countries undoubtedly go through cities.

139 Steve Lohr, October 10, 2017, "Start-up Bets on Tech Talent Pipeline From Africa," *The New York Times*, https://nyti.ms/2yD7cvA.

140 Open Badges, "About Open Badges," https://openbadges.org/about/.

141 Department of Economic And Social Affairs, 2015, "World urbanization Prospects: The 2014 Revision," United Nations, https://esa.un.org/unpd/wup/Publications/Files/WUP2014-Report.pdf.

142 Ibid.

143 World Bank, 2013, "Global Monitoring Report 2013—Chapter 2: Rural-Urban Disparities and Dynamics," World Bank, https://bit.ly/2KqQMJ5.

Figure 7.12: Increased Global Urbanization

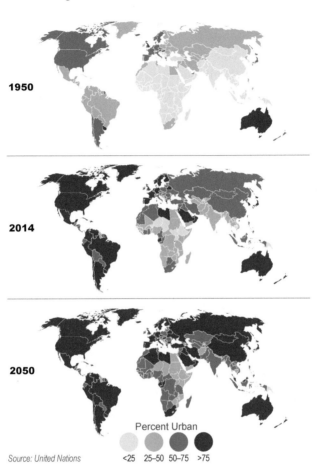

1950

2014

2050

Percent Urban

Source: United Nations   <25   25–50   50–75   >75

For developed and developing countries alike, urbanization simultaneously represents an opportunity and a challenge. The movement toward cities correlates with economic growth as concentrations of people and resources facilitate economies of scale and raise incomes.[144] Yet that same population density can contribute to problems of overcrowding, crime, and weak community net-

144 McKinsey & Company, June 2012, "Urban world: Cities and the rise of the consuming class," McKinsey & Company, https://www.mckinsey.com/featured-insights/urbanization/urban-world-cities-and-the-rise-of-the-consuming-class.

works.[145] Increased consumption can help sustain emerging market economies but lead to greater per capita waste.[146] [147]

Initiatives such as 100 Resilient Cities (100RC) bring together local government officials and city planners with NGOs and private sector partners to address the challenges of urbanization. Created by the Rockefeller Foundation in 2013, 100RC's global network helps cities achieve resilience, inclusiveness, and sustainability by promoting innovation, providing financial and logistical advice, and sharing best practices. Box 7.12 provides examples of projects 100RC member cities have implemented to (re)design healthy cities.

Box 7.12: 100RC Toward Healthy Cities

Surat, India, is making itself more resilient to disasters. Surat is reducing vulnerability to flooding by creating risk awareness centers that will use technology to track flood risk and keep communities aware of potential disasters. Surat is investing in mapping technology and enhancing its early warning system to help keep the populace informed of natural disasters and reviewing research on urban climate change and its current environmental law enforcement mechanisms to build climate change resilient infrastructure. Its approach is highly collaborative and includes participation of citizens in developing and applying innovative solutions to city problems.[148]

Quito, Ecuador, is making itself more inclusive by building local institutions that encourage citizen participation in city planning and creating more public spaces for citizens. The local government has a plan to engage citizens digitally, develop community-led neighborhood development plans, and use stakeholder engagement to develop safe parks and other spaces that people want. The effort is aligned with the SDGs and integrates actions of various levels of government, the private sector, civil society, and the scientific community.[149]

---

145 Judy L. Baker, 2008, "Urban Poverty: A Global View," World Bank, https://bit.ly/2lGOoTM.

146 Richard Dobbs, Jaana Remes and Fabian Schaer, September 2012, "Unlocking the potential of emerging market cities," McKinsey & Company, https://mck.co/2N8xolN.

147 Daniel Hoornweg and Perinaz Bhada-Tata, March 2012, "What A Waste: A Global Review of Solid Waste Management," World Bank, https://bit.ly/1mjzbQB.

148 Resilience Surat, July 2017, "Surat Resilance Strategy," 100 Resilient Cities, https://bit.ly/2KohZzB.

149 Resilience Quito, October 2017, "Resilience Strategy: Metropolitan District of Quito," 100 Resilient Cities, https://bit.ly/2KipAAn.

Buenos Aires, Argentina, is becoming more sustainable by developing a low-emission, climate-resilient urban transportation system that features eco-friendly buses, bike lanes, and bike-sharing stations. Buenos Aires is also revitalizing public spaces and housing in low-income neighborhoods with the goal of making the people who live there more economically integrated with the city, making them both happier and more productive.[150][151]

This section highlights some of the ideas and private sector solutions that address the problems and capitalize on the benefits of urbanization to increase access to jobs and services.

Access to Services in Cities

Urbanization strains resources because city residents generally consume more energy, water, and other resources per capita than their rural counterparts. Indeed, cities are responsible for two thirds of the energy used and more than 70 percent of greenhouse gases emitted globally.[152] A significant increase in investment is needed to address service gaps: urban infrastructure for water alone will require an estimated $480 billion in investment by 2025. Cities in emerging markets will need 80 percent of this investment.[153]

Urban Sprawl

Urban sprawl, resulting from the proliferation of job opportunities in urban centers coupled with poor city planning, often leads to informal settlements (slums) outside city centers. Millions of people worldwide live in slums, particularly in Sub-Saharan Africa. In 2014, more than 60 percent of the urban population in 24 countries lived in a slum.[154] By 2050, 3 billion people, nearly

---

150 World Bank, 2017, "Metropolitan Buenos Aires Urban Transformation Project," World Bank, https://bit.ly/2yPFhJN.

151 Adriana Gomez and Minakshi Seth, June 6, 2017, "IFC Supports Urban Transit Solutions for Buenos Aires with Financing and Expertise," International Finance Corporation, https://bit.ly/2KwA66c.

152 Department of Economic And Social Affairs, 2015, "World urbanization Prospects: The 2014 Revision," United Nations, https://esa.un.org/unpd/wup/Publications/Files/WUP2014-Report.pdf.

153 Richard Dobbs, Jaana Remes and Fabian Schaer, September 2012, "Unlocking the potential of emerging market cities," McKinsey & Company, https://mck.co/2N8xolN.

154 World Bank, "Population living in slums (% of urban population)," World Bank, https://bit.ly/2N8y7n1.

30 percent of the world's population, will live in slums.[155] People are often driven to live on the outskirts of urban areas by the low wages and high living costs that prevail in city centers, but informal settlements create numerous challenges for utilities, the housing sector, transportation, and health.[156] Governments are unlikely to upgrade or subsidize informal housing, while local citizens living in unauthorized areas are less likely to seek such support from the authorities because they fear the potential consequences, such as being evicted from their homes.[157] Low-income urban residents—especially women—thus spend more of their time and income to make their housing situations work, as well as on commuting expenses.[158] [159]

Urban slums have often taken root in areas threatened most by climate change and shocks, which is particularly problematic for cities. These areas, home to the most vulnerable urbanites, are more likely to suffer from natural disasters such as drought and flooding.[160] Recent refugee crises also have "urbanized." Most Syrian refugees in Lebanon and Jordan, for example, live in urban areas, straining health, education, and other public services and complicating coordination efforts.[161]

Robust city planning and significant infrastructure investments will be needed to reverse urban sprawl, but private sector players already have begun to address some of the challenges associated with it. Recognizing the pollution and congestion caused by drivers, for instance, the Chinese company Weigongjiao, or Kandi Technologies, aims to make car sharing easier. The company uses

155 Cécile Barbière, March 6, 2017, "French urban development expert: 'In 2050, 3 billion people will live in slums'," *Euractiv*, https://bit.ly/2tMM4hN.

156 Todd Litman, March 31, 2017, "Unaffordability Is a Problem, but Sprawl Is a Terrible Solution," The *City Fix*, http://thecityfix.com/blog/unaffordability-is-a-problem-but-sprawl-is-a-terrible-solution-todd-litman/.

157 Michael Spence, Patricia Clarke, and Annez Robert M. Buckley, 2009, "Urbanization and Growth: Commission on Growth and Development," World Bank, https://bit.ly/2tN7Sts.

158 Cecilia Tacoli, March 2012, "Technical Briefing: Urbanization, gender and poverty," United Nations Population Fund, http://pubs.iied.org/pdfs/G03335.pdf.

159 Suveer Sinha, January, 2018, "Combating the challenges of urbanization in emerging markets: Lessons from India," McKinsey & Company, https://mck.co/2BjKcyC.

160 Department of Economic And Social Affairs, 2015, "World urbanization Prospects: The 2014 Revision," United Nations, https://esa.un.org/unpd/wup/Publications/Files/WUP2014-Report.pdf.

161 Shelly Culbertson, Olga Oliker, Ben Baruch and Ilana Blum, 2016 "Rethinking Coordination of Services to Refugees in Urban Areas: Managing the Crisis in Jordan and Lebanon," Research and Development Corporation, https://bit.ly/2KqQ9T3.

electric cars exclusively, which it dispenses to customers through automated garages. These garages have been compared to vending machines and make the service user friendly and inexpensive.[162]

Private companies also have addressed logistical and commercial issues in expansive urban areas. Konga began as a startup to address gaps in the online shopping market in greater Lagos and has expanded to become one of Nigeria's largest online retailers.[163] Founded in 2012, Konga and its main competitor, Jumia, have even created their own distribution, logistics, and Wi-Fi centers to fulfill and deliver online orders themselves—creating jobs and closing gaps in courier, transportation, and internet services in Nigerian cities.[164]

Utilities

Urbanization can mean a poorer quality of life for many. Although access to utilities such as piped water is more attainable in urban than rural areas, coverage varies significantly and tends to be subpar in urban slums.[165] In slums or other areas of dense poverty, providing utilities and water, sanitation, and health (WASH) services can be logistically challenging.[166] Unsurprisingly, those residing in informal settlements are more prone to health problems related to environmental hazards such as pollution or unsafe water.[167] In addition, in some countries like Bangladesh, energy can cost more in slums. [168] Proof-of-residence permits can be difficult to obtain, but lacking such proof is

162 Mark Rogowsky, December 28, 2013, "Kandi Crush: An Electric-Car Vending Macjine From China Could Upen The Auto Industry," *Forbes*, https://bit.ly/2Ky7fvm.

163 NewCities, July 18, 2017, "NewCities Summit 2017 - The Unlikely Appeal of Disruptive Urbanpreneurs," NewCities, https://www.youtube.com/watch?v=pKBcofAu_wM.

164 Jake Bright, December 2, 2016, "Nigeria's Black Friday sales test the e-commerce models of startups Jumia and Konga," *TechCrunch*, https://tcrn.ch/2gVyC3e.

165 World Bank, 2017, "Reducing Inequalities in Water Supply, Sanitation, and Hygiene in the Era of the Sustainable Development Goals: Synthesis Report of the WASH Poverty Diagnostic Initiative," World Bank, http://bit.ly/2IAhTQ5.

166 Department of Economic And Social Affairs, 2015, "World urbanization Prospects: The 2014 Revision," United Nations, https://esa.un.org/unpd/wup/Publications/Files/WUP2014-Report.pdf.

167 Ibid.

168 Molla Shahadat Hossain Lipu, Taskin Jamal, Muhammad Ahad Rahman Miah, 2013, "Barriers to Energy Access in the Urban Poor Areas of Dhaka, Bangladesh: Analysis of Present Situation and Recommendations," *International Journal of Energy Economics and Policy*, https://www.econjournals.com/index.php/ijeep/article/viewFile/536/330.

a barrier to other services for those living in informal housing and increases the risk of eviction.[169] The rapid growth of cities has given rise to "urbanpreneurs" who focus on spurring (technological) innovations in their communities (see Box 7.13).[170]

Box 7.13: Urbanpreneurs Tackle Tough Problems in Cities

Entrepreneurs have come up with innovative solutions to address the gaps and market failures in providing WASH services to urban centers. SWEEP, a public-private partnership in the megacity of Dhaka, Bangladesh, has received support from UNICEF, Water & Sanitation for the Urban Poor (a London-based company), and Dhaka's municipal water agency. Of the city's 16 million people, 70 percent must use septic systems instead of metropolitan WASH services, and overflow from septic tanks pollutes local water sources. Bangladesh's first financially sustainable septic tank removal enterprise, SWEEP uses vacuum technology to eliminate its customers' waste, charging a lower rate to low-income people. It had reached 100,000 people in Dhaka by May 2017.[171] [172]

Oxygen Energy Private Limited, founded by Simbarashe Mhuriro with a support grant from the African Development Bank in 2017, has developed a 20-megawatt off-grid solar power system installed on rooftops in Zimbabwe. The company is projected to bring competitively priced, reliable, renewable energy to hundreds of small and medium-sized enterprises by partnering with a property management company to retrofit properties with the rooftop system.[173]

Urbanization also has reshaped how essential services are delivered. Currently, 65 percent of the global population—4.7 billion people—have access to mobile

169 Martina Bosi and Beatriz Eraso Puig, May 25, 2017, "From slums to neighborhoods: How energy efficiency can transform the lives of the urban poor," World Bank, http://bit.ly/2N5Li8p.

170 Richard Florida, October 20, 2016, "Rise of the 'Urbanpreneur'," *CityLab*, http://bit.ly/2MutxOU.

171 Water & Sanitation for the Urban Poor, November 17, 2016, "Promoting sanitation business models on World Toilet Day," Water & Sanitation for the Urban Poor, https://www.wsup.com/blog/is-entrepreneurship-a-solution-to-the-sanitation-challenge/.

172 Neil Jeffery, November 30, 2016, "A call for more entrepreneurs to focus on toilets," *The Huffington Post*, http://bit.ly/2tCpetO.

173 Mfonobong Nsehe, December 21, 2017, "Meet The 32 Year-Old Entrepreneur Who Is Building Zimbabwe's Largest Solar Company," *Forbes*, http://bit.ly/2Ks033C.

technology, up from around 50 percent as recently as 2012.[174] Increasingly, internet access will become a utility rather than an amenity, offering an opportunity to redesign cities, stimulate economic growth, and compete for business development. Limited internet access in Medellin, Colombia, for example, made attracting startups challenging. The city therefore made connectivity a priority, with a goal of providing 63 percent of people with internet by 2018, and it currently ranks among Latin America's top entrepreneur-friendly cities. Along with its startup-friendly policies, Medellin has become a hub for both Colombian and international entrepreneurs. The ecosystem flourishes with the likes of Ruta N incubator and accelerator Parque del Emprendimiento, co-working spaces like La Casa Redonda and NODO, and VC funds like Firstrock Capital and Capitalia.[175] Medellin brought in more than 150 companies in four years, creating more than 2,700 jobs.[176] [177] [178]

Access to Jobs in Cities

Urban areas account for a disproportionate share of global economic activity, largely due to the productivity and efficiency gains associated with cities.[179] Further, the bulk of the expected growth in global GDP between now and 2025 will come from just 600 cities—443 of them in emerging markets (Figure 7.13).[180] [181]

---

174 GSMA Intelligence, October 2016, " Global mobile trends," GSMA Intelligence, http://bit.ly/2lHjESU.

175 Nathan Lustig, December 19, 2017, "The Colombian Startup Ecosystem: Bogota, Medellin, Cali, and Barranquilla," Nathan Lustig, http://bit.ly/2lDK0Vy.

176 Jonathan Keane, August 26, 2015, "Medellin: Colombia's emerging tech hub," International Data Group Connect, http://bit.ly/2Mq6PHC.

177 Cadie Thompson, May 7, 2015, "Three growing start-up cities in South America," CNBC, https://cnb.cx/2Kroz4R.

178 Ruta N Medellín, March 22, 2017, "Medellín, World Innovation Hub," Ruta N Medellín, https://www.rutanmedellin.org/en/news/news/item/medellin-world-innovation-hub.

179 Michael Spence, Patricia Clarke, and Annez Robert M. Buckley, 2009, "Urbanization and Growth: Commission on Growth and Development," World Bank, https://bit.ly/2tN7Sts.

180 Richard Dobbs, Jaana Remes and Fabian Schaer, September 2012, "Unlocking the potential of emerging market cities," McKinsey & Company, https://mck.co/2N8xolN.

181 Ibid.

Figure 7.13: Urbanization Fuels a Growing Global Economy

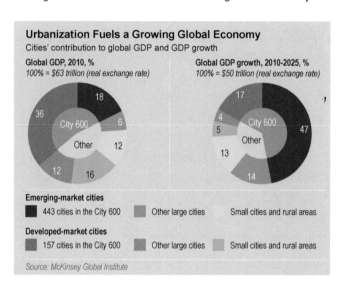

However, urbanization's economic benefits are not inevitable. Evidence from some Sub-Saharan African countries has shown urbanization can accompany lower per capita GDP and wages.[182] Urban centers often generate more informal jobs, which are less productive and more vulnerable to economic shocks.[183] [184] Informally employed people receive lower wages and less protection. Their employment is largely unregulated, making it difficult for countries to collect income tax revenue.[185]

Cities that invest in employment spaces and blend jobs with services can support inflows of younger workers, women, and migrants, creating a self-reinforcing cycle of manufacturing jobs, productivity, and employment.[186] [187] Ethiopia's

182 Remi Jedwab and Dietrich Vollrath, January 2015, "The mortality Transition, Malthusian Dynamics, and the Rise of Poor Mega-Cities," George Washington University, http://bit.ly/2KubUS1.

183 Michael Spence, Patricia Clarke, and Annez Robert M. Buckley, 2009, "Urbanization and Growth: Commission on Growth and Development," World Bank, https://bit.ly/2tN7Sts.

184 Marc Bacchetta, Ekkehard Ernst, Juana P. Bustamante, 2009, "Globalization And Informal Jobs In Developing Countries," International Labor Organization and World Trade Organization. http://www20. iadb.org/intal/catalogo/PE/2009/04308.pdf.

185 Kazuhiro Yuki, 2007, "Urbanization, informal sector, and development," *Journal of Development Economics.*

186 World Bank, 2012 "World Development Report 2013: Jobs," World Bank, http://bit.ly/2MvFILp.

187 Michael Spence, Patricia Clarke, and Annez Robert M. Buckley, 2009, "Urbanization and Growth: Commission on Growth and Development," World Bank, https://bit.ly/2tN7Sts.

Hawassa Industrial Park, for example, will create 60,000 manufacturing jobs and has been supported by affordable housing, education, and empowerment programming for female urban migrants who live and work at the park. Part of a broader effort to increase private sector investment and export-oriented growth, Hawassa's success has spurred the development of a dozen more industrial parks across Ethiopia.[188]

Advances in technology have made manufacturing less labor intensive and services more productive, leading to an increase in urban service jobs—plus a plethora of new development challenges and opportunities.[189] Countries such as India and Malaysia have increasingly begun exporting transportation, financial, and technical services, exemplifying how the service sector can bolster trade growth. [190] [191] However, providing these services often requires high-skilled workers, meaning for many developing countries these jobs alone cannot employ enough people to drive robust economic growth.[192] Similarly, studies have shown that urbanization in countries such as the Philippines has grown the informal, rather than formal, economy because of insufficient industrialization. [193]

SMEs enterprises are the primary drivers of job creation, accounting for the bulk of both manufacturing and service firms in countries such as China, Indonesia, Mexico, the Philippines, and Tunisia.[194] New enterprises can increase productivity, job creation, and technology use, making cities more economically competitive.[195] In Sub-Saharan Africa, which needs an estimated 4.6 million new jobs each year

188 Nebil Kellow, Spring 2018, "Ethiopia Stands Poised to Lead an African Industrial Revolution," DAI, http://bit.ly/2Mq8mxm.

189 Ejaz Ghani and Stephen D. O'Connell, July, 2014, "Can Service Be a Growth Escalator in Low Income Countries?," World Bank, http://documents.worldbank.org/curated/en/823731468002999348/pdf/WPS6971.pdf.

190 World Bank, 2012 "World Development Report 2013: Jobs," World Bank, http://bit.ly/2MvFILp.

191 Ejaz Ghani and Stephen D. O'Connell, July, 2014, "Can Service Be a Growth Escalator in Low Income Countries?," World Bank, http://documents.worldbank.org/curated/en/823731468002999348/pdf/WPS6971.pdf.

192 Dani Rodrik, October 14, 2014, "Can services drive developing country growth?," World Economic Forum, https://www.weforum.org/agenda/2014/10/dani-rodrik-services-manufacturing-growth/.

193 Kazuhiro Yuki, 2007, "Urbanization, informal sector, and development," *Journal of Development Economics*.

194 World Bank, 2012 "World Development Report 2013: Jobs," World Bank, http://bit.ly/2MvFILp.

195 Ejaz Ghani and Stephen D. O'Connell, July, 2014, "Can Service Be a Growth Escalator in Low Income Countries?," World Bank, http://documents.worldbank.org/curated/en/823731468002999348/pdf/WPS6971.pdf.

to employ its growing youth population, entrepreneurship will mean the difference between benefiting from urbanization and buckling under it.[196]

Fortunately, small enterprises not only create jobs but also play a significant role in narrowing the skills gap, thereby unlocking the potential of the urban services sector. Andela, for example, a startup based in Nigeria and Kenya, has developed intensive training and job placement programs to build a pipeline of computer programmers, with the goal of training 100,000 African software developers by 2028.[197] Ghanaian software developer Regina Agyare founded Tech Needs Girls through her enterprise Soronko Solutions; the startup pairs girls with women mentors who serve as both role models and teachers and has already trained more than 4,000 girls across Ghana.[198]

Coping with Climate Change

Climate change results from oceanic and atmospheric warming caused by human population and economic growth. The evidence of this warming is apparent in net glacier loss, sea level rise, decreased snow cover, and increased temperatures—April 2018 was the 400th consecutive warmer-than-average month.[199] An overwhelming scientific consensus holds that human activities cause global warming, principally through the excessive emission of greenhouse gases (GHGs), such as carbon dioxide and methane.

Climate change has disastrous consequences, particularly for those least equipped to cope. It leads to an increase in the frequency of natural disasters, prolonged drought, accelerated desertification and deforestation, ocean acidification, shifting weather patterns, melting ice and permafrost, and more. These climate and weather phenomena jeopardize agricultural output, job security, and energy supplies and pose a threat to human health and wellness for low-in-

196 Claudia Pompa, March, 2015, "Jobs for the Future," Overseas Development Institute, http://bit.ly/2tBCnU2.

197 International Finance Corporation, April, 2018, "Perspectives," International Finance Corporation, http://bit.ly/2lCDe2y.

198 Julian López, February 11, 2018, "This young entrepreneur is preparing girls to lead the tech industry in Ghana," International Research & Exchange Board, https://www.irex.org/success-story/young-entrepreneur-preparing-girls-lead-tech-industry-ghana.

199 Doyle Rice, May 17, 2018, "Earth just had its 400th straight warmer-than-average month thanks to global warming," *USA Today*, https://usat.ly/2tznlyk.

come people in developing countries. Climate change threatens to push an additional 100 to 200 million people into poverty through higher food prices, lower productivity, higher health costs from the spread of vector-borne diseases and inadequate sanitation, and natural disasters. In the face of this massive threat, policy makers are focusing on how to mitigate and adapt to climate change.[200] [201]

Mitigation refers to slowing the rate of climate change by reducing GHG emissions. A government opting to support a new wind farm instead of a more carbon-intensive coal-fired power plant for electricity is an example of mitigation. Adaptation refers to building climate resilience, such as constructing roads made of strong materials in areas prone to flooding or enforcing tougher building codes in areas susceptible to high winds.

Adequate mitigation costs could be as much as $175 billion a year by 2030, and private sector involvement will be necessary across the globe. However, this means that a business opportunity does exist; new investments, new jobs, and new technologies related to the climate all offer opportunity for more jobs and access to better services.[202]

While the lowest-income countries have historically contributed the least to global warming, they stand to lose the most, and so developing countries need to prepare for the crises that climate change will bring. Figure 7.14 shows the level of susceptibility to adverse climate change effects for each country.[203]

200 World Bank, November 8, 2015, "Rapid, Climate-Informed Development Needed to Keep Climate Change from Pushing More than 100 Million People into Poverty by 2030," World Bank, http://bit. ly/2Mx4z1k.

201 Gabe Bullard, December 1, 2015, "See What Climate Change Means for the World's Poor," *National Geographic*, https://news.nationalgeographic.com/2015/12/151201-datapoints-climate-change-poverty-agriculture/.

202 Dimitris Tsitsiragos, January 13, 2016, "Climate change is a threat – and an opportunity – for the private sector," World Bank, http://www.worldbank.org/en/news/opinion/2016/01/13/climate-change-is-a-threat---and-an-opportunity---for-the-private-sector.

203 Ian Johnston, November 7, 2016, "Map shows how climate change will hit. The economies of the world's porest countries hardest," *The Independent*, https://ind.pn/2lHpG5W.

Figure 7.14: Susceptibility to Climate Change by Country

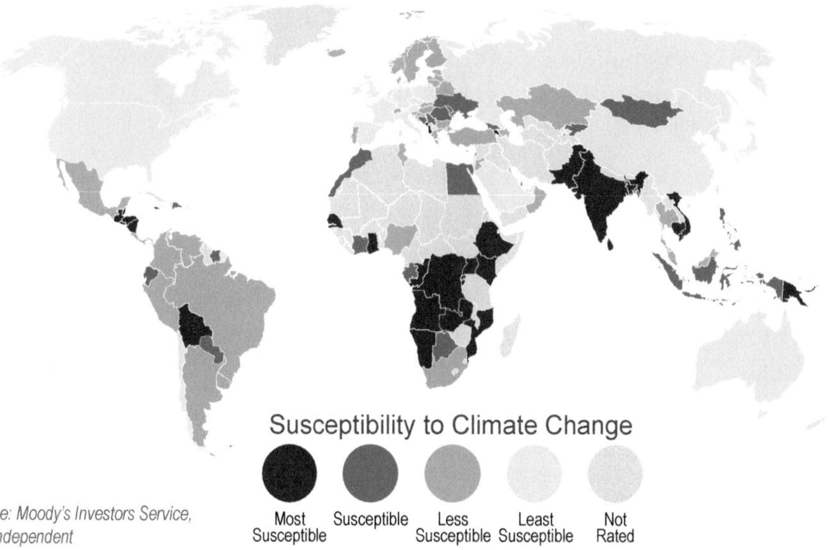

Susceptibility to Climate Change

Source: Moody's Investors Service, The Independent

Most Susceptible · Susceptible · Less Susceptible · Least Susceptible · Not Rated

Economic growth has historically relied on activities that generally contribute to global warming, and the challenge is to tackle access to services and jobs without exacerbating the climate problem going forward. If every person in the world consumed like the average American, 4.1 Earths would be required to meet this demand.[204] The world needs new paradigms for water, roads, and power—it is cheaper to mitigate GHG emissions now than it is to deal with the problem further in the future. Fortunately, many pro-poor initiatives also reduce the impacts of climate change or mitigate GHG emissions. Examples include off-grid solar powered electricity and cookstoves; improved agricultural techniques and products; clean water; and financial products such as micro-insurance that protect clients from shocks. Renewable energy is particularly attractive as it becomes less expensive every year.[205] The challenge is how to implement these initiatives in a comprehensive way.

---

204 Tim De Chant, August 8, 2018, "If the world's population lived like…," *PerSquareMile*, https://persquaremile.com/2012/08/08/if-the-worlds-population-lived-like/.

205 David Roberts, August 24, 2016, "The falling costs of US solar power, in 7 charts," *Vox*, https://www.vox.com/2016/8/24/12620920/us-solar-power-costs-falling.

Service Provision and Climate Change

Providing clean, off-grid energy can connect bottom-of-the-pyramid people to jobs and services while leapfrogging traditional power sources. When low-income consumers use solar panels or LED lights for power and lighting instead of coal and kerosene, their health and safety improves without contributing to global warming. Strategies that connect access to clean electricity with commercial activities are particularly useful for lifting people out of poverty. In India, for example, rooftop solar power is now cheaper than commercial or industrial power.[206] Annual off-grid solar investment exploded between 2012 and 2017, and annual investment in energy storage in developing markets is expected to continue to grow, likely exceeding $20 billion by 2025.[207] More than 8 million off-grid solar systems were sold between 2015 and 2016 alone.[208]

Off-grid solar products now reach 360 million people; however, millions more lack access to electricity, meaning the market still has enormous growth potential.[209] Figure 7.15 shows the growth potential by country, with 434 million households comprising the potential market.[210]

206 Bloomberg New Energy Finance, Novemeber 28, 2017, "Accelerating India's Clean Energy Transition," *Bloomberg*, https://data.bloomberglp.com/bnef/sites/14/2017/11/BNEF_Accelerating-Indias-Clean-Energy-Transition_Nov-2017.pdf.

207 World Bank, January, 2018, "Off-Grid Solar Market Trends Report 2018," World Bank, http://bit.ly/2IADAQb.

208 International Finance Corporation, 2017, "Creating Markets for Climate Business," International Finance Corporation, https://www.ifc.org/wps/wcm/connect/974eedcb-f3d9-4806-b32e-73720e6f4ca7/IFC-Climate_Investment_Opportunity_Creating_Markets.pdf?MOD=AJPERES.

209 Riccardo Puliti, February 26, 2018, "Off-grid bringing power to millions," World Bank, http://blogs.worldbank.org/energy/grid-bringing-power-millions.

210 World Bank, January, 2018, "Off-Grid Solar Market Trends Report 2018," World Bank, http://bit.ly/2IADAQb.

Figure 7.15: Countries with the Largest Potential Off-Grid Solar Markets

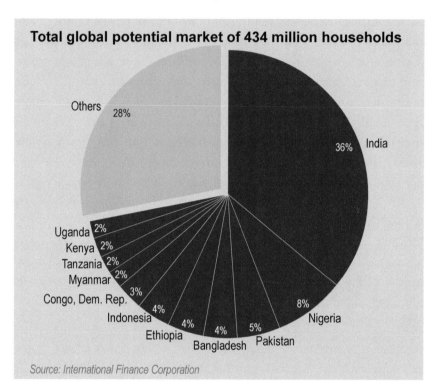

Total global potential market of 434 million households

Others 28%

India 36%

Uganda 2%
Kenya 2%
Tanzania 2%
Myanmar 2%
Congo, Dem. Rep. 3%
Indonesia 4%
Ethiopia
Bangladesh 4%
Pakistan 5%
Nigeria 8%

Source: International Finance Corporation

Constructing, adapting, or retrofitting roads, bridges, sewers, and other infrastructure to be climate resilient is one way for countries to adapt to climate change. The economic losses that stem from a lack of proper sanitation can cost some countries as much as 7 percent of their GDP, and these costs will grow as climate change causes more flooding and storms.[211]

Micro-insurance has the power to help low-income people whose livelihoods are at risk from increasingly frequent extreme weather events. In exchange for small monthly premiums, insurers provide payouts if certain conditions, such as too little rainfall, are met. R4 is a micro-insurance partnership between the World Food Programme and reinsurance giant Swiss Re that sells insurance to smallholder farmers. Swiss Re will distribute payouts if satellites detect that too

---

211 World Bank, March 20, 2013, "As Climate Change, Threatens, Water Cooperation Becomes Vital," World Bank, http://www.worldbank.org/en/news/feature/2013/03/20/climate-change-water-cooperation.

little rain has fallen in a given season. In this way, insurers do not have to make farmers prove losses, and it becomes more feasible to offer micro-insurance coverage on a grand scale.[212]

Finally, countries need to prepare themselves for the sea level to rise, the spread of vector-borne diseases, and increasingly frequent extreme weather events brought about by climate change. Rebuilding after natural disasters, however, does offer an opportunity to rebuild better. By engaging with local communities, agencies working to help communities recover after a disaster have a chance to build climate-resilient institutions to make the next disaster less devastating, as well as build social capital.[213] Box 7.14 describes the Cape Town crisis, a grim harbinger of the reality many urban centers will likely have to face in the coming decades.

Box 7.14: The Cape Town Water Crisis

In the fall of 2017, it became clear that Cape Town, South Africa, might run out of water by the following summer. Climate change is forcing many cities to reckon with their limited water resources, but none before Cape Town had ever had to reckon with what a complete lack of water would mean. To avoid this crisis—and related loss of jobs, reduced economic growth, and possibly even civil unrest—the government launched the Day Zero campaign, urging Cape Town residents to use water wisely. The plan worked, and other cities can learn from how Cape Town made its way back from the brink of disaster by reducing urban water use, upgrading water delivery infrastructure, reusing wastewater, removing foreign plant species, and applying water-efficient farming techniques.[214]

Low-Carbon Jobs and Resilient Agriculture

For developing countries, transitioning to a low-carbon economy can provide jobs and mitigate the effects of climate change without necessarily compromising growth. Ramping up investment in clean energy production and infrastructure is a common way countries are transitioning to lower-carbon economies.

---

212 Bill Lascher, November 8, 2013, "Could micro-insurance help the porrest communities deal with climate change?" *The Guardian*, https://www.theguardian.com/sustainable-business/micro-insurance-poorest-communities-climate-change.

213 World Bank, September 10, 2014, "How to Develop Effective Disaster Recovery Programs – Lessons from Vulnerable Countries," World Bank, http://bit.ly/2Kfisou.

214 Krista Mahr, "How Cape Town was saved from running out of water," May 4, 2018, *The Guardian*, http://bit.ly/2KxfQhu.

Most existing greenhouse gas emissions come from infrastructure, primarily power generation, construction, and transportation. Reforms in these areas have enormous potential for reducing climate impact. Investment in railways and urban transport projects tripled between 2010 and 2018 as developing countries began to take climate change seriously and realized that railways offer a more climate-friendly transportation option than roads for their growing populations. Low-carbon power generation is becoming a more attractive investment than traditional power sources, with investment in renewable energy projects exceeding investment in traditional projects for the first time in 2012.[215] One example of many is the Penonome wind power plant in Panama, which will reduce Panama's dependence on foreign fossil fuels, generate 448 GWh annually upon completion, and reduce carbon dioxide emissions by 400,000 tons each year.[216]

Facilities like Penonome require construction personnel, operators, and other employees and thus create jobs. Governments can create decent work by providing training and skill building to workers and entrepreneurs who can fill the demand for jobs in the clean energy sector. Many countries already provide training in fields such as forestry, sustainable agriculture, and renewable energy to meet demand generated by transitioning to a low-carbon economy. For instance, Bangladesh offers a technical and vocational education and training program for female solar engineers. Costa Rica provides training in water treatment and environmental management and has provided this training to 8,000 workers as of 2017.[217] [218] Millions of jobs that offset carbon will be created as sustainable economic projects grow in number and scope, and these new jobs have the potential to lift tens of millions out of poverty.[219]

---

215 Deblina Saha and Akhilesh Modi, 2017, "Low Carbon Infrastructure," World Bank, http://bit.ly/2tCsMfC.

216 Vanessa Bauza and Jamilette Guerrero, December 16, 2014, "IFC Closes $300 Million Financing to Support the Largest Wind Farm in Central America," International Finance Corporation, http://bit.ly/2KyaW4c.

217 International Labor Organization, April, 2017, "ILO's contribution to the objectives of the Green Climate Fund," International Labor Organization, http://bit.ly/2lCnjRI.

218 Marshall Burke, December 9, 2015, "The global economic costs from climate change may be worse than expected," Brookings Institute, https://brook.gs/2lHmtmY.

219 Fiona Harey, May 31, 2012, "Switching to a green economy could mean millions of jobs, says UN," The Guardian, https://www.theguardian.com/environment/2012/may/31/switching-green-economy-jobs-un.

Growth in the low-carbon sector will lead to structural changes in the job market; sectors that deal with green energy and climate-resilient technologies will grow, and sectors such as oil and gas are expected to shrink. These losses will often be painful. However, the alternative is more painful by orders of magnitude. The opportunity cost of not switching to a low-carbon economy globally is staggering. Global GDP could shrink by 20 percent between 2020 and 2100 if no action is taken.[220]

Many of the world's low-income people are engaged in agriculture, leaving them particularly exposed to the effects of climate change. The number of extreme weather events has escalated in recent years and put smallholder farmers at risk (see Figure 7.16).[221] Educating farmers on how to increase their resilience to climate-related shocks both protects their livelihoods and enhances food security in the regions to which they supply food.

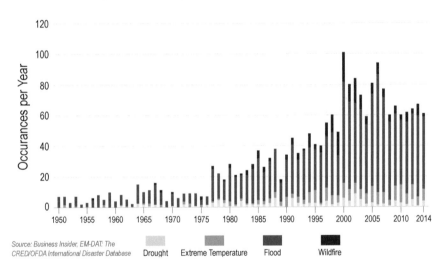

Figure 7.16: The Escalation of Extreme Weather Events

There are several ways to limit climate change's impact on agricultural livelihoods. One is by changing the types and variety of crops farmers grow. By planting both late- and early-maturing rice varieties, for example, farmers can

220 Marshall Burke, December 9, 2015, "The global economic costs from climate change may be worse than expected," Brookings Institute, https://brook.gs/2lHmtmY.

221 Elena Holodny, March 23, 2016, "Extreme weather events are on the rise," *Business Insider*, https://read.bi/2lGpynf.

hedge against an adverse shock wiping out an entire crop at once.[222] Governments, realizing the threat posed to food security, have been working to create climate-resistant crops for years. The Drought-Tolerant Maize for Africa project has resulted in research on 200 hundred kinds of maize, each suited for different climate conditions that farmers in the 13 target countries can now plant to become climate resilient.[223] Not only do these methods enhance resilience, they can improve crop yield as well (see Box 7.15 for one example from Uganda). The science and techniques underlying these seed developments and farming methods are now well established; the next challenge for governments and the development community is demonstrating to farmers the financial benefits that changing to climate-resilient crops can bring.

Box 7.15: Crop Variety and Resiliency in Uganda

Every district of Uganda produces beans. Beans provide an important source of food and income for households across the country. Periods of both droughts and floods are increasing in frequency across Uganda, and both can wipe out bean crops. The Ugandan government, in collaboration with the Pan-Africa Bean Research Alliance, has developed bean varieties that are drought-resistant or iron rich or have other favorable traits that will help farmers, especially smallholders, cope with increasingly difficult conditions. The average yield from these new crops is 60 percent higher than earlier varieties, and it is estimated that poverty would have been .1 percent higher without these more resilient varieties of beans.[224][225]

Another way the agricultural sector can adapt to climate change is by adopting more effective water management practices, in line with the adage "more crop per drop." Up to half of the global population will not have enough water to meet its needs by 2025. The relationship between agricultural output, water, and climate change is multifaceted. Climate change alters rain patterns, in-

222 OECD, 2014, "Climate Change, Water and Agriculture: Towards Resilient Systems," Organisation for Economic Co-operation and Development, http://bit.ly/2IxdCx9.

223 Edward Mabaya, June 3, 2016, "Climate change and 'smart seeds' in Africa," Aljazeera, http://bit.ly/2KyAXne.

224 California Institute of Arts & Technology, "Farmers in Uganda team up with scientists to find better beans," California Institute of Arts & Technology, http://bit.ly/2tC8XoW.

225 Standing Panel on Impact Assessment, December 2014, "Impact of Bean research in Rwanda and Uganda," CGIAR https://ispc.cgiar.org/sites/default/files/pdf/SPIA_Impact-Brief-46_Jan2015.pdf.

creases the likelihood of extreme events such as floods and droughts, affects salinity levels, and changes water quality.[226] Better irrigation techniques can help farmers withstand shocks to the water they need to remain productive. In The Gambia, despite the fact that 30 percent of GDP comes from the agricultural sector, less than 3 percent of arable land benefits from modern water management techniques. Smallholder farmers are beginning to protect themselves by using mulch and crop rotation techniques taught through government aid programs to increase water retention in soil. The private sector can complement government support by providing water conservation tools. An example is Jain Irrigation Systems in India. Jain's drip and sprinkler systems allow farmers to move away from traditional flood irrigation, and they provide water savings of up to 65 percent.[227]

Livestock and the production of animal products place an even greater strain on water resources. The demand for livestock products in 2050 is on track to be twice what it was in 2017.[228] 14.5 percent of global GHG emissions come from this sector through land destruction, the resources used for feedstock, emissions from the animals, and transport. As such, livestock will continue to be a significant contributor to global warming.[229] However, this level of emissions can be reduced with better farming and husbandry techniques. Better manure management practices, feed practices, and health management will all result in emissions reductions. Total emissions could be reduced by 18 to 30 percent if every region in the world adopted the practices of the quartile with the lowest intensity.[230]

---

226 Organisation for Economic Co-operation and Development, 2014, "Climate Change, Water and Agriculture: *Towards Resilient Systems,*" Organisation for Economic Co-operation and Development, http://bit.ly/2IxdCx9.

227 International Finance Corporation, May, 2014, "Inclusive Business Case Study: Jain Irrigation Systems Limited (JISL)," International Finance Corporation, http://bit.ly/2tCxLNz.

228 M. Melissa Rojas-Downing, A. Pouyan Nejadhashemi, Timothy Harrigan, and Sean A.Woznicki. February 12, 2017, "Climate change and livestock: Impacts, adaptation, and mitigation," *Climate Risk Management* vol. 16, https://www.sciencedirect.com/science/article/pii/S221209631730027X.

229 Gerber, P.J., Steinfeld, H., Henderson, B., Mottet, A., Opio, C., Dijkman, J., Falcucci, A. & Tempio, G., 2013, "Tackling Climate Change Through Livestock: A Global Assessment of Emissions and Mitigation Opportunities," Food and Agriculture Organization of the United Nations, http://www.fao.org/3/a-i3437e.pdf.

230 Ibid.

Chapter 8. Conclusion

Promoting inclusive economic development remains the domain of governments, international donor agencies, and philanthropists. But the landscape is changing rapidly. Today, a wider range of players seek profit with purpose, including millennials, institutional investors, and corporates. The Sustainable Development Goals (SDGs), designed to end poverty, save the planet, and ensure prosperity by 2030, offer a focal point for new players to get involved and for existing donors to revise their frameworks. None of these actors, traditional or new, can achieve truly inclusive economic systems on their own. Success will demand collaboration, often among uneasy bedfellows. It cannot be business as usual.

The good news is that the past quarter century has ushered more than a billion people out of poverty. This achievement—the result of human ingenuity, resilience, and enterprise—gives reason for optimism.

The bad news is that too many people remain excluded. When women, youth, small farmers, urban slum dwellers, refugees, indigenous peoples, and others are left out of the economy, everybody loses. The excluded cannot contribute to the economy as consumers or as workers.

Inclusive economic systems offer pathways out of poverty, primarily through access to services and jobs. This book traces these two pathways to show how the most compelling, innovative, and scalable solutions come together to drive inclusive economic growth, as summarized in Figure 8.1.

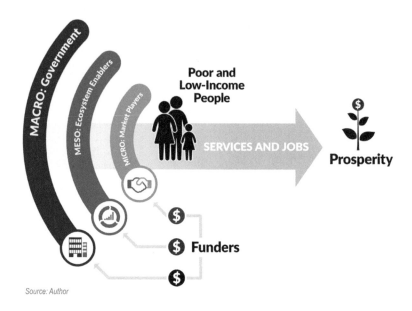

Figure 8.1: Inclusive Economic Systems Framework

Source: Author

Fátima de Jesús Carazo and her company Rosquillería Alondra (RA) show the human face of inclusive economics. Fátima was a low-income woman in Nicaragua who made her living selling corn-based baked goods called rosquillas. RA found its first major customer with the help of the Association of Producers and Exporters of Nicaragua, a business organization that helps make small businesses more competitive. Even after the association's assistance, RA still did not have financial statements or a relationship with a bank, but through her relationship with Agora Partnerships—an international small business incubator—she discovered a brand new financial product called a VPO, or variable payment option.

Here's how it works: USAID and the Dutch Argidius Foundation support a program that helps women-owned businesses in Nicaragua access finance via a regional bank called BAC. The Miller Center for Social Entrepreneurship at Santa Clara University and Agora Partnerships helped BAC introduce VPOs, a type of loan where repayment is based on the ability of the borrower to earn revenue rather than the more traditional rigid repayment structure. This loan allowed RA to improve its factory and its manufacturing practices.

Actors at every level of the economic system—micro, meso, and macro—contributed to Fátima's success. The combined efforts of BAC (micro); the Association of Producers and Exporters, the Miller Center, and Agora Partnerships (meso); the government, through reforms to improve the business climate, such as consolidating business registration processes (macro); and USAID and Argidius (funders) enabled Fátima to broaden her distribution network, nearly doubling her revenue.[1] RA now has improved financial, accounting, and cash flow practices and is more productive. Fátima can produce the same amount of rosquillas while working four hours fewer each day and has even purchased a car, which has always been a dream for her.

Fátima is not alone; between 2011 and 2017, Agora reached 156 companies in Latin America and the Caribbean, and these firms together employ more than 5,000 people.[2]

Achieving inclusive economic systems means beginning with poor and low-income people like Fátima. Their demand for services and job opportunities drives the actions—or should drive the actions—of actors at all the other levels of the economic system. But poor and low-income people are not a monolithic group. Poverty is multidimensional and complex. It affects men, women, girls, and boys in different ways at different times, depriving them of the freedom to shape their own lives and forge their own futures. In broad strokes, a poor person today is most likely to be a woman or child living in a rural village in Sub-Saharan Africa or South Asia with little to no education and working in the informal sector, especially in subsistence agriculture. Interestingly and significantly, this person is likely to have access to a mobile phone.

Micro-level market players increasingly employ promising new business models to provide services and jobs to the world's poor and low-income populations. They range from large multinational companies and commercial banks to microfinance institutions, small businesses, civil society organizations, and everything in between. Small and medium-sized enterprises (SMEs)—espe-

---

1   Miller Center for Social Entrepreneurship, January 24, 2017, "Test In Nicaragua Shifts Lending For Women Led Businesses From Collateral To Cashflow," Miller Center for Social Entrepreneurship, https://bit.ly/2wwwDM6.

2   Rachel Zurer and Marry Mazzoni, August 16, 2017, " Boost Your Social Enterprise with Advice From this Lifelong Entrepreneur," Conscious Company Media, https://bit.ly/2olYNWc.

cially those with capacity to grow—are essential service providers and employers for poor and low-income people. From financial services to energy to sanitation and beyond, entrepreneurs are finding new ways to get closer to customers, offer more reliable and relevant services, and significantly improve affordability. At the same time, the private sector supplies formal jobs, from low- to high-skilled. These jobs offer not only increased income but often additional benefits, including health insurance, retirement plans, increased morale, sense of worth, and connection to the market and the world.

Unfortunately, markets do not always connect poor and low-income people to the services and jobs they need to escape poverty. Services, from the most basic to the state of the art, do not reach all who need them, and job opportunities may be missed by those without relevant skills or information. A web of ecosystem enablers at the meso level of the economy greases the wheels of an inclusive economic system by providing either the supply or the demand side of the market—or both—with services that help these markets function more efficiently.

Although there are many ways to think about this economic scaffolding, we have focused on three types of enablers at the meso level: information champions, business boosters, and job market hackers. These three groups reflect some of the most innovative and high-impact opportunities for ecosystem enablers to facilitate access to services and jobs. Better information and transparency about the market make it easier for people to access the critical services they need; robust support to SMEs and social entrepreneurs improves their ability to offer transformative services and create jobs; and digital learning and employment platforms reduce search time and costs for job seekers and help connect them to better paying positions.

At the macro level, governments can play an important role in building an inclusive economy—or they can have the opposite effect. Appropriate legal and regulatory policies are necessary to allow innovation at the micro and meso levels, as well as attract the right kinds of resources to the system. The role of governments in spurring inclusive economic growth can fall along a spectrum from minimal involvement at one end—focusing on creating the right conditions for private investment—to directly delivering products and services to poor and low-income people on the other.

When acting to level the playing field, governments can facilitate inclusive economies by creating regulatory frameworks that equally affect all businesses and specifically make it easier for smaller businesses to operate. Some governments choose to promote certain sectors or industries by implementing policies or regulations that tilt the playing field. Such an approach strongly encourages, and sometimes forces, the private sector to invest in, offer services to, or buy from specific market segments (such as low-income) or sectors (such as light manufacturing). Finally, a more activist approach means that the government chooses to control the playing field completely by delivering services directly, sometimes to the detriment of the private sector. Government actions have been known to crowd out private initiative with cheaper but often lower-quality and/or unsustainable solutions.

International and domestic funders comprise one group of actors particularly sensitive to consistent, reliable legal and regulatory frameworks. The funding landscape for inclusive economic systems is evolving rapidly. To date, traditional donor funding and investments have played an important role in ensuring that capital reaches market players, ecosystem enablers, and governments. Increasingly, however, nontraditional funders such as venture capital funds, impact investors, corporates, and millennials are stepping up their support. Domestic capital markets are also being tapped to pay for services and generate economic opportunities.

In considering international priorities such as the SDGs, analysts have identified funding gaps of not billions but trillions of dollars. Governments and traditional bilateral and multilateral donors cannot close the $2.5 trillion annual funding gap for the SDGs on their own—private funding is required. At the same time, new business models and a recognition of the economic opportunities at the base of the pyramid have increasingly attracted commercial funders, such as banks, fund managers, and corporations. The UN identified commercial opportunities worth $12 trillion by 2030 in four SDG-related sectors: agriculture and land use, health and well-being, renewable energy, and education.

In their pursuit of inclusive economic systems, the increasingly diverse range of development actors faces several frontier issues and cross-cutting challenges. In some cases—such as the impact of disruptive technologies, pervasive urbanization, or climate change—these issues are so new that knowledge is thin when it comes to assessing the implications for developing and emerging markets. In other cases—such as women's economic empowerment, refugee integration, or consumer protections—the challenges are long-standing yet pressing concerns. In all cases, opportunities abound for expanding access to relevant services and job opportunities in a way that promotes inclusive, sustainable, and fair economic systems.

One theme that arises over and over across the entire economic system is the rapid spread of digital technologies. Indeed, cell phones and other digital delivery systems have grown faster than any other technology in modern history (see Figure 8.2). Technology has the potential to drive rapid economic inclusion in the near future—but it could also deepen the divide between the haves and have nots if we fail to purposefully address issues of equity today.

Figure 8.2: The Rapid Pace of Digital Uptake

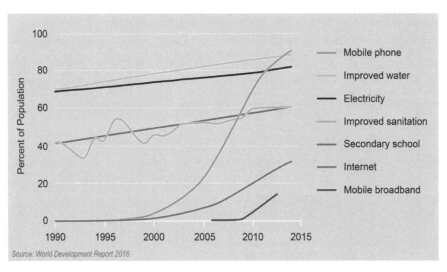

Source: World Development Report 2016

The global community has an unprecedented opportunity and a moral imperative to develop, test, and scale new business models to transform economies and more meaningfully include those currently excluded and underserved. To be successful, these business models cannot operate in a vacuum; rather, the entire economic system must be aligned so that all parts of the economy play their part for the greater good. The social entrepreneurs and small, growing businesses that will prosper in an inclusive system are those that truly understand the needs of poor and low-income people. Meeting the demand for life-changing services and high-quality jobs will not happen by magic; an ecosystem of enablers such as incubators, job search platforms, universal identification systems, and more will be required. Governments and funders can support an inclusive system by designing and executing the right policies and offering funding instruments that propel—rather than block—inclusive growth.

Building inclusive economic systems is not an easy task, and we are just learning about the most promising models at our disposal. But it is a challenge worth tackling. Realizing the vision described in this book is more important now than ever. The world simply cannot afford to continue leaving large swaths of the population behind. Our future depends on providing access for all.

Chapter 1

- Alimo, Michael. June 2, 2017. "13 Tech Startups from Ghana You Need to Know About in 2017." *Techflier*. https://www.techflier.com/2017/06/02/13-tech-startups-from-ghana-you-need-to-know-about-in-2017/.
- Aspen Network of Development Entrepreneurs. "What Is A Small And Growing Business?" Aspen Network of Development Entrepreneurs. http://www.andeglobal.org/?page=aboutandesgbs.
- B Impact Assessment. "About." http://bimpactassessment.net/.
- Bannerjee, Abhijit, Esther Duflo, and Rachel Glennerster. 2010. "Evidence from a Randomized Evaluation:
- Bill & Melinda Gates Foundation. https://www.impatientoptimists.org/Posts/2014/01/5-Reasons-Why-Muhammad-Yunus-Focuses-on-Lending-to-Women.
- Blank, Steve. January 25, 2010. "What's A Startup? First Principles." *Steve Blank*. https://steveblank.com/2010/01/25/whats-a-startup-first-principles/.
- BRAC. January 15, 2016. "Research." BRAC. http://www.brac.net/targeting-ultra-poor/item/753-research.
- Business & Sustainable Development Commission. January, 2017. "Better Business, Better World Executive Summary." Business & Sustainable Development Commission. http://report.businesscommission.org/uploads/Executive-Summary.pdf.
- DePillis, Lydia. November 3, 2017. "America's wealth gap is bigger than ever." CNN Money. http://money.cnn.com/2017/11/03/news/economy/wealth-gap-america/index.html.
- Esty, Katherine. January 10, 2014. "5 Reasons Why Muhammad Yunus Focuses on Lending to Women."
- FintechLab. 2017. "Brazil FintechLab Report." Finatech Brazil. http://fintechlab.com.br/wp-content/uploads/2017/09/Report_Fintechlab_2017_ENG.pdf.
- Forster, Michael, Ana Llena Nozal, and Celine Thevenot. January 26, 2017. "Understanding the Socio-Economic Divide in Europe." OECD Centre for Opportunity and Equality. https://www.oecd.org/els/soc/cope-divide-europe-2017-background-report.pdf.
- Gapminder Data. "List of Indicators in Gapminder World." Gapminder. https://www.gapminder.org/data/.
- Global Impact Investing Network. "About Impact Investing." Global Impact Investing Network. https://thegiin.org/impact-investing/.
- Global Impact Investing Network. "What is IRIS?" Global Impact Investing Network. https://iris.thegiin.org/.
- Global Reporting Institute. August 9, 2017. "Growing role for the private sector in the 2030 agenda." Global Reporting Institute. https://www.globalreporting.org/information/news-and-press-center/Pages/Growing-role-for-the-private-sector-in-the-2030-Agenda.aspx.
- Greenberg, Martin. September, 2014. "The Ghanaian Startup Ecosystem." *Meltwater*. http://meltwater.org/wp-content/uploads/2014/09/Ghanaian_Startup_Ecosystem_Report.pdf.
- GSMA Press Release. January 18, 2017. "GSMA Reveals Economic Impact of Mobile in Bangladesh." GSMA. https://www.gsma.com/newsroom/press-release/gsma-reveals-economic-impact-mobile-bangladesh/.

- Hagen-Zanker, Jessica. July, 2016. "Understanding the impact of cash transfers: the evidence." Overseas Development Institute. https://www.odi.org/sites/odi.org.uk/files/resource-documents/11465.pdf.
- Hashemi, Syed M. and Aude de Montesquiou. December 12, 2016. "Graduation Pathways." CGAP. http://www.cgap.org/publications/graduation-pathways.
- Karlan, Dean. October 5, 2016. "Making Microfinance More Effective." *Harvard Business Review*. https://hbr.org/2016/10/making-microfinance-more-effective.
- Lane, Barney. April, 2006. "The Economic and Social Benefits of Mobile Services in Bangladesh." GSMA. http://www.dirsi.net/english/files/Ovum%20Bangladesh%20Main%20report1f.pdf.
- Martin, Emmie. June 28, 2018. "In San Francisco, households earning $117,000 qualify as 'low income'." CNBC. https://www.cnbc.com/2018/06/28/families-earning-117000-qualify-as-low-incomein-san-francisco.html.
- Morikawa, Yuko. 2015. "The Opportunities and Challenges for Female Labor Force Participation in Morocco." Brookings Institute. https://www.brookings.edu/wp-content/uploads/2016/07/female-labor-force-participation.pdf.
- Morocco World News. July 23, 2017. "Moroccan Tourism Industry Resilient Despite Conjuncture: Oxford Business Group." *Morocco World News*. https://www.moroccoworldnews.com/2017/07/224074/moroccan-tourism-industry-resilient-despite-difficult-conjuncture-oxford-business-group/.
- Morocco World News. June 24, 2017. "Numbers of Tourists Visiting Morocco on the Rise." *Morocco World News*. https://www.moroccoworldnews.com/2017/06/221042/numbers-tourists-visiting-morocco-rise/.
- PovcalNet. "Research." World Bank, http://iresearch.worldbank.org/PovcalNet/povOnDemand.aspx.
- Rahman, Musafizur. March 19, 2017. "The SME sector has the highest opportunity to create employment in Bangladesh." Centre for Policy Dialogue, http://cpd.org.bd/sme-sector-highest-opportunity-create-employment-bangladesh-mustafizur-rahman/.
- Saugi, Aliyahdin. 2016. "Indonesia – further reforms in 2017 to promote economic growth," BNP Paribas. https://investors-corner.bnpparibas-am.com/investment-themes/indonesia-economic-recovery/.
- Schwab, Klaus. January 14, 2016. "The Fourth Industrial Revolution: what it means, how to respond." World Economic Forum. https://www.weforum.org/agenda/2016/01/the-fourth-industrial-revolution-what-it-means-and-how-to-respond/.
- Seisembayeva, Aigerim. February 1, 2017. "Kazakh Leader Outlines Five Priorities of Kazakhstan's Third Stage of Modernisation." *The Astana Times*. https://astanatimes.com/2017/02/kazakh-leader-outlines-five-priorities-of-kazakhstans-third-stage-of-modernisation/.
- Sheldon, Tony. February 7, 2017. "Can the Graduation Approach Help to end Extreme Poverty?" Yale School of Management. http://insights.som.yale.edu/insights/can-the-graduation-approach-help-to-endextreme-poverty.
- Skinner, Chris. 2017. "The State of Fintech in Brasil." *The Finanser*. https://thefinanser.com/2017/09/state-fintech-brasil.html/.
- Sreeharsha, Vinod. May 15, 2017. "Goldman Sachs Sees Big Potential for Fintech in Brazil," *The New York Times*. https://www.nytimes.com/2017/05/15/business/dealbook/goldman-sachs-sees-big-potential-for-fintech-in-brazil.html.
- State of Working America. "Poverty." State of Working America. http://www.stateofworkingamerica.org/fact-sheets/poverty/.

BIBLIOGRAPHY

- Statista. "Poverty rates in OECD countries as of 2015." Statista. https://www.statista.com/statistics/233910/poverty-rates-in-oecd-countries/.
- Sulaiman, Munshi. December, 2016. "Eliminating Extreme Poverty: Comparing the Cost-Effectiveness of Livelihood, Cash Transfer, and Graduation Approaches." Access to Finance Forum. http://www.cgap.org/sites/default/files/Forum-Eliminating-Extreme-Poverty-Dec-2016.pdf.
- Team Fintech Brazil. 2017. "Brazilian digital banks: shortlist." Fintech Brazil. http://fintechbrazil.com/brazilian-digital-banks-shortlist/.
- The Miracle of Microfinance?" Innovations for Poverty-Action. https://www.poverty-action.org/study/miracle-microfinance-evidence-randomized-evaluation.
- Thomas, Juan Carlos. June 14, 2016. "3 unorthodox lessons for Latin America's entrepreneurs." World Economic Forum. https://www.weforum.org/agenda/2016/06/3-unorthodox-lessons-for-latin-america-s-entrepreneurs/.
- Travel & Tourism Council. https://www.wttc.org/-/media/files/reports/economic-impact-research/countries-2017/morocco2017.pdf.
- Turner, Rochelle, and Evelyne Freirmuth. 2017. "Travel & Tourism Economic Impact 2017." World
- Uatkhanov, Yerbolat. February 10, 2017. "Freelancing in Kazakhstan: both stepping stone and ultimate prize." The *Astana Times*. https://astanatimes.com/2017/02/freelancing-in-kazakhstan-both-steppingstone-and-ultimate-prize/.
- Uatkhanov, Yerbolat. March 17, 2017. "Kazakhstan is fascinating place for freelancers, experts believe." *The Astana Times*. https://astanatimes.com/2017/03/kazakhstan-is-fascinating-place-for-freelancers-experts-believe/.
- United Nations. "Sustainable Development Goals." United Nations. https://www.un.org/sustainabledevelopment/sustainable-development-goals/.
- World Bank Data. "World Bank Country and Lending Groups." World Bank. https://datahelpdesk.worldbank.org/knowledgebase/articles/906519-world-bank-country-and-lending-groups.
- World Bank. "Poverty Overview." October 2, 2016 http://www.worldbank.org/en/topic/poverty/overview.
- World Bank. 2016. "World Development Report 2016: Digital Dividends." World Bank. https://openknowledge.worldbank.org/handle/10986/23347.
- World Bank. Development Indicators. World Bank. http://databank.worldbank.org/data/reports.aspx?-source=world-development-indicators.
- World Bank. June 20, 2016. "Reforms Strengthen Indonesia's Economic Resilience: World Bank Report." World Bank. http://www.worldbank.org/en/news/press-release/2016/06/17/reforms-strengthen-indonesias-economic-resilience-world-bank-report.
- World Bank. October 31, 2017. "East Asia and Pacific Economies Adopt 45 Reforms to improve business climate: Doing Business Report," World Bank. http://www.worldbank.org/en/news/press-release/2017/10/31/east-asia-and-pacific-economies-adopt-45-reforms-to-improve-business-climate-doing-business-report.

Chapter 2

- Alkire, Sabina, Nathanael Goldberg, Dean Karlan, and Aude de Montesquiou. June 2014. "Poverty in Rural and Urban Areas: Direct comparisons using the global MPI 2014," Oxford Poverty & Human Development Initiative, https://bit.ly/2GtxkOa.
- Anderson, Jamie and Wajiha Ahmed. February 2016. "Smallholder Diaries: Building the

Evidence Base with Farming Families in Mozambique, Tanzania, and Pakistan." CGAP. https://bit.ly/1pl5QNA.

- Baer, Drake. February 22, 2016. "This map shows the percentage of people around the world who own smartphones." *Business Insider*. https://read.bi/1oDTDDp.

- Banerjee, Abhijit V. and Esther Duflo. October 2006. "The Economic Lives of the Poor," Massachusetts Institute of Technology. https://economics.mit.edu/files/530.

- Bernard, Tanguy. April 21, 2014. "The Future in Mind: Aspirations and Forward-Looking Behaviours in Rural Ethiopia." World Bank. https://bit.ly/1lTkOp5.

- Bullen, Piroska Bisits. "Measuring poverty using the Progress out of Poverty Index." tools4dev. http://www.tools4dev.org/resources/progress-out-of-poverty-index-tool-review/.

- Clifton, Jon and Ben Ryan. August 12, 2014. "Only 1.3 Billion Worldwide Employed Full Time for Employer."

- Collins, Daryl, Jonathan Morduch, Stuart Rutherford and Orlanda Ruthven. December 19, 2010. "Portfolios

- de Medina, Rafael Diez. June 2012. "Statistical update on employment in the informal economy." ILO Department of Statistics. https://bit.ly/2q2pboJ.

- Deloitte. https://bit.ly/2GtiQxH.

- Devictor, Xavier. September 15, 2016. "How many years do refugees stay in exile?" World Bank. http://blogs.worldbank.org/dev4peace/how-many-years-do-refugees-stay-exile.

- Dobbs, Richard, Anu Madgavkar, Dominic Barton, Eric Labaye, James Manyika, Charles Roxburgh, Susan Lund, and Siddarth Madhav, June 2012, "The world at work: Jobs, pay, and skills for 3.5 billion people," McKinsey Global Institute, https://www.mckinsey.com/global-themes/employment-and-growth/the-world-at-work.

- Dubush, Grace. July 27, 2015. "How Mobile Phones Are Changing the Developing World." Consumer Technology Association. https://bit.ly/29NCbtZ.

- Dziadosz, Alex. November 21, 2016. "Syrian exiles in Lebanon seek a refuge in work." *The Financial Times*. https://on.ft.com/2q4kgnS.

- Edwards, Adrian. June 19, 2017. "Forced displacement worldwide at its highest in decades." UNHCR. https://bit.ly/2GxspHE.

- Evans, David. May 27, 2014. "Do the Poor Waste Transfers on Booze and Cigarettes? No." *Development Impacts*. https://blogs.worldbank.org/impactevaluations/do-poor-waste-transfers-booze-and-cigarettes-no.

- Food and Agriculture Organization, International Fund for Agricultural Development, UNICEF, World Health Organization, and World Food Program. 2017. "The State of Food Security and Nutrition in the World 2017, Building resilience for peace and food security." http://www.fao.org/state-of-food-security-nutrition/en/.

- Gakidou, Emmanuela. 2010, "Increased Educational Attainment and its Effect on Child Mortality in 175 Countries between 1970 and 2009: A Systemic Analysis." *The Lancet*. http://bit.ly/2L9m0ce.

- Gallup, http://news.gallup.com/poll/174791/billion-worldwide-employed-full-time-employer.aspx.

- Global Basic Income Foundation, "Facts," http://www.globalincome.org/English/Facts.html.

- Global Partnership for Education. "Education Data." Global Partnership for Education. http://www.globalpartnership.org/data-and-results/education-data.

- Grojec, Anna. July 12, 2017. "Progress on Drinking Water, Sanitation, and Hygiene." World Health Organization and UNICEF. http://www.who.int/mediacentre/news/releases/2017/launch-version-report-jmp-water-sanitation-hygiene.pdf.

- GSMA Intelligence. September 2017. "Global Mobile Trends 2017." GSMA. https://bit.ly/2h72M58.
- Hall, Gillette. April 2010. "Indigenous Peoples, Poverty, and Development." Cambridge University Press. http://siteresources.worldbank.org/EXTINDPEOPLE/Resources/407801-1271860301656/full_report.pdf.
- Hall, Gillette. August 9, 2016. "Poverty and exclusion among Indigenous Peoples: The global evidence." World Bank. https://blogs.worldbank.org/voices/poverty-and-exclusion-among-indigenous-peoples-global-evidence.
- Hammond, Allen L., William J. Kramer. 2007. "The Next 4 Billion: Market Size and Business Strategy at the Base of the Pyramid." International Finance Corporation and World Resources Institute.https://bit.ly/2q1v9Hj.
- Hodal, Kate. October 5, 2016. "UN warns universal education goal will fail without 69 million new teachers." *The Guardian*. https://bit.ly/2dQYBqR.
- International Labour Office. 2013. "Women and Men in the Informal Economy: A Statistical Picture." International Labor Organization. https://bit.ly/1xDj9vG.
- International Labor Organization. 2017. "Economic Impacts of Reducing the Gender Gap," International Labor Organization. https://bit.ly/2C2Ujsx.
- Internet Live Stats. "Internet Users." http://www.internetlivestats.com/internet-users/.
- Jahan, Selim. 2016. "Human Development Report 2016." United Nations Development Programme. http://hdr.undp.org/sites/default/files/2016_human_development_report.pdf.
- Kenny, Charles. September 25, 2015. "Give Poor People Cash." *The Atlantic*. https://www.theatlantic.com/international/archive/2015/09/welfare-reform-direct-cash-poor/407236/.
- Larivee, Michelle, Kristen Dobson, and Allie O'Shea. June 2017. "Reaching Deep in Low-Income Markets."
- Leopold, Aaron, Lucy Stevens, and Mary Gallagher. 2014. "Poor people's energy outlook 2014." Practical Action. https://bit.ly/2uLI6d7.
- Lucini, Barbara Arese and Kalvin Bahia. September 22, 2017. "2017 Mobile Industry Impact Report: Sustainable Development Goals." GSMA. https://bit.ly/2JiIH9o.
- Martin, Will. November 5, 2010. "Food Security and Poverty – a precarious balance." World Bank. http://blogs.worldbank.org/developmenttalk/food-security-and-poverty-a-precarious-balance.
- Matthews, Brett. July 2017. "Design for Oral Financial Inclusion," Briefing Note #2. My Oral Village. http://myoralvillage.org/research/publications/.
- Matthews, Brett. October 31, 2014. "Oral Information Management Tools: Lighting the Path to Financial Inclusion." My Oral Village. https://bit.ly/2uLpb20.
- McHale, Brandee. "Youth Optimism, Meet Opportunity: Bridging the Gap between Young People's Career Aspirations & Ability to Succeed." CECP. https://bit.ly/2JfOfkV.
- Murphy, David. February 4, 2017. "2.4BN Smartphone Users in 2017, Says Emarketer." *Mobile Marketing Magazine*. http://mobilemarketingmagazine.com/24bn-smartphone-users-in-2017-says-emarketer.
- of the Poor: How the World's Poor Live on $2 a Day." Princeton University Press.
- Organisation for Economic Co-operation and Development. May, 2012. "Gender Equality in Education, Employment and Entrepreneurship; Final Report to the MCM 2012." Organisation for Economic Co-operation and Development. https://www.oecd.org/employment/50423364.pdf.
- Poushter, Jared. February 22, 2016. "Smartphone Ownership and Internet Usage Continues to Climb in Emerging Economies." Pew Research Center. https://pewrsr.ch/1RX3Iqq.

- Rangan, V. Kasturi, Michael Chu, and Djordjija Petkoski. June 2011. "The Globe: Segmenting the Base of the Pyramid." *Harvard Business Review*. https://hbr.org/2011/06/the-globe-segmenting-the-base-of-the-pyramid.
- Robinson, Lorriann. July 8, 2014. "Early marriage and poverty: Why we must break the cycle." ONE. https://www.one.org/us/2014/07/08/early-marriage-and-poverty-why-we-must-break-the-cycle/.
- Roser, Max and Esteban Ortiz-Ospina. March 27, 2017. "Global Extreme Poverty." Our World in Data. https://ourworldindata.org/extreme-poverty/#the-demographics-of-extreme-poverty.
- Scommegna, Paola and Marlene Lee. April 2014. "Aging in Latin America and the Caribbean." Population Reference Bureau.
- The Economist Intelligence Unit. February 2015. "Global Trends Impacting the Future of HR Management:Engaging and Integrating a Global Workforce." SHRM Foundation. https://bit.ly/2uOlHeW.
- The Water Project. August 31, 2016. "Facts About Water: Statistics of the Water Crisis." The Water Project. https://thewaterproject.org/water-scarcity/water_stats.
- UN Stats. 2015. "The World's Women." The United Nations. https://unstats.un.org/unsd/gender/chapter8/chapter8.html.
- UNESCO Institute for Statistics. July 2016. "Leaving no one behind: How far on the way to universal primary and secondary education?" UNESCO. https://bit.ly/29IlbFG.
- UNESCO Institute for Statistics. June 2017. "Reducing global poverty through universal primary and secondary education." https://bit.ly/2gOP6zn.
- UNICEF and World Bank. October 3, 2016. "Nearly 385 million children living in extreme poverty, says joint World Bank Group – UNICEF study." UNICEF. https://www.unicef.org/media/media_92856.html.
- UNICEF Data. "Nutrition." UNICEF https://data.unicef.org/topic/nutrition/malnutrition/.
- UNICEF, World Health Organization, and World Bank. 2017. "Levels and Trends in Child Malnutrition." https://data.unicef.org/wp-content/uploads/2017/05/JME-2017-brochure-1.pdf.
- United Nations Department of Economic and Social Affairs. 2014. "World Urbanization Prospects: The 2014 Revision, Highlights." United Nations. https://bit.ly/2gYlppO.
- United Nations Department of Economic and Social Affairs. 2015. "The World's Women 2015: Trends and Statistics." United Nations, https://unstats.un.org/unsd/gender/downloads/WorldsWomen2015_report.pdf.
- Watkins, Kevin. 2006. "Human Development Report 2016." United Nations Development Program. http://hdr.undp.org/sites/default/files/reports/267/hdr06-complete.pdf.
- World Bank, "World Bank Development Indicators," World Bank, http://databank.worldbank.org/data/reports.aspx?source=world-development-indicators.
- World Bank. 2012. "World Bank Development Report 2012: Gender Equality and Development." World Bank. https://bit.ly/2GN1ISO.
- World Bank. 2014. "Women, Business and the Law 2014, Removing Restrictions to Enhance Gender Equality." World Bank. https://bit.ly/2q29Fdp.
- World Bank. 2016. "Poverty and Shared Prosperity 2016: Taking on Inequality." https://bit.ly/2cL20LI.
- World Bank. October 2, 2016. "Poverty Overview." http://www.worldbank.org/en/topic/poverty/overview.
- World Health Organization and the World Bank. 2015. "Tracking Universal Health

Coverage: First Global Monitoring Report." http://www.who.int/mediacentre/news/releases/2015/uhc-report/en/.

- World Health Organization Media Centre. November 2017. "Violence against women."
- World Health Organization. http://www.who.int/mediacentre/factsheets/fs239/en/.
- Zollman, Julie. 2014. "Kenya Financial Diaries – Shilingi kwa shilingi, the financial lives of the poor." FSD Kenya. http://fsdkenya.org/publication/kenya-financial-diaries-shilingi-kwa-shilingi-the-financial-lives-of-the-poor/.

Chapter 3

- Aakar Innovations website. "Impact Measurement." https://aakarinnovations.com/impact-measurement/.
- Abrams, Jeff, Maelis Carraro, Wajioha Ahmed. March, 2017. "Alternative Delivery Channels for Financial Inclusion." The Mastercard Foundation and Bankable Frontier Associates. https://mastercardfdn.org/wp-content/uploads/2018/06/BFA_ADC_FIpaper_April2017-Accessible.pdf.
- Ahmed, Wajiha. November 15, 2017. "How fintech is changing lives in the global south." World Economic Forum. https://www.weforum.org/agenda/2017/11/how-fintech-is-changing-lives-in-global-south/.
- Alexander, Alex J. Lin Shi, and Bensam Solomon. March, 2017, "How Fintech is Reaching the Poor in Africa and Asia," International Finance Corporation, https://bit.ly/2fus9xQ.
- Alvarez, Gabriela Zapata and Martha Casanova. November 30, 2016. "How a Retail Chain Became Mexico's No. 1 Bank Account Supplier." CGAP. https://bit.ly/2IFzxTi.
- Babban Gona. "Our Solution." http://www.babbangona.com/our-solution/.
- Balancing Act Africa staff. November, 2015. "Group TigoPaare accounts in Chad may lead to Peoples' Banks for communities across Africa." Balancing Act Africa. https://bit.ly/2qoHiFp. Beneficial Returns website. "News." http://www.beneficialreturns.com/news.
- Butcher, Mike. October 23, 2015. "Angaza Raises $4M To Make Clean Energy Affordable For World's Poorest." *TechCrunch.* https://tcrn.ch/2Hhjfme.
- Byun, Jungwon. August, 2015. "Zoona: A Case Study on Third Party Innovation in Digital Finance." Financial Sector Deepening Zambia. https://bit.ly/2kBRhWS.
- CFI Staff. January 18, 2018. "How Technology Is Propelling Inclusive Insurance." Center for Financial Inclusion. https://cfi-blog.org/2018/01/18/how-technology-is-propelling-inclusive-insurance/.
- Chemonics International Inc. June 18, 2010. "Ethiopia Coffee Industry Value Chain Analysis." USAID. https://bit.ly/2v1T4Ls.
- Chen, Cecilia and Marcus Haymon. 2016. "Realizing the potential of digital job seeking platforms."Brookings Blum Roundtable. https://brook.gs/2bEECiO.
- Cheston, Susy, Tomás Conde, Arpitha Bykere and Elisabeth Rhyne. July, 2016. "The Business of Financial Inclusion: Insights From Banks in Emerging Markets." Institute of International Finance. https://bit.ly/29zWLM7.
- Cheston, Susy. January, 2018. "Inclusive Insurance: Closing the Protection Gap for Emerging Customers." Center for Financial Inclusion at Accion and Institute of International Finance. https://bit.ly/2GNVWRV.
- Cook, William. October 3, 2017. "In Kenya, Bank Accounts Again More Popular Than M-Pesa." CGAP. http://www.cgap.org/blog/kenya-bank-accounts-again-more-popular-m-pesa---why.
- D.light website. "About Us." http://www.dlight.com/about-us.

- Dassel, Kurt and John Cassidy. June, 2017. "Reaching deep in low-income markets." Deloitte, https://bit.ly/2qo6gVD.
- de la Mata, Guadalupe. July 21, 2012. "What is inclusive business?: World Bank's definition and resources." Innovation for Social Change. https://innovationforsocialchange.org/what-is-inclusive-business-world-banks-definition-and-resources/.
- Dell'Amore, Christine. October 28, 2011. "Human Waste to Revive Haitian Farmland?" *National Geographic*. https://bit.ly/2IHZvW1.
- Demirguc-Kunt, Asli and Leora Klapper. 2013. "Measuring Financial Inclusion: Explaining Variation in Use of Financial Services across and within Countries." Brookings Institute. https://brook.gs/2GPr83f.
- Demirguc-Kunt, Asli, Leora Klapper, Dorothe Singer, Saniya Ansar and Jake Hess. April, 2018. "The Global Findex Database 2017: Measuring Financial Inclusion around the World." World Bank. http://bit.ly/2M6zHF9.
- Dercon, Stefan, Tessa Bold and Cesar Calvo. 2008. "Insurance for the Poor?" UNICEF. https://www.unicef.org/socialpolicy/files/Insurance_for_the_Poor.pdf
- Dietz, Miklos Vivayak HV, and Gillian Lee. November, 2016. "Bracing for seven critical changes as fintech matures." McKinsey & Company. https://bit.ly/2qJTzFE.
- Euromonitor statistics. January 11, 2017. "Caffeine (Coffee) Consumption By Country." *Caffeine Informer*. https://www.caffeineinformer.com/caffeine-what-the-world-drinks.
- Ferreira, David and Scott Featherston. 2017. "The Business of Education in Africa." Caerus Capital. http://edafricareport.caeruscapital.co/thebusinessofeducationinafrica.pdf.
- Flemming, Peyton Fiona Messent, Christine Eibs Singer, and Stacy Swann . 2017. "Energizing Finance: Scaling and Refining Finance in Countries with Large Energy Access Gaps." Sustainable Energy for All. https://bit.ly/2HaB7PH.
- Flores, Gabriela, Daniel Hogan, Gretchen Stevens, Justine Hsu, Tessa Tan-Torres Edejer, Sarah Thomson, Tamás Evetovits, Agnès Soucat, and John Grove. December, 2017. "Tracking Universal Health Coverage: 2017 Global Monitoring Report." World Health Organization and World Bank. https://bit.ly/2ACuGmb.
- Franco, Adriana Barrera and Alejandro Pulido Moran. 2016. "The Mexican Automotive Industry: Current Situation, Challenges, and Opportunities." ProMexico. https://bit.ly/2sdFd1R.
- Global Impact Investing Network. "Bridge International Academies." Global Impact Investing Network. https://thegiin.org/research/profile/bridge-international-academies.
- Global Off-Grid Lighting Association website. "About Us." https://www.gogla.org/about-us.
- Grey Global. "Life Saving Dot Case Study." Grey Global. http://grey.com/global/work/key/singapore-life-saving-dot/id/5623/.
- GSMA Blog. January 1, 2013. "Urban Planet Mobile." GSMA. https://www.gsma.com/mobilefordevelopment/topic/digital-literacy/urban-planet-mobile/.
- GSMA Staff. 2015. "2015 Mobile Insurance, Savings & Credit Report." GSMA. https://bit.ly/2v3b8Fd.
- GSMA Staff. 2016. "State of the Industry Report on Mobile Money." GSMA. https://bit.ly/2DxsiPf.
- Gustafson, Sara and Manuel Hernandez. May 19, 2017. "The Ethiopia Commodity Exchange: A coffee success story?" International Food Policy Research Institute. https://bit.ly/2HfsuDu.
- Hutton, Guy and Mili Varughese. January, 2016. "The Costs of Meeting the 2030 Sustainable Development Goal Targets on Drinking Water, Sanitation, and Hygiene." World

Bank and UNICEF. https://bit.ly/2GOiEVD.

- Hynes, Casey. August 24, 2017. "India's Domestic Workers Have A New Ally In This Innovative Fin-Tech Startup." Forbes. https://bit.ly/2EBnmEn.
- Ilumexico website. "Home." https://ilumexico.mx/home/.
- Innovations in Healthcare. "Livewell." https://www.innovationsinhealthcare.org/profile/livewell-(previously-viva-afya)/.
- Iwai, Mariko Higaki. Flo website. http://marikoproduct.com/Flo.
- Kabuya, Francois I. August, 2015. "The Rotating Savings and Credit Associations (ROSCAs): Unregistered Sources Of Credit in Local Communities." *IOSR Journal of Humanities and Social Science*. http://www.iosrjournals.org/iosr-jhss/papers/Vol20-issue8/Version-4/M020849598.pdf.
- Karmali, Naazneen. March 5, 2010. "Aravind Eye Care's Vision for India." Forbes. https://bit.ly/2qo6gVD.
- Karnani, Aneel Aneel Karnani, Bernard Garrette, Jordan Kassalow, & Moses Lee. 2011. "Better Vision for the Poor." *Stanford Social Innovation Review*. https://ssir.org/articles/entry/better_vision_for_the_poor.
- Kaye, Leon. January 22, 2016. "How This Solar Startup Became a Multinational Social Enterprise." *Triple Pundit*. https://www.triplepundit.com/2016/01/m-kopa-pay-as-you-go-solar-africa/.
- Kjorven, Olav. September, 2011. "Remittances, Towards Human Resilience: Sustaining MDG Progress in an Age of Economic Uncertainty." United Nations Development Programme. https://bit.ly/2EAukK0.
- Laboratoria website. "Our Impact." www.laboratoria.la/en.
- Lake, Andrew. 2014. "Alternative Delivery Channels and Technology Handbook." International Finance Corporation. https://bit.ly/2ILytNM.
- Lauer, Kate and Timothy Lyman. October, 2014. "Digital Financial Inclusion: Implications for Customers, Regulators, Supervisors, and Standard-Setting Bodies." CGAP. https://bit.ly/2JCzw3B.
- Living Goods website. "Measuring Impact." https://livinggoods.org/what-we-do/measuring-impact/.
- LR Group website. "Adama Aldeia Nova, Angola." http://lr-group.com/project/adama-aldeia-nova-angola-2/.
- M-KOPA, 2018, "Our Impact," M-KOPA, http://solar.m-kopa.com/about/our-impact/.
- M-KOPA. "Products." M-KOPA. http://www.m-kopa.com/products/.
- Manyika, James, Susan Lund, Marc Singer, Olivia White, and Chris Berry. September, 2016. "Digital Finance for All." McKinsey Global Institute. http://bit.ly/2xA0R37.
- Mas, Ignacio and Dan Radcliffe. 2011. "Mobile Payments go Viral: M-PESA in Kenya." *The Capco Institute Journal of Financial Transformation*.
- Mazzi Container website. "Our Container." http://www.mazzican.com/.
- McKay, Claudia. January 28, 2012. "Banking Services Transforming a Town in the Amazon." CGAP. http://www.cgap.org/blog/banking-services-transforming-town-amazon.
- McKay, Claudia. November 3, 2010. "Branchless Banking 2010: What Price?" CGAP. http://www.cgap.org/blog/branchless-banking-2010-what-price.
- Milford, Anna. 2004. "Coffee, Co-operatives and Competition: The Impact of Fair Trade." The Chr. Michelsen Institute. https://www.cmi.no/publications/file/1802-coffee-co-operatives-and-competition.pdf.

- Millicom blogs. 2015. "How a mobile money solution is born." Millicom. http://www.millicom.com/media-room/blogs/blog-tigo-paare/.
- PesaLink website. "What sets us apart?" https://ipsl.co.ke/pesalink/.
- Porter, Michael E. 1985. "Competitive Advantage." The Free Press.
- Price, Susan. July 6, 2017. "Lending Pioneer Kiva Hits The One Billion Mark And Launches A Fund For Refugees." *Forbes.* https://bit.ly/2HrMKzx.
- Rosenberg, Richard. June, 2007. "CGAP Reflections on the Compartamos Initial Public Offering."CGAP. https://bit.ly/2v1GxYt.
- Rosenberg, Tina. June 14, 2016. "Liberia, Desperate to Educate, Turns to Charter Schools." *The New York Times.* https://www.nytimes.com/2016/06/14/opinion/liberia-desperate-to-educate-turns-to-charter-schools.html.
- Runde, Daniel. August 12, 2015. "M-Pesa And The Rise Of The Global Mobile Money Market." *Forbes.* https://bit.ly/2HoFNPE.
- Safaricom. 2014. "Safaricom Limited FY14 Presentation." Safaricom. https://www.safaricom.co.ke/images/Downloads/Resources_Downloads/FY_2014_Results_Presentation.pdf.
- Salian, Priti. May 19, 2015. "The Little Red Dot Saving Lives in India." *Takepart.* http://www.takepart.com/article/2015/05/19/life-saving-dot-iodine-india.
- Samhita staff. "Sarvajal Case Study." Samhita Better CSR. www.samhita.org/water-for-all/.
- Sarvajal website. "Home." www.sarvajal.com/.
- SCALA. 2015. "The Power of Downstream." Inter-American Development Bank. https://observatorioscala.uniandes.edu.co/images/The-Power-of-Downstream-SCALA-5.pdf.
- Siroya, Shivani. February, 2016. "A smart loan for people with no credit history (yet)." TED. https://www.ted.com/talks/shivani_siroya_a_smart_loan_for_people_with_no_credit_history_yet#t-351517.
- SistemaB. September 13, 2017. "FINAE Is Creating New Avenues for First-Generation University Grads in Mexico." B the Change. https://bthechange.com/finae-mexico-on-campus-3160de4e82dd.
- Staritz, Cornelia and Jose Guilherme Reis. January, 2013. "Global Value Chains, Economic Upgrading, and Gender." World Bank. https://bit.ly/2JAFG48.
- Taylor, Allen. August 15, 2017. "The Growth of Lending-as-a-Service." *Lending Times,* https://lending-times.com/2017/08/15/the-growth-of-lending-as-a-service/.
- The Alliance for Clean Cookstoves. "Impact Areas: Health." The Alliance for Clean Cookstoves. http://cleancookstoves.org/impact-areas/health/.
- The Economist Group. January 18, 2017. "Bridge International Academies gets high marks for ambition but its business model is still unproven." The Economist. https://econ.st/2GNJBgy.
- Ushahidi Staff. 2010. "Crisis Mapping Haiti: Some Final Reflections." Ushahidi. https://www.ushahidi.com/blog/2010/04/14/crisis-mapping-haiti-some-final-reflections.
- Ushahidi Staff. 2010. "Mapping Honduras Hospitals." Ushahidi. https://www.ushahidi.com/blog/2010/09/27/mapping-honduras-hospitals.
- van den Heever, Claire. "China's Mobile Payment Revolution Is Going to Africa." *The Huffington Post.* https://www.huffingtonpost.com/claire-van-den-heever/china-mobile-payment-africa_b_9329126.html.
- VisionSpring. December 20, 2010. "VisionSpring Releases New Research on the Positive Effects of Eyeglasses on Low-Income Consumers in India." VisionSpring. https://bit.ly/2v3Jh7J.

- Ward, Catherine. September 3, 2012. "Six Innovations Lifting the World's Agricultural Workers out of Poverty." Worldwatch Institute. https://bit.ly/2EAVeBt.
- Wheatley, Jonathan. November 6, 2017. "Nigeria's 'great farm' model bears fruit in time of high insecurity." *Financial Times.* https://www.ft.com/content/a32b0c58-a75a-11e7-ab66-21cc87a2edde.
- Wolfe, Eli. April 5, 2014. "'Academies-in-a-Box' Are Thriving – But Are They the Best Way to School the World's Poor?" *California Magazine.* https://bit.ly/2GOi3aT.
- World Bank. April 5, 2017. World Bank. "Financial Inclusion Overview." http://www.worldbank.org/en/topic/financialinclusion/overview.
- Y Media Labs. March 14, 2017. "Developing Nations Take Aim With Fintech: What Elite Economies Can Learn." Y Media Labs. https://ymedialabs.com/developing-nations-fintech/.
- Yang, Jennifer. November 22, 2012. "Why Haiti sees hope in a toilet bowl." The Star. https://www.thestar.com/news/world/2012/11/22/why_haiti_sees_hope_in_a_toilet_bowl.html.

Chapter 4

- Adkins, Sam S. August, 2016. "The 2016-2021 Worldwide Self-paced eLearning Market: Global eLearning Market in Steep Decline." Ambient Insight. http://www.ambientinsight.com/Resources/Documents/AmbientInsight_The%202016-2021_Worldwide_Self-paced%20eLearning_Market.pdf.
- AID: Tech. 2017. "What We Do." AID: Tech. https://aid.technology/what-we-do/.
- Anders, George. July 27, 2015. "India Loves MOOCs." *Technology Review.* https://www.technologyreview.com/s/539131/india-loves-moocs/.
- Ashley, Caroline and Aline Menden. November 15, 2015 "Business Incubation FAQs." International Business Innovation Association. https://web.archive.org/web/20151115190341/https://inbia.org/resources/business-incubation-faq.
- Asilia Africa. 2011. "About Asilia Africa." http://www.asiliaafrica.com/about-asilia/.
- Aspen Network of Development Entrepreneurs. 2011. "About ANDE." Aspen Network of Development Entrepreneurs. http://ande.site-ym.com/?page=AboutANDE
- Aspen Network of Development Entrepreneurs. November 21, 2014. "Measuring Value Created: By Impact Incubators & Accelerators." Aspen Network of Development Entrepreneurs. https://bit.ly/2lbqZd9.
- B Impact Assessment. June, 2012. "Jeroen Harderwijk." http://bimpactassessment.net/case-studies/jeroen-harderwijk.
- Baird, Ross, Lily Bowles and Saurabh Lall. June, 2013. "Bridging the 'Pioneer Gap': The Role of Acelerators in Launching High-Impact Enterprises." Aspen Network of Development Entrepreneurs and Village Capital. https://bit.ly/2LRtzA2.
- Banerjee, Shweta. December 2015. "World Development Report 2016 Digital Dividends: Aadhaar: Digital Inclusion and Public Services in India." World Bank. https://bit.ly/2lb9rOk.
- Bangladesh Women Chamber of Commerce and Industry. "BWCCI at a glance." http://bwcci-bd.org/index.php?option=com_content&view=article&id=46&Itemid=34.
- BanQu App. 2018. "Our Solutions: How It Works." http://www.banquapp.com/our-solutions/how-itworks/.
- Brown, Martin, Tullio Jappelli, and Marco Pagano. 2007. "Information Sharing and Credit: Firm-Level Evidence from Transition Countries." European Corporate Governance Institute. https://papers.ssrn.com/sol3/papers.cfm?abstract_id=967485.
- Bruhn, Miriam, Dean Karlan, and Antoinette Schoar. 2013. "The Impact of Consulting

Services on Small and Medium Enterprises: Evidence from a Randomized Trial in Mexico."
World Bank. https://bit.ly/2MsU5Rm.

- Certified B Corporation. 2018. "Why B Corps Matter." https://www.bcorporation.net/what-are-bcorps/why-b-corps-matter.

- Chandy, Laurence. January 31, 2016. "The Future of Work in the Developing World."
Brookings Institute. https://www.brookings.edu/research/the-future-of-work-in-the-developing-world/.

- Chattopadhyay, Sahana. June 26, 2014. "11 Differences between a MOOC and an Online course." *ID and Other Reflections*. http://idreflections.blogspot.com/2014/06/11-differences-between-mooc-and-online.html.

- Christiaensen, Luc, Siddhartha Raja, and Esteve Sala. June 1, 2017. "Can technology reshape the world of work for developing countries?" World Bank. http://blogs.worldbank.org/jobs/can-technology-reshape-world-work-developing-countries.

- Dahan, Mariana, and Alan Gelb. 2015. "The Role of Identification in the Post-2015 Development Agenda. World Bank." https://siteresources.worldbank.org/EXTGLOBALFINREPORT/Resources/8816096-1361888425203/9062080-1361888442321/sme_consulting_mexico-Paper.pdf.

- Deloitte. 2014. "Value of Connectivity: Economic and social benefits of expanding internet access." Deloitte. https://www2.deloitte.com/content/dam/Deloitte/br/Documents/technology-media-telecommunications/ValorConectividade.pdf.

- Dempwolf, C. Scott, Jennifer Auer and Michellle D'Ippolito. October, 2014. "Innovation Accelerators: Defining Characteristics Among Startup Assistance Organizations." Small Business Administration. https://fr.slideshare.net/eddodds/innovation-accelerators-report.

- Desai, Vyjayanti, Mattias Witt, Kamya Chandra, and Jonathan Marskell. 2017. "Counting the uncounted: - billion people without IDs." World Bank. http://blogs.worldbank.org/ic4d/counting-uncounted-11-billion-people-without-ids.

- Devex. 2018. "The Eleos Foundation." Devex. https://www.devex.com/organizations/the-eleos-foundation-23546.

- Dichter, Sasha, Robert Katz. Harvey Koh and Ashish Karamchandani. 2013. "Closing the Pioneer Gap." *Stanford Social Innovation Review*. https://ssir.org/articles/entry/closing_the_pioneer_gap.

- Diop, Makhtar. May 24, 2017. "Making everyone count: how identification could transform the lives of millions of Africans." World Economic Forum. https://www.weforum.org/agenda/2017/05/making-everyone-count-the-case-for-national-identification-systems/.

- Djankov, Simeon, Caralee McLiesh and Andrei Shleifer. January, 2005. "Private Credit in 129 Countries." National Bureau of Economic Research. http://www.nber.org/papers/w11078.pdf.

- Djankov, Simeon, Oliver Hart, Caralee McLiesh and Andrei Shleifer. 2006. "Debt Enforcement Around the World." National Bureau of Economic Research. http://dx.doi.org/10.3386/w12807.

- Egyptian Banking Institute. "I-Score." http://sme.ebi.gov.eg/supportingactivities/Pages/I-Score.aspx.

- Fayomi, Toks. March 3, 2015. "Online outsourcing is creating opportunities for job seekers and job creators." World Bank. http://blogs.worldbank.org/ic4d/online-outsourcing-creating-opportunities-job-seekers-and-job-creators.

- Fitzgerald, Nicholas. October 11, 2012. "Women Entrepreneurs Focus of New Collaboration Between Agora Partnerships and the Eleos Foundation." Accelerate the Shift. http://agorapartnerships.org/acceleratetheshift/2012/10/11/women-entrepreneurs-focus-of-new-collaboration-between-agora-partnerships-and-the-eleos-foundation/.

- Frey, Carl Benedikt, and Ebrahim Rahbari. July 20, 2016. "Do labor-saving technologies spell the death of jobs in the developing world?" Brookings Blum Roundtable. https://www.brookings.edu/wp-content/uploads/2016/07/Global_20160720_Blum_FreyRahbari.pdf.

- Geromel, Ricardo. December 12, 2011. "You must know THIS before investing in Brazil." *Forbes*. http://bit.ly/2O4FLQ3.

- Global Impact Sourcing Coalition. "What is the Global Impact Sourcing Coalition." BSR Collaboration. https://gisc.bsr.org/files/BSR_GISC_Factsheet.pdf.

- Global Opportunity Network. July 8, 2016. "The Digital Labour Market." Global Opportunity Network. https://web.archive.org/web/20160708052511/http://www.globalopportunitynetwork.org/report-2016/the-digital-labour-market/#.Wh78saJc-dU.

- Gutierrez, Karla. November 29, 2012. "18 Mind-Blowing eLearning Statistics You Need To Know." Shift Learning. https://www.shiftelearning.com/blog/bid/247473/18-Mind-Blowing-eLearning-Statistics-You-Need-To-Know.

- Handa, Mudit. March 20, 2018. "What are the impacts of linking Aadhaar to personal info?" *E-Startup India*. https://www.e-startupindia.com/blog/what-are-the-impacts-of-linking-aadhaar-to-personal-info/10118.html.

- Hathaway, Ian. March 1, 2016. "What Startup Accelerators Really Do." *Harvard Business Review*. https://hbr.org/2016/03/what-startup-accelerators-really-do.

- infoDEV. 2015. "Business Incubation Basics" https://www.infodev.org/infodev-files/m1_traineemanual_20101029.pdf.

- Innovation, Science and Economic Development Canada. October 4, 2017. "Minister Bains addresses B Corp community at its annual retreat." *Newswire*. https://bit.ly/2JOjxDc.

- International Finance Corporation. 2006. "Credit Bureau Knowledge Guide." International Finance Corporation. https://bit.ly/2sXPnmJ.

- Internet World Stats. December 31, 2017. "Internet Users Statistics for Africa." Internet World Stats. http://www.internetworldstats.com/stats1.htm#africa.

- Klapper, Leora and Dorothe Singer. August 24, 2014. "The Opportunities of Digitalizing Payments." World Bank. https://bit.ly/2JM9FpI.

- Klapper, Leora. November 27, 2015. "Can digital financial services help close the gender gap?." World Economic Forum. https://www.weforum.org/agenda/2015/11/can-digital-financial-services-help-close-the-gendergap/.

- Kuek, Siou Chew, Cecilia Paradi-Guilford, Toks Fayomi, Saori Imaizumi, Panos Ipeirotis, Patricia Pina, and Manpreet Singh. June, 2015. "The Global Opportunity in Online Outsourcing." World Bank. https://bit.ly/2HOQzgE.

- Lilenstein, Adaiah. June, 2016. "In West Africa, education = jobs and jobs = development." World Bank. http://blogs.worldbank.org/jobs/psd/west-africa-education-jobs-and-jobs-development.

- Love, Inessa, and Nataliya Mylenko. October, 2003. "Credit Reporting and Financial Constraints." World Bank.

- Lynk. "About Us.". https://lynk.global/aboutus.

- Manyika, James, Susan Lund, Kelsey Robinson, John Valentino, and Richard Dobbs. June, 2015. "Connecting talent with opportunity in the digital age." McKinsey & Company. https://www.mckinsey.com/global-themes/employment-and-growth/connecting-talent-with-opportunity-in-the-digital-age.

- Martini, Maira. 2013. "The role of business associations and chambers of commerce in the fight against corruption." Transparency International. https://bit.ly/2sZyZCh

- Mastercard. September, 2017. "Building Electronic Payment Acceptance at the Base of the Pyramid to Advance Financial Inclusion." Mastercard. https://mstr.cd/2yyZkMd.
- McCarthy, Rory. September, 2009. "Text messaging helps young Palestinians find work." *The Guardian.* https://www.theguardian.com/world/2009/sep/21/souktel-jobs-west-bank.
- McCord, Mark. "The Business Association Development Guidebook." USAID. http://pdf. usaid.gov/pdf_docs/pnaeb607.pdf.
- McKinsey & Company. September, 2014. "Offline and falling behind: Barriers to Internet adoption." McKinsey & Company.https://www.mckinsey.com/industries/high-tech/our-insights/offline-and-falling-behind-barriers-to-internet-adoption.
- Menden, Aline. May 30, 2017. "More than money: mapping the landscape of advisory support for inclusive business." Practioner Hub for Inclusive Business. http://www. inclusivebusinesshub.org/money-mapping-landscape-advisory-support-inclusive-business/.
- Mishra, Sumit. July 31, 2017. "The conomics of Aadhaar." Live Mint. http://www.livemint. com/Home-Page/s22gUzxOULwQxqukfcBMiM/The-economics-of-Aadhaar.html.
- Mounir, Hossam. Jan 22, 2016. "72m Credit facilities registered in I-Score database as of October 2015." *Daily News Egypt.* https://bit.ly/2l86QV2.
- Puin, Karolina. February 1, 2012. "Introduction to SEBRAE." *The Brazil Business.* http:// thebrazilbusiness.com/article/introduction-to-sebrae.
- Reach Project, Mastercard Center for Inclusive Growth, and The Munk School of Global Affairs. 2017. "India Case study: Aahaar – providing proof of identity to one billion." Mastercard. https://bit.ly/2MCUjph.
- Reuben, William and Flávia Carbonari. May, 2017. "Identification as a National Priority: The Unique Case of Peru." Center for Global Development. https://www.cgdev.org/sites/ default/files/identification-national-priority-unique-case-peru.pdf.
- Rockefeller Foundation. June, 2011. "Job Creation Through Building the Field of Impact Sourcing." World Bank. https://olc.worldbank.org/sites/default/files/Impact%20Sourcing_0. pdf.
- Salela, Pumela. July 23, 2014. "The Business Case for Impact Sourcing." Global Sourcing Council. https://www.gscouncil.org/the-business-case-for-impact-sourcing/.
- Saxena, Rishabh. May 2, 2017. "E-learning challenges and trends in developing regions." Totara. https://www.totaralms.com/blog/e-learning-challenges-and-trends-developing-regions.
- SEBRAE. "700 Service Centers throughout Brazil." Sebrae. http://www.sebrae.com.br/sites/ PortalSebrae/canais_adicionais/sebrae_english.
- Shortlist. "About Us." https://shortlist.net/about-us/.
- Shu, Catherine. July 30, 2014. "Pricey Data is a Barrier to Internet Access in Developing Countries." *Techcrunch.* https://techcrunch.com/2014/07/30/pricey-data-is-a-barrier-to-internet-access-in-developing-countries/.
- Solomon, Shoshanna. September 7, 2017. "Israeli startup Fiverr sees Amazon as model for growth." *The Times of Israel.* https://www.timesofisrael.com/israeli-startup-fiverr-sees-amazon-as-model-for-growth/.
- Souktel. January 20, 2016. "World Bank: Souktel's Job-Find Solution Boosts Wages, Closes Gender Gaps." Souktel. http://www.souktel.org/media/news/world-bank-souktel%E2%80%99s-job-find-solution-boosts-wages-closes-gender-gaps.
- Sparreboom, Theo, and Anita Staneva. December, 2014. "Is education the solution to decent work for youth in developing economies?" United Nations. http://www.un.org/youthenvoy/ wp-content/uploads/2014/10/Work4Youth-Publication.pdf.

- Sundararajan, Arun. April 24, 2012. "India's Unique Identity (UID) Reaching Underprivileged Households That Have No Existing ID." New York University Stern. http://www.stern.nyu.edu/experience-stern/faculty-research/sundararajan-uid-results.
- Unique Identification Authority of India. May 31, 2018. "State/UT wise ranking based on Aadhaar saturation as of 31st May, 2018" AADHAAR. https://uidai.gov.in/images/StateWiseAge_AadhaarSat_24082017.pdf.
- United States Development Programme. 2016. "Goal 16 Targets." United States Development Programme. http://www.undp.org/content/undp/en/home/sustainable-development-goals/goal-16-peace-justice-and-strong-institutions/targets/.
- Universitat Autonóma de Barcelona. 2017. "Differences between a MOOC and an online course." Universitat Autonóma de Barcelona http://www.uab.cat/web/study-abroad/mooc/differences-between-a-mooc-and-an-onlinecourse-1345668290741.html.
- Van Hilten, Lucy Goodchild. July 27, 2015. "Higher education is key to economic development (but it's not as simple as you think)." Elsevier. https://www.elsevier.com/atlas/story/people/higher-education-is-key-to-economic-development.
- Verma, Aditya. September 18, 2014. "Impact Sourcing 101: The Fundamentals of a Powerful Global Sourcing Model." Everest Group. http://www.everestgrp.com/2014-09-impact-sourcing-101-the-fundamentals-of-a-powerful-global-sourcing-model-sherpas-in-blue-shirts-15558.html/.
- Wilson, Lily. July 8, 2015. "Utilizing eLearning In Developing Countries: eLearning Breakthroughs In 2015." eLearning Industry. https://elearningindustry.com/utilizing-elearning-in-developing-countries-elearning-breakthroughs-2015.
- World Bank. 2016. "World Development Report 2016: Digital Dividends." World Bank. http://documents.worldbank.org/curated/en/896971468194972881/pdf/102725-PUB-Replacement-PUBLIC.pdf.
- World Bank. 2017. "Identification for Development (ID4D)." World Bank. http://www.worldbank.org/en/programs/id4d.
- World Bank. August 28, 2014. "World Bank Report: Digital Payments Vital to Economic Growth." World Bank. https://bit.ly/Z62dxU.
- World Bank. January 14, 2013. "Pakistan: Uplifting Lives and Livelihoods Through Cash Transfers." http://www.worldbank.org/en/results/2013/04/15/pakistan-uplifting-lives-and-livelihoods-through-cash-transfers.
- World Bank. June 2, 2015. "Jobs Without Borders." World Bank. http://www.worldbank.org/en/news/feature/2015/06/02/jobs-without-borders.

Chapter 5

- Access to Finance Rwanda. March 2016. "FinScope Rwanda 2016." National Institute of Statistics of Rwanda. http://www.statistics.gov.rw/publication/finscope-rwanda-2016.
- Altenburg, Tilman and Claudia Assmann. 2017. "Green Industrial Policy: Concept, Policies, Country Experiences." Partnership for Action on Green Economy. http://www.un-page.org/files/public/green_industrial_policy_book_aw_web.pdf.
- Argent, Jonathan, James A. Hanson and Maria Paula Gomez. August, 2013. "The Regulation of Mobile Money in Rwanda." International Growth Centre. https://www.theigc.org/wp-content/uploads/2014/09/Argent-Et-Al-2013-Working-Paper.pdf.
- Arthur, Peter and Emmanuel Arthur. Winter, 2014. "Local Content and Private Sector Participation in Ghana's Oil Industry: An Economic and Strategic Imperative." *Africa Today*. http://bit.ly/2uaKciV.

- Azerbaijan-Central Asia Financial Markets Infrastructure Advisory Services Project. August, 2010."Development of the First Private Credit Information Bureau." IFC Central Asia – Azerbaijan Financial Markets Infrastructure Project. https://bit.ly/2MCkLiU.
- Baer, Tobias, Massimo Carassinu, Andrea Del Miglio, Claudio Fabiani, and Edoardo Ginevra. December 2009. "The national credit bureau: A key enabler of fionancial infrastructure and lending in developing economies." McKinsey and Company. https://mck.co/2ynUcuK.
- Barder, Owen, Toby Eccles, and Elizabth Littlefield. October 2013. "Investing in Social Outcomes: Development Impact Bonds The Report of the Development Impact Bond Working Group." Center for Global Development. https://www.cgdev.org/sites/default/files/investing-in-social-outcomes-development-impact-bonds.pdf.
- Barder, Owen. June 11, 2012. "What If You Could Invest in Development?" Center for Global Development.https://www.cgdev.org/blog/what-if-you-could-invest-development.
- Basu, Avik. April 15, 2005. "Urban & Regional Planning Economic Development Handbook: Import substitution as economic development." Taubman College of Architecture and Regional Planning.
- Behuria, Pritish. June 12, 2017. "The Cautious Return of Import Substitution in Africa." London School of Economics. http://blogs.lse.ac.uk/africaatlse/2017/06/12/the-cautious-return-of-import-substitution-in-africa/.
- BetterWork. May 28, 2018. "Compliance Data." BetterWork. https://portal.betterwork.org/transparency/compliance#.
- Blattman, Christopher, Natrhan Fiala, and Sebastian Martinez. 2013. "Generating Skilled Self-Employment In Developing Countries: Experimental Evidence from Uganda." Oxford University Press. https://chrisblattman.com/documents/research/2014.GeneratingSkilledEmployment.QJE.pdf.
- Brown, Drusilla. September, 2016. "Highlights: Progress and Potential – Findings from an independent impact assessment." Better Work Global Programme. https://betterwork.org/dev/wp-content/uploads/2016/09/BW-ProgressAndPotential-Highlights.pdf.
- Buen, Jørund. January 8, 2018. "The Danger of Subsidized Solar: How government and Donors Unwittingly Hobbled Our Business." Next Billion. https://nextbillion.net/danger-subsidized-solar-government-donors-unwittingly-hobbled-business/.
- Cheney, Catherine. January 23, 2018. "Rwanda could become a model for drone regulation." Devex. https://bit.ly/2yoI8sX.
- Cheney, Catherine. May 23, 2016. "Filling the gaps between financial access and financial inclusion." Devex. https://www.devex.com/news/filling-the-gaps-between-financial-access-and-financial-inclusion-88036.
- Cleary, Siobhan, Stefano Alderighi, Jacqueline Irving and Jim Woodsome. July 18, 2017. "Small and Medium-Sized Enterprises and SME Exchanges." World Federation of Exchanges and Milken Institute. https://bit.ly/2I1H5Pm.
- Creehan, Sean. September 2014. "Asia Focus: Priority Sector Lending in Asia." Federal Reserve Bank of San Francisco. https://www.frbsf.org/banking/files/Asia-Focus-Priority-Sector-Lending-in-Asia-September-2014.pdf.
- Da Rita, Paul. May 4, 2017. "What are the new trends driving private infrastructure investment in emerging markets?." World Bank. http://blogs.worldbank.org/ppps/what-are-new-trends-driving-private-infrastructure-investment-emerging-markets.
- DAI. 2016. "The Capo Verde Land Project." DAI. https://bit.ly/2lkBqe8.
- DAI. 2017. "Tanzania – Advancing Youth Activity." DAI. https://www.dai.com/our-work/projects/tanzania-youth-economic-empowerment-activity.

- Dasmani, Adam, 2011. "Challenges facing technical institute graduates in practical skills acquisition in the Upper East Region of Ghana." *Asia-Pacific Journal of Cooperative Education*. https://www.ijwil.org/files/APJCE_12_2_67_77.pdf.
- del Ninno, Carlo, Kalanidhi Subbarao and Annamaria Milazzo. May, 2009. "How to Make Public Works Work: A Review of the Experiences." World Bank. http://documents.worldbank.org/curated/en/465371468155125564/pdf/485670Replacem138914B01PUBLIC100905.pdf.
- Demirgüç-Kunt, Asli, Leora Klapper, Dorothe Singer, Saniya Ansar, and Jake Hess, 2018. "The Global Findex Database 2017: Measuring Financial Inclusion and the Fintech Revolution." World Bank. https://globalfindex.worldbank.org/#data_sec_focus.
- Deringer, Hanna, Fredrik Erixon, Philipp Lamprecht and Erik van der Marel. January, 2018. "The Economic Impact of Local Content Requirements: A Case Study of Heavy Vehicles." European Centre For International Political Economy. http://ecipe.org//app/uploads/2018/01/LCR-Paper-final-2-KL.pdf.
- Desai, Sasi and Nipun Jasuja. October 27, 2016. "India Stack: The Bedrock of a Digital India." Wharton FinTech. https://medium.com/wha rton-fintech/the-bedrock-of-a-digital-india-3e96240b3718.
- Dias, Denise. August, 2017." FinTech. Regtech and Suptech: What They Mean for Financial Supervision." Toronto Centre. https://bit.ly/2JP4fOT.
- Donigan, Thomas. June, 2017. "Rural Tanzanians Map Their Country's Future." Frontlines. USAID. https://bit.ly/2ll6rio.
- Elsayed, Mohamed. October 16, 2017. "New import substitution initiatives in the Middle East – 2017. The year of new policies." IHS Markit. https://bit.ly/2JXX0Qp.
- Farole, Thomas. September, 2011. "Special Economic Zones: What Have We Learned?" *Economic Premise*. http://siteresources.worldbank.org/INTPREMNET/Resources/EP64.pdf.
- Faucon, Benoit and Sarah Kent. July 30, 2014. "ConocoPhillips Sells Nigerian Oil Assets to Oando." *The Wall Street Journal*. https://www.wsj.com/articles/conocophillips-sells-nigerian-oil-assets-to-oando-1406741704.
- Faz, Xavier, Denise Dias, Carlos Lopez-Moctezuma and Brenda Samaniego. May 19, 2011. "A Bold Move Toward Simplifying AML/CFT: Lessons from Mexico." CGAP. http://www.cgap.org/blogbold-move-toward-simplifying-amlcft-lessons-mexico.
- Faz, Xavier. June 25, 2013. "Mexico's Tiered KYC: An Update on Market Response." CGAP. http://www.cgap.org/blog/mexicos-tiered-kyc-update-market-response.
- Fialka, John. December 19, 2016. "Why China Is Dominating the Solar Industry." *Scientific American*. https://www.scientificamerican.com/article/why-china-is-dominating-the-solar-industry/.
- International Monetary Fund. April, 2018. "Fiscal Monitor." International Monetary Fund. https://www.imf.org/~/media/Files/Publications/fiscal-monitor/2018/April/pdf/fm1801.ashx?la=en.
- Steenbergen, Victor and Beata Javorcik. August, 2017. "Analysing the impact of the Kigali Special Economic Zone on firm behavior." International Growth Center. https://www.theigc.org/wp-content/uploads/2017/10/Steenbergen-and-Javorcik-working-paper-2017_1.pdf.
- FinTech Global. 2017. "London Leads Growth in Regtech Investments as Sector set to Soar in 2017." FinTech Global. https://bit.ly/2xRB4Dc.
- Fisher-French, Maya. February 17, 2012. "Mzansi accounts reach dead end*." Mail & Guardian*. https://mg.co.za/article/2012-02-17-mzansi-accounts-reach-dead-end.
- Freschi, Arianna. November 27, 2017. "Trialling mobile-enabled PAYG energy in a greenfield market: lessons from Brighterlite in Myanmar." Global System for Mobile

Communications. https://bit.ly/2MBlNeO.

- Frey, Carl, Ebrahim Rahbari, Harry Patrinos, Cecilia Chen, Marcus Haymon, Louise Fox, Eric Simonson, Michael Grimm. August 1, 2016. "2016 Brookings Blum Roundtable: The future of work in the developing world." Brookings Institute. https://www.brookings.edu/multi-chapter-report/the-future-of-work-in-the-developing-world/.

- Gereffi, Gary. 1990. "Manufacturing Miracles: Path of industrialization in Latin America and East Asia." Princeton University Press.

- Google Public Data. April 24, 2018. "GDP per capita (current US$) 1960-2016." https://www.google.com/publicdata/explore?ds=d5bncppjof8f9_&met_y=ny_gdp_pcap_cd&hl=en&dl=en.

- Görlich, Dennis. March, 2016. "Growth and Jobs by investing in Sustainable Special Economic Zones."Council of Global Problem-Solving. https://bit.ly/2tacyKI

- Government of Punjab. March, 2015. "Punjab Skills Development Sector Plan 2018: Providing skills for productive employment." Planning & Development Department. http://www.pndpunjab.gov.pk/system/files/Punjab_Skills_Sector_Plan_2018_0.pdf

- Guay, Jennifer. June 10, 2017. "Brazil lifts millions out of poverty with direct cash transfer scheme."Apolitical. https://apolitical.co/solution_article/brazil-lifts-millions-poverty-direct-cash-transfer-scheme/

- Gustafsson-Wright, Emily, Izzy Boggild-Jones, Dean Segell and Justice Durland. September, 2017."Impact Bonds in Developing Countries: Early Learnings from the Field." Brookings Institute and Convergence. https://www.brookings.edu/wp-content/uploads/2017/09/impact-bonds-in-developing-countries_web.pdf

- Hanouch, Michel. October 19, 2012. "Beyond the Mzansi Acount in South Africa – Targeting Usage." CGAP. http://www.cgap.org/blog/beyond-mzansi-account-south-africa-%E2%80%93-targeting-usage

- Harwood, Alison and Tanya Konidaris. January, 2015. "SME Exchanges in Emerging Market Economies: A Stocktaking of Development Practices." World Bank. https://bit.ly/2K2MCao

- IFC's Global Credit Reporting Team. 2012. "Credit Reporting Knowledge Guide." International Finance Corporation. https://bit.ly/2JReSQW.

- International Labor Organization, 2018. "Employment Intensive Investment Programme: Creating jobs through public investment." International Labor Organization. http://www.ilo.org/wcmsp5/groups/public/---ed_emp/---emp_policy/---invest/documents/publication/wcms_619821.pdf

- Irving, Jacqueline, John Schellhase, and Jim Woodsome. 2017. "Can Stock Exchanges support the Growth of Small and Medium-Sized Enterprises?" Milken Institute. https://bit.ly/2t9pCzX

- Kamali, Wilson and Douglas Randall. August 6, 2017. "Leveraging 'suptech' for financial inclusion in Rwanda." World Bank. http://blogs.worldbank.org/psd/leveraging-suptech-financial-inclusion-rwanda

- Kluve, Jochen. March, 2016. "A review of the effectiveness of Active Labour Market Programmes with a focus on Latin America and the Caribbean." International Labour Office. https://bit.ly/2taxAbT

- Kumar, Muneesh, Neetika Batra, and Florent Deisting. 2016. "Determinants of Priority Sector Lending: Evidence From Bank Lendiong Patterns in India." *The International Journal of Business and Finance Research*. ftp://ftp.repec.org/opt/ReDIF/RePEc/ibf/ijbfre/ijbfr-v10n2-2016/IJBFR-V10N2-2016-5.pdf

- Kwibuka, Eugène. April 4, 2018. "Agric will remain a priority sector – Premier." *The New*

Times. http://www.newtimes.co.rw/rwanda/agric-will-remain-priority-sector-premier

- Lyman, Timothy, Tony Lythgoe, Margaret Miller, Xavier Reille, and Shalini Sankaranarayan. September, 2011. "Credit Reporting at the Base of the Pyramid Key Issues and Success Factors." CGAP. http://www.cgap.org/sites/default/files/CGAP-Forum-Credit-Reporting-at-the-Base-of-the-Pyramid-Oct-2011.pdf.

- Maimbo, Samuel Munzele and Claudia Alejandra Henriquez Gallegos. October, 2014. "Interest Rate Caps around the World: Still Popular, but a Blunt Instrument." World Bank. http://documents.worldbank.org/curated/en/876751468149083943/pdf/WPS7070.pdf.

- Maritz Africa Intelligence. August 30, 2016. "Ethiopia: Import substitution likely to be a growing theme." *East Africa Consumer Industries Quarterly*. https://www. howwemadeitinafrica.com/ethiopia-import-substitution-likely-growing-theme/55584/.

- Mbengue, Djibril Maguette. November 11, 2013. "The Worrying Trend of Interest Rate Caps in Africa." CGAP. http://www.cgap.org/blog/worrying-trend-interest-rate-caps-africa

- Mckinsey & Company. April, 2017. "Deepening capital markets in emerging economies." McKinsey &Company. https://mck.co/2tazr0t.

- Mutabazi, Junior Sabena. September 3, 2014. "TVET schooling the answer to youth unemployment?" The New Times. http://www.newtimes.co.rw/section/read/380.

- Nabi, Ijaz. January 11, 2017. "Course correcting learning in the provision of skills." Brookings Institute. https://www.brookings.edu/blog/future-development/2017/01/11/course-correcting-learning-in-the-provision-of-skills/.

- National Bank of Rwanda. July, 2014. "Rwanda's Financial Inclusion Success Story: Umurenge SACCOs." Alliance for Financial Inclusion. https://www.microfinancegateway. org/library/rwanda%E2%80%99s-financial-inclusion-success-story-umurenge-saccos.

- Newhouse, Sean. April 3, 2018. "Utkrisht Bond Aims to Prevent Maternal Mortality in India." The Borgen Project. https://borgenproject.org/utkrisht-bond-maternal-mortality-india/.

- Nwaokoro, Joseph Nna Emeka. April, 2011. "Nigeria's National Content Bill: The Hype, the Hope and the Reality." *Journal of African Law*. http://bit.ly/2KWReyX.

- Organization For Economic Co-Operation and Development. February, 2016. "The economic impact of local content requirements." Organization For Economic Co-Operation and Development. https://www.oecd.org/tad/policynotes/economic-impact-local-content-requirements.pdf

- Oxford Business Group. 2016. "Oman's in-country value scheme expected to broaden domestic industry." Oxford Business Group. https://oxfordbusinessgroup.com/analysis/adding-value-country-value-icv-scheme-expected-broaden-domestic-industry.

- Packman, Andrew and Augusto Lopez-Claros, 2016. "Paying Taxes 2016." PricewaterhouseCoopers. https://www.pwc.com/gx/en/paying-taxes-2016/paying-taxes-2016.pdf.

- Pessino, Carola. December 7, 2016. "El Salvador will improve tax and customs management with IDB support." Inter-American Development Bank. https://bit.ly/2M5xMQK

- Pilat, Dirk. 2012. "Resurrecting industrial policy." Organisation for Economic Co-Operation and Development. http://oecdobserver.org/news/fullstory.php/aid/3814/Resurrecting_industrial_policy.html

- Piskadlo, Danielle. May 21, 2018. "The Politics (and Varied Experiences) of Interest Rate Caps." Center for Financial Inclusion, Client Focus, Governance, Policy. https://cfi-blog. org/2018/05/21/the-politics-and-varied-experiences-of-interest-rate-caps/

- PK, Jayadevan. September 5, 2017. "Consent, the final layer in India's ambitious data regime, falling in place." *Factory Daily*. https://factordaily.com/consent-architecture-indiastack/

- Proctor, Shonika. May 3, 2013. "Chile launches one day business incorporation online portal." *Andes-Beat*. http://andesbeat.com/2013/05/03/chile-one-day-business-incorporation-online-now-possibl/

- Rani, Shilpa and Diksha Garg. January, 2015. "Priority Sector Lending: Trends. Issues and Strategies." *International Journal of Management and Social Sciences Research*. http://www.irjcjournals.org/ijmssr/Jan2015/4.pdf.

- Republic of Rwanda. March, 2015. "Domestic Market Recapturing Strategy." Ministry of Trade and Industry. http://www.minicom.gov.rw/fileadmin/minicom_publications/Planning_documents/Domestic_Market_Recapturing_Strategy.pdf

- Reserve Bank of India. April 18, 2018. "Frequently Asked Questions." Reserve Bank of India. https://www.rbi.org.in/scripts/FAQView.aspx?Id=87

- Reyes, Joes-Daniel and Miguel Eduardo Sanchez. November, 2016. "Special Economic Zones in the Dominican Republic: Policy Consideration for a More Competitive and Inclusive Sector." World Bank. https://bit.ly/2tk7J0x.

- Rodrik, Dani. 2014. "Green industrial policy." Oxford Review of Economic Policy. https://drodrik.scholar.harvard.edu/files/dani-rodrik/files/green_industrial_policy.pdf

- Rodrik, Dani. January 6, 2011. "The Return of Industrial Policy." Ethos Insights. https://bit.ly/2K3Rhf9

- Rojas-Suarez, Liliana and Lucía Pacheco. June, 2017. "An Index of Regulatory Practices for Financial Inclusion in Latin America: Enablers. Promoters and Preventers." BBVA Research. https://bit.ly/2tm1zNp.

- Rojas-Suarez, Liliana and Lucía Pacheco. October, 2017. "An Index of Regulatory Practices for Financial Inclusion in Latin America: Enablers. Promoters. and Preventers." Center for Global Development. https://www.cgdev.org/sites/default/files/index-regulatory-practices-financial-inclusion-latin-america_0.pdf.

- Rosas, Nina and Shwetlena Sabarwal. February, 2016. "Can You Work it?: Evidence on the Productive Potential of Public Works from a Youth Employment Program in Sierra Leone." World Bank. http://documents.worldbank.org/curated/en/105531467996736274/pdf/WPS7580.pdf

- Saha, Deblina. June, 2017. "Private Participation in Infrastructure (PPI): Half Year Update: January-June 2017." World Bank. https://ppi.worldbank.org/~/media/GIAWB/PPI/Documents/Global-Notes/PPI2017_HalfYear_Update.pdf.

- Schellhase, John, Eric Bundugu and Jim Woodsome. December, 2015. "Capital Markets in Rwanda:Assessment and Aspirations." Milken Institute. https://bit.ly/2K13Ftl.

- Schellhase, John, Moutusi Sau, and Apanard Prabha. June 2014. "Capital Markets in Developing Countries: The State of Play" Milken Institute: Center For Financial Markets. https://bit.ly/2taZ2X9.

- Shiller, Robert J. October 14, 2016. "What's Behind a Rise in Ethnic Nationalism? Maybe the Economy." *The New York Times*. https://www.nytimes.com/2016/10/16/upshot/whats-behind-a-rise-in-ethnic-nationalism-maybe-the-economy.html.

- Jaya Shukla. March 21, 2017. "Embrace priority sector lending to enhance financing of the agric sector." *The New Times*. http://www.newtimes.co.rw/section/read/209279.

- The Skuld P&I Club. January 19, 2016. "Algeria: Restriction on import of vehicles, cement and steel debars." The Skuld P&I Club, https://safety4sea.com/algeria-restriction-on-import-of-vehicles-cement-and-steel-debars/.

- Smeenk, Gaby, Yi Duan, and Dulijon Veldhoen. July 24, 2017. "China's Free Trade Zones – Overview of 2017 Developments." Mondaq. https://bit.ly/2I1jRZK
- Smith, Henry. August 8, 2017. "Algeria: Regulatory changes in automotive sector to favour domestic production over imports." Control Risks. https://www.controlrisks.com/our-thinking/insights/automotive-algeria
- Start-Up Chile. May 5, 2013. "Chile's new law: incorporate your business in just one day, in one step, and for free." Start-Up Chile. https://bit.ly/2I0Nbzy
- Subbarao, Kalandihi, Carlo del Ninno, Colin Andrews, and Claudia Rodríguez-Alas. 2013. "Public Works as a Safety Net: Design, Evidence, and Implementation." World Bank. https://bit.ly/2MDGy9T
- Temkin, Benjamin. January, 2016. "The impact of labor informality on subjective well-being." *Global Labour Journal.* https://bit.ly/2JZPeWi.
- The Central Bank of Nigeria IFC. February 28, 2017. "The Credit Crunch: How the use of movable collateral and credit reporting can help finance inclusive economic growth in Nigeria." World Bank. https://bit.ly/2K5vmUQ
- The Economist. August 24, 2006. "Of property and poverty." *The Economist.* http://www.economist.com/node/7830252.
- The Economist. August 5, 2010. "The global revival of industrial policy: Picking winners, saving losers." *The Economist.* http://www.economist.com/node/16741043.
- The Economist. June 4, 2015. "Dubai's Economy: Growing up." *The Economist.* https://www.economist.com/middle-east-and-africa/2015/06/04/growing-up.
- The Economist. September 8, 2016. "Interest-rate caps: Cut-price logic." *The Economist.* https://www.economist.com/news/leaders/21706528-bad-idea-remarkably-common-cut-price-logic.
- Thornett, Robert. October 14, 2015. "In Brazil, a City's Waste Pickers Find Hope in a Pioneering Program." Yale School of Forestry & Environmental Studies. https://e360.yale.edu/features/in_brazil_a_citys_waste_pickers_find_hope_in_a_pioneering_program.
- Timm, Stephen. July 20, 2015. "Is forcing banks to lend to SMEs a good idea?." Ventureburn. http://ventureburn.com/2015/07/forcing-banks-to-lend-to-smes-a-good-idea/.
- USAID. November, 2017. "The Utkrisht Impact Bond – Improving Maternal and Newborn Health Care in Rajasthan. India." USAID. https://www.usaid.gov/sites/default/files/documents/1864/Utkrish-Impact-Bond-Brochure-November-2017.pdf.
- Whalley, John. February 24, 2015. "The impact of China's new free trade zone." World Economic Forum. https://www.weforum.org/agenda/2015/02/the-impact-of-chinas-new-free-trade-zone/.
- Winter, Preston. January 9, 2018. "Land Rights Open Economic Opportunities in Cabo Verde." Millenium Challenge Corporation. https://www.mcc.gov/blog/entry/blog-010918-land-rights-cabo-verde.
- World Bank. 2012. "Doing Business 2012: Economy Profile: Macedonia. FYR." World Bank. https://bit.ly/2JMajaC
- World Bank. 2014. "Doing Business 2015: Economy Profile: Macedonia. FYR." World Bank. https://bit.ly/2M65yW9
- World Bank. 2016. "Doing Business 2017: Economy Profile: Macedonia. FYR." World Bank. https://bit.ly/2tmoIPE.
- World Bank. 2017. "Doing Business 2017: Equal Opportunity for All – Economy Profile 2017: Rwanda." World Bank. https://bit.ly/2ta61Qe
- World Bank. 2018. "Doing Business 2018: Reforming to Create Jobs." World Bank. http://

www.doingbusiness.org/~/media/WBG/DoingBusiness/Documents/Annual-Reports/
English/DB2018-Full-Report.pdf
- World Bank. April 28, 2015. "Tajikistan's First Credit Bureau Contributes to Private Sector Development." World Bank. http://www.worldbank.org/en/results/2015/04/28/tajikistans-first-credit-bureau-for-private-sector-development
- World Bank. June, 2017. "Starting a Business: Reforms." World Bank. http://www.doingbusiness.org/data/exploretopics/starting-a-business/reforms
- World Bank. February 22, 2017. "Free-Trade Zones in the Dominican Republic, an Engine for Competitiveness and Jobs: World Bank." World Bank. http://www.worldbank.org/en/news/press-release/2017/02/21/zonas-francas-republica-dominicana-competitividad-empleos
- World Bank. July 5, 2016. "Vietnam: Improving Efficiency and Transparency in Land Administration Services." World Bank. https://bit.ly/29l8DhS.
- World Bank. June 12, 2016. "Vietnam: Improved Land Governance and Database Project." World Bank. https://bit.ly/2MCBEty.
- World Bank. March 24, 2017. "Why Secure Land Rights Matter." World Bank. http://www.worldbank.org/en/news/feature/2017/03/24/why-secure-land-rights-matter.
- World Bank. March, 2017. "Public Works and Welfare: A Randomized Control Trial of a Cash for Work Program Targeting the Poor in a Lower Income Country." Impact Evaluation to Development Impact.
- World Bank. October 10, 2016. "Government Objectives: Benefits and Risks of PPPs." World Bank. https://ppp.worldbank.org/public-private-partnership/overview/ppp-objectives.
- Zeng, Douglas Zhihua. May 5, 2015. "Why are more countries embracing industrial zones?." World Bank. http://blogs.worldbank.org/trade/why-are-more-countries-embracing-industrial-zones-video.
- Zhan, James. February 21, 2018. "Growing popularity of SEZs demonstrates the raft of benefits they offer." *World Finance*. https://www.worldfinance.com/markets/growing-popularity-of-sezs-demonstrates-the-raft-of-benefits-they-offer.

Chapter 6
- Accion website. What We Do: Investments." https://www.accion.org/frontier.
- Acumen. "Our Portfolio: Our Companies Create Sustainable Solutions That Enable the Poor to Transform Their Lives." Acumen. https://acumen.org/companies/.
- Asian Development Bank. January 30, 2018. "ADB, India Sign $250 Million Loan to Improve Rural Connectivity in 5 States." Asian Development Bank. https://www.adb.org/news/adb-india-sign-250-million-loan-improve-rural-connectivity-5-states.
- Asian Development Bank. October 7, 2016. "ADB and Citi Partner to Provide $100 Million for Microfinance in Asia." Asian Development Bank. https://www.adb.org/news/adb-and-citi-partner-provide-100-million-microfinance-asia.
- Asian Development Bank. September 30, 2013. "Who Will Pay for Asia's $8 Trillion Infrastructure Gap?." Asian Development Bank. http://www.adb.org/news/infographics/who-will-pay-asias-8-trillion-infrastructure-gap.
- Balkus, Jenna, Maria Luque, and Trent Van Alfen. January, 2014. "The Intersection of Impact Investing and International Development: A Primer." Accelerating Market-Driven Partnerships. https://bit.ly/2tq3i-Co.
- Banco Bilbao Vizcaya Argentaria. February 28, 2018. "BBVA to mobilize €100 billion by 2025 to fight climate change and drive sustainable development." BBVA. https://bbva.info/2tA0AcA.

- Bank of America. July 27, 2015. "Bank of America Announces Industry-leading $125 Billion Environmental Business Initiative." Bank of America. https://bit.ly/2MVOVhe.
- Bank, David. April 23, 2018. "Rise Fund's Impact Multiple of Money: A conversation with TPG's Bill McGlashan." *ImpactAlpha*. https://impactalpha.com/the-rise-funds-impact-multiple-of-money/.
- Bank, David. October 30, 2017. "Universal Ownership: The supertankers of global finance are shifting course." *ImpactAlpha*. https://bit.ly/2ImeTa9.
- Bernholz, Lucy, Edward Skloot and Barry Varela. May, 2010. "Disrupting Philanthropy: Technology and the Future of the Social Sector." Duke University. http://cspcs.sanford.duke.edu/sites/default/files/DisruptingPhil_online_FINAL.pdf.
- Biao, Huang. August 7, 2017. "China, People's Republic of: Green Transport Finance." Asian Development Bank. https://www.adb.org/projects/51056-001/main#project-overview.
- Bill & Melinda Gates Foundation. "Alliance For A Green Revolution." https://www.gatesfoundation.org/How-We-Work/Resources/Grantee-Profiles/Grantee-Profile-Alliance-for-a-Green-Revolution-in-Africa-AGRA.
- Birdsall, Nancy and Anna Diofasi. May 18, 2015. "Global Public Goods for Development: How Much and What For." Center for Global Development. https://www.cgdev.org/publication/global-public-goods-development-how-much-and-what.
- Brest, Paul and Kelly Born. August 14, 2013. "Unpacking the Impact in Impact Investing." *Stanford Social Innovation Review*. https://ssir.org/articles/entry/unpacking_the_impact_in_impact_investing.
- Bruce-Lockhart, Anderson June 26, 2017. "China's $900 billion New Silk Road. What you need to know." World Economic Forum. https://www.weforum.org/agenda/2017/06/china-new-silk-road-explainer/.
- Buchner, Barbara, Padraig Oliver, Xueying Wang, Cameron Carswell, Chavi Meattle and Federico Mazza. October, 2017. "Global Landscape of Climate Finance 2017." Climate Policy Initiative. https://climatepolicyinitiative.org/wp-content/uploads/2017/10/2017-Global-Landscape-of-Climate-Finance.pdf.
- Business & Sustainable Development Commission. January, 2017. "Better Business Better World." Business & Sustainable Development Commission http://report.businesscommission.org/report.
- CB Insights. 2018. "The 2017 Global CVC Report." CB Insights. https://www.cbinsights.com/research/report/corporate-venture-capital-trends-2017/.
- CB Insights. March 13, 2018. "Hungry for Investment: Big Food Races Toward Startups." CB Insights. https://bit.ly/2KmwPU1.
- Chami, Ralph, Dalia Hakura, and Peter Montiel, April 2009. "Remittances: An Automatic Output Stabilizer?" International Monetary Fund. http://www.imf.org/external/pubs/ft/wp/2009/wp0991.pdf.
- Chan Zuckerberg Initiative, 2018. "About." Chan Zuckerberg Initiative. https://www.chanzuckerberg.com/about.
- Chow, Daniel C.K. February 25, 2016. "Why China Established the Asia Infrastructure Investment Bank." Vanderbilt *Journal of Transnational Law*. https://www.vanderbilt.edu/jotl/wp-content/uploads/sites/78/7.-Chow_Paginated.pdf.
- Citigroup. February 18, 2015. "Citi Announces $100 Billion, 10-Year Commitment to Finance Sustainable Growth." Citigroup. http://www.citigroup.com/citi/news/2015/150218a.htm.
- Clark, Cathy and Ben Thornley July 5, 2016. "Cracking the Code of Impact Investing."

Stanford Social Innovation Review. https://ssir.org/articles/entry/cracking_the_code_of_impact_investing.

- Clean Technology Fund. December 14, 2017. "Scaling Up: Low Carbon Technologies." http://www.climateinvestmentfunds.org/sites/default/files/knowledge-documents/ctf_factsheet.pdf.

- CrowdExpert. February 29, 2016. "Crowdfunding Industry Statistics 2015-2016" CrowdExpert. http://crowdexpert.com/crowdfunding-industry-statistics/.

- Crunchbase. April 6, 2018. "Overview of Vox Capital." Crunchbase. https://www.crunchbase.com/organization/vox-capital-llc#section-overview.

- Cubo website. https://cubo.network/en.

- DAI. 2016. "Mexico – Technical assistance Perogram for Rural Microfinance (PATMIR)." DAI. https://www.dai.com/our-work/projects/mexico-technical-assistance-program-rural-microfinance-patmir.

- DAI. April 30, 2018. "USAID East Africa Trade and Investment Hub: Quarterly Report (2018. Q2)." DAI.

- DAI. June 30, 2016. "USAID East Africa Trade and Investment Hub: Quarterly Report (2016. Q3)." DAI.

- Desai, Raj and James Vreeland. July 17, 2014. "What the new bank of BRICS is all about." *The Washington Post*. https://wapo.st/2lyOgFQ.

- DeSilver, Drew. January 29, 2018. "Remittances from abroad are major economic assets for some developing countries." Pew Research Center. http://www.pewresearch.org/fact-tank/2018/01/29/remittances-from-abroad-are-major-economic-assets-for-some-developing-countries/.

- Detrixhe, John. October 26, 2017. "Big tech firms like Amazon are eager to eat the banking industry's lunch." *Quartz*. https://bit.ly/2xqbzGr.

- Devex. "Emerging Donors 2.0." Devex.

- Emerging Capital Partners. http://www.ecpinvestments.com/.

- Emerging Market Private Equity Association, 2018. "Industry Statistics: Year-end 2017." EMPEA. https://www.empea.org/app/uploads/2018/02/EMPEA-Industry-Statistics-YE-2017-Official-Member.pdf.

- Entrepreneur Staff. February 15, 2017. "What Corporate Incubators and Accelerators Can Mean for Your Business." *Entrepreneur*. https://www.entrepreneur.com/article/287495.

- Equator Principles website. http://equator-principles.com/.

- FMO. March 27, 2018. "Major Development impact and profitability FMO in 2017." FMO. https://bit.ly/2lw023P.

- Fomin. https://www.fomin.org/en-us/.

- Fullenkamp, Connel. February 10, 2015. "Do remittances drive economic growth?." World Economic Forum. https://www.weforum.org/agenda/2015/02/do-remittances-drive-economic-growth/.

- Gizitdinov, Nariman and David Malngha Doya. September 7, 2017. "Nigerian Soveraign Welath Fund Grows to $2 Billion, CEO Says." *Bloomberg*. https://www.bloomberg.com/news/articles/2017-09-06/nigerian-sovereign-wealth-fund-now-at-2-billion-ceo-orji-says.

- Global Impact Investing Network, 2018. "What You Need To Know About Impact Investing." Global Impact Investing Network. https://thegiin.org/impact-investing/need-to-know/#s2.

- Global Innovation Fund. "Stages of funding." https://globalinnovation.fund/what-we-do/stages-of-funding/.

- Goldman Sachs, 2018. "Environmental Market Opportunities: Green Bonds and Impact Investing." Goldman Sachs. http://www.goldmansachs.com/citizenship/environmental-stewardship/market-opportunities/green-bonds-impact-investing/.
- Greene, Sean. September 2014. "A Short Guide to Impact Investing." The Case Foundation. https://bit.ly/2MlFztR.
- Heinemann, Florian. January 14, 2016. "Focus areas of Corporate Accelerators." Corporate Accelerator DB. https://www.corporate-accelerators.net/database/focus-areas.html.
- Helms, Brigit and Kanini Mutooni. Summer 2018. "Blended Finance in Action - How USAID Leveraged $100 Million in East Africa." DAI. http://dai-global-developments.com/articles/blended-finance-in-actionhow-usaid-leveraged-100-million-in-east-africa/.
- IDC website. "Africa Unit." https://www.idc.co.za/africa-strategic-business-unit.html.
- IFC Asset Managment Company. December 31, 2016. "Emerging Markets. established expertise: 2016 Review." International Finance Corporation. https://bit.ly/2IpzhqO.
- Impact Capital Managers website. https://www.impactcapitalmanagers.com/.
- ImpactAssets. "ImpactAssets 50: An Annual Showcase of Impact Investment Fund Managers - Vox Capital." Impact Assets. http://www.impactassets.org/ia50_new/fund.php?id=a01E000000TzYWrIAN.
- Kenny, Charles, Jared Kalow, and Vijaya Ramachandran. January 17, 2018. "Inside the Portfolio of the International Finance Corporation: Does IFC Do Enough in Low-Income Countries?" Center for Global Development. https://www.cgdev.org/publication/inside-portfolio-international-finance-corporation-does-ifc-do-enough-low-income.
- Knox, Duncan. July 13, 2016. "Measuring aid to global public goods (GPGs)." Development Initiatives. http://devinit.org/post/measuring-aid-to-global-public-goods-gpgs/.
- MacBride, Elizabeth. July 31, 2017. "Kiva Hits $1B In Loans. $25 At A Time. Here's One Of The Hidden Keys To Its success." *Forbes*. https://www.forbes.com/sites/elizabethmacbride/2017/07/31/canonline-lenders-assess-your-character-to-a-certain-extent-yes/#7a8c28cb1b2f.
- Matsukawa, Tomoko, Robert Sheppard, and Joseph Wright. December 2003. "Foreign Exchange Risk Mitigation for Power and Water Projects in Developing Countries." World Bank. http://documents.worldbank.org/curated/en/433171468779677009/pdf/280940Energy0Exchange0EMS0no-09.pdf.
- Mittelman, Melissa. October 3, 2017. "TPG Seals Record $2 Billion for Fund Co-Led by Bono." *Bloomberg*. https://bloom.bg/2Kiy1HE.
- Monaco, Julie. July 18, 2017. "Why addressing FX risk could hold the key to infrastructure investment." World Bank. http://blogs.worldbank.org/ppps/why-addressing-fx-risk-could-hold-key-infrastructure-investment.
- Mudaliar, Abhilash, Hannah Schiff, Rachel Bass and Hannah Dithrich. May 2017. "Annual Impact Investor Survey 2017." Global Impact Investing Network. https://thegiin.org/assets/GIIN_AnnualImpactInvestorSurvey_2017_Web_Final.pdf.
- Mudaliar, Abhilash, Rachel Bass and Hannah Dithrich. June 2018. "Annual Impact investor Survey 2018." Global Impact Investing Network. https://thegiin.org/assets/2018_GIIN_Annual_Impact_Investor_Survey_webfile.pdf.
- Multilateral Development Banks. June, 2018. Mobilization of Private Finance 2017: By Multilateral Development Banks and Development Finance Institutions. https://www.edfi.eu/wp/wp-content/uploads/2018/06/201806_Mobilization-of-Private-Finance_v2.pdf.
- Ndong-Obiang, Olivia. May 2, 2018. "African Development Bank approves ZAR 140-million loan to support African Local Currency Bond Fund." African Development Bank Group. https://www.afdb.org/en/news-and-events/african-development-bank-

approves-zar-140-million-loan-to-support-africanlocal-currency-bond-fund-17813/.

- New Development Bank website. 2017. "History." New Development Bank. https://www. ndb.int/about-us/essence/history/.
- Organisation for Economic Co-Operation and Development. 2018. "Private Philanthropy for Development, 2013-15." Tableau. https://tabsoft.co/2IosTAh.
- Organisation for Economic Co-Operation and Development. March 23, 2018. "Private Philanthropy for Development." Organisation for Economic Co-Operation and Development. https://read.oecd-ilibrary.org/development/private-philanthropy-for-development_9789264085190-en#page4.
- Overseas Private Investment Corporation. February 22, 2018. "Investment As A Stabilizing Force: Highlights From OPIC's 2017 Annual Report." Overseas Private Investment Corporation. https://www.opic.gov/blog/opic-action/investment-stabilizing-force-highlights-opics-2017-annual-report.
- Overseas Private Investment Corporation. March 24, 2016. "Partner Spotlight: How microvest Combines A Commerical and Social Approach to Microfinance Investing." Overseas Private Investment Corporation. https://bit.ly/2lvZFpX.
- Parplies, Kay, Y. Ehlert, A. Efiong, P. Horrocks, J. Sedemund, and W. Bartz, S. Andreasen, C. Clubb, J.Durland, and H. Hirschhofer. February 1, 2017. "The Need to Reduce FX Risk in Development Countries by Scaling Blended Finance Solutions." European Commission, OECD, EDFI, Convergence, and TCX. https://assets.ctfassets.net/bbfdx7vx8x8r/3UYrVVpyqckCsw802wWoOi/e5ca01a8c2109991e15a0c9509067e0c/FX_Risk_in_Development_Primer.pdf.
- Pazarbasioglu, Ceyla. May 2, 2017. "Developing local capital markets to fund domestic long-term financing needs." The World Bank. http://blogs.worldbank.org/voices/developing-local-capital-markets-fund-domestic-long-term-financing-needs.
- Ramachandran, Vijaya and Charles Kenny. January 17, 2018. "The International Finance Corporation's Mission is Facilitating Risky Investments – So Why Is It Taking on Less and Less Risk?" Center for Global Development. https://www.cgdev.org/blog/international-finance-corporation-mission-facilitating-risky-investments-so-why-it-taking.
- Salesforce. October 3, 2017. "Salesforce Ventures Introduces New $50 Million Impact Investment Fund." Salesforce. https://www.salesforce.com/company/news-press/press-releases/2017/10/171003/.
- Savoy, Conor M., Paddy Carter, and Alberto Lemma. October, 2016. "Development Finance Institutions Come of Age: Development Finance Institutions Come of Age Policy Engagement, Impact, And New Directions." Center for Strategic and International Studies. https://csis-prod.s3.amazonaws.com/s3fs-public/publication/161021_Savoy_DFI_Web_Rev.pdf
- SME Finance Forum. 2018. "About: What We Do." SME Finance Forum. http://www.smefinanceforum.org/about/what-we-do.
- Swart, Richard. December, 2013. "World Bank: Crowdfunding Investment Market to Hit $93 Billion by 2025." Media Shift. http://mediashift.org/2013/12/world-bank-crowdfunding-investment-market-to-hit-93-billion-by-2025/.
- Tableau. December 2, 2017. "Gross bilateral ODA, 2015-2016 average." Organisation for Economic Co-Operation and Development. https://tabsoft.co/2KD3E28.
- Tew, Rob. April 20, 2018. "Aid spending by DAC donors in 2017." Development Initiatives. http://devinit.org/post/oda-data-2017/.
- The Impact Programme. December, 2017. "The Impact Programme: Annual Report." UK AID, 2016." http://www.theimpactprogramme.org.uk/wp-content/uploads/2017/12/Impact_AR_2016.pdf.

- Thees, Anderson. September 15, 2017. "Corporate venture in Brazil gains steam as giants amp up startup investments." *Techcrunch*. https://tcrn.ch/2xp1hZW.
- Thornley, Ben and Brian Locasio. June 18, 2018. "Best Practices in Impact Management Begin to Take Hold." *Stanford Social Innovation Review*. https://bit.ly/2yyjXIH.
- Tillemann, Tomicah and Scott Kalb. October 13, 2017. "Bretton Woods II Responsible Asset Allocator Initiative: Bretton Woods II Leaders List." *New America*. https://www.newamerica.org/in-depth/bwii-responsible-asset-allocator/bretton-woods-ii-leaders-list/.
- Trieu, Huy Nguyen. May 26, 2018. "Alibaba Becomes Top 10 Global Bank." *Disruptive Finance*. http://www.disruptivefinance.co.uk/2018/05/26/alibaba-becomes-top-10-global-bank/.
- Turner, Matt. January 26, 2018. " Everyone at Davos is talking about 'Larry's letter'." *Business Insider*. http://www.businessinsider.com/everyone-at-davos-is-talking-about-larry-finks-letter-to-ceos-2018-1.
- Tyson, Jeff. May 23, 2016. "Inside the World Bank's Pandemic Emergency Facility." Devex. https://www.devex.com/news/inside-the-world-bank-s-pandemic-emergency-facility-88195.
- U.S. Trust. 2017. "U.S. Trust Insights on Wealth and Worth: Annual survey of high-net-worth and ultra-high-net-worth Americans - 2017 The Generational Collide." U.S. Trust. https://ustrustaem.fs.ml.com/content/dam/ust/articles/pdf/FindingsOverview_Broch_Final.pdf.
- Urquhart, Angus and Luminita Tuchel. 2018. "Global Humanitarian Assistance Report 2018." Development Initiatives. http://devinit.org/wp-content/uploads/2018/06/GHA-Report-2018.pdf.
- USAID Development Credit Authority. September 30, 2017. "Empowering Returning Afghans and Internally Displaced Persons." USAID. https://usaid-credit.exposure.co/empowering-returning-afghans-and-internally-displaced-persons.
- USAID. 2014. "Domestic Resource Mobilization: El Salvador Tax Reform Boosts Revenues for Development." USAID. https://bit.ly/2cQ2ErI.
- USAID. February, 2018. "USAID East Africa Trade and Investment Hub." USAID. https://bit.ly/2ttG3XQ.
- USAID. May, 2018. "INVEST Project: Mobilizing Private Investment for Development Overview Presentation." USAID.
- Vox Capital website. "Portfolio." Vox Capital. http://www.voxcapital.com.br/new-gallery-1/p6k9hvkzgt3i46rxk0g8mdjto4u3al.
- Weiss, Martin A. February 3, 2017. "Asian Infrastructure Investment Bank (AIIB)." Congressional Research Service. https://fas.org/sgp/crs/row/R44754.pdf.
- World Bank. "Small and Medium Enterprises (SMEs) Finance." World Bank. http://www.worldbank.org/en/topic/smefinance.
- World Bank. November 27, 2012. "World Bank approves $500 million to accelerate Tunisia's economic recovery. pave way for more inclusive growth." World Bank http://www.worldbank.org/en/news/press-release/2012/11/27/world-bank-approves-fiv-million-accelerate-tunisias-economic-recovery-pave-way-more-inclusive-growth.
- World Bank. October 3, 2017. "Remittances to Recover Modestly after Two Years of Decline." World Bank. http://www.worldbank.org/en/news/press-release/2017/10/03/remittances-to-recover-modestly-after-two-years-of-decline.
- Zhang, Junyi. July 19, 2016. "Order from Chaos: Chinese foreign assistance, explained." Brookings Institute. https://www.brookings.edu/blog/order-from-chaos/2016/07/19/chinese-foreign-assistance-explained/.

Chapter 7

- Addati, Laura, Florence Bonnet, Ekkehard Ernst, Rossana Merola and Pei Man Jessica Wan. 2016. "Women at Work: Trends 2016." International Labor Organization. https://bit.ly/2Kvtn9E.

- Al-Fuqaha, Ala. 2015. "Internet of Things: A Survey of Enabling Technologies. Protocols and Applications." Institute of Electrical and Electronic Engineering.

- Alfred, Charlotte. April 17, 2017. "The Future of Refugee Education: A Roundup." *NewsDeeply.* https://bit.ly/2pctO1v.

- Alimi, Eyitayo. February 21, 2018. "A practical look at virtual reality in Nigerian education." TEDxGbagadaSalon. https://www.youtube.com/watch?v=40gesn6Sgec.

- Apolitical. April 20, 2017. "Case Study: Can Jordan's special economic zones give jobs to Syrian refugees?" Apolitical. https://apolitical.co/solution_article/can-jordans-special-economic-zones-gives-jobs-syrian-refugees/.

- Arntz, Melanie, Terry Gregory, and Ulrich Zierahn. 2016. "The Risk of Automation for Jobs in OECD Countries: A Comparative Analysis." Organisation for Economic Co-Operation and Development Social. https://bit.ly/2aL60tC.

- Association of Southeast Asian Nations. November 2017. "ASEAN Consensus On The Protection And Promotion Of The Rights Of Migrant Workers." Association of Southeast Asian Nations. https://bit.ly/2KqPh0J.

- Attanasio, Orazio, Matthew Bird, and Pablo Lavado. 2017. "Tablet-based financial education in technology." Innovations for Poverty Action. https://www.poverty-action.org/study/tablet-based-financial-education.

- Bacchetta, Marc, Ekkehard Ernst, Juana P. Bustamante. 2009. "Globalization And Informal Jobs In Developing Countries." International Labour Office and World Trade Organization. http://www20.iadb.org/intal/catalogo/PE/2009/04308.pdf

- Baker, Aryn, 2017. "The American Drones Saving Lives in Rwanda." *Time Magazine.* https://ti.me/2yQME3O.

- Baker, Judy L. 2008. "Urban Poverty: A Global View." World Bank. https://bit.ly/2lGOoTM.

- BanQu. "Current BanQu Case Studies." BanQu App. http://www.banquapp.com/our-solutions/pilots/.

- Barbelet, Veronique, Jessica Hagen-Zanker and Dina Mansour-Ille. February 2018. "The Jordan Compact: lessons learnt and implications for future refugee compacts." Overseas Development Institute Policy Brief. https://bit.ly/2Mwf0Cq.

- Barbière, Cécile. March 6, 2017. "French urban development expert: 'In 2050. 3 billion people will live in slums'." *Euractiv.* https://bit.ly/2tMM4hN.

- Bauza, Vanessa and Jamilette Guerrero. December 16, 2014. "IFC Closes $300 Million Financing to Support the Largest Wind Farm in Central America." International Finance Corporation. http://bit.ly/2KyaW4c

- Beauchamp, Zach. "9 Maps and Charts that Explain the Global Refugee Crisis." *Vox.* January 30, 2017.

- Biegel, Suzanne, Sandra M. Hunt and Sherryl Kuhlman. October, 2017. "Project Sage –Tracking Venture Capital with a Gender Lens." Social Impact Initiative. https://whr.tn/2N5ni5n

- Bloomberg New Energy Finance. November 28, 2017. "Accelerating India's Clean Energy Transition." Bloomberg. https://data.bloomberglp.com/bnef/sites/14/2017/11/BNEF_Accelerating-Indias-Clean-Energy-Transition_Nov-2017.pdf

- Bosi, Martina and Beatriz Eraso Puig. May 25, 2017. "From slums to neighborhoods:

How energy efficiency can transform the lives of the urban poor." World Bank. http://bit.ly/2N5Li8p.

- Bright, Jake. December 2, 2016. "Nigeria's Black Friday sales test the e-commerce models of startups Jumia and Konga." *TechCrunch*. https://tcrn.ch/2gVyC3e.

- Brown, Donald. April 2016. "The urban informal economy. local inclusion and achieving a global green transformation." Habitat International.

- Brynjolfson, Erik and Andrew McAfee, 2016. "The Second Machine Age: Work. Progress and Prosperity in a time of Brilliant Technologies". WW. Norton and Company.

- Bullard, Gabe. December 1, 2015. "See What Climate Change Means for the World's Poor." *National Geographic*. https://news.nationalgeographic.com/2015/12/151201-datapoints-climate-change-poverty-agriculture/

- Burke, Marshall. December 9, 2015. "The global economic costs from climate change may be worse than expected." Brookings Institute. https://brook.gs/2lHmtmY

- California Institute of Arts & Technology. "Farmers in Uganda team up with scientists to find better beans." California Institute of Arts & Technology. http://bit.ly/2tC8XoW.

- Castro, Ramiro Postigo. "Caja Arequipa." Women's World Banking. https://bit.ly/2KsWRIu.

- Chen, Martha and Jenna Harvey. January 23, 2017. "The Informal economy in Arab Nations: A Comparative Perspective." Women in Informal Employment: Globalizing and Organizing. http://www.wiego.org/sites/default/files/resources/files/Informal-Economy-Arab-Countries-2017.pdf

- Citi GPS, 2016. "Technology at Work v2.0. The Future Is Not What It Used to Be." https://bit.ly/2KhYfyg.

- Collins, Kate. March 1, 2015. "Vodafone 'Instant Classroom' is digital school in a box for refugees." *Wired Magazine*. http://www.wired.co.uk/article/vodafone-instant-classroom.

- Commission on the Status of Women [Fifty-fourth session]. March 8, 2010. "Interactive expert panel on 'Women's economic empowerment in the context of the global economic and financial crisis'." United Nations. https://bit.ly/2KenO33.

- Convergence. October 12, 2017. "Impact Bond For Syrian Refugee Livelihoods Recieves Funding For Structuring and Launch." Convergence. https://www.convergence.finance/news-and-events/news/9JWH3yAel2Gekq0MqEoy6/view.

- Cooper-Knock, Sarah Jane. February 26, 2016. "Gender. politics. and parliament in Rwanda." *openDemocracy*. https://www.opendemocracy.net/westminster/sarah-jane-cooper-knock/gender-politics-and-parliament-in-rwanda.

- Cruz del Rosario, Teresita. February 19, 2018. "Abuse of foreign domestic workers must end now." *Aljazeera*. https://www.aljazeera.com/indepth/opinion/abuse-foreign-domestic-workers-180219082433652.html

- Culbertson, Shelly, Olga Oliker, Ben Baruch and Ilana Blum, 2016 "Rethinking Coordination of Services to Refugees in Urban Areas: Managing the Crisis in Jordan and Lebanon." Research and Development Corporation. https://bit.ly/2KqQ9T3.

- D-Rev. "Mobility Impact Dashboard." http://d-rev.org/impact/remotion/.

- Dalberg. November 2017. "Privacy On the Line." https://bit.ly/2D72w3U.

- Darnton, Hannah. June 20, 2016. "Promising Innovations for Tackling the Refugee Crisis." Skoll Foundation. http://skoll.org/2016/06/20/promising-innovations-for-tackling-the-refugee-crisis/

- De Chant, Tim. August 8, 2018. "If the world's population lived like…." *PerSquareMile*. https://persquaremile.com/2012/08/08/if-the-worlds-population-lived-like/.

- Demirgüç.-Kunt, Asli, Leora Klapper, Dorothe Singer, Saniya Ansar and Jake Hess, 2017. "The Global Findex Database." World Bank. https://globalfindex.worldbank.org.
- Department of Economic and Social Affairs. 2015. "World urbanization Prospects: The 2014 Revision." United Nations. https://esa.un.org/unpd/wup/Publications/Files/WUP2014-Report.pdf.
- Dobbs, Richard. Jaana Remes and Fabian Schaer. September 2012. "Unlocking the potential of emerging market cities." McKinsey & Company. https://mck.co/2tC80Nv.
- Drones For Development. "The Dr.One Concept." https://www.dronesfordevelopment.org.
- Duffy, Gary. May 25, 2010. "Family Friendly: Brazil's scheme to tackle poverty." BBC. https://www.bbc.com/news/10122754.
- Dughi, Paul. February 3, 2018. " A simple explanation of how blockchain works." Medium. https://bit.ly/2xGMICL.
- Embrace. "Our Story." http://embraceglobal.org/about-us/
- Farnworth, Cathy Rozel, Clare M. Stirlinga, Amon Chinyophiroc, Andrew Namakhomac and Rebecca Morahand. February 2018. "Exploring the potential of household methodologies to strengthen gender equality and improve smallholder livelihoods: Research in Malawi in maize-based systems." *Journal of Arid Environments*. https://bit.ly/2yNdJ85.
- Ferrant, Gaëlle, Luca Maria Pesando, and Keiko Nowacka. December 2014. "Unpaid Care Work: The missing link in the analysis of gender gaps in labour outcomes." OECD Development Centre. https://bit.ly/2ICWUw6.
- FinCoNet. "About us." FinCoNet. http://www.finconet.org/about/
- Florida, Richard. October 20, 2016. "Rise of the 'Urbanpreneur'." *CityLab*. http://bit.ly/2MutxOU.
- Frey, Carl Benedikt and Ebrahim Rahbari. August 2016. "The Future of Work in the Developing World: Do labor-saving technologies spell the death of jobs in the developing world?" Brookings Institute.https://brook.gs/2tJ8z7p.
- Fundacíon Capital. 2017 "LISTA Initiative." Fundacíon Capital. https://fundacioncapital. org/our-work/lista-initiative/.
- GALS at Scale. http://www.galsatscale.net.
- Gender at Work. "Gender Action Learning: Gender at Work Action Learning Program as an Approach to Furthering Gender Equality." Gender at Work. http://genderatwork.org/gender-action-learning/.
- Gerber, P.J., H. Steinfeld, B. Henderson, A.Mottet, C. Opio, J. Dijkman, A. Falcucci and G. Tempio. 2013. "Tackling Climate Change Through Livestock: A Global Assessment of Emissions and Mitigation Opportunities." Food and Agriculture Organization of the United Nations. http://www.fao.org/3/ai3437e.pdf
- Ghani, Ejaz and Stephen D. O'Connell. July, 2014. "Can Service Be a Growth Escalator in Low Income Countries?." World Bank. http://documents.worldbank.org/curated/en/823731468002999348/pdf/WPS6971.pdf
- Goodier, Rob. July 1, 2016. "How the Internet of Things Is Improving Lives and Livelihoods in Developing Countries." Engineering for Change. https://bit.ly/2KeqH3T.
- Grupo Antolin, 2016. "Informe Anual 2016." Guimedic. http://www.grupoantolin.com/sites/default/files/informe_anual_2016_es_0.pdf.
- GSMA Intelligence. October 2016. "Global mobile trends." GSMA Intelligence. http://bit.ly/2lHjESU.
- Harey, Fiona. May 31, 2012. "Switching to a green economy could mean millions of jobs. says UN." *The Guardian*. https://www.theguardian.com/environment/2012/may/31/

switching-green-economy-jobs-un

- Haus Leo and Haus der Kulturen der Welt. "Arriving In Berlin." https://arriving-in-berlin.de.
- HelpMeSee. "Our Progress." https://helpmesee.org.in/Home
- HelpMeSee. "Simulation-Based Training Program." https://helpmesee.org.in/OurTechnology#anchorCollapse.
- Holodny, Elena. March 23, 2016. "Extreme weather events are on the rise." Business Insider. https://read.bi/2lGpynf.
- Hoornweg, Daniel and Perinaz Bhada-Tata. March 2012. "What A Waste: A Global Review of Solid Waste Management." World Bank. https://bit.ly/1mjzbQB.
- Huang, Cindy. February 7, 2018. "New Opportunities for Bangladeshi Citizens and Rohingya Refugees: A Refugee Compact for Bangladesh." Center for Global Development. https://bit.ly/2tDgiV4.
- Human Development Report Office Research Team. March 2016 "Valuing Care Work." United Nations Development Programme. http://hdr.undp.org/en/content/valuing-care-work.
- International Finance Corporation. "Banking on Women." International Finance Corporation. https://bit.ly/2tCiexi.
- International Finance Corporation. 2017. "Creating Markets for Climate Business." International Finance Corporation. http://bit.ly/2tBlfOi.
- International Finance Corporation. April, 2018. "Perspectives." International Finance Corporation. http://bit.ly/2lCDe2y.
- International Finance Corporation. May, 2014. "Inclusive Business Case Study: Jain Irrigation Systems Limited (JISL)." International Finance Corporation. http://bit.ly/2tCxLNz.
- International Labour Organisation. "Statistics on forced labor, modern slavery and human trafficking." https://bit.ly/1MRrt2y.
- International Labour Organisation. 2017. "Global Estimates of Modern Slavery: Forced Labour and Forced Marriage." International Labour Organisation.
- International Labour Organisation. 2017. "SDG NOTE: Engaging The Private Sector On Decent Work - Business operation And Investments." International Labour Organisation. https://bit.ly/2KyCOYS.
- International Labor Organization. April 12. 1999. "ILO Estimates Over 1 Million Work-Related Fatalities Each Year." International Labor Organization. http://www.ilo.org/global/about-the-ilo/newsroom/news/WCMS_007969/lang--en/index.htm
- International Labor Organization. April, 2017. "ILO's contribution to the objectives of the Green Climate Fund." International Labor Organization. http://bit.ly/2lCnjRI.
- International Telecommunications Union. 2016. "Harnessing the Internet of Things for Global Development." https://bit.ly/23wI5nN.
- International Youth Foundation. February 18, 2016. "At Work in Rural Communities to Prevent the Spread of the Zika Virus." International Youth Foundation. https://www.iyfnet.org/blog/work-rural-communities-prevent-spread-zika-virus.
- Jagannathan, Sheila. March 7, 2017. "Virtual Reality: The Future of Immersive Learning for Development." World Bank. https://blogs.worldbank.org/publicsphere/virtual-reality-future-immersive-learning-development
- Jedwab, Remi and Dietrich Vollrath. January 2015. "The mortality Transition, Malthusian Dynamics and the Rise of Poor Mega-Cities." George Washington University. http://bit.ly/2KubUS1.

- Jeffery, Neil. November 30, 2016. "A call for more entrepreneurs to focus on toilets." *The Huffington Post.* http://bit.ly/2tCpetO.
- Johnston, Ian. November 7, 2016. "Map shows how climate change will hit. The economies of the world's porest countries hardest." Independent. https://ind.pn/2lHpG5W.
- Juskalian, Russ April 12, 2018. "Inside the Jordan refugee camp that runs on blockchain." *MIT Technology Review.* https://www.technologyreview.com/s/610806/inside-the-jordan-refugee-camp-that-runs-on-blockchain/.
- Keane, Jonathan. August 26, 2015. "Medellin: Colobia's emerging tech hub." International Data Group Connect. http://bit.ly/2Mq6PHC.
- Kellow, Nebil. Spring 2018. "Ethiopia Stands poised to Lead an Africa Industrial Revolution." DAI. http://bit.ly/2Mq8mxm.
- Kluge, John. September 20, 2016. "Over 50 U.S. Businesses Step Up For Refugees." *Forbes.* https://www.forbes.com/sites/johnkluge/2016/09/20/u-s-businesses-step-up-for-refugees/#532a9b8b3a9e
- Lascher, Bill. November 8, 2013. "Could micro-insurance help the porrest communities deal with climate change?" The Guardian. https://www.theguardian.com/sustainable-business/micro-insurance-poorest-communities-climate-change
- Lipu, Molla Shahadat Hossain, Taskin Jamal, Muhammad Ahad Rahman Miah. 2013. "Barriers to Energy Access in the Urban Poor Areas of Dhaka. Bangladesh: Analysis of Present Situation and Recommendations." *International Journal of Energy Economics and Policy.* https://www.econjournals.com/index.php/ijeep/article/viewFile/536/330
- Litman, Todd. March 31, 2017. "Unaffordability Is a Problem. but Sprawl Is a Terrible Solution." *The City Fix.* http://thecityfix.com/blog/unaffordability-is-a-problem-but-sprawl-is-a-terrible-solution-toddlitman/
- Loaiza, Edilberto and Mengjia Liang. January, 2016. "Universal Access to Reproductive Health: Progress and Challenges." United Nations Population Fund. https://www.unfpa.org/sites/default/files/pub-pdf/UNFPA_Reproductive_Paper_20160120_online.pdf.
- Lohr, Steve. October 10, 2017. "Start-up Bets on Tech Talent Pipeline From Africa." *The New York Times.* https://nyti.ms/2yD7cvA.
- López, Julian. February 11, 2018. "This young entrepreneur is preparing girls to lead the tech industry in Ghana." International Research & Exchange Board. https://www.irex.org/success-story/young-entrepreneur-preparing-girls-lead-tech-industry-ghana
- Lustig, Nathan. December 19, 2017. "The Colombian Startup Ecosystem: Bogota, Medellin, Cali, And Barranquilla." Nathan Lustig. http://bit.ly/2lDK0Vy.
- Mabaya, Edward. June 3, 2016. "Climate change and 'smart seeds' in Africa." *Aljazeera.* http://bit.ly/2KyAXne.
- Mahr, Krista. May 4, 2018. "How Cape Town was saved from running out of water." *The Guardian.* http://bit.ly/2KxfQhu.
- Manyika, James. Susan Lund, Michael Chui, Jacques Bughin, Jonathan Woetzel, Parul Batra, Ryan Ko, and Saurabh Sanghvi. November 2017. "Jobs lost. jobs gained: What the future of work will mean for jobs. skills. and wages." McKinsey Global Institute. https://mck.co/2lE8uhx.
- Mattern, Max. June 21, 2018. "How Ghana Became One of Africa's Top Mobile Money Markets." CGAP. http://www.cgap.org/blog/measuring-women's-financial-inclusion-2017-findex-story.
- Mayes, Jonathan and Andrew White. November 1, 2016. "How Smartphone Technology Is Changing Healthcare In Developing Countries." *Journal of Global Health.* http://www.

ghjournal.org/how-smartphone-technology-is-changing-healthcare-in-developing-countries/.

- Mayoux, Linda. September, 2014. "Gender Action Learning System (GALS)." GALS@ Scale. https://bit.ly/2lF5nG4.

- Mazer, Rafe, Katharine McKee and Alexandra Fiorillo. June 2014. "Applying Behavioral Insights in Consumer Protection Policy." CGAP. https://bit.ly/2MuZLtu.

- McKay, Claudia and Rafe Mazer. October 1, 2014. "10 Myths About M-Pesa: 2014 Update." CGAP. https://bit.ly/2KsLEYo.

- McKinsey & Company. June 2012. "Urban world: Cities and the rise of the consuming class." McKinsey & Company. https://mck.co/2tIK0HL.

- McKinsey & Company. September 2015. "The Power of Parity: How Advancing Women's Equality Can Add $12 Trillion to Global Growth." McKinsey & Company. https://mck.co/2twK4Kq.

- Ministry of Manpower. April 15, 2016. "Medical insurance requirements for foreign worker." Ministry of Manpower. http://www.mom.gov.sg/passes-and-permits/work-permit-for-foreign-worker/sector-specific-rules/medical-insurance

- Ministry of Manpower. June 21, 2018. "Employers' Orientation Programme (EOP)." Ministry of Manpower. https://bit.ly/2mh91aB.

- Moxley, Harry. February 24, 2016. "At Work in Rural Communities to Prevent the Spread of the Zika Virus." Youtube. https://www.youtube.com/watch?v=gTksWjbUVoE.

- Nedelkoska, Ljubica and Glenda Quintini. March 2018. "Automation. skills use and training." Organisation for Economic Co-operation and Development. https://bit.ly/2N1xNXr.

- NewCities. July 18, 2017. "NewCities Summit 2017 - The Unlikely Appeal of Disruptive Urbanpreneurs." NewCities. https://www.youtube.com/watch?v=pKBcofAu_wM.

- NexLeaf Analytics. "Coldtrace helps health workers get safe vaccines to kids." NexLeaf Analytics http://nexleaf.org/vaccines/

- Nourse. Timothy H. November 2003. "Microfinance for Refugees: Emerging Principles for Effective Implementation." United Nations Human Rights Council. http://www.unhcr.org/3fc47f78d.pdf

- Nsehe, Mfonobong. December 21, 2017. "Meet The 32 Year-Old Entrepreneur Who Is Building Zimbabwe's Largest Solar Company." *Forbes*. http://bit.ly/2Ks033C.

- Okonkow, Judith. June, 20, 2017. "An immersive and accessible tool for education." TED Archive. https://www.youtube.com/watch?v=5-KWeRmdklY

- Open Badges. "About Open Badges." https://openbadges.org/about/

- Organisation for Economic Co-operation and Development. 2014. "Climate Change. Water and Agriculture: Towards Resilient Systems." Organisation for Economic Co-operation and Development. http://bit.ly/2IxdCx9.

- Patrinos, Harry Anthony. August 2016. "The skills that matter in the race between education and technology" Brookings Institute. https://www.brookings.edu/wp-content/uploads/2017/01/global_20170131_future-of-work.pdf

- Pompa. Claudia. March, 2015. "Jobs for the Future." Overseas Development Institute. http://bit.ly/2tBCnU2.

- Puliti, Riccardo. February 26, 2018. "Off-grid bringing power to millions." World Bank. http://blogs.worldbank.org/energy/grid-bringing-power-millions

- Rands, Kevin. November 14, 2017. "How blockchain technology is disrupting the remittance industry." CIO Magazine. https://bit.ly/2KsyeLW.

- Refugee Council. November 13, 2016. "The 7 Largest Refugees Camps in the World." Refugee Council USA. http://www.refugeecouncilusa.org/the-7-largest-refugee-camps-in-the-world/.
- Resilience Quito. October 2017. "Resilience Strategy: Metropolitan District of Quito." 100 Resilient Cities. https://bit.ly/2KipAAn.
- Resilience Surat. July 2017. "Surat Resilience Strategy." 100 Resilient Cities. https://bit.ly/2KohZzB.
- Rice, Doyle. May 17, 2018. "Earth just had its 400th straight warmer-than-average month thanks to global warming." *USA Today*. https://usat.ly/2tznlyk.
- Roberts, David. August 24, 2016. "The falling costs of US solar power. in 7 charts." Vox. https://www.vox.com/2016/8/24/12620920/us-solar-power-costs-falling
- Rodrik, Dani. October 14, 2014. "Can services drive developing country growth?." World Economic Forum. https://www.weforum.org/agenda/2014/10/dani-rodrik-services-manufacturing-growth/
- Rogowsky, Mark. December 28, 2013. "Kandi Crush: An Electric-Car Vending Macjine From China Could Upen The Auto Industry." *Forbes*. https://bit.ly/2Ky7fvm.
- Rojas-Downing, M. Melissa, A. Pouyan Nejadhashemi, Timothy Harrigan, and Sean A.Woznicki. February 12, 2017. "Climate change and livestock: Impacts, adaptation, and mitigation*." Climate Risk Management*. https://www.sciencedirect.com/science/article/pii/S221209631730027X
- Ruta N Medellín. March 22, 2017. "Medellín. World Innovation Hub." Ruta N Medellín. https://www.rutanmedellin.org/en/news/news/item/medellin-world-innovation-hub.
- Saha, Deblina and Akhilesh Modi. 2017. "Low Carbon Infrastructure." World Bank. http://bit.ly/2tCsMfC.
- Schuettler, Kirsten. November 9, 2017. "Refugees' right to work: Necessary but insufficient for formal employment of refugees." World Bank. https://bit.ly/2KvD2Qy.
- SenseFly. "The professionals drone mapping choice. "https://www.sensefly.com.
- Senthilingam, Meera. November 29, 2017. "Sexual harassment: How it stands around the globe." CNN. https://www.cnn.com/2017/11/25/health/sexual-harassment-violence-abuse-global-levels/index.html.
- Sinclair, Hugh. October 8, 2014. "Does microfinance really help poor people?" *The Guardian*. https://bit.ly/2d5LNR8.
- Sinha, Suveer. January 2018. "Combating the challenges of urbanization in emerging markets: Lessons from India." McKinsey & Company. https://mck.co/2BjKcyC.
- Skoll, 2018. "Mothers2Mothers." Skoll. http://skoll.org/organization/mothers2mothers/.
- Solli, Jami. January, 2015. "What Happens to Microfinance Clients who Default." Smart Campaign. https://bit.ly/1nvqx8l.
- Spence, Michael, Patricia Clarke, and Annez Robert M. Buckley, 2009. "Urbanization and Growth: Commission on Growth and Development." World Bank. http://bit.ly/2Mx2PoO.
- Standing Panel on Impact Assessment. December 2014. "Impact of Bean research in Rwanda and Uganda." CGIAR https://ispc.cgiar.org/sites/default/files/pdf/SPIA_Impact-Brief-46_Jan2015.pdf
- Suri, Tavneet and William Jack. December 8, 2016. "The Long-Run Poverty and Gender Impacts of Mobile Money. *Science Magazine*. http://www.microfinancegateway.org/sites/default/files/publication_files/new_jack_and_suri_paper_1.pdf.
- Tacoli, Cecilia. March 2012. "Technical Briefing: Urbanization. gender and poverty." United Nations Population Fund. http://pubs.iied.org/pdfs/G03335.pdf

- Tent Partnership for Refugees. "About." Tent. https://www.tent.org/about/
- The Smart Campaign. http://www.smartcampaign.org/
- The White House. June 30, 2016. "Fact Sheet: White House Launches a Call to Action for Private Sector Engagement on the Global Refugee Crisis." The White House. https://bit.ly/2Kug755.
- Thomason, Jane. August 11, 2017. "7 ways to use blockchain for international development." Devex. https://bit.ly/2KipXe8.
- Thompson, Cadie. May 7, 2015. "Three growing start-up cities in South America." CNBC. https://cnb.cx/2Kroz4R.
- Tsitsiragos, Dimitris. January 13, 2016. "Climate change is a threat – and an opportunity – for the private sector." World Bank. http://www.worldbank.org/en/news/opinion/2016/01/13/climate-change-is-a-threat---and-an-opportunity---for-the-private-sector
- United Nations High Commissioner for Refugees. "UNHCR Statistics Population Statistics Database." United Nations High Commissioner for Refugees http://popstats.unhcr.org/en/overview#_ga=2.71656465.344681890.1525814728-24605281.1523638495.
- United Nations High Commissioner for Refugees. "What We Do." United Nations High Commissioner for Refugees. http://www.unhcr.org/en-us/what-we-do.html.
- United Nations High Commissioner for Refugees. 2016. "Story Maps: Refugee Camps." United Nations High Commissioner for Refugees. https://storymaps.esri.com/stories/2016/refugee-camps/#.
- United Nations High Commissioner for Refugees. 2017. "Left Behind: Refugee Education In Crisis." United Nations High Commissioner for Refugees. http://www.unhcr.org/59b696f44.pdf
- United Nations High Commissioner for Refugees. June 19, 2018. "Figures at a Glance." United Nations High Commissioner for Refugees. http://www.unhcr.org/en-us/figures-at-a-glance.html.
- United Nations High Commissioner for Refugees. September 2016. "Missing Out: Refugee Education In Crisis." United Nations High Commissioner for Refugees. http://www.unhcr.org/57d9d01d0.pdf
- United Nations Population Fund, 2017. "State of the World's Population 2017." United Nations Population Fund. https://www.unfpa.org/swop.
- United Nations Relief and Works Agency. July 1, 2014. "Where We Work: Lebanon." United Nations Relief and Works Agency. https://www.unrwa.org/where-wework/lebanon
- United Nations Women. "Commission on the Status of Women." United Nations Women. http://www.unwomen.org/en/csw.
- United Nations Women's Economic Empowerment. "Leave no One Behind: A Call To Action For Gender Equality And Women's Economic Empowerment." United Nations Women's Economic Empowerment. https://bit.ly/2KtcTBR.
- United Nations. Department of Economic and Social Affairs, 2017. "Goal 4: Ensure inclusive and equitable quality education and promote lifelong learning opportunities for all." United Nations. https://unstats.un.org/sdgs/report/2017/goal-04/.
- Wachiaya, Catherine. March 14, 2017. "Innovation transforms education for refugee students in Africa." United Nations High Commissioner for Refugees. https://bit.ly/2yPPHJz.
- Water & Sanitation for the Urban Poor. November 17, 2016. "Promoting sanitation business models on World Toilet Day." Water & Sanitation for the Urban Poor. https://www.wsup.com/blog/is-entrepreneurship-a-solution-to-the-sanitation-challenge/.

- Women Effect. "Women Effect: What is Gender Lens Investing." www.womeneffect.com.
- Women Watch. "IFAD: Good Practice Example: Household-based Approaches to Training and Extension." United Nations. http://www.un.org/womenwatch/feature/ruralwomen/ifad-good-practice.html.
- Women's World Banking. "Women's World Banking Capital Partners. LP." Women's World Banking https://www.womensworldbanking.org/about-us/capital-partners-gender-lens-investing/.
- World Bank, 2012 "World Development Report 2013: Jobs." World Bank. http://bit.ly/2MvFILp.
- World Bank, 2013. "Global Monitoring Report 2013—Chapter 2: Rural-Urban Disparities and Dynamics." World Bank. https://bit.ly/2KqQMJ5.
- World Bank, 2014. "Global Survey on Consumer Protection and Financial Literacy: Oversight Frameworks and Practices in 114 Economies." World Bank. https://bit.ly/2KeRjlf.
- World Bank, 2016. "World Development Report 2016: Digital Dividends" World Bank. http://documents.worldbank.org/curated/en/896971468194972881/pdf/102725-PUB-Replacement-PUBLIC.pdf.
- World Bank, 2017. "Employment in agriculture (% of employment) (modeled ILO estimate). https://bit.ly/2KvPw7w.
- World Bank, 2017. "Good Practices for Financial Consumer Protection, 2017 Edition." World Bank. https://bit.ly/2Kj1dlS.
- World Bank, 2017. "Reducing Inequalities in Water Supply. Sanitation. and Hygiene in the Era of the Sustainable Development Goals: Synthesis Report of the WASH Poverty Diagnostic Initiative."World Bank. http://bit.ly/2IAhTQ5.
- World Bank. "Population living in slums (% of urban population)." World Bank. https://bit.ly/2N8y7n1.
- World Bank. August 31, 2016. "Uganda's Progressive Approach to Refugee Management." World Bank. http://www.worldbank.org/en/topic/fragilityconflictviolence/brief/ugandas-progressive-approach-refugee-management
- World Bank. January, 2018. "Off-Grid Solar Market Trends Report 2018." World Bank. http://bit.ly/2IADAQb.
- World Bank. June 2018. "Financial Education Program (FEP)—Ghana: Needs Assessment Report." World Bank. http://documents.worldbank.org/curated/en/331891528817424815/pdf/127119-WP-P155002-PUBLIC.pdf.
- World Bank. March 20, 2013. "As Climate Change Threatens, Water Cooperation Becomes Vital." World Bank. http://www.worldbank.org/en/news/feature/2013/03/20/climate-change-water-cooperation
- World Bank. November 8, 2015. "Rapid. Climate-Informed Development Needed to Keep Climate Change from Pushing More than 100 Million People into Poverty by 2030." World Bank. http://bit.ly/2Mx4z1k.
- World Bank. September 10, 2014. "How to Develop Effective Disaster Recovery Programs – Lessons from Vulnerable Countries." World Bank. http://bit.ly/2Kfisou.
- World Economic Forum. 2016. "The Global Gender Gap Report 2016." World Economic Forum. http://www3.weforum.org/docs/GGGR16/WEF_Global_Gender_Gap_Report_2016.pdf.
- World Economic Forum. 2017. "Worlds Apart: Global Gender Gap Report 2017." World Economic Forum. http://reports.weforum.org/global-gender-gap-report-2017/key-findings/.
- World Health Organization. "Blindness and Vision Impairment Prevention." https://bit.ly/1rTbp2S.

- World Health Organization. "Global Health Observatory (GHO) data." World Health Organization. http://www.who.int/gho/maternal_health/skilled_care/skilled_birth_attendance_text/en/.
- World Health Organization. November 30, 2017. "Protecting workers' health." World Health Organization. https://bit.ly/2lDEr9C.
- Yeung, Bernice. March 13, 2018. "How the most vulnerable workers are targeted for sexual abuse." *The Guardian*. https://www.theguardian.com/news/2018/mar/13/how-the-most-vulnerable-workers-are-targeted-for-sexual-abuse
- Young African Refugees For Integral Development. "Young African Refugees For Integral Development Young African Refugees For Integral Development. http://www.yarid.org/index.php
- Yuki, Kazuhiro. 2007. "Urbanization. Informal sector and development" *Journal of Development Economics*.
- Zevin Asset Management LLC. "Investors 'Take the Lead' on Advocating for Gender Equality." Zevin Asset Management LLC https://www.zevin.com/documents/Take%20 The%20Lead%20Article%20 Final%20Draft%2017-1103.pdf.

Chapter 8

- Miller Center for Social Entrepreneurship, January 24, 2017. "Test In Nicaragua Shifts Lending For Women Led Businesses From Collateral To Cashflow" Miller Center for Social Entrepreneurship. https://bit.ly/2wwwDM6.
- Zurer, Rachel and Marry Mazzoni. August 16, 2017. " Boost Your Social Enterprise with Advice From this Lifelong Entrepreneur." Conscious Company Media. https://bit.ly/2olYNWc.